GRAPHIC GESTURE
CREATIVE GESTURE

Scriptor Books

The British Academy of Graphology would like to express its immense gratitude to Mr Michael Coultas and Mrs Edwina Franceschini for their invaluable contribution to the translation of this important book, which will be much appreciated by gaphologists worldwide.

The Academy also wishes to thank most sincerely all its members, in particular Brother George Searles, for their generous financial contribution to this enriching publication.

RENNA NEZOS
Principal of The British Academy of Graphology

London, 1 July 2004

"Il gesto grafico
gesto creativo"
Copyright © 1998, Edizioni Borla s.r.l., Rome, Italy

English Edition first published in 2004
by SCRIPTOR BOOKS,
an imprint of
The British Academy of Graphology (Limited by Guarantee)
in association with The London College of Graphology Ltd.,
11 Roundacre, London SW19 6DB, U.K.

Editorial Office: 123 Bickenhall Mansions, London W1U 6BT

English Edition Copyright © 2004
The British Academy of Graphology Ltd.

A CIP catalogue record for this book is available
from the British Library.

ISBN 1-8996539-5-3

Typesetting and layout by

EuroBuro '92 Brigitte Froud
London, Tel 020-8788 3289

Nicole BOILLE

GRAPHIC GESTURE
CREATIVE GESTURE

Translated by
EDWINA FRANCESCHINI & MICHAEL COULTAS

Edited by
Michael Coultas

Scriptor Books

an imprint of
The British Academy of Graphology
London

In respectful memory of Jean-Charles Gille-Maisani,
an unforgettable teacher of ethics and graphology

With thanks to Renato Perrella for his encouragement and
practical suggestions in the course of completing this books,
and to my daughter, Emanuela, for her constant assistance.

NICOLLE BOILLE

Cover image: a painting by Wassily Kandinsky

CONTENTS

8

PREFACE

This absorbing book is a complete graphological treatise without equal at both a general and an expert level. Dr Boille graduated in psychology and received a diploma from the Société Française de Graphologie (SFDG) as well as a certificate from the Graphologues-Conseils de France. The author has developed an enviable competence and professional commitment for analysing handwriting, particularly in the scholastic and professional fields, along with business consultation and judicial work. Settling in Rome for family and artistic reasons, she founded there in 1981 Arigraf (Associazione di ricerca grafologica). By opening the school she became involved in national and European graphological debate, attending conferences and conventions throughout Europe. It is thanks to Nicole Boille, ably assisted by her daughter Emanuela, that French textbooks have been translated into Italian, such as *Psicologia della scrittura* by J.-C. Gille-Maisani [105 in the Bibliography] and *Manuale di grafologia* by J. Peugeot, A. Lombard, and M. de Noblens [200].

Of pivotal importance for the development of Dr Boille's methodology was her friendship over many years with Professor Gille-Maisani, who, I believe, was the most eminent expert in world graphology. Gille-Maisani, Professor of Mathematical Sciences at the University of Quebec, always used to spend a few weeks of the summer vacation at Urbino (Graphological Institute G. Moretti) and Rome (Arigraf) to give lectures. Nicole Boille became an essential collaborator in the publication of some of his scholarly texts in Italian. When Professor Gille-Maisani died, he bequeathed to her his very extensive graphology library (all the books in the world, in all editions). The library, now in Rome, is considered by Boille a cultural heritage and is available to researchers in the subject. This present publication clearly expresses the richness of knowledge and the breadth of experience gained during her long scholarly association with Professor Gille-Maisani, whose influence makes the work of Dr Boille especially important.

The author has also been influenced by Crépieux-Jamin and the French school's excellent methods and ideologies in the field of general handwriting analysis. In this publication, however, the author embraces the other important European methodologies of the German Klages, the Central European Pulver, and the Italian Girolamo Moretti. The Morettian method is given a particularly prominent role, because, as she writes, "having participated in Italian life for many years, we have gradually taken to the Morettian teaching method of the University of Urbino." She adds, "we will concentrate essentially on the observation of differences in handwriting between France and Italy", in which context she discusses the sociocultural habits which contribute to differentiate in some way our handwriting from those on the other side of the Alps. It is important for the professionally employed graphologist to have such a rich source of information, because even within the field of graphic stroke in its universal configurations, there are diversities connected with the specific sociocultural context. The graphologist in search of objectivity must take into consideration, as pointed out in the book, that these conditions influence from the very start the writing of schoolchildren.

Boille warns graphologists not to be taken in by easy eclecticism acquired by knowledge of other methodologies. "Each method has its own structural order, and even if one single aspect can be borrowed from another method, the in-depth examination of writing must concentrate on each methodology in its entirety and not on a hotchpotch which will risk either superficiality or the alteration of basic concepts."

Much knowledge on foreign methodologies has been acquired in Italy, in particular since the initiative started by the Graphological Institute G. Moretti through international conferences and translation of textbooks, but always to deepen the knowledge of students and certainly not to encourage that "hotch-potch" so disparaged by the author. This book can be used, among other things, as a useful organ for the teaching of comparative graphology to broaden the scope of both experts and pupils, but in an epistemologically correct way, without improper interpolations which only succeed in causing confusion.

Part I contains clearly the Basic Principles and the Key Concepts of graphology which unite all methodologies. Part II firstly describes specific methodologies. Right from the beginning Dr Boille is keen to demonstrate two unavoidable concepts for the development of graphological analysis: the interaction between the *graphic signs* and the importance of the *graphic context* in assigning correct values to single signs, because "such a principle alerts us to the interpretative dangers based on the single sign and confers on the graphological discipline its own scientific complexity."

The fundamentals of graphological analysis proper then occupy the central part of the book, according to Crépieux-Jamin's lines and the French school in general but enriched by a close look at the Italian and German schools. These schools are explored because, apart from Crépieux-Jamin, only Moretti and Klages have formulated an organic and autonomous method (in time improved by their followers) for handwriting analysis. Hence the reason for the many references to the Morettian method and the various Italian handwritings interspersed with French samples in describing signs, as well as in the more organic methods of analysis.

Part III considers the evolution of handwriting in relation to age and other influencing factors such as maturity and the psychophysical equilibrium of the individual. This is an aspect noticed by everyone when looking at an individual's handwriting and provokes many questions from the layman, to which graphologists must give clear and convincing answers in their analyses.

Part IV discusses the relationship between psychology and graphology, particularly in the context of reciprocal knowledge and collaboration. The two disciplines share common ground in discovering personal individuality, but use different means in accordance with their specific methodologies. The book concludes with an essential bibliography with references to the most important publications by the graphological schools, in particular those cited within the book.

I believe that this interesting publication will enrich all those who include graphological science within an overall cultural interest as well as at a professional level. The book also has great merit for teaching because the considerations on the various aspects of the graphic stroke are followed by clear summary tables, and numerous handwriting examples of notable explanatory relevance accompany the text. This book is indeed an essential study of the subject, and we are extremely grateful to the author for filling a gap with such authority.

P. LAMBERTO TORBIDONI
Founder of the Graphological Institute G. Moretti
Lecturer in the Graphological School at Urbino University

Osimo 4 June 1997

INTRODUCTION

Writing is a symbolic activity, spatial and temporal, in which the graphic stroke inscribed on a surface leaves its own imprint, rhythm, and energy to express the individual's response to cultural graphic models. While writing, the graphic stroke obeys time: not just linear time with its successions, sequences, duration, and speed, but also subjective time, our internal temporal state, encompassing past experiences, memories, dreams, projects, and the potential of becoming.

The *graphic form* also obeys present reality, those *"solitary instants, carriers of tension towards fulfilment, which draw upon past forces"*, as expressed by Gaston Bachelard [14]. The graphic stroke shares in the solitary instant, as well as in the tension and cohesion between different instants.

Writing is the result of motor learning as well as an intellectual and emotional development that allows the achievement of an individual writing rhythm. The written stroke results therefore from a higher brain activity, from specialized centres in the cerebral hemispheres.

Writing expresses the lived and the evolution of being, growing in a given context and participating in a socializing process. The graphic stroke expresses the most hidden individuality of being and is the witness, and forerunner, of evolutionary processes. It varies in its own form, as it is itself a creative process.

Graphology has now qualified itself as a *human science* linked to psychology, but it does distinguish itself by its own methodological principles and techniques. Like psychology, graphology investigates the character and dynamics of the personality, but as its analytical material – the written medium – is so specific, it needs largely different theories and techniques, which make the discipline autonomous. This point is confirmed in article 1.5 of the Deontological Code of Graphologists promulgated by the AGI [1]: *"Graphology must find within itself its validation criteria and its control methods. It must hence give itself its own epistemological status in order to justify an autonomous scientific space."*

The empirical investigation of the first graphologists has certainly not been in vain. It has allowed the gathering of rich materials, from which base various teams of graphologists have enlarged their experimental techniques and adapted them for verification and control.

Contemporary graphology defines its epistemological status and organizes, consequently, its own technical-scientific parameters. European research is very useful for this purpose, and many present initiatives, international conventions, seminars, magazines, meetings, publications, and schools of teaching, create a climate for emulation. This is not always devoid of a competitive spirit, but it also presents an opportunity to specify the relationship between different methodologies and overcome unnecessary rivalries between national schools.

One speaks of European research because the principal methods used have a European origin. In reality studies have already been carried on at a wider level. Many countries are involved in achieving better understanding in the discipline of graphology, such as Canada, the United States, Latin and Central America, and many Eastern countries.

We can perhaps summarize the epistemological perspective: graphology as an autonomous discipline has already defined its scientific objectives, methods, and techniques. It must, however, intensify its experimental and statistical examination to consolidate itself as a human science. Collaboration with various arms of psychology and the participation of authoritative psychologists can only improve these two parallel disciplines, *graphology and psychology*, while remaining within their own ethical and scientific domains.

*   *   *

Notwithstanding the use of personal computers, which have replaced the pen, writing still remains an imperative and complex human activity at the level of physiological need and psychological expression. Writing continues to be a unique and irreplaceable medium for the discovery of personality, for following the development of child and adolescent, and for their better guidance.

The correlation of graphology with graphotherapy, understood as re-education of the writing in cases of motor dysfunction, has been well known for some time, just as that of psychology in relation to handwriting. There are many graphological applications relating to certain psychological tests, in particular those of Rorschach, the tree test, Wartegg, Szondi, and other graphic tests. We also emphasize the intense use of graphology in personnel selection, especially in business, where in France the take-up is 80% of all companies, though in Italy the response is less.

Other research areas are now being opened. After Lurija's study [157], new perspectives between graphology and physiology, hitherto reserved to specialists given the complexity of the subject and the current reworking of theories in the field of neuropsychophysiology, are under scrutiny. Research between graphology and informatics, and more recent experiments with lasers which allow dating of old documents, is also being pursued.

Connected to graphology, but a discipline in itself, is expert judicial assessment. Although it has elaborated its own repertory in the investigation of handwriting and established its particular research and technical parameters, it is underpinned by the laws of graphology.

*   *   *

The graphologist's code of conduct is similar to that of the doctor and psychologist: professional secrecy, practice of the profession only after qualifying, and follow-up training. Some strict codes have been promulgated. In addition to the already mentioned AGI code, the Groupement des Graphologues-Conseils de France (GGCF) proclaimed in 1946 a stringent code of practice. In 1992, on an initiative by the GGCF, a new European Deontology Code was proposed. Two years later in 1994 the ADEG or European Graphologists Deontological Association was founded. The Association unites the most qualified European associations, which all subscribe to the European Deontology Code, an event of significant importance.

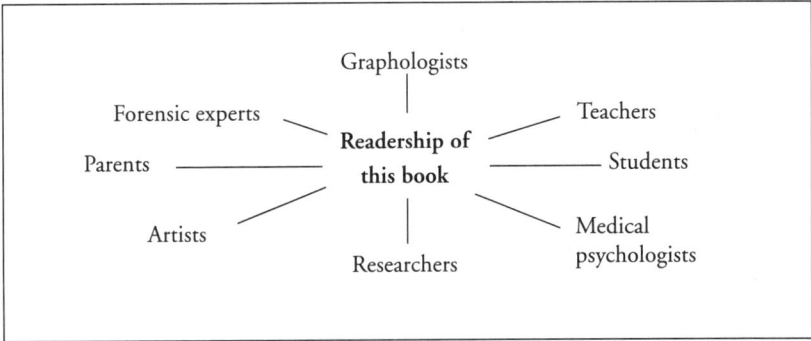

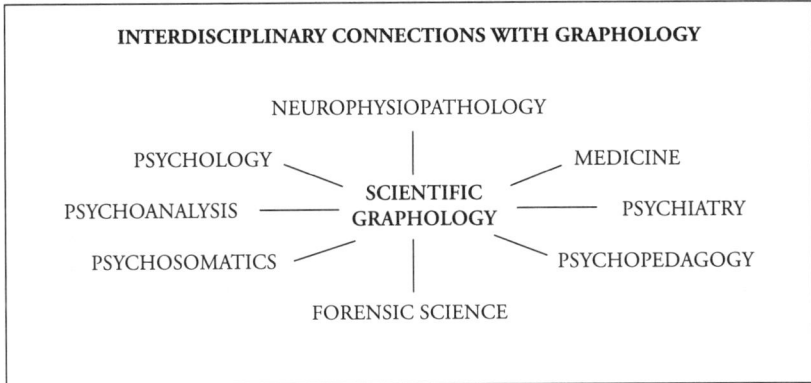

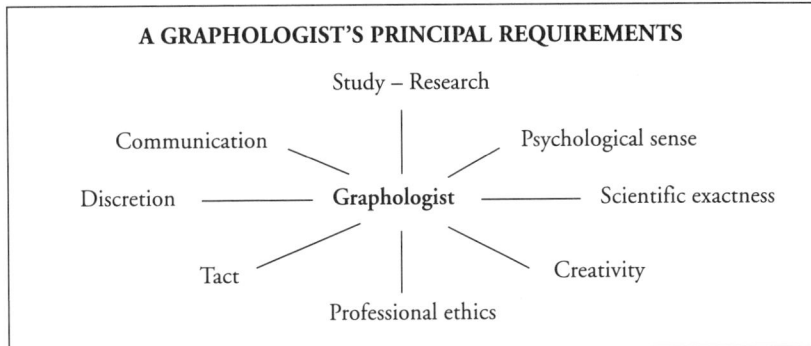

Graphologists

Forensic experts **Readership of** Teachers

Parents **this book** Students

Artists Medical
Researchers psychologists

INTERDISCIPLINARY CONNECTIONS WITH GRAPHOLOGY

NEUROPHYSIOPATHOLOGY

PSYCHOLOGY MEDICINE

PSYCHOANALYSIS **SCIENTIFIC GRAPHOLOGY** PSYCHIATRY

PSYCHOSOMATICS PSYCHOPEDAGOGY

FORENSIC SCIENCE

A GRAPHOLOGIST'S PRINCIPAL REQUIREMENTS

Study – Research

Communication Psychological sense

Discretion **Graphologist** Scientific exactness

Tact Creativity

Professional ethics

Table 1

GRAPHOLOGICAL DISCIPLINES

I   GENERAL OR BASIC GRAPHOLOGY
  - methodology for graphological analysis
  - classification of graphic characters
  - terminology (without requiring interpretation)

II   HISTORICAL GRAPHOLOGY
  - paleography (antique handwriting)
  - calligraphy schools
  - graphological schools

III PHYSIOLOGICAL GRAPHOLOGY
  - laws and mechanisms of handwriting

IV   PATHOLOGICAL GRAPHOLOGY
  - organic disorders
  - psychopathological disorders

V   PSYCHOLOGICAL GRAPHOLOGY
  - personality analysis

VI   COMPARATIVE GRAPHOLOGY
  - comparison between schools and methods

VII SPECIALIST GRAPHOLOGY
  - scholastic evaluation
  - professional tests
  - aptitude selection

VIII JUDICIAL (FORENSIC) GRAPHOLOGY

PRINCIPAL APPLICATIONS FOR GRAPHOLOGY

Personality analysis	Scholastic and professional orientation Analysis of interpersonal dynamics Personnel selection
Clinical tests	Diagnostic and prognostic contribution Graphic re-education and graphotherapy
Judicial/forensic expertise	Evaluation of graphomotor rhythm and analysis of Signs

Table 2

PART I

GRAPHOLOGICAL METHODS
AND PRINCIPLES

Chapter One

FUNDAMENTALS OF GRAPHOLOGY

I. HISTORICAL DEVELOPMENT OF GRAPHOLOGY IN EUROPE

This chapter will outline the main authors or pioneers, mostly in Europe, who made possible the structure of graphology before the Second World War, as a scientific discipline. This chapter does not therefore reproduce the entire history of graphology, which has been covered already by a large number of manuals and is very well documented in a publication by Salvatore Ruzza [216]. For the precursors of graphology a recent work by Joseph Seiler [220] is exhaustive and informative.

MAIN EUROPEAN SCHOOLS AND SEMINAL BOOKS (1870–1948)			
FRANCE	*GERMANY*	*ITALY*	*SWITZERLAND*
1870 MICHON *1875 Système de graphologie*			
1885 CRÉPIEUX-JAMIN *L'Écriture et le caractère* ↓	1904 KLAGES *1917 Handschrift und Charakter*	1914 MORETTI (Koch) *Manuale di grafologia*	
1929 *ABC de la graphologie*	1929 MENDELSSOHN (Teillard)		1931 PULVER *Symbolik der Handschrift*
	1939 POPHAL 1943 HEISS		
1948 TEILLARD *L'Âme et l'écriture*		1948 *Trattato di grafologia*	

Table 3

During the second half of the nineteenth century, along with the social, medical, and scientific development which heralded modern times, graphology as a discipline acquires its name, identity, and status. Around 1870 in France, Abbé Jean-Hippolyte Michon coined the name *graphology*, from the Greek *graphe* "writing" and *logos*, bringing this discipline, as he explained, "to the state of reasoned science, with its own laws, principles and classifications." These ideas are found in his book *Système de graphologie* published in 1875 after 35 years of study. He was able to remove graphology from a menacing occultism which was trying to absorb it, and placed it instead in the realm of a purely experimental method. In 1871, Michon founded the Société Française de Graphologie and published the first journal, *La Graphologie*.

Following Michon's steps, at the end of the century, Jules Crépieux-Jamin, who became head of the French graphological school, built a method regarded even today as the basis for the study of graphology in France. After publishing various titles, and after 30 years of research, he set out a classification of seven *categories* which grouped 175 graphological *signs*, included in his 1929 book *ABC de la graphologie*. Crépieux-Jamin established basic principles as a guide to handwriting, and in particular to *sign interaction* within the graphic environment. Crépieux-Jamin's psychological vision restored the principles of Gestalt theory for which each element in a structural group is evaluated and interpreted in the context of the whole. In other words, the *graphic environment*, parallel with medicine's *clinical context*, as expressed by Dr Gille-Maisani [105], attributes an appropriate value to the single graphic stroke.

We are therefore a long way from the graphology of the *small sign/stroke* of fixed value and the atomistic psychology of the nineteenth century. Although at the beginning of the twentieth century Gestalt principles had already taken hold, and had influenced early graphology, it is astonishing to note that even today, certain types of publication give fixed values to graphic aspects. This misinforms and discourages the reader or researcher with superficial interpretations.

At the end of the nineteenth century in Germany and Switzerland, several graphology books were published by authors such as Langenbruch, W. Preyer, Hans Busse, and Georg Meyer. These authors precede the man who became pivotal to the German school, the philosopher Ludwig Klages. The first of his books, *Writing and Character*, appeared in 1917 and set out a method placing *rhythm* as the focal point of graphic observation, a global principle, which still remains a universal and immovable point in graphology.

German graphology sides early on with German scientific psychology of the period, in other words, with neurophysiology and pathology, helped by the work of the neurologist Rudolph Pophal and Robert Heiss, professor of philosophy and psychology, who succeeded in creating a graphology department at the University of Freiburg. In ideology, however, both took Klages' lines. The hypothesis that Pophal proposed, concerning the cerebral locations of graphic movement, has today been surpassed, but his researches on the tension of handwriting remain fundamental.

In Italy, after Cesare Lombroso's 1875 publication, Father Girolamo Moretti, under the pseudonym Umberto Koch, in 1914 published *Manual of Graphology*. His influence dominates Italian graphology and in the 1920s he was its leading pioneer spirit. Moretti seems to have studied French methods, but preferred to elaborate his own system. His strong personality and intuition certainly pushed him to research with fervour the question of character and its correlations in graphology, avoiding Crépieux-Jamin's systems and methods, though they were probably in contact. His most important book, *Treatise on Graphology*, appeared in 1948 and in a series of later editions. Moretti classified logically 80 graphic types, making distinctions between substantial, modifying, and accidental signs. In the Morettian view, the graphic sign does not have just one meaning and his attentions also focused beyond the psyche onto the human body, of which Moretti discerned, through the writing, several modes of expression. The neurophysiological aspects of the graphic stroke are at the heart of his research and illuminate physical as well as mental conditions.

During the 1930s two outstanding graphologists, heirs to the Middle European culture, introduced the psychology of the unconscious into graphology. Ania Teillard was of Baltic descent, a follower of Jung and a psychoanalyst. The other was a Swiss philosopher called Max Pulver. They were both born in 1889 and contemporaneously developed their own research methods. They both located graphology in the realm of psychology, observing a firm link to the unconscious. They did not introduce a new method of graphology, instead they established a different level of interpretation, based on both French and German methods. As followers of Freud, Jung, and Adler they were not satisfied to test mere character descriptions. Instead they focused their studies towards the hidden dynamics of personality.

Ania Mendelssohn (Teillard) in 1929 published her first book in Leipzig together with her brother. Her second book *The Soul and Handwriting* was published in 1933 in her own name. This book appeared in French in 1948 as *L'Âme et l'écriture* in the name of Ania Teillard. It had great success after the war and its influence still resonates today. Ania Teillard was the first to establish a graphological connection with Freud's *psychosexual* stages and Jung's *psychological types.*

Pulver's outstanding work, *Symbolism of Writing*, was published in 1931 and supplied graphology with an incomparable means of working out the symbolic value of the stroke in its relation to space. Pulver, a man of immense humanistic culture, was appointed graphology lecturer at Zurich's Institute of Applied Psychology. A short time before his death in 1952, he obtained a chair of graphology at the University of Zurich.

Concerning the analysis of child and adolescent graphology, a special impulse was created in the 1950s by Hélène de Gobineau's statistical researches, followed by the psychiatrist Jean de Ajuriaguerra and his team in the Experimental Psychology Department of the Henry Rousselle Hospital in Paris. These experiments conducted over ten years or more established a solid scientific basis in this area.

European graphology therefore has its roots in the work of these major pioneers. From the end of the Second World War, contacts between the various schools have intensified and as a result a profitable comparison between the differing methods, which in many ways integrate, has increasingly given graphology the status of *discipline.*

Contributions by the latest graphologists, the opening of new teaching schools, mainly in France, Italy, Germany, and Switzerland, and new uses for graphology such as management personnel selection, especially common in France, have also created a momentum that now seems unstoppable. These pioneering methods are spreading throughout Europe, where countries such as Belgium, Spain (the stimulating work of Augusto Vels), Portugal, and England are making original contributions. Most other European countries, even from Eastern Europe, are involved. European graphology has had in particular a strong impact on the most interesting developments across the Atlantic, in the United States, Canada, and Latin America.

This growing interest has also affected the judicial use of graphology, giving the expert in this field a boost in professional quality and analytical depth, overtaking the fixed basis of previous methods. Judicial (or forensic) expertise is well established as a separate graphological specialization.

Graphology has achieved in just over a century its own space as a companion discipline to psychology, but with its own epistemology, laws, and techniques. It is therefore the fruit of Western culture, allowing the delineation of universal principles to transcend any difference between the schools.

France has been greatly advantaged because graphology has gained credit in the workplace and consequently the consultant graphologist has reached the status of a qualified professional. Teaching the subject has also become extremely rigorous and is governed by the Société Française de Graphologie (SFDG) and by the Groupement des Graphologues-Conseils de France (GGCF), whose diploma from 1978 has been approved by the French Ministry as a degree level. The GGCF is part of UNAPL, Union des Professions Libérales, of SEPLIS, Secrétariat Européen des Professions Libérales, and is the only professional group of graphologists affiliated to ORDINEX, Organisation Internationale des Experts, whose headquarters is in Geneva, and as a body embraces the 53 most represented professions.

The school at Urbino in Italy has recently acquired official recognition as a School for Special Needs, which has improved the status of the qualified graphologist. Other schools inspired by Morettian graphology have also emerged in Italy, among them the school of Rolando Marchesan in Milan. Another initiative aims to group qualified Italian graphologists in a single national association, Associazione Grafologi Professionisti (AGP).

This short summary is not intended to cover the contributions and the quality of many graphologists who have been working since the end of the Second World War, nor does it deal with the ramifications and influence of the various schools. Our only intention is to give an overview of the present situation of graphology and to outline in the following sections the basic principles of the subject, then to lay out the essential information necessary for further research.

II. BASIC PRINCIPLES OF GRAPHOLOGY

Graphology as a scientific discipline is based on the processing of theories and techniques unique to it. Its aim is the study of personality, behaviour, and depth psychology on the evidence of the subject's graphic processes and in particular the handwriting. Many factors are involved in the graphic act and consequently in ways of learning to write. In first place and fundamentally important are the *neurophysiological* factors of motor energy, strength, muscular tension or relaxation which principally affect the cerebral circuits, and which change with age and state of health.

It is also important to consider the *sociocultural* factors which apart from defining the school model of writing also determine cultural habits which influence graphic perceptions and organization, logical ability, aesthetic taste, and even the desire for learning how to write.

Finally *psychodynamic* factors specific to the life of each subject bring with them endless variables which interact with other basic factors. These are linked to education, motivation, communication ability, inhibition, and so on. All these aspects will be examined implicitly or explicitly in the course of this book.

During the past 120 years we have seen how successive generations of graphology have evolved and how the principal European schools have debated some of the fundamental theories. All schools however agree to certain basic criteria, which could presage a future unification of methods (see Table 4).

SOME UNIVERSAL PRINCIPLES: SUMMARY		
1.	Correspondence: *brain* — — — — —→ *hand* — — —→ *graphic gesture*	
2.	Phases of: *evolution – organization – involution*	
3.	Relation: *graphic gesture* ←— — — — — — — — —→ *graphic space*	
4.	Interaction of: *signs*	
5.	Interrelation: *space* ←— — — — — —→ *time* *movement* *form*	
6.	Symbolism: *forms – tendencies*	
7.	Four factors affecting writing ability: Development of: — *motor ability* — *mind* — *language* — *social ability*	

Table 4

Principle of brain–hand correspondence

Writing as a motor gesture depends directly on upper cerebral activity. The cerebral circuits involved are extremely complicated and are still not very well known. The hand is only an instrument, and in fact after a certain amount of training, writing produced with an instrument held in either mouth or foot, for example, shows the same graphodynamic as writing by hand. After the initial cerebral impulse, learning and practice produce what we call writing, the final result of a spatio-temporal activity.

Principle of the interaction of signs

A graphic stroke or sequence of strokes called a *sign* reveals its own meaning only together with other signs present in the graphic field, and each modification of a sign generates a new graphic configuration or graphic "Gestalt". From this the notion of *graphic environment* has become one of the key points in graphological study. Such a principle removes the dangers of interpretation based on any individual sign, and confers on graphology its scientific complexity.

Principle of graphic symbolism

Our graphic stroke interacts with space. Writing follows a basic learnt calligraphic model but also reflects the cultural symbolism acquired by our collective unconscious, which in Western civilization is reinforced in many spheres. The child's first doodle is the first step that develops through playful drawing and finally evolves into stroke and form arranged within space under differing pressure, in other words into the relationship between the communicated message and the implicit, unexpressed one. From religion to myth, art, and science the same meanings are attributed to the symbolism of top, bottom, left, and right, likewise to horizontal or vertical, to rounded, looped, angular, cruciform, and wavy forms.

III. GRAPHOLOGICAL ANALYSIS AND SOCIOCULTURAL CONTEXT

To study the handwriting of any nationality or period, we have to have precise information such as the writer's gender and age. Even though there are some typically feminine or masculine writing styles, in many cases they are not necessarily certain to belong to either woman or man. One can only give an opinion which at times can be absolutely wrong. According to Ania Teillard, "*writing reflects only the psychological and not the physiological gender.*"

As for the determination of age, Alfred Binet, inventor with Dr Simon of the IQ scale of intelligence to evaluate the *mental age* of the subject, undertook at the beginning of the last century a scientific investigation into the attribution of age to a particular script [31]. He concluded that because the error percentage was very high this possibility had to be excluded. Experience of graphologists has in fact confirmed that adult writing reflects "psychological age" and not the physical age.

Having said that, we can easily recognize in a writing the signs of senility, arteriosclerosis, or Parkinson's disease, for example. Without any of these specific conditions however, we have found extremely young writing styles in people over 70. By contrast cases of younger people with conditions like tremors or writing impediments, whether due to nervous tension or transient organic causes, present great difficulties in the determination of age.

In most cases knowledge of the two basics, gender and age, is sufficient to proceed with a normal graphological analysis. To obtain a more specific analysis for academic or professional guidance, further information about educational level is required. For a psychopathological analysis it is advisable to know the subject's clinical history in order to collaborate with the clinical and psychotherapeutic team.

If we want to undertake the study of *foreign* writing it is absolutely essential to find additional and precise information on local teaching models and cultural norms.

Copybook school models of handwriting

A school handwriting style is defined as that taught in schools and belongs to a particular period in history. We know how the style of writing changes greatly at different times. Principal European models of recent times will be analysed later (Chapter Eight). Exercise books have a precise system of lines, spaces, and margins which change according to class level, schools, and countries. The graphologist must take into account precisely all these factors, before drawing a conclusive analysis. Basic teaching methods cover writing and reading together because they relate to each other. Depending upon the country, these methods can be more or less uniform over the national territory, or the style may vary regionally according to circumstances, as appears to be the case in Italy.

All these points concern essentially technical methods of schoolteaching and are particularly useful in the analysis of children's writing. We shall concentrate further on these particular points in the following chapters.

Sociocultural customs

Children's school life, in particular during the first years, is mostly influenced by educational and cultural aspects peculiar to the country itself, and we need to take these into consideration. Factors such as discipline, permissiveness, flexibility, aims, and timescales condition not only teaching methods but also attitudes to learning, and these are reflected in the handwriting. Sociocultural customs in their turn contribute to the development of the writing style of a particular country. These customs could also vary according to region, type of school, or aspects of school writing performance such as neatness and calligraphy. These determining factors could influence, at motor level, greater or lesser writing agility or inhibition.

Teaching demands and regulations are to be judged over the whole schooling span, up to late adolescence, taking into consideration rapid changes in mentality and objectives that shape new school generations – in cycles of three or four years – and also considering "fashions" which condition graphic styles during adolescence.

Sociocultural customs whether embracing family, school, or professional life, certainly influence graphic performance. The conditions change not only with the country and sociopolitical period but much more at a family level. We are not proposing to discuss here such wide questions, rather we aim to make the graphologist aware of the complexity of the parameters in question. The graphologist's evaluation and analysis should not be linked or restricted to preconditioned theories, but should be changed by the subject's social conditions after carefully studying the information.

In the case of families belonging to high socioeconomic and cultural status, there will not be any relevant educational or professional differences between Italy and France, for example. Differences however may arise concerning work structures that exist in either country in relation to the job market. On the contrary, the student and future professional from disadvantaged social levels may fare better in some countries, for example France, than in others.

On a more psychological plane consideration must be taken of child rearing differences. For example, the tendency to overprotect the small child in Italy contrasts with the less maternal French tradition. On the other hand during adolescence there is in general a greater independence of spirit in a young person in a French family. By contrast, in the Italian relationship between adolescents and parents uncertainty and a feeling of loss prevails.

It is important to ascertain, for general research, what value certain subjects are given by a country's culture: for example, humanities, sciences, arts, technical studies. The most encouraged subjects may tend to foster either individualism or a more collective culture. It is also important to pick out cultural customs which are not necessarily explicitly defined but which are intrinsically part of the nation's customs and uses. These affect ways of writing, the perception of graphic space (of greater or lesser significance in communication, as a way to address others), and the understanding of the relationship between legibility and spontaneity in the written message. In Italy legibility is regarded more highly than in France, where legibility is sacrificed much more to personalized graphic rhythms. For personnel selection and careers advice these cultural customs play a fundamental role in the analysis of a subject's writing and the consultant graphologist must not ignore them.

* * *

Having dealt with the historical, methodological, social, and cultural presuppositions which must guide graphologists with long experience and strict professional ethics, we now turn to the specifics of graphology, in such a way that the reader can follow, step by step, the development of the graphic stroke both in its universal configuration and seen within a given cultural context. During the course of this treatise we shall limit ourselves to the major Western European models and in particular concentrate on the differences between France and Italy as they are better documented. The following chapter covers commonly used graphological concepts and terms, while the ensuing chapters will cover the principal graphological methods developed in the course of the twentieth century.

Chapter Two

KEY CONCEPTS IN GRAPHOLOGY

We must now define various concepts terms used in graphology, relating both to the graphic elements of writing proper and to the basic movements of the graphic stroke, in normal situations. This chapter will not deal with the psychological significance of the terms. These primary definitions will be kept short enough to familiarize the reader with a vocabulary that will be explained in depth in the following chapters, while avoiding simplifications or assumptions that may reduce their clarity. We have also avoided sample writings.

The quotations of linguist and poet Roland Barthes, taken from his book on oriental writing *L'Empire des signes* [16], are poetic evocations of plastic and concrete concepts related to the graphic field. We use these to balance the lapidary effect which pure definitions often have. The following are the first three quotations. They suggest perfectly both the heart and the intellectual synthesis of graphic observation.

The two primordial materials of writing: the surface and the instrument

Elementary writing signifiers: the blank page and the groove of its incisions

The outline of the sign

I. THE MAIN CATEGORIES

Gesture   *track of light*

Automatic or deliberate neurophysiological impulse, which leaves an outline on a surface. The impulse is released by cerebral commands from the upper cortex, though it is influenced by the more archaic subcortical centres which favour spontaneity but also unpredictability of execution. The neurophysiology of the graphic movement is extremely complicated and not well understood, and is still a subject for specialist research following on the work of Lurija [157].

Sign   *the sign is a fracture which never opens*
                                            except on the face of another sign

Mark left by every movement, every graphic manifestation, whether large or small, clear or faint, independent of linguistic meaning. By extension, synonymous with *graphic species* (see Section V below). In Morettian graphology the term "sign" indicates both simple and complex characteristics. Abstract art has often conferred on the *sign* the individualizing value of the painter's hand, a type of "algorithm" and unique to the artist.

Layout   *the white which cancels out in us*
                                            the kingdom of rules

The linking together of letters and words – the *blacks* – interrupted by breaks, spaces, gaps, silences – the *whites*. In a written text the layout arranges sentences or phrases, but for a doodle or drawing it arranges strokes. In writing the layout is represented by a graphic thread, which unravels and rewinds on the line. Kandinsky (*Reflections on Abstract Art*, 1931): "Sometimes silence speaks louder than sound and dumbness has an eloquent voice."

Space   *the page of life,*
                                            the silk of language

The total surface space on which one is writing. Sometimes one distinguishes between *internal* space, within and between letters, between words and lines; and *external* space, margins around the text, paragraph spacing, indentation. According to Pulver the space on the paper on which we write or draw symbolizes our life space, the space we make between ourselves and our surroundings.

Stroke   *the stroke freed of any advantageous image*
                              that the writer wants to portray does not
                              express, but simply exists

Substance and constituent of the sign. By extension, synonymous with *pressure*, consistent with the amount of ink, the pen's structure and form, the position of the hand and fingers which hold it. The *stroke* is the first concrete witness of the movement becoming sign.

Gille-Maisani: "Stroke is to layout as material is to form (according to Pophal): if stroke shows the writer's essence as 'psychic raw material', the layout will indicate how the writer's personality has organized and arranged this raw material."

Form   *Where does writing start? Where does painting begin?*

Form is the final product of *sign* and *layout*. Form depends on linguistic meaning and represents the most conscious graphic element. From simplicity to artifice, form resides in a microcosm: *stroke – sign – layout*.

Around the age of three the small child, having mastered horizontal and vertical lines, expresses in its movement a new intention, playing with curves. The child then discovers *form* with a sketch of the *matchstick man*. This particular image, according to Widlöcher [249], is "the meeting of mastery of form and the ability to recognize the reality behind this form."

Symbol   *a chiselled thought … frees the symbol*

Each sign can contain within itself a symbolic value, be an expression with an implicit, concealed, content or be itself a *symbol*. A cross is a symbolic sign. In this way the letter *t* formed in the shape of a cross can implicitly contain the symbolic value of the cross: the meeting of vertical and horizontal. Symbolism contained in the main directions of high–low, left–right, has acquired in Western civilization universal archetypal values, which are part of our collective unconscious.

Leitbild

Leitbild is the unconscious image which is already in us even before starting to write. According to Klages it is an impressed image which wants to produce an effect, an *impression*, in opposition to *expression* which emanates from a writing without any implicit intention. *Leitbild* is shaped by instincts, by the need to imitate, personal preferences, likes and dislikes.

II. GRAPHIC BODY

Zones: Writing and outline, word and phrase, develop in three zones.

In the *middle zone* lies the body of all lowercase letters and the entirety of small letters such as *a, e, i, o, u, c, m, n, r, s, v, w, x, z.*

The *upper zone* contains the *upper strokes* or *upper extensions*, in the letters *b, d, f, h, k, l, t,* capital letters, and accents.

The *lower zone* contains the *lower strokes* or *lower extensions* on the letters *f, g, j, p, q, y, z,* and sometimes on capital G.

Garland: mainly seen in the cup form of the letters *m* and *n*.

Angle: seen both in forms of letters and in connecting strokes.

Arcade: mainly on the arched forms of letters *m* and *n*, but also in some connecting strokes. A final arched movement can also be construed as a leftward stroke.

Slant, inclination: denotes the angle to the vertical of the stroke.

Initial and final strokes: the initial and final strokes of a letter may be treated as of lesser or greater significance in the teaching of graphology.

Paraph: denotes a line supplementary to the signature. In general it is an underline, but may be an overline, or may almost or totally enclose a signature.

III. BASIC MOVEMENTS

Writing movement

Three fingers assist in the act of writing but as a rule it is the *index* finger which mostly directs the instrument/pen and controls the pressure. Vertical writing from top to bottom is achieved through the index finger's flexing middle phalanx. In this way a continuous vertical movement of "coming and going" is created, whose width generally thins out in the upward movement. Rotational movement allows us to make loops and curves, the hand being semi-flat [51]. There are, consequently, four main types of writing movement: *extending* from bottom to top; *flexing* from top to bottom; *movement away* from the main body; *movement towards* the main body.

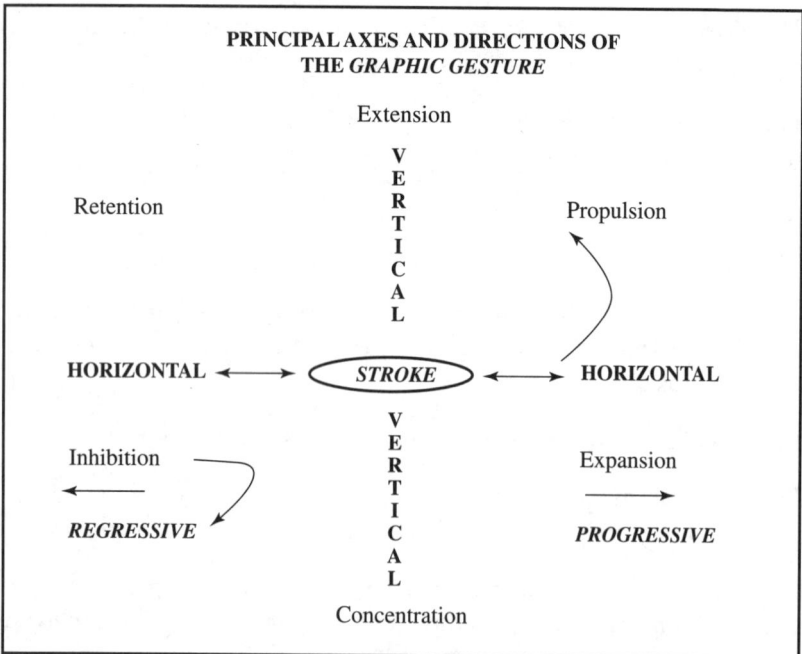

PRINCIPAL AXES AND DIRECTIONS OF THE *GRAPHIC GESTURE*

Extension

Retention — Propulsion — HORIZONTAL — STROKE — HORIZONTAL — Inhibition — Expansion — REGRESSIVE — PROGRESSIVE — Concentration (VERTICAL)

Table 5

Cursive movement

In countries using the Roman alphabet a cursive style has developed, starting from left to right with joining strokes which favour a logical linking of one letter to another. The coordination of the writing movement and its cursive flow allows the flexibility and speed normally necessary for the spontaneity and legibility of the stroke.

Progressive or *rightward* movement

Once one has acquired the *cursive* movement, writing inclines towards the right in the most logical, economical, and rapid way without any alteration in structure of either letter or word. The economic movement which favours connections towards the right and avoids unnecessary returns to the left, is called *graphic progression*, provided it also maintains a suitable firmness of stroke.

Progressive strokes are principally found in the lower zones, the letters *f*, *p*, *q* in particular; in connections between letters (simplification and sobriety of the letters themselves allows an economy of form in linking them); in some forms, for example in *ovals* which instead of being closed remain open or tend to stretch towards the right. *Progressive* movements are also called *rightward* movements.

Regressive or *leftward* movement

Regressive movements are those with a tendency to lean to the left, contrary to the basic teaching models. This is therefore called *graphic regression* because it hinders the stroke's movement to the right and ignores the basic model's writing logic. It can also accentuate some returns to the left, in particular in the looped letters.

Regressive strokes are found principally in the lower strokes of the letters *f*, *g*, *j*, *p*, *q*, *y*, *z*; in accessory signs, initial or final stroke of a letter, which comes from the left, stops, or returns to the left; in forms, all those which increase curving to the left or impede movement to the right, sudden stops or retrograde movements. *Regressive* movements are also called *leftward* movements.

• For Pulver "the generic significance of accentuated leftward tendency is that of a direction towards the ego and the past far stronger than normal", in other words "an inhibition of expression".

Centrifugal and centripetal stroke

The *centrifugal* stroke tends to prolong the end of a letter or part of a letter in a north- east direction. The *centripetal* stroke tends to prolong the end of a letter or part of a letter towards the base. These definitions are independent from those used in physics.

IV. BASIC NOTIONS

Concept of *regularity*

Pulver proposes three measurable criteria which, when their presence is constant and simultaneous, determine a *regular* handwriting: middle zone height (*i*-height), width–compression ratio, inclination of the line. For Pulver regularity is the expression of will in its dual nature: principle of organization and principle of inhibition. One needs to assess the relationship between expression of spontaneous energy and self-control, between excessive impulsiveness and reserve, between creative activity and conformity, between authenticity and artifice or pretence.

Concept of *irregularity*

Irregularity is a concept which assumes in Crépieux-Jamin's theory a positive value when it is moderate and derives from a dynamic movement. In this case it is close to the Morettian notion of "methodical irregularity", which enlivens the graphic rhythm. Irregularity concerns each graphic aspect, from organization of space to width and proportion of the letters, to pressure, connection, etc. It becomes negative when the writing is disturbed and *arrhythmic*. As a notion it is important, but difficult to judge except by the experienced graphologist. It deals with a global quality which is quintessentially gestalt. To measure it would be like attempting to measure sensitivity in numerical values. Human science cannot entertain such a task, instead it is more a matter of appreciating its quality.

It does not mean that the Morettian evaluation of the sign in quantitative terms cannot be given, but the notion of irregularity seen within the complexity of the interactions which occur must, in the final analysis, be judged by the graphologist with the help of experience.

Concept of *discordance*

When irregularities in general, or a specific type of irregularity, are found to the point where they cause complete disharmony, we may introduce the concept of discordance. Dr Gille-Maisani has explained this type fully [105], outlining the psychopathological aspects which underpin it, often in terms of character or sexual anomalies. If the writing environment is either too strict or weak it constitutes fertile ground for the growth of discordance. Statistical studies on sexual criminals, researched by Roda Wieser, have shown discordances in pressure in writings of childish or low Formlevel and lacking in rightward movement, or in monotonous writing in which spasms, exaggerations, sharp points, and centrifugal strokes are found.

Concepts of *spontaneity* and *artifice*

These are essential concepts about the genuineness or not of a writing, but difficult to quantify; they require perception on the part of the graphologist. They are widely used in judicial analysis, with other nuances, as artifice is synonymous with faking or hiding. In graphology *spontaneity* is often related to speed of writing but the two notions are not necessarily correlated. Someone manifesting motor or psychological difficulties can write "spontaneously" as well as slowly. *Artifice* goes against simplicity and spontaneity. Even before "expressing" itself artificial writing has the aim of "representing" itself. It emanates from choice, or at least from the writer's voluntary impulse.

Concepts of *simplicity* and *simplification*

Simplicity defines a writing that respects sobriety and clarity, while *simplification* involves a personalized evolution which reduces forms and strokes, favouring a rightward slant, without particularly altering the rhythm or legibility. These two notions are in reality almost in opposition and must not be confused.

V. OTHER TECHNICAL TERMS

Species *(= Sign, see Section I above)*

According to Crépieux-Jamin, "All writing manifestations are included within the seven generic categories. The categories are subdivided into *species* which express the specific qualities of each category." The French expert listed 175 species, which have seen later additions or deletions. The *Manual of Graphology* [200] contains around 155, including H. de Gobineau's "movement types" but excluding the free strokes, and initial or final strokes. Extracting the more significant species from various books by Moretti, Torbidoni and Zanin [230] propose 83 species or signs, including various types of free stroke.

Graphic environment *(see Chapters Three and Four)*

This is determined by the four main graphological categories: degree of graphic *Harmony*, quality of *Stroke*, relationship between *Form* and *Movement*, and *Rhythm*. The graphic environment establishes the relative weight of interdependence between the signs and therefore their final interpretation.

Definition *(see Chapter Five)*

The description of the graphic elements of a particular writing, which are later summarized in the "graphic synthesis", also called "technical plan". The first stage summarizes the evaluation of the graphic environment, while the second lists the signs in order of importance and checks the particular signs, accents, punctuation, signature, etc. From this, five or six *syndromes* are extracted which group together in a logical and articulate way the previously identified graphic traits, so building for each syndrome an interpretative synthesis which will be used as a guide to draw up the final portrait. Lastly the main psychological aspects are correlated: Freudian categories and the resulting psychopathological configurations, Jungian psychological types, and other aspects of character, of temperament, and of personality considered most appropriate.

• Crépieux-Jamin: "We have to exercise rigorous discipline to find out in each handwriting the dominant signs, before we can consider interpretation." See also Chapter Three, Section IV, "The fifteen principles of Crépieux-Jamin."

Graphic level

The level of a handwriting must be evaluated objectively following rigorous criteria. In general an elementary writing level is seen in people who have little education, whereas a higher standard is achieved by those with further education. Studying and above all the habit of writing gives one a greater graphomotor agility and a more personal style.

In graphological literature, the term *level* sometimes takes on a qualitative significance of "general superiority" according to some classic graphologists (today a highly questionable notion). For Crépieux-Jamin the level must be linked to *harmony* with an original, comfortable, and simplified writing, for example. Klages instead believes that it is the *rhythm* which provides the correct yardstick to judge the vitality of the writing. However there are people who present a good level of writing without much education (see e.g. Fig. 25). The graphologist acquires the perception of graphic level with practice, working on many writing styles from the same level of education or belonging to the same professional category or cultural background, etc.

PART II

GRAPHOLOGICAL METHODOLOGIES

Chapter Three

BASIC THEORIES

This chapter offers a panoramic view of the principal European theories that make up the greater part of the graphological corpus common to all practitioners. The graphologist who principally uses a particular method needs to study further in order to turn it into a sensitive instrument. In addition an overall picture can benefit the graphological culture as well as illustrate the complexity of the field.

To make it easier, we start with the Swiss school, which thanks to Pulver's theory on the symbolism of space exerts a special and immediately understood attraction. It also has the merit of putting graphology in touch with deep psychology and the dimension of the *unconscious*, without being tied up in complex psychodynamic theorizing.

We continue with the German school and the figure of Ludwig Klages in the first place, continuing with his successors Robert Heiss and Rudolf Pophal. A careful examination of the Italian school, also called Morettian in honour of its founder Father Girolamo Moretti, follows. For maximum scientific precision, we have relied on the helpful supervision of Father Lamberto Torbidoni, the current head of Italian thinking. Lastly we look at the French school and its methodology, which has usefully worked towards the integration of the findings of the Swiss and German schools. In this way we shall be prepared for the study of the categories and signs in the next chapter.

To conclude this introduction to the study of the main schools, it must be clearly pointed out that knowledge of the developmental lines of a methodology, at the level of a specialist work such as this, is one thing, but quite another to know how to apply them and test them in depth over years of experiment.

I. THE SWISS SCHOOL

Max Pulver's symbolism of space

> "The man who writes draws subconsciously his internal nature. Conscious writing is an unconscious drawing, a drawing of self, a self-portrait." (Pulver)

Max Pulver (1889–1952) was a humanist, philosopher, and poet as well as a graphologist (see Fig. 1 for his handwriting). He brought to the fore many "constants" relating to the symbolism of space which are part of our culture and in some way have been interiorized over millennia and become our collective inheritance. He applied them to the graphological field in a manner that now seems inevitable, but in reality he introduced a variable "unconscious" into a discipline still attached to mechanisms of cause and effect belonging to the positivist view of character.

We must remember that Pulver's graphology was based on the teachings of the French expert Crépieux-Jamin, as well as on Klages, of whom he was often critical. The French school in its turn has, we repeat, totally integrated Pulver's theories, probably because he – along with his contemporary Ania Teillard – had started with already known graphological methods, to which he added a level of graphological interpretation which took into account hidden dynamics of personality, the interaction between conscious and unconscious.

Pulver's fundamental book *The Symbolism of Handwriting* [207], in addition to illustrating the symbolic values relating to all graphic aspects, offered in-depth explanations on graphic and psychological themes from a very interesting viewpoint. His notions for example of *regularity* and *irregularity* demonstrate basic ways of being and lead on to concepts of *ambivalence* and *dissimulation*. He also contributed greatly to the study of *pressure* as well as the delicate problems of sincerity and honesty, presenting a list of *insincere* signs, restated later by Saudek.

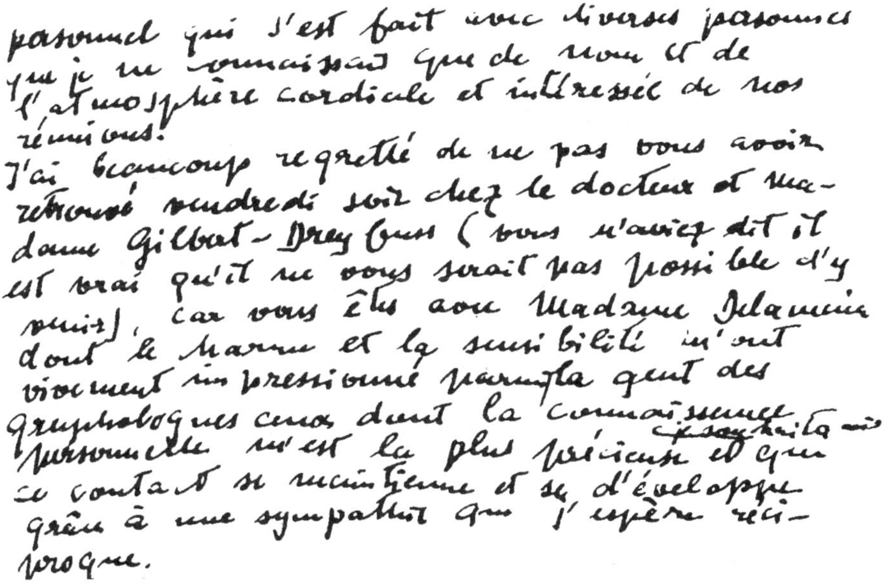
personnel qui s'est fait avec diverses personnes
que je ne connaissais que de nom et de
l'atmosphère cordiale et intéressée de nos
réunions!
J'ai beaucoup regretté de ne pas vous avoir
retrouvé vendredi soir chez le docteur et madame Gilbert-Dreyfuss (vous m'aviez dit il
est vrai qu'il ne vous serait pas possible d'y
venir), car vous êtes avec Madame Delamain
dont le charme et la sensibilité m'ont
vivement impressionné parmi la gent des
graphologues ceux dont la connaissance
personnelle m'est la plus précieuse et que
ce contact se maintienne et se développe
grâce à une sympathie que j'espère réci-
proque.

Figure 1
Max Pulver's handwriting (reduced)

SPATIAL SYMBOLISM

"He thought that he had to look for the bell on the right, because everything that was great and wonderful came from that side." (Andersen)

The spatial symbolism that Pulver made the pivot of his own methodology, represents a conceptual tool which graphologists cannot possibly ignore, even if it can be subjected to further verification. Let us consider the quote above from Andersen's tale *The Bell*, an emblematic story concerning the absorption of spatial symbolism from our collective unconscious. This shows clearly how much archaic symbolism transmitted by myths and legends is anchored within us.

In the story two children leave together to search for an extraordinary sound whose origin no one had ever been able to discover, because those who went searching for the answer had never returned. This magical and deep sound seemed to come from a distant bell on the other side of the forest that bordered the village. One day two little boys, one the son of a prince, the other of a peasant, go along together to resolve the mystery. On the edge of the forest they must choose between two paths, to the left and to the right. The peasant's son chooses the one to the right "because everything that was great and wonderful came from that side." The prince's son on the other hand chose the left path because "the sound came from the left, where the heart is." At the end of the forest, which both boys succeed in crossing, their paths meet again at sunset at the edge of the sea, and at this point they both realize that the wonderful sound is the sound of the universe itself, which they contemplate before them in all its power, holding hands "in front of the great church of nature and poetry."

In this tale Andersen does not accord any duality or priority between left and right, he transcends the notion of good and evil and grasps the union of opposites, the circular way between interior and exterior actions. To graphologists, the spontaneous attribution of power and wonder to the *right* reflects the Western symbolic tradition which puts the active, masculine, values to the right.

We cannot linger here on the many interpretations of symbolism and its cultural variations, but see Ania Teillard's corresponding chapter [227] that touches upon symbolism in other cultures, with special reference to burials.

Pulver states that at the level of our intuition "writing emerges bodily from the paper, creating a space around itself." This symbolizes our own *internal* space which delimits a primary sense of order, a *symbolic* order which is intuitive before it is intellectual. According to Pulver this is part "of an original mythic representation".

The *line* on which our writing instrument leans and moves can be a *real* or *ideal* line, symbolically similar to the horizon. The horizon divides day from night, the sky from the depths, it separates the visible and invisible, conscious and unconscious, real and imaginary, top and bottom, rise and fall, inspiration and depression. In addition, the horizontal axis of writing crosses the vertical and where they join – a point which for Pulver represents the *ego* – writing flows towards the right, at least that is the usual way for right-handed people in the West. Such a point of intersection symbolizes therefore the centre of the body, the umbilical centre from which curvilinear movements begin. Notwithstanding many returns to the left, these movements, following a graphic route which proceeds from the Self to the You, tend to the right, towards extroversion, the future, and fulfilment.

Graphic development, according to Pulver, forms an intentional act, "a psychic act that *goes towards an aim.*" The graphic stroke "crosses time-space, starting from the individual's past, involving itself in the lived of the Self and taking in the future which is devoured as the present and left behind as the past." Therefore, on the one side the past, origins, mother, dependency, and on the other side father, future, fulfilment, autonomy, are all connected and interdependent symbolisms (Table 6).

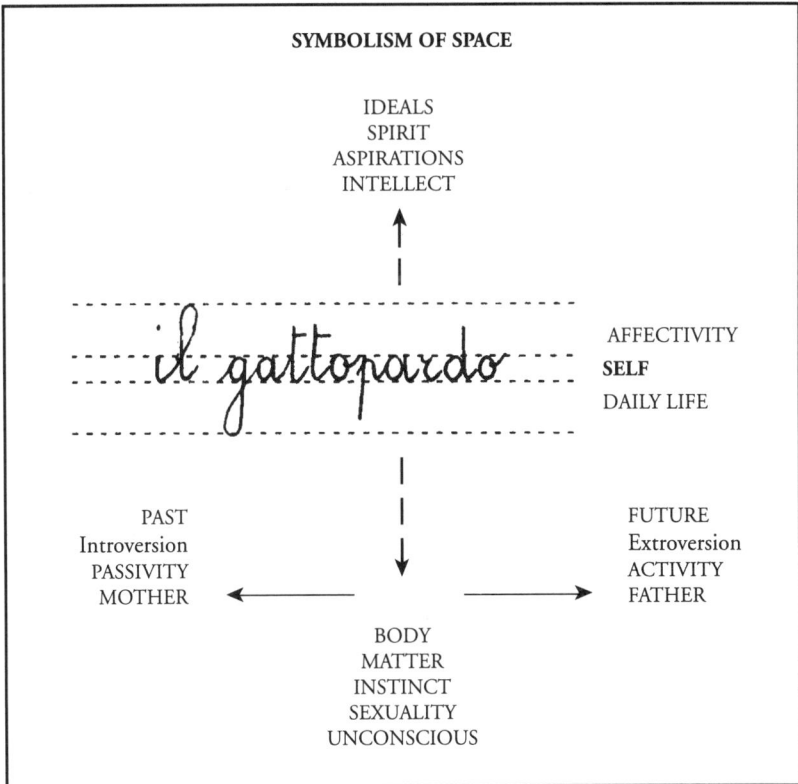

Table 6

The symbol on the other hand does not have a purely individual connotation, as Pulver explains: "my strokes could be considered as a condensed
self-portrait, but in my self-portrait the moulding forces of my antecedents
mingle with the influences of my education and environment."

In respect to writing, spatial symbolism involves the whole of the graphic
Gestalt along with the structure of the graphic body itself. The distribution
of the graphic imprint in relation to free space determines intervals and
concentrations independently from graphic forms. Therefore a structure
of space formed mainly by intervals and blank areas emerges.

GRAPHIC BODY

A single word, letter, or sign alone are all elements touched by spatial
symbolism. Rigidity, fluidity, untidiness are all aspects of the graphic
environment covered by spatial dynamics and are essential elements in
reaching a final evaluation.

The *graphic body* is made up of three zones, with the middle zone (*i*-
height) internationally established at 3 mm, and illustrates, as Pulver said,
"the old threefold division: spirit – soul – body." We must be aware, however,
that the development of the upper zone, for example, could indicate an
interest in intellectual or spiritual values, but without presupposing any
other qualitative value, or it could also be a sign of great pride or psychic
over-enthusiasm.

In the same way a prolonged lower zone will not necessarily be an
indication of materialism but could instead indicate an interest in a
deepening contact towards unconscious forces. It is necessary to bear in
mind a fundamental principle not only held by Pulver but shared by all
major experts, the *polyvalence of meanings*.

In other words the development of particular zones indicates the
intensity of certain traits but does not indicate the use made of them.

PAGE LAYOUT

By observing the written page and its margins one can immediately see the
relationship between margins and text. The weight of a deep ***upper margin***
evokes an authoritarian touch; the subject has internalized hierarchical

respect, the law of the father. If the writing is rigid, it will be at the mercy of a demanding Superego – to the point of castration – leading to problems tied to inhibition and weakness of the Self. If the writing is vivacious with signs of creativity the subject will have internalized respect for authority and the law, with a respect for rules and conventions, without any alteration in creative freedom and ability to decide. Indeed one has to recognize the positive role of the Superego in the process of *creation* which allows the artist to work tenaciously in perfecting composition and style. This process was explained by the French psychoanalyst Didier Anzieu in an extremely interesting book [7].

The *left margin* supplies much information, although this must be reviewed in the context of the cultural habits of the country or period as well as physical age. It supplies many indications of the tensions in play between past and future: attachment to values and family or escape from one's own past, capacity for autonomy, tendency to withdraw or to take up challenges, hope or fear for the future.

Absence of margin, similar to *invasive* writing in the adult hand, signals a difficulty in clear thinking and a tendency to let spontaneous images and associations of ideas run uncontrolled. By contrast, *wide spacing*, with large white gaps, may indicate loss of contact with others and with reality, or painful isolation, particularly in adolescence.

Relationships between space and text (see Lexicon: Aerated, Compact, Invasive, Tangled, Punctured) are treated by Pulver in his theory of space. To evaluate them he imagines an internal system of structuring spaces. "Those who do not allow sufficient intervals between words and lines, let themselves be guided by impulses rather than intellectual thought. This intense closeness can derive from either a richness of images arising out of a creative nature, or a simple lack of mental order."

In Fig. 2 we observe two different styles of page layout, by an artist specializing in engraving. This example confirms the need for the graphologist to have extensive documentation before pronouncing an opinion, especially when in-depth graphological analysis is required.

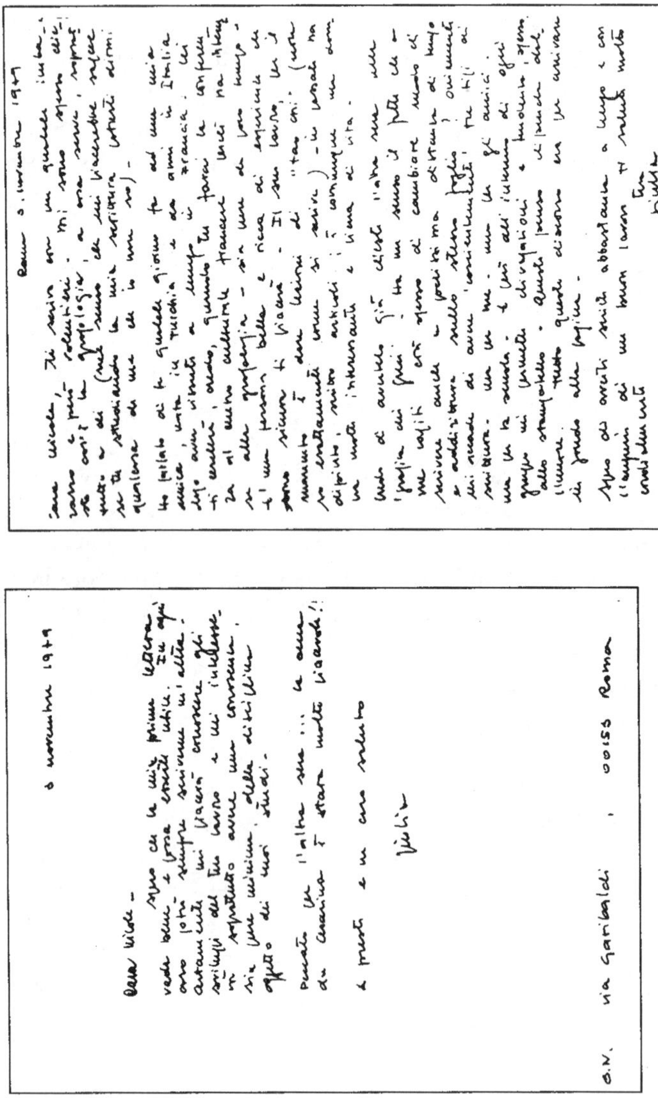

Figure 2
Writing style of the artist Giulia Napoleone: two ways of page layout

Regularity and irregularity

According to Pulver will-power in its double nature creates a *principle of organization* and a *principle of inhibition*, both modelled by the intellect. He distinguished therefore three measurable criteria whose simultaneous presence defines regularity:

(a) middle zone height (*i*-height);
(b) middle zone width–compression ratio;
(c) inclination of the line of writing.

"When the lower-case letters have roughly the same height, the intervals between them are practically identical, and the base lines appear approximately parallel", explains Pulver, the writing is *regular*. When these three criteria return different values, on the other hand, *irregularity* dominates.

The task of the graphologist confronted with *regular* writing is to see whether the resulting *organization*, with its own principles of moral ethics, allows creative energy to flow freely, or whether implicit *inhibition* carries the writing towards automatism or the building of an artificial personality, and sometimes pretence.

In the same way, with *irregularity* the graphologist must evaluate whether the sensibility is lively, with depth of reaction, or whether lack of discipline and of resistance to stimulation indicates the tendency to be at the mercy of extreme excitement or inconstancy in affection and commitment. Pulver states: "The authenticity of the sensibility (in the broad sense) cannot be judged sufficiently on just *irregularity*. It is also necessary to take into account the way in which *forms* are created, together with *rhythmic* distribution and the appearance of the *stroke*."

Signs of insincerity

From the notion of irregularity we turn to *ambivalence*, a theme that Pulver treated thoroughly. The signs of insincerity which Pulver proposed (as listed by Saudek; see Table 7) may certainly now be reviewed in the light of the subsequent evolution of writing and the findings of the French and Italian schools of graphology, more than the German. (See the article by Catherine

Dupuis [86] who has picked out five types of "fraudulent writings".) We take upon our own authority the suppression of some of Pulver's signs which we believe must be placed in a more general context, like the following (see Lexicon):

- *structural* writing;
- some cases of *artificial* writing;
- what Pulver has called *shark's tooth* writing, which can indicate repressed aggression in an adolescent: it implies a tendency to conceal but does not necessarily translate into dishonesty;
- *arcaded* writing in general: as well as conformism it can reveal the need to be constructive;
- *leftward slant*, which can represent a defensive mechanism.

Other signs must be contemporaneously present to reach the conclusion of dishonesty. Signs to be excluded are those caused by pathological or motor deterioration.

Pulver identifies the presence of these signs according to whether the writing is either "slow" or fluid (or rather "not slowed down"). It would appear now that his distinction does not have much importance. In fact in both classes many signs are suspicious. The fact that a particular writing is slowed down deliberately is already an indication, even if not sufficient proof, of a possible manipulative tendency. See [207] for a detailed treatment of the subject.

SIGNS OF INSINCERITY (after Pulver and Saudek)	
In SLOW writing	**In writing NOT SLOWED DOWN**
Artificial writing	Unexpected filiform strokes
Covering strokes	Wavy base line
Arcades curved back	Ambiguous forms
Coarseness and strange complications	Receding connections
Omission of letters	Omission of letters
Substitution of letters	Substitution of letters
Retouching	Dissimilarity between text and signature
Inversions	Various exaggerations
Leftward tendency	Coarseness and strange complications

Table 7

II. THE GERMAN SCHOOL

The principles of Ludwig Klages

Ludwig Klages (1872–1956) studied chemistry then dedicated himself to philosophy and psychology, moving away from the accepted thinking of his own time. His energies and ability were concentrated on the creation of a "natural philosophy" which would catch life's meaning. The core of Klages' philosophical thought, the juxtaposition between *Seele* (soul) and *Geist* (spirit), owes its basic direction to the works of Nietzsche and Bachofen.

Giampiero Moretti [174] wrote: "With Bachofen, Klages discovers the existence of an original natural right founded on principles which seem to return us to a stage in human civilization not yet conditioned by the spirit. Interpreting the oldest myths, Bachofen had traced in his works the uncertain history of the *development*, from an original right which guaranteed basic equality, to principles dictated by the spirit as a force which separates, divides, and 'assigns' according to canons that only man established by the power of the will."

But having arrived at this stage, Klages goes further, appealing to Nietzsche's concept of the *dionysiac*, but freeing it, juxtaposing to it the spirit and so placing the *soul* as a repository of life in its dionysiac essence. According to Klages, in effect, the spirit's wilful interference tends to overwhelm the creative spontaneity of the *soul*, the *soul* and body forming life's vital nucleus. Klages therefore intends to reach this fundamental nucleus of the character by studying a sublime expression of it whose outline endures through time – namely an individual's handwriting.

THE SCIENCE OF EXPRESSION

Klages as a philosopher of the science of expression, propounds some philosophical criteria that underlie the *rhythm of life* and by extension the rhythm of writing, as an expressive manifestation. Klages considers that "writing is an outline, better still an *image*, and by examining it one can to some extent reveal the mode, or the 'place' where the spirit has 'met' (and often attacked) the unitary body-soul of the self who is writing."

The essence of being human is also shown through other expressive means, from the way of walking, of greeting and shaking hands, as well as facial expression, tone of voice, the mode of conversation, etc. But graphic expression is unique because of its "durable" imprint, which challenges the present, takes account of the past, and foresees the future.

MOVEMENT OF EXPRESSION AND MOVEMENT OF REPRESENTATION

Klages intended to track, in the varied movements of writing, those expressing the *soul* so as to distinguish them from the constricted movements which the spirit tends to impose. Movement is the result of two opposing forces, the first *expressive*, the other *representative* or *impressed*, which are mostly guided by personal *Leitbild* (individual directional image or *anticipatory* image, see Chapter Two). *Leitbild* anticipates an effect that one wants to create, by the intervention of the will.

Expressive writing is therefore that which presents itself with spontaneity and naturalness, expressing the subject's emotions and sensations. The impressed type of writing mostly obeys "rules" or tries to produce an effect on others, and ultimately becomes "acquired", a concept which is linked with the notion of artificiality (see Chapter Two). As in every aspect of human behaviour, writing feels the effects of two tendencies: expression and representation.

KLAGES' FUNDAMENTAL PRINCIPLES

The following principles were summarized from Klages [120] by Bernhard Wittlich.

1. Each graphic sign is capable of more than one meaning; it takes on its specific significance *only* within the framework of a group of signs.
2. Principle of duality (or bipolarity): each expressive movement contains a dual interpretation according to what is produced:
    (a) by force of the instinct (positive meanings);
    (b) by either stopping or limiting the instinct (negative meanings).

3. The graphologist's perception of expressive content must not rely solely on rational evaluation, but also on personal ability to tune in with the rhythm of the writing, and therefore with its author.

DUALITY (BIPOLARITY) OF GRAPHIC INDICATORS

One of Klages' famous examples illustrates the theme of *duality* better than any other explanation: two small boys A and B find themselves suddenly in front of a field of tulips. A starts to pick a bunch of flowers, whereas B hesitates and abstains from picking. How do we judge them? Perhaps A is gifted with a stronger impulsive force, a greater ability to participate? Or does he prove weak at resistance? Does B have a lesser desire to pick flowers? Can he perhaps control himself better? Or is he afraid of punishment – the punishment of which A is also frightened but whose desire is greater? Perhaps B demonstrates an internalized and contemplative emotion, whose indifference only conceals the intensity of his feeling?

Facts can be noted, but what needs to be found after that is the play of instinctive or antagonistic forces moving behind a particular type of behaviour. For Klages, writing, as every human expression, is conditioned as much by the force of a psychic impulse, to which he attributes a plus value (+), as by weakness in psychic resistance, assigned a minus value (–).

How then can the true quality of life, hidden beneath an assumed attitude, be found through writing? To clarify the problem, the key concept will be that of Formlevel, which is itself the basis of studying writing. In order to establish Formlevel, Klages proposes the conception of *rhythm*, connecting this directly to the evaluation of *regularity* and the degree of *proportion*. We shall postpone until Section IV of this chapter the technical study of rhythm and Formlevel, within the framework of the total evaluation of *writing environment*. Now however we shall try to understand the vitality of a writing and how this is expressed visually through rhythm.

RHYTHM IN LIFE AND IN WRITING

Rhythm according to Klages is itself the expression of life. Different forms of life are governed by temporal and spatial rhythms, whether days, seasons, or the waves of the sea which reproduce themselves constantly, always similar but never identical. "Through imperceptible transformations between two limits, the incessant alternation of mountains and valleys follows each other without pauses, jumps, or breaks", stated Klages.

Rhythm is the opposite of *cadence*. Rhythm is free from constrictions, leaving the deep spring of the *soul* to break free and manifest its vital fullness. Cadence keeps always the same time and space imposing the law of the *spirit*.

To better explain the notion of rhythm we will now look at writing samples of the historical figures Nietzsche, Napoleon, and Beethoven, taken from Klages' studies. These samples are very evocative and favour therefore a first perception of graphological rhythm, even though other writing aspects (covered later on) will be brought in so as not to be too simplistic. In this way the reader will begin to be attuned to the vitality of handwriting without being at this stage influenced by specific technicalities.

Klages defines Nietzsche's rhythm (Fig. 3) as a *chiselled rhythm* and gives the philosopher the highest grade of Formlevel. He observes in this writing "natural proportions, optimal and original organization of the body of the writing combined with neat and refined forms", whereas in the writing

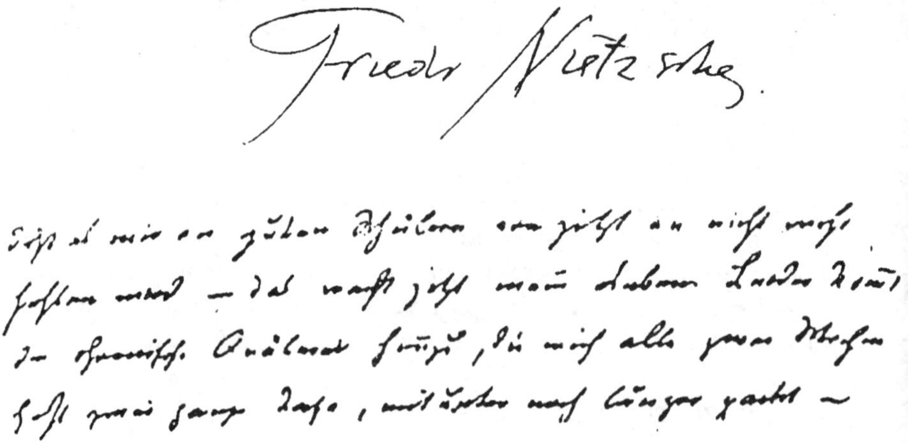

Figure 3
Writing of Friedrich Nietzsche (reduced)

of Napoleon (Fig. 4) he sees "the powerful but blind expression of the intensity of life, constricting those possessed of it." Two very different types of rhythm are seen here, but both are highly personalized. Independently from any value judgement, the rather obsessive aspect of Nietzsche's writing and the overexcitement of Napoleon's are not concealed from the modern graphologist. But let us not enter further into the complex question of play between psychic forces and their interference with character.

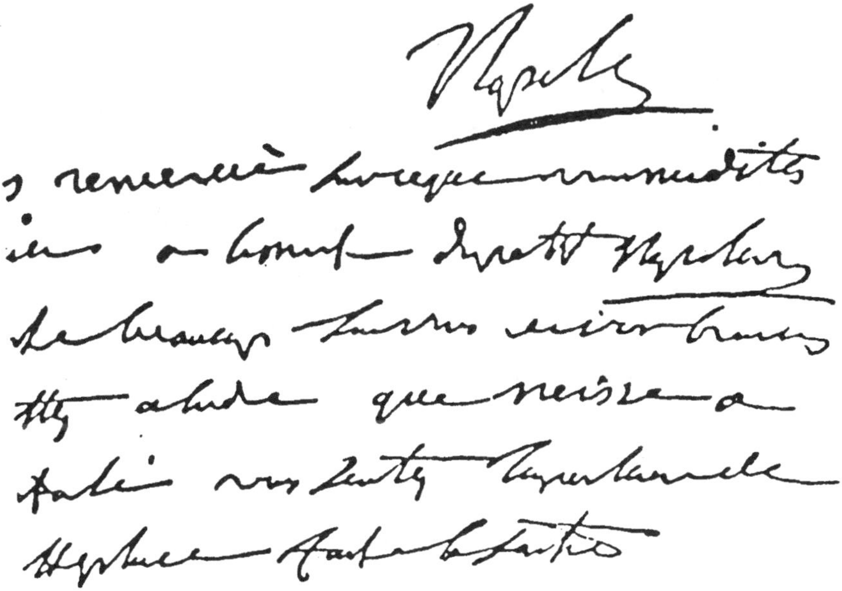

Figure 4
Writing of Napoleon Bonaparte (reduced)

Beethoven's writing has been a target of many authors (see Dr Gille-Maisani's bibliography on Beethoven [108]). Crépieux-Jamin included it among *harmonious* writings, describing it as follows: "Beethoven's writing is not like any other ... Beethoven is a whole being in his harmonious, simple, simplified, comfortable, uninhibited, semi-angular, firm, resolute writing, always moving but remaining noble in its strokes." To view the style as harmonious the Frenchman had obviously seen a text by Beethoven written in French and as a result written less exuberantly and in a more studied fashion than usual (Fig. 5a). For Klages, on the other hand, Beethoven's writing (Fig. 5b) becomes the prototype of writing with strong *rhythm* but without *harmony* through lack of regularity and proportion. It reaches heights of "original spirituality in the language of its forms." It expresses the overflowing of the *soul* which upsets the spirit, and for Klages his Formlevel approaches the highest grade.

Figures 5a and 5b
Writing of Ludwig van Beethoven (reduced)

Klages measured his Formlevel in five stages, a system that graphology has not maintained. Now Formlevel is only judged high, medium, or low. In the few samples to which Klages gave the highest grade "1" he included his *own*, which certainly can only amuse us (Fig. 6).

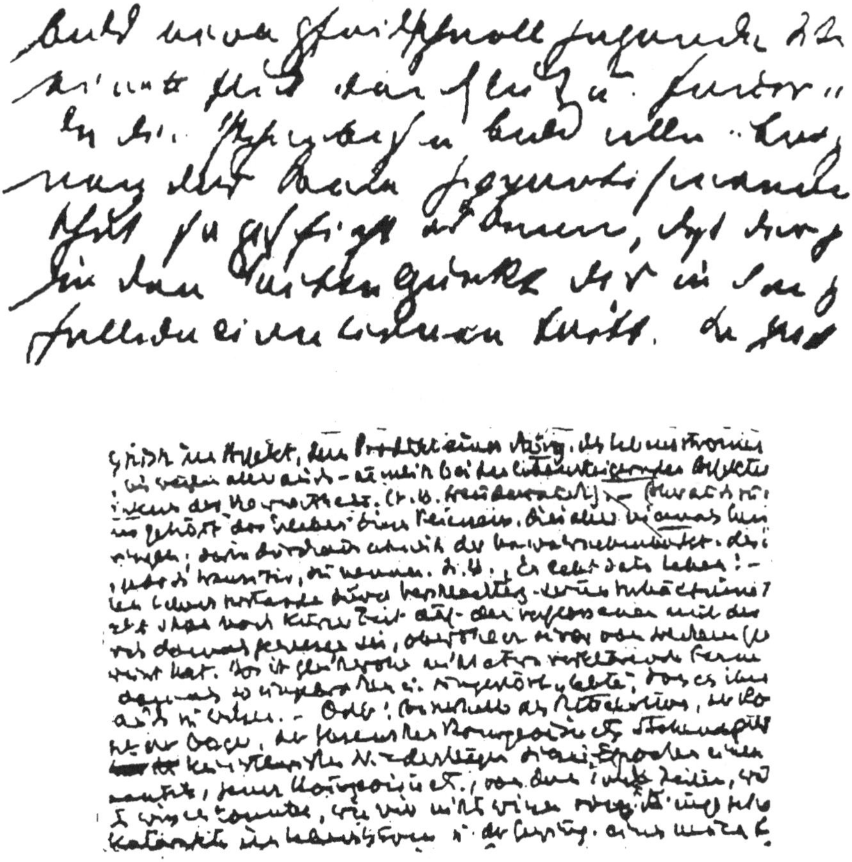

Figure 6
Writings of Ludwig Klages (18 and 44 years old)
(Taken from *La Graphologie* 175)

The major hazard for the evaluation of rhythm consists in the risk of subjective evaluation. In this, the Cartesian Crépieux-Jamin could only clash with the German master's opinions, and their exchanges during the 1928 Congress in Paris testify to the bitterness of their discussions. Klages and Ania Teillard believed that the *rhythm* of a handwriting had to be *felt* because it cannot be understood in relation to descriptive and objective categories. Even if the German expert preferred empathic participation with writing, at the same time he placed some limits to subjectivity. These are today under review; however, one must remember them because they draw attention to the delicacy of certain approaches.

VALUE AND LIMITATIONS OF GRAPHOLOGY ACCORDING TO KLAGES

- ELEMENTS NOT RECOVERABLE THROUGH HANDWRITING
  - sex, profession, illness;
  - ingenuity, creative ability;
  - some components of character (only discernible through reasoning);
  - harmony of characters between partners;
  - criminality.

- VALIDITY (as regards other psychological research)
  - subject must be independent, free from artificial examination situations;
  - availability of an existing and spontaneous writing;
  - possibility of identifying the greatest diversity of character aspects as well as their harmonious and conflicting interactions.

- SUBJECTIVE LIMITS OF THE GRAPHOLOGIST
  - necessity of acquiring a "specific and delicate sensitivity in looking at writing";
  - ability in exposition and argument.

With this last point Klages focuses on the graphologist's ability as a determining factor and the need to be on top of any theoretical and technical training. This concerns the capacity not only to talk in a general way but to express oneself in writing in a clear but informed style – in particular a style that must communicate with the interlocutor.

LAWS OF ACQUIRED WRITING (KLAGES–MEYER)

Klages in his principal book *Handschrift und Charakter* reiterates the laws of Georg Meyer which mostly concern the field of judicial expertise but which every graphologist must know. These are the "Laws of acquired writing" which explain the relationship between attention and spontaneity in the assessment of masked writing.

The Klages–Meyer view is useful for two reasons: firstly for the light it sheds on the relationship between graphic stroke, intention, and attention, secondly for the distinction between the "acquired-representational" type, that is to say a self-imposed writing style, with mastery of its own forms of stroke (more representational than expressive), and writing "acquired" in Klages' sense of tending to conceal. According to Georg Meyer's studies on masked writing, "a graphic property is much more difficult to remove if it belongs to the imagery expressive of the will, or rather it is much more difficult to produce the less it belongs to the imagery expressive of the will." Therefore three basic laws come out of this:

1. *Law of the direction of the attention*

This law allows us to identify the properties representative of a script from those which are not. How does one act generally when wishing to modify one's own writing? By modification of capital letters, which are immediately obvious to the eye; modification of long lower-case letters (*f, p*...), then the medium-sized ones (*b, d, t*...), then the low ones (vowels, *c, m*...), in size, width, position; modification especially at the beginning of words and phrases; no interest in accessory elements.

2. *Law of the difficulty or ease of producing graphic properties*

Some properties are more difficult to change in a mechanical manner because the graphic impulses resist to a certain degree the directions of the will. To begin with it seems easy enough: changing the direction of lines or the difference in length of consonants, changing the position of the dot of the *i*; however, the attention span cannot last long enough.

When altering handwriting it is easier to substitute voluntarily signs of *resistance* than the other way around. The following signs of resistance are therefore more readily produced: *strong pressure – narrowness – verticality – disconnection – double angles – arcades – thin forms – leftward strokes – great differences in length – strengthening of lower strokes – organization – lack of speed – regularity* (the *acquired* movement being slower than the natural one).

Consequently the following properties are not generally *acquired* properties: *light pressure – width – inclination – double curves – garlands – full forms – rightward strokes – little differences in length – lack of organization – speed – irregularity.*

3. *Law of concomitant modifications*

Some typical accessory effects are triggered off during the course of an intentional attempt to influence one's own writing. "Each act of transformation is accompanied by accessory effects which testify to an increasing progressive effort, such as the regularity of the general aspect, frequency of interruptions, and growing vigour", said Klages.

AFTER KLAGES

German graphologists after Klages have grounded the concept of rhythm through other verifiable criteria. Rudolf Pophal and Roda Wieser studied the properties of *movement* as an "index of rhythm", establishing the degrees and modes of its elasticity and rigidity. Robert Heiss described three main rhythms: of *movement, space,* and *form.* These perspectives also allowed another problem to be overcome, that of level of *culture.* There is no doubt that a high cultural level enhances the expression in writing of a more personalized rhythm, in Klages' sense.

The differentiation between the various rhythms along with the theory of tension or release in writing allows us to better catch the play between spontaneity and graphic constriction, even in writings called elementary. These difficulties in the evaluation of spontaneous elements are better resolved now thanks to the psychodynamic researches of Pulver and Ania Teillard, which allow us to penetrate the dynamics of personality by using a variety of approaches.

Even if Pophal seems to precede Heiss on the German graphology stage, we shall first outline Heiss's theories because they are easier to understand than those of Pophal.

The three rhythms of Robert Heiss

While writing, the hand expresses and impresses a *movement* which uses and organizes the surrounding *space* at an overall and a specific level, creating, by means of gesture and stroke, a *form*. The interaction of these three aspects characterizes the graphic physiognomy and produces a unique *rhythm* for every handwriting. Heiss takes up an idea from Carl Gross (a graphologist who died young) and divides rhythm into three aspects, rhythm of *movement*, *space*, and *form*, each capable of assuming different degrees of organization (*underdeveloped – accentuated – disturbed*).

From the interaction of the three rhythms the graphic personality emerges, which springing from a *movement* confronts a *space* and synthesizes itself in the rhythm of the *structuring of form*. The prevalence of one rhythm over the others is indicative of the personality, which favours one type of adaptation and demonstrates a particular behaviour.

1. RHYTHM OF MOVEMENT

One needs to observe, says Catherine de Bose [71], how "the movement projects itself forward or slips, advances or hesitates, climbs, blocks itself, etc.; the strength or weakness of its course; and the different directions and sequences of the strokes. In practice, it is easier to discover the movement by observing the writing in a mirror or upside down. Forms soften and details of the movement stand out better." The rhythm of movement throws light on the deep personality structure, with its impulses, its unconscious reflexes, its emotional flow uncontrolled by the will.

Rhythm of movement underdeveloped

Graphic dynamism is poor and uneasy: awkward stroke, connections hesitant, jerky, or tight, blocked or unsteady rhythm. Pressure is weak with thin stroke. This expresses a personality of weak character with poor or blocked impulses and tendencies of resignation.

connaisse pas grand chose c'est
l'entreprise et son développemen
qui m'intéressen.

Je souhaiterais vous rencontrer

J'ai 41 ans, titulaire du bre
vitaire au long cours, j'ai quitté la Marine
Industrie, après quelques années à la compag
Transatlantique.

Etant donné que vous cherchez un jeune Ingénieur
de diagnostic et de l'étude critique des installations,
soumettre ma candidature.

rimation de l'artisanat. Pour ce fai
Créé en 1967, a divisé le Québec en
ayan de mieux connaître le monde
le pousser vers une plus grande pro-
en se souciant de lui garder son

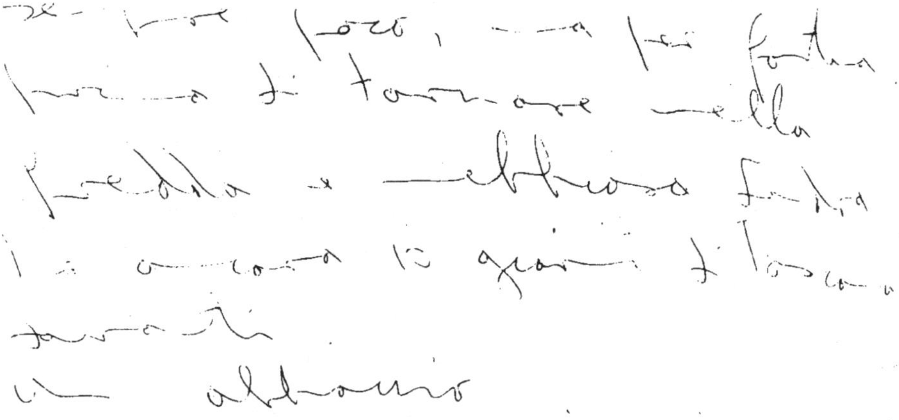

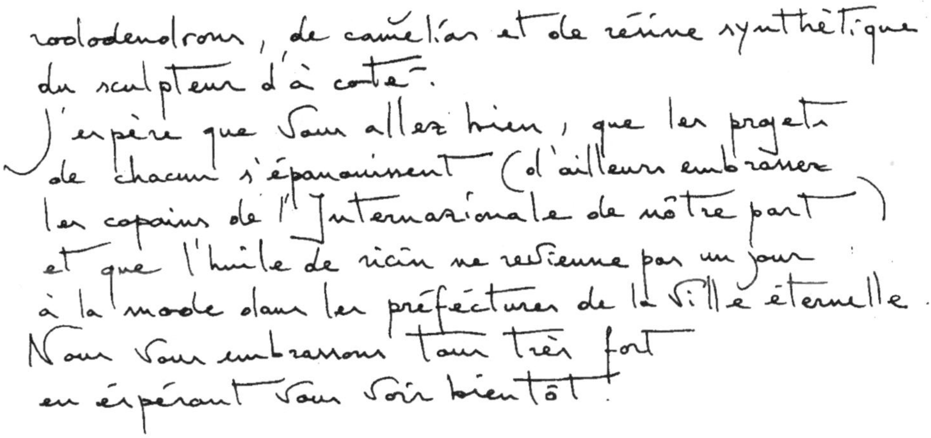

rododendron, de camélias et de résine synthétique du sculpteur d'à côté.
J'espère que vous allez bien, que les projets de chacun s'épanouissent (d'ailleurs embrasser les copains de l'Internationale de notre part) et que l'huile de ricin ne revienne pas un jour à la mode dans les préfectures de la Ville éternelle. Nous vous embrassons tous très fort en espérant vous voir bientôt.

Figure 8 (above)
Relationship between movement and form:
(a) 32 year old left-handed financial agent: rhythm of movement prevails over form;
(b) 30 year old painter, rhythm of form prevails

◄ Figure 7 (left)
In the first two samples the rhythm of movement prevails over that of form; in the last two the rhythm of form prevails

Rhythm of movement accentuated

Diversified graphic dynamic: supple, spontaneous gesture, assured and fluid connections. Firm elastic stroke (rhythmic tension). Variety of connections. Full dynamic forms (originating spontaneously from a flowing movement). Open personality expressing with ease all its potential. The person is able to assimilate, change, and evaluate experiences and influences, by adjusting and adapting behaviour to reality.

Figure 9 (see opposite page)
Accentuated and personalized rhythm of space (page: 15 x 21 cm)
Writing of Hélène Mottis Planet, graphologist: balanced relationship
between rhythm of movement and form: forms flow from the movement

Rhythm of movement disturbed

Uncoordinated and agitated. Lack of control and homogeneity. Uneven stroke, too rigid or too loose, shaky or broken. Spasmodic pressure. Forms muddled by the movement. Often conceals a pathology and needs an in-depth study.

2. RHYTHM OF SPACE

One needs to see how the writing laid out on the page manages spaces, between lines, words, letters, and also the margins. One needs to understand how the graphic stroke deals with space in relation to the vertical or horizontal axis of the graphic flow, and with what proportions.

Rhythm of space underdeveloped

Space is arranged according to passive or conventional or casual criteria with no particular choice. The manner of direction or inclination can be purely schoolbook, rigid, or awkward. The distribution of white space and text is untidy, the graphic body is poorly defined, and margins are neglected. Such underdeveloped spatial rhythm indicates the writer's dependence on environment and lack of autonomy. One must however consider nationality differences, cultural habits, and learning models (see Arigraf survey on invasive writings [55]).

8 janvier 62

Chère Madame —

Voici le second corrigé —
Dans l'ensemble — et sauf
quelques erreurs bien excusables
au départ — c'est bien —

Je comprends très bien que
vous vouliez attendre, pour les
analyses. Mais vous verrez vous-
même. par la suite, combien une
analyse approfondie demande
d'heures de travail — et c'est la
raison des tarifs qui peuvent
paraître élevés à première vue.

Croyez à mes meilleurs
sentiments.

L. Mottis Plant

Rhythm of space accentuated

When space is extremely personalized, active, and shows control of what is put on the page, without rigidity, such a rhythm of space is often proof of successful adjustment and a satisfactory exchange between the writer and the environment. Other criteria may show us whether the adjustment is easy, or derived from a conscious will to show individuality, which does not always lead to an harmonious relationship of subject and environment.

We can see, for example, how the graphic space of a poet can be "accentuated" with the deliberate arrangement of lines, margins, or spaces. The relationship with the environment is not necessarily easy, rather the poet has created a "protective island" which allows a positive exchange between the depths of being and the outside environment, but only within a complex personal vision of existence.

Fig. 9 well illustrates an accentuated rhythm of space. It is the writing of a famous graphologist, Hélène Mottis Planet, a student of Ania Teillard who continued to study for a long time with her by correspondence, and who died prematurely.

Rhythm of space disturbed

The spacing shows a disorderly and almost incoherent appearance: the rhythm attests obstacles to social inclusion. The subject adopts a situation of conflict with the environment, without being especially antisocial: this is often a trait in people who have psychopathological problems. One however must be careful! Sometimes those who have a highly creative talent use writing beyond bounds of normal criteria, as a means of expression, of mental release, and the disorder can be complete.

3. RHYTHM OF FORM

Rhythm of form underdeveloped

Forms are schoolbook, impersonal, awkward, boring. They have remained on the whole strictly at an elementary level. It could also indicate an illiterate person. In the case of those who are reasonably educated, the lack of personalized writing style shows straightaway a conventional mental structure. One need not apply the term "underdeveloped" to those very "simple", applied hands, faithfully emulating schoolbook forms, but with a strong and differentiated stroke, which could belong to personalities of great refinement and reliability, who remain internalized without any desire to stand out.

Rhythm of form accentuated

Forms are liberated from the strictly schoolbook, tending to individualism by inventive means, the stroke is well controlled. The result is easy forms, at the same time structured, dynamic, and different. When form flows from movement it is called a *rhythm of creation of form*. The personality interacts with its impulses and the need to structure life. The Ego leans towards stability and assimilation. If form inhibits movement, the personality lacks spontaneity and freedom. One may be afraid that suddenly the repressed flow will break its banks.

Rhythm of form disturbed

Exaggerated forms prevail, either confined by rigidity or monotony or veering towards absurd ornament. Some take on aspects of dissolution and graphic imbalance by the fact that the invasive forms neutralize both the space and the flow of the movement. These are automatic "strokes" more than forms. The "obsessive" or "overornamented" rhythms of form are found in schizophrenic handwriting.

In graphological practice an evaluation is based above all on whether the movement prevails over form and vice versa, or if one overwhelms or constrains the other.

Rudolf Pophal's degrees of tension

The neurologist Pophal established a classification of the movement's *tension* and formulated the hypothesis that the tension of the writing, and consequently of the stroke, is developed and controlled by precise localized cerebral commands. This theory is today contested because of discoveries of more complicated mechanisms. Nevertheless, Pophal's correlations between degrees of writing tension and personality traits remain an important element in graphological research. Studies conducted by W. H. Müller and A. Enskat [178] along with continuing studies by other independent graphologists are testimony to the fertile field of discovery opened up by the Germans Klages, Pophal, and Heiss. We mention as examples Thea Stein-Lewinson, Ursula Avé-Lallemant, Rosa Wieser, Hans Knobloch, Bernard Wittlich, and Gerhardt Grünwald, authors whom Catherine de Bose has introduced into France through the journal *La Graphologie* [71] over many years, and whose ideas she has summarized further in a recent book [72].

In this book she states: "Pophal's method of degrees of tension is certainly the essential element of present German graphology ... the elasticity which it categorizes is an essential condition of rhythm. All in all one may think that the observation of tension compensates in part for our present inability to understand exactly what lies behind the graphic stroke."

The focal point of Pophal's theory is the distinction that he makes between "tension" produced by *pressure* and "tension" which comes from the process of *stiffening*. If both pressure and stiffening represent at the physiological level states of tension, the voluntary struggle that is expressed by both directs itself in a different way. In practice "the general sense of pressure is activity, that of stiffening is resistance." According to Pophal's theory five principal classifications define the *management of movement* and are called *degrees of tension*. They inform on the subject's adaptability to reality.

Grade I: *weak tension.* The stroke and layout is weak, slack, with uncertain hesitant forms. Personality lacks structure and does not get involved much.

Grade II: *adequate suppleness.* Stroke and layout is fluid and elastic. Easy adaptability and availability (even excessive) characterizes the subject. Adaptability stems from natural disposition rather than will.

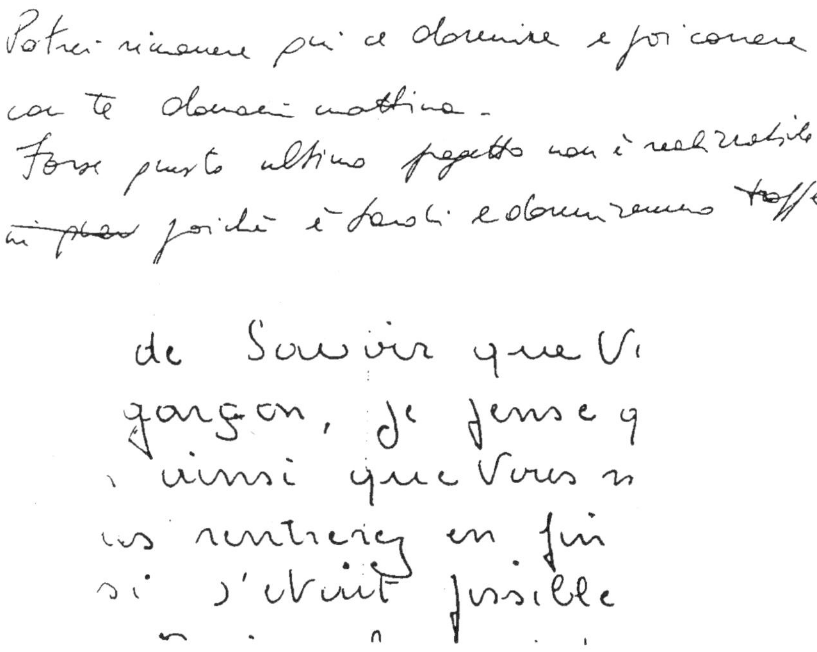

Figure 10 (reduced)
Insufficient tension: Pophal's Grade I

Grade III: *adequate control* in the management of movement. Firmness and flexibility join up to give the writing body. The personality shows a type of decisive and rational adaptability. The intervention of a programmed will comes into play, but without rigidity, defence is proportionate to the attack. In Grade III one can identify three different styles, called *stylizations*: *logical, ethical,* and *aesthetic stylization.*

The *logical* stylization responds to a prevailing intellectual precept: writing is clear and aerated, sober, concentrated, with a neat stroke and a tendency to closeness. The *ethical* stylization produces a more impersonal writing style similar to schoolbook, and at times can mask antisocial tendencies when the "covering" stroke predominates. The *aesthetic* stylization denotes a "receptive aesthetic sensitivity", where studied simplification sets into relief some aesthetic forms. The writer wants to be valued, but Klages has rightly warned us not to overestimate these hands, which however express a need "to be artistic". Excessive stylization produces a mechanized movement, with structured forms (see Heiss above), which is therefore assigned to Grade IVa.

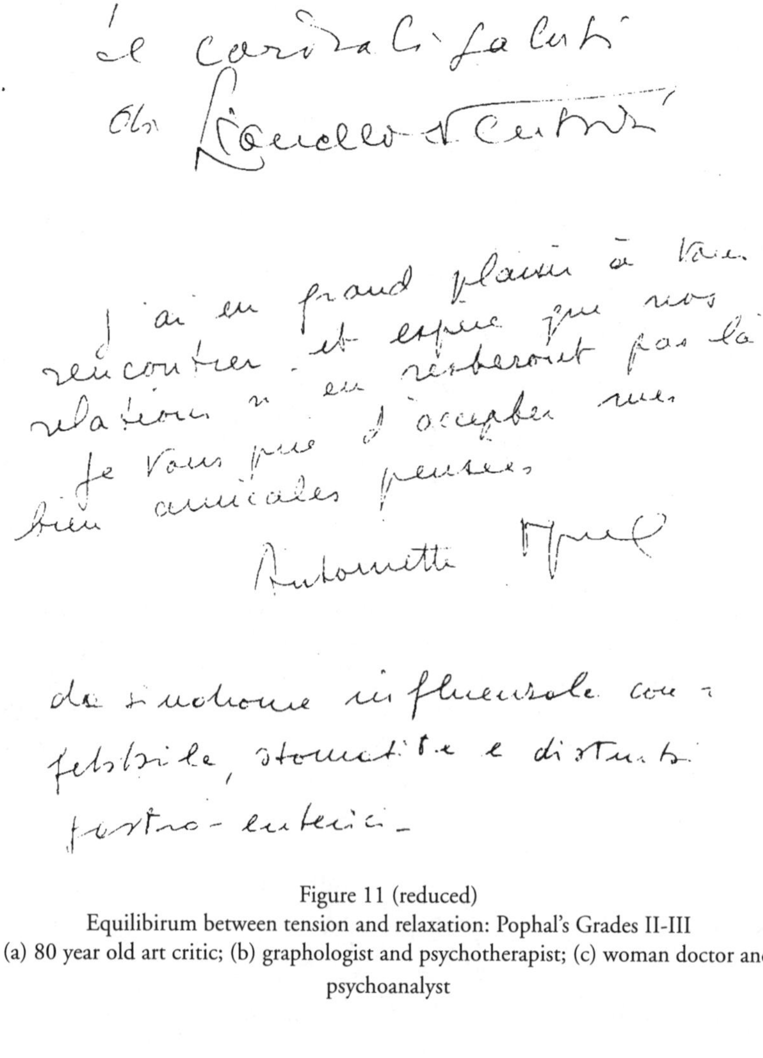

Figure 11 (reduced)
Equilibirum between tension and relaxation: Pophal's Grades II-III
(a) 80 year old art critic; (b) graphologist and psychotherapist; (c) woman doctor and psychoanalyst

Grade IVa: *stiffening, insufficient suppleness.* The stroke is tight and the layout barely elastic, it presents a deliberate or monotonous pace. The adaptability of the subject is of a voluntary kind, with little flexibility; it remains however a voluntary discipline.

Grade IVb: *inhibition.* Strokes are "jerky" and the layout is inhibited or rigid, static. The subject is anxious, distressed, and unable to confront reality. Mood is dark, obstinate, diffident, and at times depressed.

Grade V: *rigidity, contraction.* The stroke is no longer controlled because of excessive tension or because forms dissolve. Adaptability is entirely problematic: deep anxiety, outbursts of inadequacy; often a symptom of a pathological state.

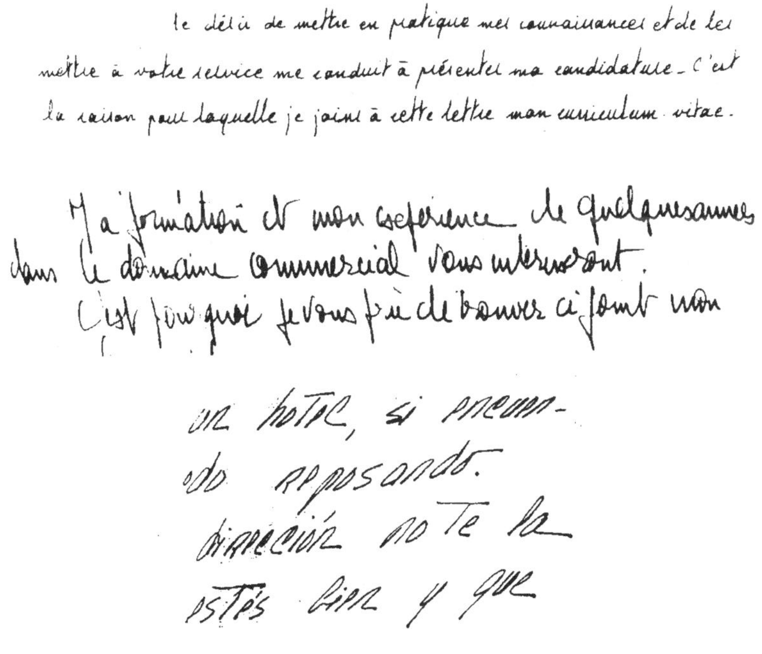

Figure 12 (reduced)
Excessive tension, voluntary rigidity: Pophal Grade IVa
(a) young engineer; (b) secretary; (c) 30 year old Spanish lady

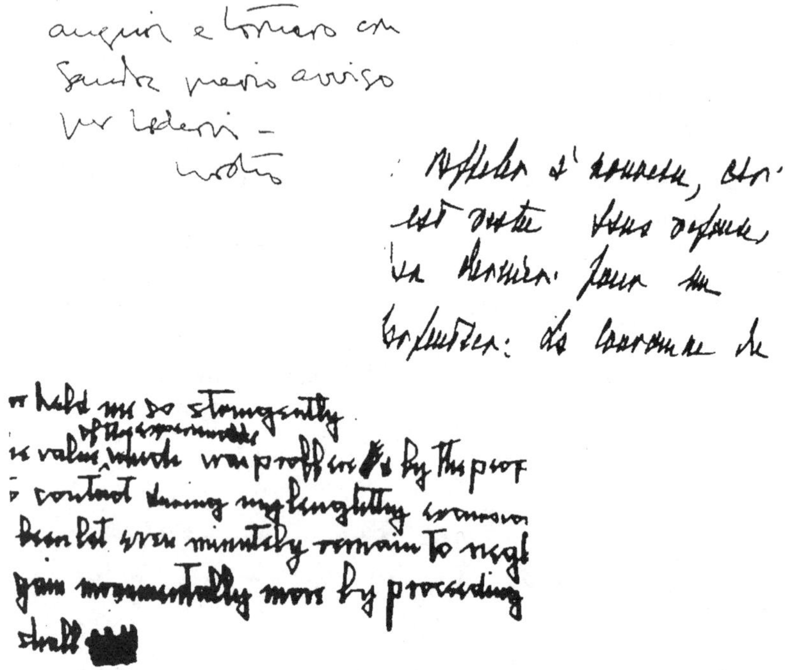

Figure 13 (reduced)
Excessive tension, involuntary contraction/feebleness: Pophal Grade IVb and V
(a) Latin-American artist; (b) industrialist; (c) severe pre-schizophrenic pathology

The German school supplies, as we have seen, a wide and very distinct graphological view which concentrates on what happens to the graphic stroke as it unfolds in the graphic space. The elasticity of its movement; timing and polarity of its sequences; presence or absence of spatial rules which govern it; and the relationship between form and movement – accentuation of impulsiveness when the movement prevails or, when form prevails, an emphasis on disposition controlled through mental imagination.

For wider explanations, Müller and Enskat [178] have set out in tables the elasticity, modality, and timing of movement. We may also refer to the well-illustrated book of Catherine de Bose [72].

III. THE ITALIAN SCHOOL

1. The method of Girolamo Moretti

With the exception of the Morettian method, the instruction used in this book is mostly drawn from the teachings of the French school, where we received our basic graphological education. However, because we have lived an Italian life for many years, we have little by little absorbed also the teaching methods of the Morettian School at the University of Urbino.

In this section we shall try not to elicit comparisons with the German or French schools but simply expound the Morettian method. Each method, as mentioned before, has its own structural order. Any serious examination of writing must be framed by one of the complete methodologies. One can certainly borrow a single aspect from another method, but should not adopt a general mixture that might risk superficiality or the alteration of basic concepts. Dr Gille-Maisani in the preface to the French edition of Torbidoni and Zanin wrote: "In graphology as in other human sciences each school is complete in itself, given that none can pretend to possess all of the Truth."

We shall refer as a principal source of information to this practical and theoretical text by Torbidoni and Zanin [230], authors who have the merit, according to Giancarlo Galeazzi in the preface, "of organizing in a simple and systematic manner the richness of Morettian graphology." Our approach can only be synthetic but also tries to be objective and, it must be explained, comes from knowing from the outside how much we do not always apply such a method in our analyses.

GIROLAMO MORETTI

Father Girolamo Moretti was born at Recanati in 1879 and died in Ancona in 1963. He not only created the Italian graphological method but also founded the present Istituto Grafologico "G. Moretti" based in Ancona and Urbino. Father Lamberto Torbidoni succeeded him as director, followed in 1982 by Father Fermino Giacometti.

Girolamo Moretti may be unique in the history of graphology for creating a new method on his own and also forming a group of true scholars, moreover in a Franciscan monastic environment, and therefore full of dedication without the need for social recognition. His ideas spread quickly and openly without any tendency to a "sect" mentality. Moretti had none of the attributes of the "shaman" surrounded by meek disciples, on the contrary he was a pioneer with exceptional charisma, a stimulating source of constructive creativity. This was reflected in the high quality of the School at Urbino, an offshoot of the Institute and later attached to the University of Urbino, offering a diploma in consulting graphology.

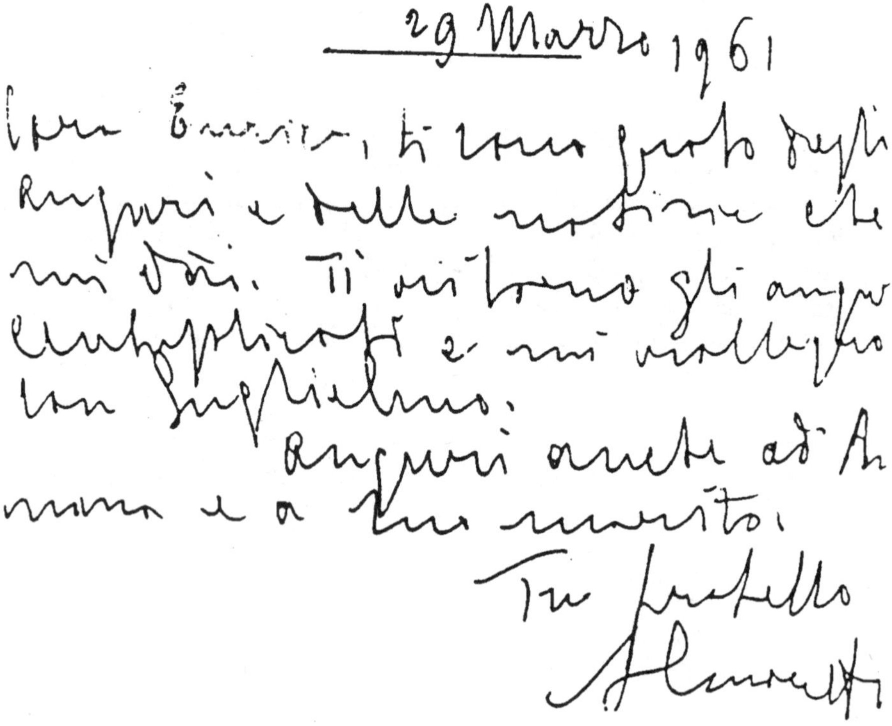

Figure 14
Girolamo Moretti's writing

The graphological work of Moretti was the result of 50 years of observation, research, and activities both scientific and popular. Moretti combined the Franciscan friar's lifestyle with a passionate commitment to discover the vital sources of graphology, wishing to be completely independent from any outside influence. An intuitive character, as his writing demonstrates (Fig. 14), he followed his own internal direction, seeming to experiment on the spot and catching immediately his interlocutor's psychology. From the sum of his observations he obtained an organic vision of graphic characteristics and developed his own graphological method. It is here that his pivotal merit is found – that is to have translated intuition into a communicable method.

In 1914 under the pseudonym Umberto Koch the future leader of Italian graphology published *Manuale di grafologia*, in which he outlined his brilliant intuitions. In later works he submitted these ideas to continual tests leading to an eventual scientific formulation, such as the quantitative measurement of each graphic sign in tenths. Moretti therefore put in place, as Torbidoni and Zanin stress, "a method which pinpointed not only the characteristics of his signs, but which would also measure the frequency and intensity of any given writing."

MORETTIAN METHODOLOGY

Moretti's method examines and then connects diverse personality aspects, recognizing in the graphic sign, and above all in its combinations, the somatic projection, the psychic strength, and the resulting behavioural elements, leading to a synthesis of individual personality which avoids mere classification.

Categories of signs

Moretti distinguishes three sign categories: the substantial, the changeable, and the accidental.

Substantial: the signs which mostly inform us of the individual's psychophysical make-up.

Changeable: signs which change or vary the substantial signs.

Accidental: signs which introduce additional but separate elements.

Concerning this, Torbidoni and Zanin comment: "Moretti's distinction is an important methodological pointer not seen by other graphologists. It corresponds to one of psychology's most modern discoveries, seeing in man basic fundamental attitudes susceptible to growth or change according to the incidence of other factors (see E. H. Erikson, *Insight and Responsibility*, New York, Norton, 1964, chap. IV). In any case it is essential to keep in mind that each sign and every detail, even if not fundamental or basic, has its importance in the graphic and psychosomatic context."

In addition, each sign points to certain indications mostly linked to either will or intelligence, even when they are always interactive in establishing an overall view of the writer's personality.

Neurophysiology of the graphic stroke

Moretti's distinction between graphic stroke and graphic act is emphasized by Pacifico Cristofanelli [68]. "The graphic act is the controlled writing movement, that is 'calligraphy' and not spontaneous writing, writing which is 'more drawing than handwriting', the object of calligraphy not graphology. The graphic stroke, instead, is the spontaneous and automatic graphic movement, the specific study of graphology." (We refer readers to the two works cited above for a neurophysiological approach to the writing process, as we cannot enlarge on it here.)

Examination of the signs

According to the Morettian method the principal signs with their degree of presence and intensity are surveyed, and then comes the interplay of simple or complex combinations between them, which especially qualifies the writer's pressure, graphic stroke, and fleeting stroke. An important factor for a Morettian graphological reading is the definition of "sign". The "sign" can be revealed by a single graphic characteristic, or may derive from more than one of these, or even from a combination of "signs". According to Cristofanelli: "the sign Small is constituted from various factors (small dimension, width of letter above average, fluidity and smoothness)."

Measurement of the signs

The decimal scale of Moretti specifies the following gradation:
0/10: absence of sign;
5/10: average presence of sign;
10/10: maximum grade.

The system foresees diversified criteria in conformity with the signs: this measurement is therefore precise but it must never be either rigid or mechanical, because the aim of this measurement is the best way of identifying the intensity and therefore the quality of a characteristic. For practical purposes it is sufficient to identify and evaluate whether the grade of a sign is under, on, or above the average. The gradation of each sign must be deduced by the various requirements that define the sign.

Turning to Torbidoni and Zanin's text, let us take the example of the sign Laboured, which expresses difficulty in continuity. It needs four requirements:
- disconnected letters within words;
- sudden hindrances of stroke;
- thickenings;
- twisting within the body of the same letter.

"If in a script the above four occur we have 10/10 of the sign Laboured; if there are only sudden hindrances, thickening, and twisting without disconnected letters we have 9/10. If these three are not in all the writing but are scattered here and there over most of it, we have 8/10; if there are only hindrances and twisting, we have 6–7/10 according to frequency; if only twisting occurs we have 5/10; if hindrances or thickening strokes occur we still have 5/10; if there are disconnected letters with some sudden hindrances or twisting, we have 4/10; if only thickening we have 3/10; if only disconnection, we have 2/10, but the writing then approaches the concept of Broken."

Combinations of signs

In stating the relationship of signs with each other, Moretti affirmed that each sign affects the other signs in various ways. Some signs act as supports (increasing the value of the sign), some are contrary (diminishing the value of the sign), others are indifferent (giving their own specificity to the signs which they dominate through their high grade in a writing).

Torbidoni and Zanin insist in a particular way on the combinations, presenting as an example a table relating to Curved and Angular, these being the two fundamental signs in Morettian graphology. The first expresses altruism, the second egoism. It is clearly shown that the grade of a sign and its combination with other signs bring about modifications which nuance the basic meaning.

Cataloguing of signs

Signs are ordered according to the following arrangement: Curvilinearity and Angularity – Pressure – Width – Connections – Dimension – Slant and Axial Direction – Lateral extensions – Clarity and Confusion – Speed – Form and Accuracy – Curls (see below) and Convolutions. Cristofanelli suggested this order in a table indicating the nature of every sign (Substantial, Changeable, or Accidental) as well as its significance in relation to the four Morettian temperaments (Stopping, Waiting, Resistance, Aggression).

Among the most characteristic and original signs of the system, not taken up by other methodologies, we must mention in this brief synthesis at least the following: Width of letters, Space between letters, Space between words (considered singly and in their reciprocal relationship), Methodically irregular, Flexible, Twisted, Hesitant, Wavering, Laboured, Straight extension, Extensions concave to left, Extensions concave to right, Curls.

THE TWO FUNDAMENTAL SIGNS: CURVED AND ANGULAR

We present a brief account of the Curved and Angular signs. The Curved and Angular strokes, being basic graphic movements, play a fundamental role in the Morettian perspective. Moreover, as Cristofanelli reminds us, they also share a wider symbolic conception of reality according to which the enfolding curve represents the feminine, while the angular is intrusive and represents the masculine. For a better understanding we show examples (Figs 15–16) taken from the chapter "Sign Combinations" in Torbidoni and Zanin's book, because they show clear examples of various signs in the Morettian method.

Angularity in its turn can be subdivided into different types which bring greater clarity to its specification: Angles A, B, C, and Dry.

Angle A. Occurs with a blunted or pointed movement at the lower part of letters. It is noted above all in the letters which have ovals (in particular *a*) and in letters which turn up at their base such as *r, u, v, e, l, c, i, m, n.* These are letters whose curvilinearity is expected in the copybook school model. An angle of 45°, for example, defines an Angle A grade of 7/10. However, the measurement should be flexible, because it must consider all the letters and find an average.

Angle B. It is found in a blunted or pointed shape at the bottom and the top of oval letters (in particular the letter *o*).

Angle C. Is the result of blunted Angles A and B and other important elements such as continuity, fluidity, and any other "embellishment" which is not too showy and in the same place.

Dry. Very angular writing; tight letters and narrow spaces between letters; total absence of flourishes.

Curved (Fig. 15)

Supporting signs:

Angle C, for the sense of opportunity and discernment of the most suitable means of externalizing altruism.

Thickened type II, not more than 3/10, for feeling very solicitous towards others.

Space between letters, 5/10 upwards, for generosity in giving.

Profuse, for increased generosity which transforms altruism into prodigality.

Angular (Fig. 16)

Supporting signs:

Angle A, for facility of resentment and irritability.

Angle B, for tenacity in defence of the rights of the Ego.

Thickened type I, for the ambition to prevail over others.

Thickened type II, 4/10 upward, for increased negative feeling about the Ego.

Sharp, for narrowness of mind in considering the demands of others.

Spiky, for quibbling and cavilling in opposing the demands of others.

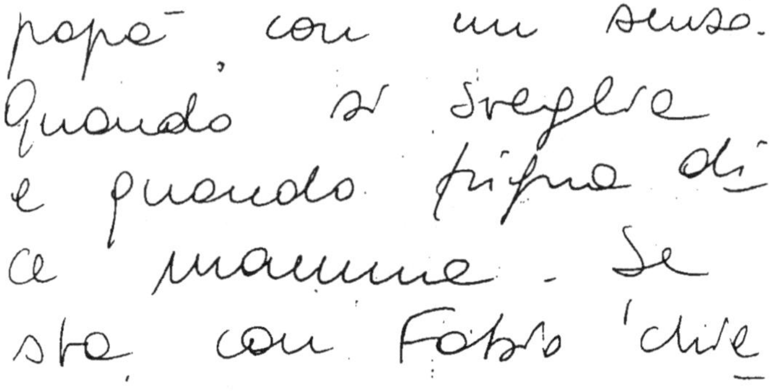

Figure 15
Combination of *Curved – Triple width – Angle C*

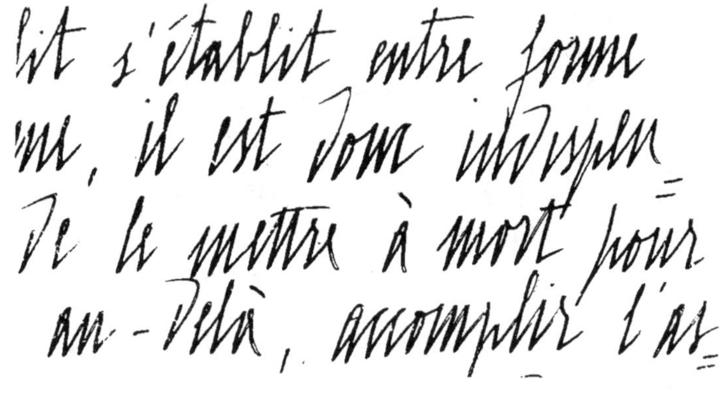

Figure 16 (reduced)
Combination of *Angular – Sharp – Thickened type I*

We also quote a few definitions for already mentioned signs, from the "reference book of signs", which contains around 80 all told.

Sharp: horizontally tight writing, with pointed angles at the top and bottom of letters = intellectual subtlety, contrary attitude.

Thickened type I: writing with downstrokes more marked than upstrokes = ambition to command, independent spirit, imposition of will.

Thickened type II: writing with sudden heavy pressure or alternation of light and heavy pressure on the upstrokes = excitability, sudden impulsiveness, tendency to exaggeration.

Spiky: all tops and bottoms of letters very pointed and very reduced horizontal movement = contrary and cavilling spirit, exasperating sophistry.

Profuse: writing horizontally and to lesser degree vertically extended, with thrusting strokes and free strokes = accentuated expansion of thought and feelings, lack of equilibrium and restraint.

Pacifico Cristofanelli, in an eloquent and amusing article [67], shows several of Moretti's writing samples, taken from his own books to illustrate some signs, which are in the hand of none other than Moretti himself. As an example Fig. 17 shows the sign Methodically irregular.

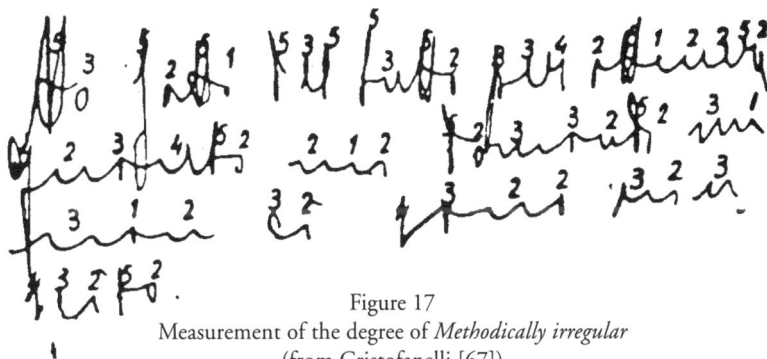

Figure 17
Measurement of the degree of *Methodically irregular*
(from Cristofanelli [67])

2. Moretti's "fleeting" strokes or "curls" (Fig. 18)

The Morettian concept of the "fleeting" stroke is extremely rich in meaning because it responds to a spontaneous and often unconscious expression of the "writer's biotype". In general one individuates oneself in the "curls", that is in the initial, ending, or surrounding strokes of letters, *t*-bars, *i*-dots, accents, punctuation. Note that Moretti's "curls" broaden the normal Jaminian definition of "free strokes" given in Chapter Five, Section II.

Figure 18
Some "curls" in the handwriting of the composer Camille Saint-Saëns

Torbidoni and Zanin examine the strokes associated with Sobriety, Concealment, Subjectivism, Affectation, Phlegmatism, Pomposity, Mythomania, and Confusion. The strokes must be evaluated according to their frequency and extent, that is in their tendency to invade the space of other letters or words. They need to be interpreted in relation to the graphic context.

Cristofanelli [68] writes: "All curls, being the decoration of the personality as well as the writing, on the whole point to particular aspects in the formation of character, and to defensive and compensatory mechanisms learnt by experience that is not always positive. Some of the most useful indicators of (psychological) *insincerity* are therefore the various types of curls" (see also Figs 8b, 39, 40b).

3. Moretti's four temperaments

The principal exponents of the Urbino school – following Moretti's position – have always been extremely reluctant about general classifications. Consequently they are rather critical on "characterology" (Heymans–Le Senne school), once widely used in France, though now somewhat less popular. Father Moretti nevertheless identified four categories of temperament emerging from the mix of various signs: Waiting, Stopping, Resistance, and Aggression.

It must be well understood that these "temperaments" have not been imported from outside (that is not from psychology and characterology) but derive from the internal graphological system strictly linked to the nature of the signs. To each temperament correspond groups of principal and secondary signs, some of which could also be linked to another temperament. The harmonious personality, explains Cristofanelli, implies a "fusion of elements from the four temperaments."

Such a classification by Moretti results from an original vision and does not imitate other existing typologies. One can perhaps draw an analogy with the four temperaments of Hippocrates (lymphatic, sanguine, nervous, bilious), but one cannot speak of a direct correspondence. Hippocrates' typology is based on a temperamental biology whereas Moretti's temperaments come from psychological determinants.

For example the temperament of Waiting, the most complex of the four, is characterized by Moretti from specifications which comprise the essential signs: (1) Twisted and Flexible, (2) Laboured and Wavering, (3) Deliberate, Calm, and Sober, (4) Light, Fine, and Naturally graceful, (5) Thick and Gross with Curves, (6) curls of Affectation and Artificially graceful, (7) Careful, Smooth, and curls of Concealment.

Thus the same temperament Waiting, according to which group of signs identifies it, orients itself either towards cautious delicacy, or towards indecision or even hypocrisy. Each temperament therefore corresponds to a deep psychological attitude that, according to the ethics, character tendencies, and life experiences of the subject, leads to the outward display of various sorts of behaviour. Nothing in common with a temperamental mould that would predict equivalent behaviour.

SYNTHESIS OF ORIENTATION

The chapter "Synthesis of orientation for the graphologist", apart from advising "useful regulations" and recapping on graphological laws and the method of analysis, contains a section "Predispositions" which seems to us extremely specific to the Morettian viewpoint and a source of reflection for the graphologist.

"For *predisposition*, we mean those factors which are hereditary in nature and favour development of morbid mental conditions or illnesses. This state becomes active only under favourable environmental conditions." A description of character aspects which are "indices of morbidity" follows, including prodigality, avarice, suggestibility, impetuosity, rigidity, doubt, instability, diffidence, erotic internalization, megalomania, pedantry. Every excessive or deficient level of a sign obviously alters graphic harmony, and "each combination of heavily used supporting signs, even if they are of a positive nature, can be a sign of morbidity."

The chapter ends with the affirmation: "Graphological reflections of a predisposition to illnesses are:

(a) *Nervous*: each sign pointing to irritability, susceptibility, excitability, and difficulty in adapting, and much more if pronounced;

(b) *Mental*: each sign pointing to the inability to compensate or to anomaly, even indirectly, of the *animus*;

(c) *Organic*: each sign indicating disorder, lack of ease, irregularity."

Conclusion

Moretti's seminal work, updated by students at the Moretti Institute, along with the founding first of a High School of Graphology and then a School for Special Needs, now transformed into a University Diploma course in Consulting Graphology (short degree), and the organization of many international conferences, have placed the Italian school in the mainstream of graphology. Various branches have developed, but all derive from the Morettian method.

In the preface to the French edition of Torbidoni and Zanin [230], Dr Gille-Maisani underlines a fundamental aspect of the Morettian method: "one of the fundamental characteristics of Morettian graphology is that of being *concrete* ... The writer is described as a *concrete whole*; this makes him alive in front of us, his concrete behaviour is shown in his familiar environment, with his subordinates, with his superiors, with the opposite sex, etc."

IV. THE FRENCH SCHOOL

Jean-Hippolyte Michon and Jules Crépieux-Jamin

The French school had a lightning start at the end of the nineteenth century under the aegis of the brilliant pioneer Jean-Hippolyte Michon. Michon has still not received full recognition because he was followed by the solid achievements of Jules Crépieux-Jamin, who provided a structure and logical basis to the immense field opened up by Michon. Crépieux-Jamin has partly obfuscated the original ideas of Michon, whose personality could be compared with that of Girolamo Moretti. Both were great proselytizers with creative and innovative visions, sometimes risky but always of great depth. For a better understanding of Michon we recommend the authoritative articles by Colette Coblence [59] from the journal *La Graphologie*.

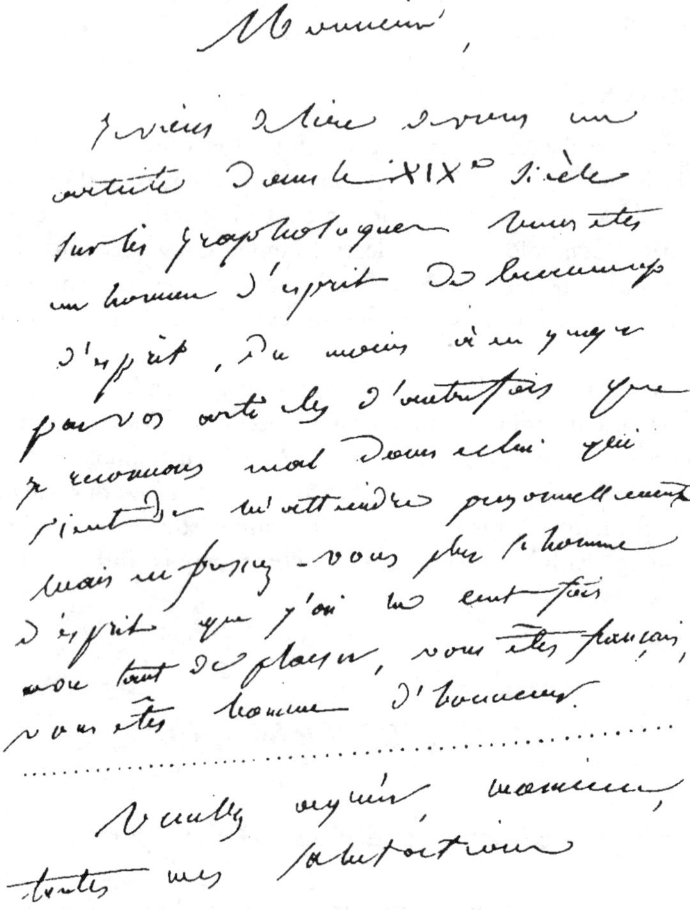

Monsieur,

Je viens de lire de vous un article dans le XIXe siècle sur les graphologues. Vous êtes un homme d'esprit, de beaucoup d'esprit, du moins si on juge par vos articles d'autrefois que je reconnais mal dans celui qui s'entend à m'atteindre personnellement. Mais ne froissez-vous pas l'homme d'esprit que j'ai lu cent fois avec tant de plaisir, vous êtes français, vous êtes homme d'honneur.

....

Veuillez agréer, monsieur, toutes mes salutations

J. H. Michon

Figure 19
Handwriting of Jean-Hippolyte Michon (reduced)

Crépieux-Jamin, more a Cartesian thinker, laid down certain "principles", established precise definitions, and wanted to give a sort of moral guide – under the banner of Harmony in writing – where those who analyse writing and those who are analysed become involved with each other. If we look at Crépieux-Jamin's handwriting (Fig. 20) we notice that the criteria for *harmony* have all been observed. Not having actually seen the original text we can only deduce some hypotheses on the consistency of the stroke, which appears to be neat and a little "dry". The French master brought his critical perspicacity and moral courage to the fore defending Dreyfus (the Jewish captain unjustly accused of high treason) and in so doing he lost friends and clients of his dental practice.

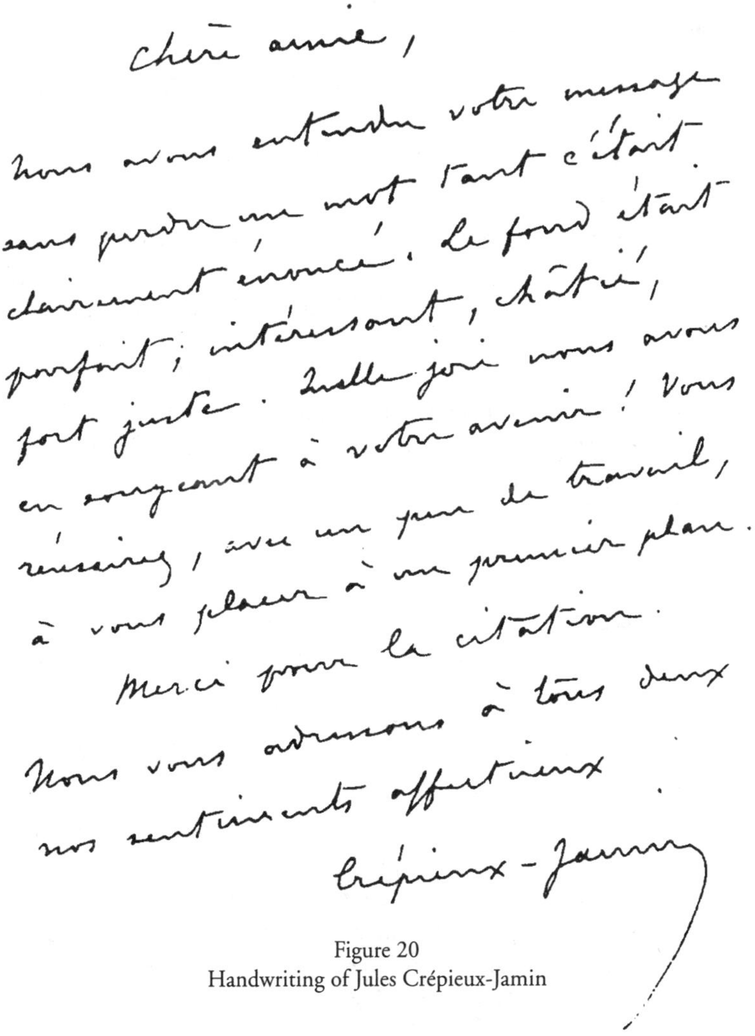
Chère amie,

Nous avons entendu votre message sans perdre un mot tant c'était clairement énoncé. Le fond était parfait; intéressant, châtié, fort juste. Quelle joie nous avons en songeant à votre avenir! Vous réussirez, avec un peu de travail, à vous placer à un premier plan.

Merci pour la citation.

Nous vous adressons à tous deux nos sentiments affectueux.

Crépieux-Jamin

Figure 20
Handwriting of Jules Crépieux-Jamin

The broad organization of the French school along with its rigorous teaching methods has continuously perfected the Jaminian method by introducing where appropriate ideologies from the Swiss and German schools, which are now an integral part of the French methodology.

THE FIFTEEN PRINCIPLES OF CRÉPIEUX-JAMIN

We summarize here the fifteen principles devised by the French master, which every graphologist must take into account during the course of their work. The full listing is found in his major tract [65].

- Not to make a judgement if only one sample is available
- Thoroughly research the graphic characteristics and list them in order of intensity
- Define the writings through their graphic characteristics rather than their psychological qualities
- Try to retrace the graphic movements of the writer
- There are no particular signs independent from the major movements of the writing; there are only general signs used in different ways
- Small signs acquire value only if they are repeated
- The classification of individual aspects occurs according to a hierarchical order
- Check whether some characteristics show the same degree of intensity
- Some aspects can be measured: dimension, spaces, angles, etc.
- Major errors: forgetting less important signs and not noticing the dominant ones
- Observe the relationship between text and signature
- The number of aspects suitable to describe a handwriting must not be too small or too high (between 6 and 10 principal ones)
- The absence of a sign does not confer any quality opposite to that which such a sign would express
- A "definition" is well made when it allows us to find without hesitation, among say 20 others, the writing which is its subject
- One must not deal with the detailed graphological picture unless one is able to make a "definition"

After Crépieux-Jamin the French school continued to insist on a prior summary evaluation from objective criteria. This must not be confused with an analytic enumeration; in fact it concerns the ability to pick out the dynamics of writing from all the graphic gestures, within their graphic environment. We shall therefore now consider the fundamental aspect of graphological study within the framework of the French school, the evaluation, which must precede the "definition" of a handwriting (Table 8).

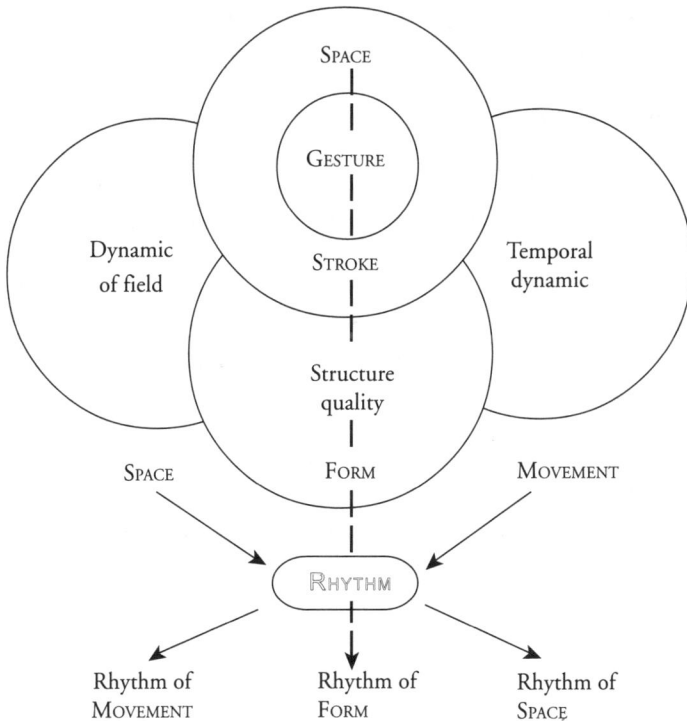

Table 8

THE GRAPHIC ENVIRONMENT: CRITERIA OF EVALUATION

Global perception

This approach does not aim at or reach psychological conclusions, but helps us feel the *life* of a writing. The graphologist must learn to observe before passing judgement. The foundations of interpretation spring from intelligent observation. Consequently answers given using a computer on a few lines or a signature can only be fragmentary and practically interchangeable within the writing sample, with insufficient parameters subjected to an electronic brain. One must hope that the graphologist's mind can add to a technical framework the sense of the complexity of psychological refinement and discernment.

It is essential to evaluate the graphic environment in order to give the right value to graphic signs, beyond any subjective impression. We must have a global view of the dynamic field in which many graphic gestures interact with each other, and in their turn interact with space. Different principles can help us to free our perceptions, to make them active and objective.

Leroy-Gourhan [145] invites us to look at space through two different viewpoints. The first is the *itinerant* view, which he compares to a dog walking along a street sniffing his way. This is a sensory vision, which stimulates the muscles and the olfactory sense, resulting in an active and linear vision. The second is a *wide range view*, corresponding to a bird's-eye view from a stationary body. This radiates a circular, receptive, and global vision from one fixed point. A combination of these two viewpoints is best for understanding writing. The graphologist who keeps to only the itinerant vision risks losing himself in detail without ever perceiving the whole picture. Vice versa, keeping only to a wide range view risks losing details, all the small things which meticulously define a particular writing.

We see a similar approach in the *psychology of form* or *Gestalt theory*, which has shown that a *whole* is not just the simple sum of its parts but that its configuration is the result of the interaction of its elements. If only one element is removed the dynamic is modified, in other words the *whole* is different. We are dealing therefore with the second fundamental principle, already mentioned, in which a given *graphic environment* can be totally modified by the weight of a single graphic sign, such as *flying strokes, light pressure, heavy pressure*, etc.

To allow an objective evaluation of the graphic environment, precise criteria have been identified, as summarized in Table 9. Various broad graphological categories must be taken into consideration:

- the degree of evolution: *unorganized, organized, disorganized*
- the degree of *harmony*
- the quality of *stroke*
- relationship between *form* and *movement*
- *rhythm*

Finally, according to the German term now in common use, the vitality of a writing, its *Formlevel*, is established.

HARMONY

The concept of *harmony* has been for a long time the main criterion of the French school. It allowed a favourable or unfavourable global interpretation of a writing. This idea was certainly connected both with the psychology of French classicism which still permeates French good taste, and with the strictness demanded in written presentation, in school life, and in general culture.

Today however some parameters concerning harmony can be toned either up or down. The strong need to personalize one's own writing is so important for the French that, since the Second World War, the notions of legibility or order necessary to obtain good harmony have become less important than in Crépieux-Jamin's time. On the contrary, a lively unevenness associated with a very individual stroke no longer disturbs harmony as it once did. It is regarded instead as a type of *rhythmic* harmony. We therefore find that the notion of *rhythm* drawn from German graphology has been assimilated by the French, and finds parallels too with the Morettian idea of "methodical irregularity".

OBSERVATION OF THE GRAPHIC ENVIRONMENT:
GLOBAL EVALUATION

1. Observe writing in a receptive way

2. Define the degree of *Harmony:*   Spontaneity
                                      Clarity
                                      Proportion
                                      Order
                                      Simplicity

3. Evaluate the quality of *Stroke:*   Strength   Heavy
                                                       Light

                                       Consistency   Pasty
                                                       Precise

4. Evaluate the *Pressure:*   Firm
                              Weak
                              In relief
                              Deviated

5. Establish the level of *Tension* of the stroke:

Low tension	Grade I
Adequate tension	Grade II
Elasticity	Grade III
Constriction	Grade IVa
High tension	Grade IVb
Rigidity	Grade V

6. Evaluate the relationship between *Form* and *Movement:*

Movement	which breaks up Form
Rhythm	of dominant Movement
Movement	that carries the Form
Form	that springs from Movement
Rhythm	of structuring of Form
Form	which constricts Movement

7. Evaluate *Rhythm* and *Formlevel:*   Originality – Individualism
                                        Intensity
                                        Control
                                        Freedom
                                        Warmth

Table 9

A further note on the criterion of creative harmony is that of "*combined writing*" whose graphic agility, according to Crépieux-Jamin, reflected mental sharpness. Today the criterion of sobriety has led to reappraisal of the positivity of this type.

Criteria for the evaluation of Harmony

For the evaluation of the degree of harmony in writing there are five graphic aspects to be considered:

- *spontaneity* which is born from a free flowing and natural movement found predominantly when contrary signs like rigidity, constriction, or artificiality are lacking
- *clarity* which presumes a certain degree of legibility or at least is without ambiguity of form
- *proportion* between the three zones of writing, between capital and lower-case letters, between text and signature
- *order* which concerns the balance between the graphic masses – the harmonious spatial relationship between text and writing surface – as well as a certain organization of layout and control of the flow of writing
- *simplicity* which corresponds to sobriety and excludes ornamentation or superfluity

When one of these elements is clearly missing or if their overall presence is scarcely relevant, the degree of harmony is lowered and may even lead to total disharmony.

For Crépieux-Jamin, *Harmony* (with a capital H) reflected a level of *superiority*, and *disharmony* a state of *inferiority* in personality, even in the moral sense, according to the vocabulary of the time. Today a certain degree of harmony is considered a sign of balance and unity of the personality, elements which obviously favour social relationships. This notion does not however show cultural level. *Harmonious* writing can be produced by educated or nearly illiterate writers. The contrary, *disharmony* with its discordance, confusion, or exaggeration is no longer regarded solely as a profile of unsuitable or unreliable personality. Instead consideration must be made of its freedom of expression and emotion, which could be – if the graphic environment confirms it – a sign of pathological confusion, but also one of creative originality and genius, as is demonstrated in Beethoven's writing (Fig. 5).

We are certainly indebted to the German *Gestalt* theory, which places *rhythm* at the focal point for the observation of writing, for having enlarged the Jaminian concepts that had for too long remained anchored to a type of cultural good manners.

Crépieux-Jamin as already mentioned attributed a very positive value to *combined* writing, represented as a graphic synthesis of originality, inventive freedom in the choice of connection between letters, speed, and economy of stroke. As witness to the balance and reliability of personality, this style of writing maintains a high qualitative value insofar as it respects the criteria of sobriety and clarity necessary to the principle of harmony (see Fig. 21: the beautiful writing of the Swiss graphologist Gustave Magnat).

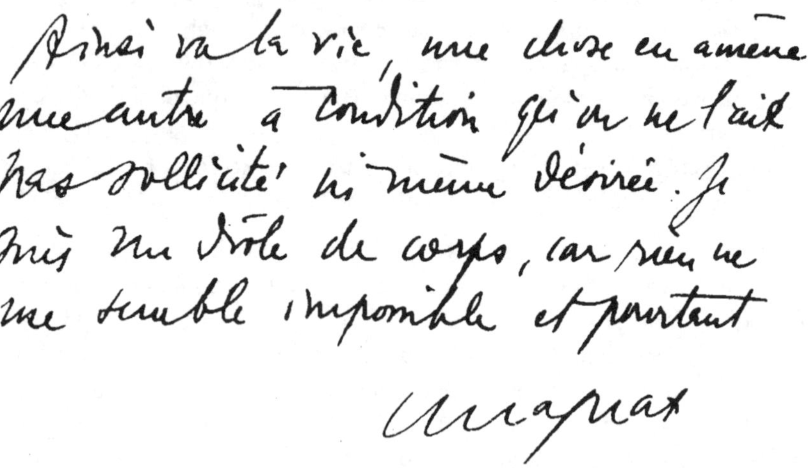

Figure 21
The writing of Gustave Magnat (reduced)

If instead combined writing generates a type of inextricable graphic texture and if the stroke lacks flexibility, it is possible that the inventiveness and creativity could be linked to a psychic disturbance of an almost pathological kind. In reality only the graphologist's experience and practice can prevent interpretative dangers such as confusion between monotony and simplicity, originality and artificiality, or extreme simplification and near illegibility.

Concerning this last point one must have experience of the writing habits of the particular country. The use of simplification in France, which makes single letters thin and reduced to skeletal proportions, is considered completely compatible with adequate legibility. Instead in Italy the dominant preoccupation is that of good legibility. Because we are dealing essentially with qualitative values, there is no doubt that the evaluation of these criteria can be extremely difficult.

QUALITY OF THE STROKE (Figs 22 - 23)

As already stated in Chapter Two, the *stroke* is both *support* and *substance* of a primordial graphic gesture, a gesture which becomes form after confronting a space, after relating with other gestures, after achieving its autonomous reality. The *gesture-stroke* represents the synthesis of cerebral *inputs* in the intellectual, affective, motor, and propulsive regions; all essential impulses for the graphic act.

It is indispensable to observe the stroke on the original document. Reproductions can only give approximate evaluations, by deduction. The *stroke* is the first witness to the "health" of a writing, whether it is firm or shaky, straight or distorted, flexible or rigid, bold or hesitant, homogeneous or mixed up. The stroke through its consistency, dynamics, and structure influences and indeed determines the whole graphic configuration. From the very first hesitant and shaky childish attempts at writing to the tremors of old age, the stroke records all the psychological and physical strengths and disadvantages.

For the evaluation of the graphic environment, some aspects of stroke must be dealt with immediately, namely motor energy, *heavy* or *light* stroke; thread or consistency, *pasty* or *precise* stroke. Also one must assess tension, *tight* or *loose*; and *general firmness* of outline. Walter Hegar, who directed many of his observations to the study of stroke, picked out eight fundamental aspects, in opposing pairs. The first four, *heavy-light* and *pasty-precise*, are easily picked out on an original document. When at first sight their observation is very clear, these two pairs are extremely useful in ascertaining the graphic environment.

Heavy or light stroke

According to the writing instrument – generally chosen by the individual – the stroke made by the pressure on the instrument is more, or less, thick. The ball pen for example allows greater pressure to be applied, whereas a felt-tip tends to slip more on the paper. The *heavier* stroke is easily picked out by observing above all the verticals, where the pressure leaves a noticeable groove; this can be seen best by turning the paper over. The writer who skims the paper produces a *light* stroke with a rather pallid inking, which need not prevent it from being also pasty, like a light brushstroke which expands while barely touching the surface.

Pasty or precise stroke

The *pasty* stroke widens on the paper and its borders are softened. A type of osmosis occurs with the physical support of the instrument, a fluid and sharing contact. The *precise* stroke remains neat, thin, and its borders are clear. A certain detachment from the support occurs and the contact is *guarded*. In both, the pressure of the stroke can be either light or heavy.

Rigid or loose movement

To evaluate *graphic environment* in relation to the amount of rigidity, the graphologist must observe the *tension* of the stroke. According to Pophal this tension is grounded in the *management of the stroke.*

General firmness

A *firm* stroke is spotted at first sight: it corresponds to a tone in the graphic stroke whereby the graphomotor impulse consistently applies ink in the verticals from top to bottom. Such a dominant aspect of the pressure of the stroke reflects a favourable graphic environment and suggests firmness and reliability of character.

We must remember that the absence of a positive graphic characteristic does not necessarily mean the presence of its opposite in the personality.

An uneven stroke could according to circumstance mean the lack of good physical or psychological health, vulnerability of feeling, lack of will-power and enterprise, slovenliness, not forgetting also underdevelopment in writing.

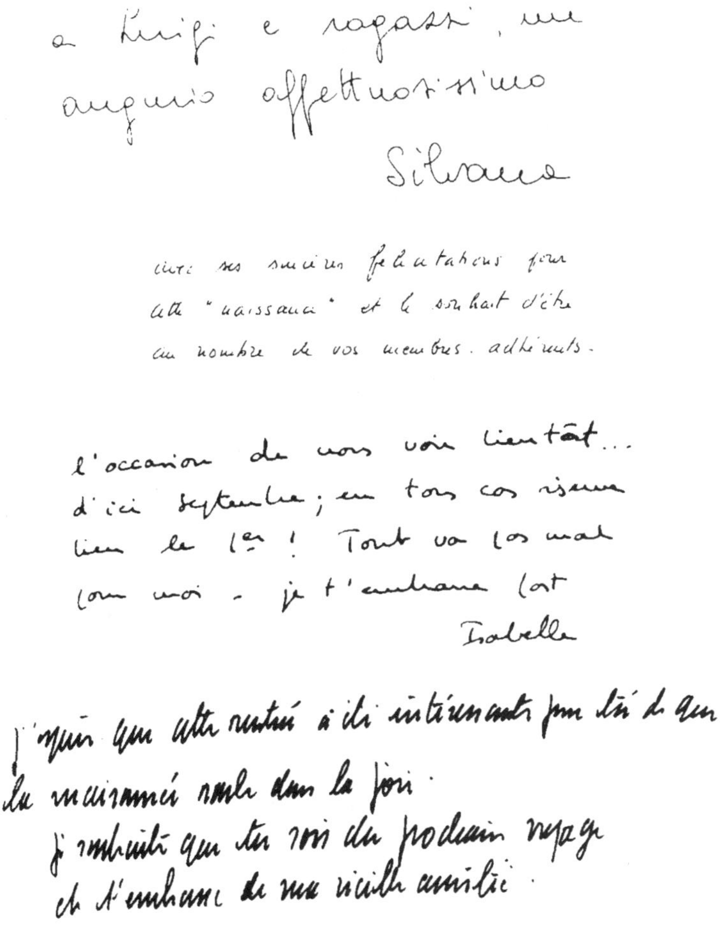

Figure 22 (reduced)
Feminine writing: (a–b) light and precise; (c) light and pasty;
(d) pasty and heavy on the vertical lines (felt-tip)

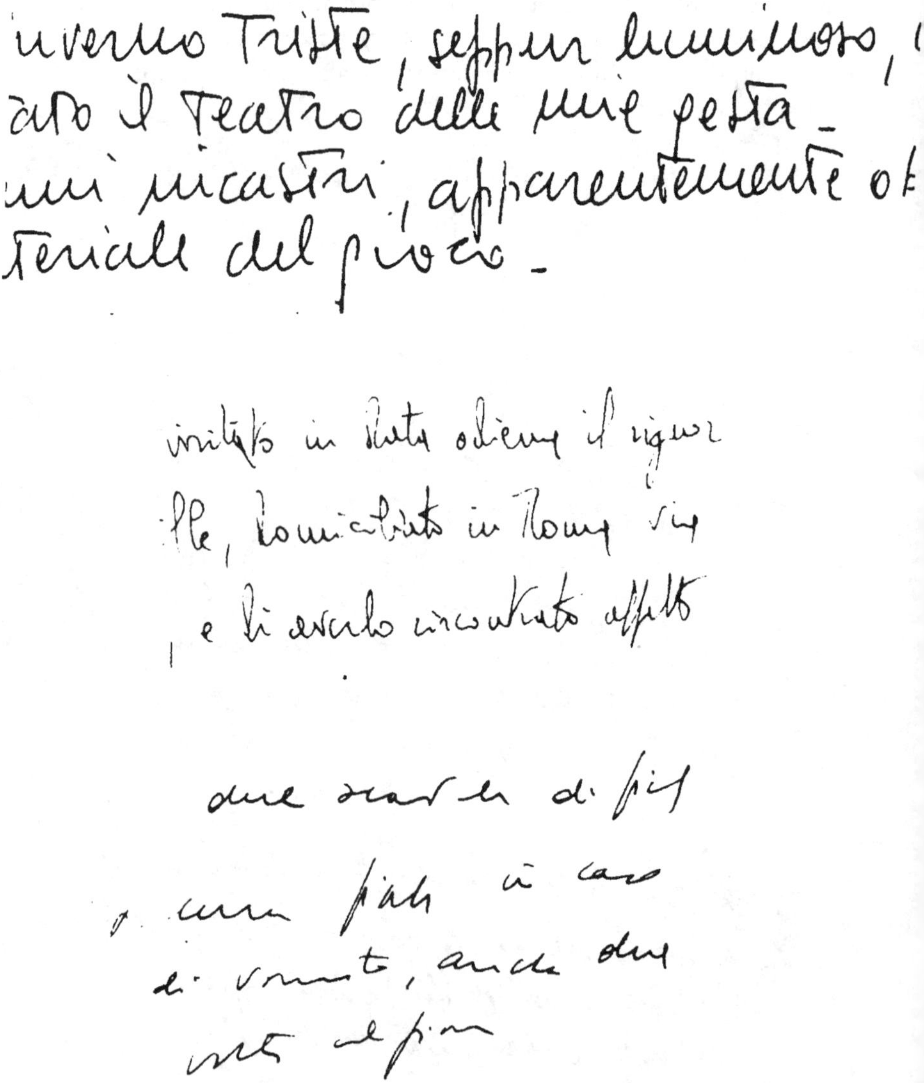

inverno Triste, seppur luminoso,
aro il Teatro delle mie pessa-
mi micastri, apparentemente ot-
teriale del fioco -

Figure 23
Masculine handwriting: (a) precise and heavy (60 year old artist);
(b) precise and light; (c) pasty and light

RELATIONSHIP BETWEEN FORM AND MOVEMENT

On the basis of Heiss's theory one determines whether *form* prevails over movement, and if at times it even constricts it. Where form predominates one must assess if it is a form of "structure". If the *movement* dominates the form, one must see whether it breaks down the structure, or simply provides dynamism. If however a balance is seen, form flows from the movement. For clarification see under Heiss in Section II of this chapter.

RHYTHM

As in music, rhythm in writing picks up unpredictability and originality in the chain of movement. Rhythm impregnates and irradiates each graphic element with energy. It excludes therefore rigidity and monotony as well as unevenness caused by excessive irregularities and exaggerations. To identify rhythm the following graphic categories are taken into consideration:

Intensity: this involves qualitative evaluation ensuring absence of signs of weakness, spatial uncertainty, weakness of pressure, in other words observing movement, stroke, and space in intrinsic coherence.

Originality: often a subjective concept, which must however be defined precisely in the most objective terms possible. Originality does not mean the bizarre or ostentatious. In practice it refers to a simple individualizing of writing, moving away from school types and remodelling itself as a personal style without artificiality or vulgarity.

Freedom: spontaneity and variation, flexibility of stroke, and fluidity of movement. Tendency to progressive writing.

Control, also called *constriction*: opposing liberating forces, control assumes a force of regulation necessary to rhythm and without which writing would become a sort of battlefield. Seen above all in final signs, such as the last strokes of the words when they are short, and in signs of spatial order and proportion.

Warmth: an overall aspect found principally in pasty or nourished strokes and wide and curved forms. This excludes dry strokes and tall and angular forms.

FORMLEVEL

This is the term Pulver replaced with "existential quality". It stems from
rhythm and defines the intensity and substantial quality of a writing. It is
now assessed using the terms high, medium, or low, no longer by the value
judgements Klages proposed. As an illustration we have taken the writing
of the Russian poet Mayakovsky, which is extremely expressive in its graphic
dynamics (Fig. 24). We can look at it without being distracted by the
meaning of the words, thus better revealing its graphic rhythm.

> *"I walk loosely grumbling softly, nearly without words and sometimes I*
> *shorten my step so as not to disturb the grumbling, and sometimes I*
> *grumble more quickly following the pace of my footsteps. In this way*
> *rhythm takes form, as basis to any rhyme and follows it like a buzz.*
> *Slowly from this buzz emerge words ... Where the source of this rhythmic*
> *buzzing comes from is impossible to say ... Rhythm is the essential force,*
> *the essential energy of verse. It is inexplicable. We can say the same*
> *about magnetism and electricity: they are forms of energy."* (Mayakovsky)

We are struck by the rapid gesture, which is simplified and leans to the
right, and develops in a continuous graphic line between single words. All
these signs tell us immediately the speed of a conceptual intelligence
determined in its course. The gesture thrusts itself in space impulsively,
but also stops sharply like a brake: this is a tense gesture and totally
antagonistic to the flexibility of the previous word which offered receptive
and soft curves. The meeting of these two gestures, the propulsive and
braking gestures, produces a very individualized *rhythm*.

The pressure is rather irregular, sometimes heavy with firmness on the
descending strokes, sign of great energy, sometimes lightened, particularly
in the middle zone, expressing vulnerability of feeling. The pressure often
changes *spasmodically* indicating in this case a deep conflict and menacing
nervous resistance.

We also notice the so-called "lasso", a sign of ability to seduce, but
sometimes these become real *knots*. According to the *knot* symbolism on

Figure 24
Writing and a (reduced) poster by the Russian poet Mayakovsky
(from Claude Frioux, *Majakovskij par lui-même*, Éditions du Seuil)

which Bernson wrote [27], there is a "useful knot" which ties and reconnects, an "acquisitive knot" which enslaves, and the "dangerous knot" which strangles, the latter being the type closest to the poet. We find the same kind of symbolism in drawings and posters of the knotted "serpent" used by Mayakovsky for his theatrical enterprises. Note the poet's wide regressive strokes, nostalgic of things past and of the mother, strokes antagonistic to the decisive verticals, stating a virile and autonomous assertiveness.

There are alternating extremes: full, decisive, and proud capital letters next to depressions in graphic flow, in which the middle zone often presents a concave waviness with weak connections between letters and a delicate pressure. There is no doubt that the great poet was suffering from contradictory and threatening states of mind.

SAMPLES OF PRESENT-DAY WRITINGS

Fig. 25, belonging to a domestic worker, shows a high degree of *harmony* with a high level of space control and stroke flexibility. Only the "uncouth" style of the signature reveals a lack of education.

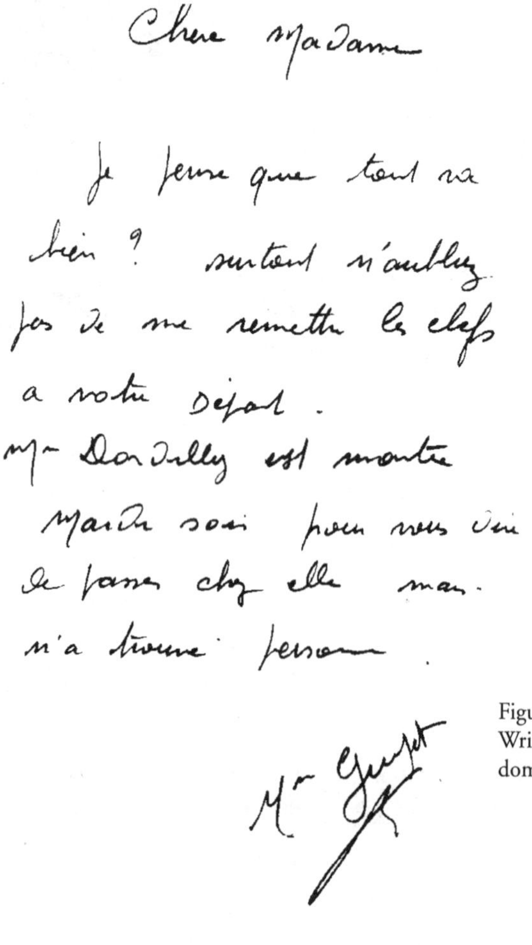
Chère Madame

Je pense que tout va
bien ? surtout n'oubliez
pas de me remettre les clefs
a votre départ .
Mme Dondilly est montée
Mardi soir pour vous dire
de passer chez elle mais
n'a trouvé personne .

Mme Guyot

Figure 25 (reduced)
Writing of a female
domestic worker aged 38

The writing in Fig. 26, although belonging to a woman of higher social level, shows a distinctly lower "graphic level" than the previous sample. The lack of spatial organization – with intertwined lines, absence of margins – and discordance concerning the exuberant *t*-crossings make this writing *inharmonious*. This is not the creative untidiness generated by the amount of original ideas, but an internal disharmony which places the *self* at the centre of its preoccupations. In this case the presumed motherly love has become a trap turning children into victims of its own crushing egocentricity.

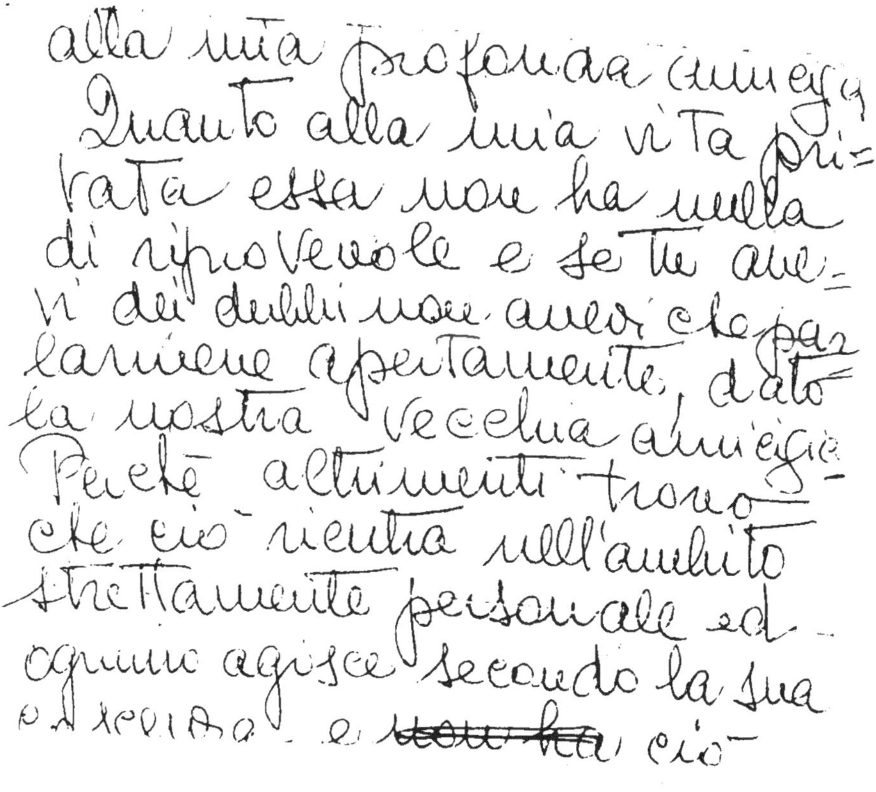

Figure 26 (reduced)
Writing of a 60 year old woman: firstly teacher, then clerk

Hegar and stroke theory

In his principal book [112], published in Paris in 1938, Walter Hegar critically confronted existing studies on stroke, and in particular those of Margret Hartge and Magnat, which Hegar regards as too tied to the symbolic aspect of stroke. He focuses on a *quantitative* evaluation, objectively observed and psychologically interpreted, based on Klages' *theory of expression*. As Hegar put it: "The formation of the stroke is essentially determined by the deepest layers of the subconscious which are outside the directive image [of Klages]. The movements which produce strokes are reflex movements." Hegar's theory is founded basically on the interpretation of drawings (see Stora on the interpretation of the tree test [224]).

Hegar's theory was obviously based on writing instruments of his era. Today graphologists are deprived of the amount of information and the subtleties on which Hegar developed his theories. However his basic considerations are still extremely useful, given meticulous scrutiny of original writings, then of suitable enlargements, and an experienced understanding of modern writing instruments. A ball pen allows a valid observation of the stroke, whereas the felt-tip often eliminates the differences in shading. It is therefore important to be very cautious and informed on the type of pen used.

HEGAR'S EIGHT ASPECTS OF STROKE

Hegar's theory groups together eight aspects of stroke in opposing pairs:

Active	Passive
Heavy	Light
Precise	Pasty
Straight	Curved
Rapid	Slow

The first four aspects are those we are mainly concerned about in estimating graphic environment. They reveal at a glance the play of contrast in a writing, the touchstone of sensitivity and vitality (Table 10). However the predominance of either the "straight" or "curved" stroke could sometimes be given primary importance. We recall that the two fundamental signs of the Morettian method are "curved" and "angular", and the angle derives from the meeting of two of Hegar's "straight" strokes. Hegar opposed *curved* and *straight*, Moretti *curved* and *angular*, and Pophal *tense* and *loose*. These three authors have therefore grounded fundamental aspects in relation to the dynamic perception of the development of the graphic flow.

HEGAR'S STROKES
Basis for evaluation of the graphic environment

Light
- Precise = *intellectual and cerebral sensitivity*
- Pasty = *impressionable senses, emotional delicacy*

Heavy
- Precise = *strong energy, incorruptibility*
- Pasty = *energy and demands of the senses, conflict*

Table 10

One can say that Hegar, through his sixteen combinations of stroke, defines the relationships between *energy, decision,* and *moral principles* on one side, and *sensitivity, world of the senses, imagination* on the other.

The coincidence of "active" elements points to energy and activity, if both somewhat rigid, turning into insensitivity and coldness, whereas the accumulation of "passive" elements points to sensory impressionability and imagination, turning into mythomania and anxiety. The "precise" and "straight" strokes belong to a moral world, intransigent and ruthless, while the "pasty" and "curved" strokes are of a sensory world of sensual imagery.

If Hegar's theory represents a good summary of aspects intrinsic to the "stroke", it does not pretend to and cannot be a complete methodology of writing analysis. It does not consider a variety of "pressure" types (spasmodic, deviated, shaky, etc.). It concentrates on *speed* taken as a single element, but not on the overall writing speed. In Table 11 we summarize various combinations with "straight" strokes, according to Hegar.

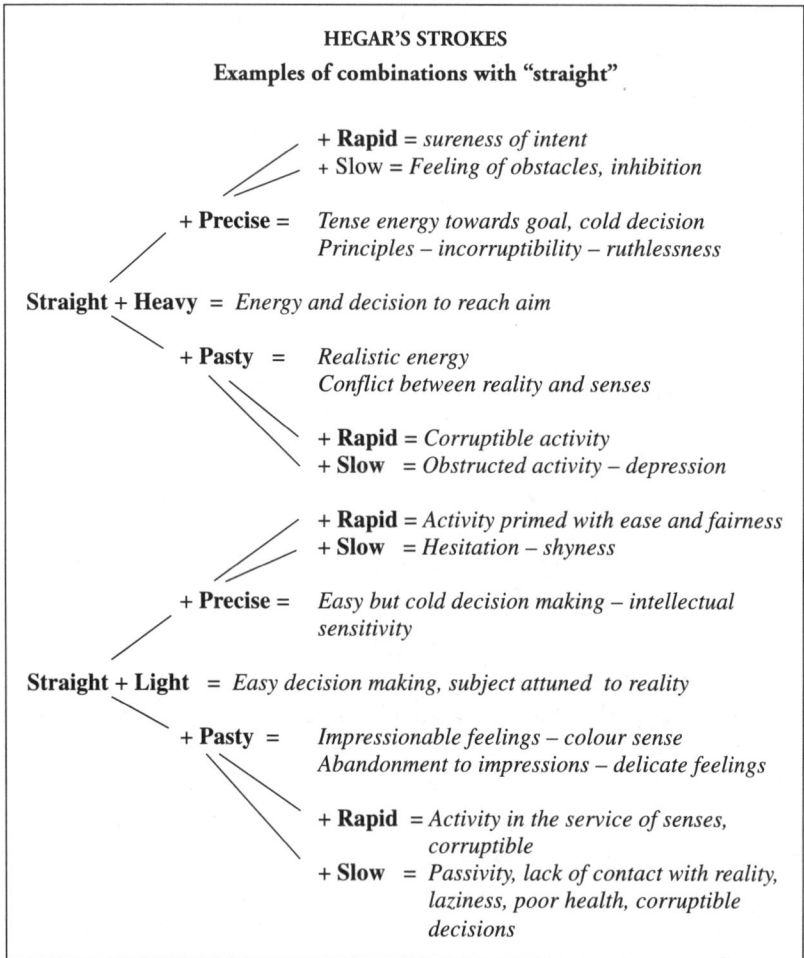

HEGAR'S STROKES
Examples of combinations with "straight"

+ **Rapid** = *sureness of intent*
+ Slow = *Feeling of obstacles, inhibition*

+ **Precise** =   *Tense energy towards goal, cold decision*
                  Principles – incorruptibility – ruthlessness

Straight + Heavy = *Energy and decision to reach aim*

+ **Pasty** =   *Realistic energy*
                 Conflict between reality and senses

+ **Rapid** = *Corruptible activity*
+ **Slow** = *Obstructed activity – depression*

+ **Rapid** = *Activity primed with ease and fairness*
+ **Slow** = *Hesitation – shyness*

+ **Precise** =   *Easy but cold decision making – intellectual*
                  sensitivity

Straight + Light = *Easy decision making, subject attuned to reality*

+ **Pasty** =   *Impressionable feelings – colour sense*
                 Abandonment to impressions – delicate feelings

+ **Rapid** = *Activity in the service of senses,*
               corruptible
+ **Slow**   = *Passivity, lack of contact with reality,*
               laziness, poor health, corruptible
               decisions

Table 11

HEGAR'S THEORY OF ZONES AND CONNECTIONS

We also consider very interesting Hegar's reflections on zones and connections. Hegar distinguishes two zones in relation to the sheet of paper: "the zone under or behind the paper, on which the pressure of the pen is concentrated, which symbolizes reality, material objects, destructible things and essences, works or actions to be carried out"; and "the zone in front of or above the paper, symbolizing internal life, sensitivity, the immaterial world, spirituality." In the graphic field Hegar also distinguishes between "simple connections" and "connections in space".

Simple connections: rounded, looped, or regressive garlands, arcaded, filiform, angular, double arcade, and forms of uncertain connection.

Connections in space: generated by pressure differences, "they connect the lower zone which symbolizes reality and action to the surface zone which symbolizes receptive tendencies." The subject needs to value himself, and to identify himself with his functions.

Concave arch in space: "it begins with a light stroke which gradually reinforces itself to maximum pressure then decreases to a light stroke." This is an arch open to the surface zone – zone of interior life – and closed to the lower zone of reality. The interior life however could be of variable quality. The precise, *rapid*, "inky" concave arch in space, without any heaviness, is found in subjects who fulfil projects, work with pleasure, and are active physically. The *slow* concave arch in space, full of ink, is seen in materially gross subjects, sometimes criminals, or people who are either tired or old and not open to the problems of others.

Convex arch in space: "fullness becomes more and more thin and then returns slowly wider." The convex arch is closed to the surface zone and open to the deeper zone. "The writer feels strong contact with reality. Sensibility is high." Where fullness is frequently interrupted, it could be due to a physical illness and in this case a visit to the doctor is recommended.

Lack of connections in space: indicates lack of specific ambition. If strokes are always "thick", the subject always tries to act physically on reality through his own presence.

Angle in space: "more or less sharp passage from light stroke to heavy or vice versa." "The relations and exchange between receptive and sensible life and fulfilling energy are disturbed and altered. The writer falls prey to many sentiments and impressions which he is unable to express adequately." "If they are creative their thought tends to compartmentalize things, showing intellectual stubbornness."

Thread in space: a sort of subtle arch, without any sharp change, frequent in creative persons.

WRITING SAMPLES

We now examine some significant writing samples noted by Hegar. Gandhi's writing (Fig. 27) shows very different forms of connection, even if they follow the English model: "the rigidity of the precise stroke is balanced by a very flexible layout."

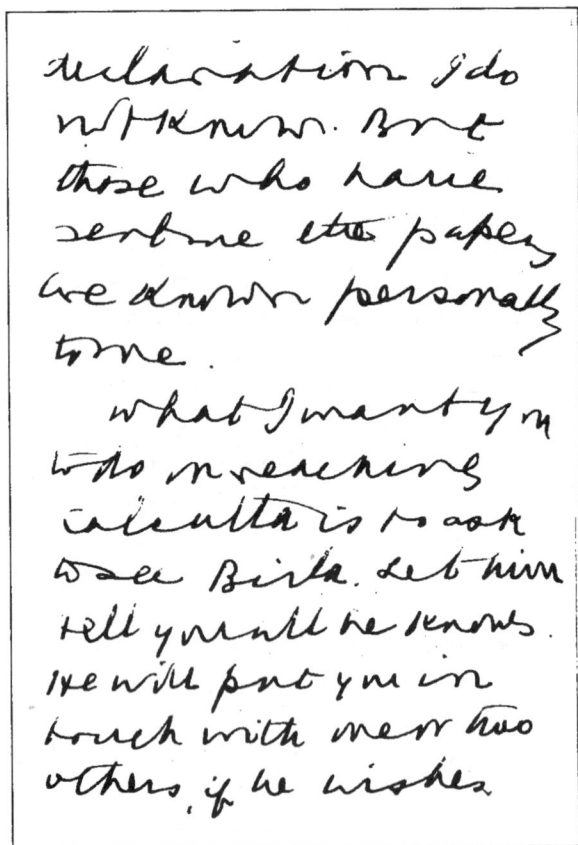

Figure 27 - Gandhi's writing (reduced)

A young person's writing (Fig.28a) (a natural son very attached to the mother): with "numerous pasty strokes to the right, a personality therefore with labile instincts finding great difficulty in reconciling his contradictory impulses. Through tests the young man showed very high intelligence. However, the psychologist and graphologist Jacoby gave an extremely unfavourable diagnosis which was later confirmed. The analysis of pastiness points to one of the most important roots of psychosis."

Freud's writing (Fig. 28b), although not mentioned by Hegar, illustrates some aspects of stroke well:

Heavy + Precise + Curved + Rapid: in middle zone;
Heavy + Precise + Straight + Rapid: in the extensions;
Rapid concave arch and angle in space.

The stroke therefore puts the emphasis on fulfilling energies and intellectual persistence.

Hélène de Gobineau and graphometry

Hélène de Gobineau's untimely death has certainly deprived graphology of a heavyweight academic. Her graphometric researches with the psychologist Perron were among the highest level of work conducted after the Second World War. She was the first graphologist to introduce into France, in 1952, statistical research on the *genesis* of writing.

She was fortunate to have the support of René Zazzo, director of the École des Hautes Études in Paris and of the Psychology Laboratory of the Henri Rousselle Hospital. Following the Laboratory's scientific methods and with the assistance of Roger Perron, who was a colleague of Zazzo, she began an important validation of graphological theories. Her exceptionally interesting book [110] reports all the procedures and results of these tests, which lasted more than six years and took into consideration 1500 cases.

The originality of Hélène de Gobineau's work, explains Zazzo in the preface to her book, "is not only to have combined a pathological method with the genetic, as this was the practice in our laboratory for some time. Her merit was to have developed such validation with the constant aim of not detaching herself from her first intuition. She undertook quantification and gradation in the quality of writing, without throwing away anything that appeared valid and irreplaceable in the descriptions of these qualities."

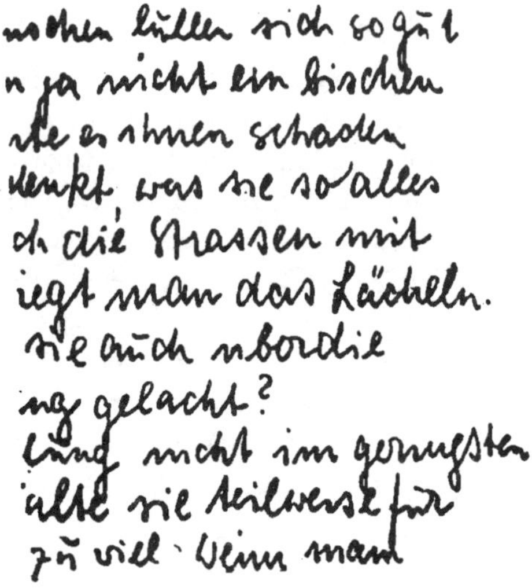

wachen hüllen sich so gut
n ja nicht ein bischen
ite es ihnen schaden
denkt was sie so alles
ch die Strassen mit
iegt man das Lächeln.
sie auch ubordie
ng gelacht?
lung nicht im geringsten
ällte sie teilweise für
zu viel. Wenn man

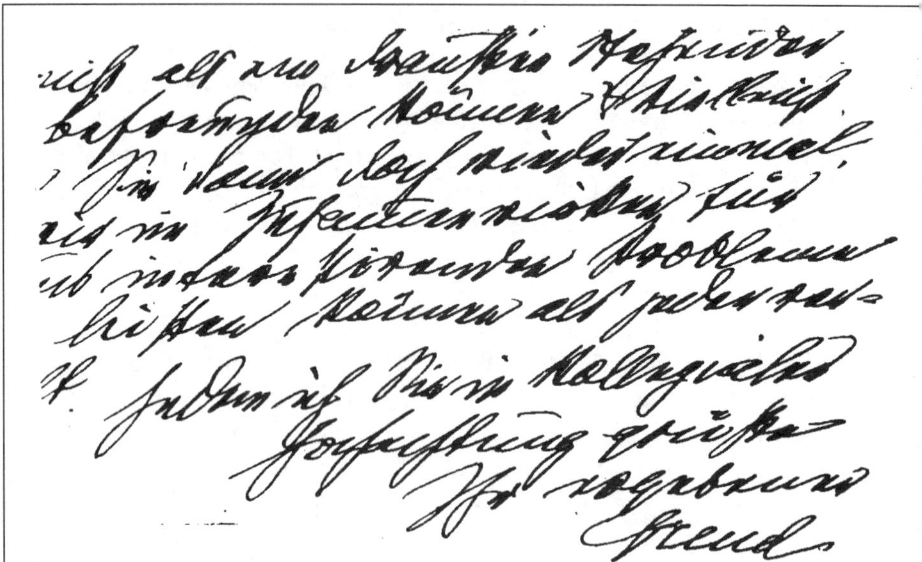

Figure 28
(a) Young person's writing, with psychological problems;
(b) Freud's handwriting (reduced)

This statement gets to the heart of the matter. How does one quantify without losing the quality of graphological values, such as rhythm, movement, or speed itself, which represents one of the most quantifiable variables, using graphometric tests, but which assumes *qualitatively* different meanings, if for example the writing is structured or loose?

VARIABILITY AND DIFFERENCE

To get away from these problems, de Gobineau developed a method of research adapted to take account of the complexity and variability of phenomena: intra-individual and inter-individual variability, and differences between groups. "One needs", she said, "to make an effort at quantification, without being enslaved by the measurement, which is only an instrument. The rough result must therefore be developed and refined with more subtle means."

Intra-individual variability

This is checked to see whether a particular writing characteristic is permanent or occasional. Hysterical tendencies for example provoke substantial changes in writing, whereas in the same space of time, epileptics rarely change, even if the instructions are suitably modified.

Inter-individual variability

These are defined by homogeneous sets, by sex, age, educational, social, intellectual, scholastic, and professional standing, and a standardization of the test is established leading to the measurement of the variation.

Differences between groups

As used in differential psychology, a comparison between defined groups is made to identify "constants" within a group. A diagnostic test is used, allocating a given subject to a particular group. On the basis of this test two types of research are carried out. The first is on the "genetics of writing", in other words, how the development of "infantile modes" evolves into adult script. The other is on the syndromes which define a particular type of personality or pathology.

De Gobineau unfortunately died at 55 and her death caused the break-up of the research group, a reduction of confidence in the French scientific programme, and the gradual suspension of the work she was developing. The work she had undertaken on children's handwriting was however carried on and perfected by Ajuriaguerra, which we shall discuss in Chapter Ten. Her so-called *Autonomy* scales remain interesting. These contain 31 elements for evaluating an adolescent's development. These scales however are a little arduous to compile, given that a "definition" of writing similar to that used for adults takes less time and has a similar outcome. We concentrate instead on the following research which makes an interesting contribution to the study of graphopathology, bringing forward the subject to this chapter so as to treat de Gobineau's work together.

PERSONALITY COMPONENTS

On the basis of a thorough statistical study, researchers catalogued 14 "components of personality" (P), easily observable and suitable for outlining a personality profile (Table 12). De Gobineau then established the degree of presence of these components in reference groups: for example groups of intellectuals, of paranoids, of people with retarded emotions, and of hysterics. Each chosen and studied P component has been broken up into "items", in a sufficiently high number to reduce errors and allow a more precise evaluation. The interpretation of these writing aspects is based on the method of inter-group differences. On the one hand, the pathological method, with the prominence of the P components in specific pathological groups with wider character references. On the other hand, a normal method which considers different socio-cultural groups. The groups are as follows:

Normal adults

Without qualification – with secondary education – with college or university studies (doctors, lecturers in humanities and sciences, business people with professional qualifications).

The mentally ill (based on medical diagnosis)

1) *paranoids* very aggressive-defensive; strong social demands
2) *epileptics* (not mentally defective)
3) *hysterics* (childish and dramatic behaviour, emotionally demanding with neuropathic crises)

4) *manic-depressives* (highly charged in manic phase in words and actions)
5) *schizophrenics* (a less homogeneous group, obsessives, with hallucinations and depersonalization, all beyond reality in a different way to other groups)
6) *emotionally deprived* (without intellectual deficit but incapable of independent life: shy, withdrawn, defenceless, childish, neither retarded nor psychotic, but requiring help).

To conclude this brief treatment of Hélène de Gobineau's work we point out the section on "Precautions and limitations" in which she discussed the problem of "imitation", which according to her observations "can lead to a true and proper graphic mimicry." She cited the case in which numerous adolescents imitate a teacher they admire. One therefore needs prudence before interpreting their personality.

GOBINEAU'S 14 PERSONALITY COMPONENTS (evaluated in 5 grades)	
1. Outline structure	1a Degree of structure of letters: 5 items 1b Degree of outline firmness: 15 items
2. Organization	Spaces – proportions: 18 items
3. Angularity	Line or surface predominance: 7 items
4. Closed or open ovals	Connections: 7 items
5. Extension	Dimension of letter and extensions: in 5 grades
6. Spaces	Aerated or compact: 6 items
7. Slant	From leftward to rightward slant: 5 grades
8. Turning to the right/progressive 6 items Turning to the left/regressive 12 items	
9. Speed	Number of letters in 30 seconds: 5 grades
10. Movement	I Static II Floating III Fluid IVa Blocked IVb Feathered V Dynamic
11. Irregularity	Dimension – slant: 5 grades
12. Connection	According to amount of lifting of the pen: 5 grades
13. Pressure	Evaluated with carbon paper: 5 grades
14. Rigidity/flexibility	According to firmness: 10 items

Table 12

She also stated that in 1500 writing samples of mentally ill patients in psychiatric hospitals, the illness of 25% of patients had not been detected in their writing.

Finally, she predicted that the disputes between psychologists and graphologists will cease: we must eliminate methods based on a specific psychological "church", and also eliminate every graphological method giving character significance to every graphic detail. She also recommended not to end an assessment with coded evaluations: codes being a beginning and not a conclusion. "Intuition and flexibility are indispensable to soften an otherwise sterile technique if used on its own. They must round it out as art rounds out science, not only in research but also in application. Only then will a great number of good ideas drawn from master graphologists be obtained."

To complete this chapter Table 13 illustrates the three main European methodologies.

PRESENT EUROPEAN GRAPHOLOGICAL METHODS

ITALIAN Moretti	GERMAN Klages --> Müller and Enskat	FRENCH Crépieux-Jamin Pulver–Klages
A. Surveying signs *Dynamic vision*	A. Variables of whole *Synthetic vision*	A. Graphic environment *Gestalt vision*
B. Measurement of degree of sign presence	I. Movement/form measurement II. Degree of tension III. Rhythm IV. Originality V. Homogeneity	I. Organization II. Harmony III. Rhythm IV. Ratio Form/ Movement
I. Substantials II. Modifiers III. Accidentals	B. Quantifiable variables	B. Type hierarchy
C. Sign combinations	3 2 1 0 1 2 3 slow ‖‖‖ rapid disconnected ‖‖‖ connected small ‖‖‖ large precise ‖‖‖ pasty	C. Graphic syndromes D. Psychological correlations
INTERPRETATION	INTERPRETATION	INTERPRETATION

Table 13

Chapter Four

CLASSIFICATION OF GRAPHIC SIGNS

I. INTRODUCTION

Having covered the criteria for the evaluation of the graphic environment, we can now enter upon the more analytic study of graphic signs. After many years of observation Crépieux-Jamin had singled out 175 *signs* divided into seven *categories*. After publication of his book *ABC de la Graphologie* in 1929 – a kind of dictionary of signs – many French or Francophone graphologists used and developed further the work of their master.

The modern French method, begun by Crépieux-Jamin, was completed by Gille-Maisani and regularized by the Société française de graphologie, with particular contributions by the following graphologists: Bresard, Delamain, Desurvire, Faideau, Lombard, Peugeot, Pinon, among others.

The German method begun by Klages, Heiss, and Pophal was systematized by Müller and Enskat, whose work is at the heart of the Bavarian school in Munich directed by Helmut Ploog, currently the principal school in Germany. In Italy the work of Moretti has been systematized at Urbino by Torbidoni and Palaferri in particular and more recently by Cristofanelli.

The classification given here is essentially the one adopted by the French school but with some reference to the Italian and German schools. One has to bear in mind that each school presents its own method organically and uniquely and that one cannot be reduced to another. Today, emulation and cross-fertilization could be very beneficial. Gille-Maisani's work has always been towards this object, to enrich the French classification without detracting from its origins.

The French school has adopted a classification of eight *categories* each grouping a number of *signs*. This classification represents for the graphologist a very useful tool because of its ease of use and above all for its didactic clarity. This must not however detract from the basic Crépieux-Jamin principle according to which a *sign* does not have in itself a fixed value, but is affected by the graphic environment. We are therefore a long way from a graphology based on the interpretation of a number of unconnected signs. On the contrary, there is always dynamic interaction between various signs acting in a graphic context.

For greater clarity and with respect for historic tradition we shall present the *categories* according to their classical groupings. Based on our own experience, we shall make an in-depth examination of those *signs* we consider indispensable. We shall leave to the Lexicon, at the end of the book, the task of summarizing the basic interpretations that we use, because the point of this chapter is about understanding the dynamic between the signs. In practice, students can understand the interpretations only once they have mastered the theory of the graphic environment, the quality of stroke, and the meaning of space, and have learnt to observe the graphic gesture.

This chapter deals with the systematic application of interpretations transmitted from previous generations of graphologists, without being rethought or reworked. The exceptions to this rule come from the graphologists whose works we cite. Students must obviously take care not to repeat phrases already used by graphologists for a particular writing and transfer it to another. This habit encourages very bad graphology, which is aired in second-rate publications, lacking reflection or consideration of graphic context, and with a minimum of creative reasoning.

II. THE CATEGORIES

The eight *categories* of graphic gesture used by the French school are the following: *Space – Dimension – Direction – Slant – Continuity – Speed – Pressure – Form.*

It can be said that each category gives information on one global aspect of personality and of behaviour. The order of categories here is arbitrary. The French authors of the *Manual of Graphology* [200] first treated *Pressure* and *Form* and concluded with *Space*.

The important factor is to consider the interaction between all the categories, and not give a partial analytical description. We have to remember that the smallest stroke derives from a solid dynamic play of *force – speed – connection – fullness – direction – propulsion – formative movement.* Suzanne Bresard [46] defined the *psychology of movement* as a dynamic intrinsic to the graphic stroke, opening the way for a wholesale rethinking of graphological theories and techniques.

Space (also called Layout)

As we have already seen in Chapter Three, in the spatial symbolism of Max Pulver, the organization of space reflects adaptability to the environment and social inclusion. The relationship between paper and writing (between the "whites" and the "blacks" as it is often expressed) shows immediately the relationship between the writer and the outside world, the capacity for decision-making and emotional response, the amount of involvement and identification with the environment, together with the subject's feeling for time, present, past, and future.

Dimension

The fullness of the gesture, the enlargement of the forms, the straight or looped extensions, the vertical or horizontal movement, are indicators of the subject's assertiveness and ability to externalize, according to temperament and motivation: self-esteem, emotional and physical needs, freedom or inhibition.

Direction

Supplies elements regarding the writer's conduct in the context of sensibility. The flow of writing, flexibility, use of space, slant of the line, indicate how the writer reacts and struggles in relation to the environment and to self, to present and past experiences and future prospects.

Slant

Indicates self-control and sensitivity to relationships. The slant of the letters reveals the forces in play between spontaneity and control, impulsiveness and restriction, thought and passion. Continuous and rapid variations of slant point to a battle between contradictory forces: this is a statement of uncertainty about one's own identity and choices, and is reinforced by repeated and uncontrollable changes in the style of writing.

Continuity

Shows the relationship between thought and action. The degree of graphic cohesion, homogeneity of arrangement, fluidity, rhythm of the "whites" and "blacks", arising from the writer's psychomotor coordination, reflects intellectual and relational capabilities in both functional and emotional aspects.

Speed

This category influences all the others as it pervades every aspect of writing. Experimental research has shown that it can be measured precisely. Graphic dynamism, dexterity, impetus of stroke, and regularity of flow indicate the degree of efficiency of one's actions and reactions.

Pressure

According to classic graphology this is the key element which conveys mental energy and the writer's vitality. However, one must consider several factors: the writing tool, speed of writing, the energy available in the precise mental-physical moment, and the paper being used. These are all variables that often make the evaluation of pressure very difficult, especially today.

The consistency of the *stroke*, its strength and quality, its contact or lack of contact with the paper, alterations in its distribution, point to the condition of the writer's vital resources. In brief, the graphic gesture in its interaction *Continuity – Speed – Pressure* indicates the individual's psychomotor dynamics.

Form

Supplies us with important elements on self-realization and individuality. The formal structure, the ultimate aim of the graphic stroke, offers through its specific style a true synthesis between intention and possibility, between voluntary and forced behaviour.

III. SPACE/LAYOUT

Bearing in mind the basic school writing model and the cultural influences of a writer's country, we can say that the *management of space* is partly guided by personal and conscious choice, but partly also by an unconscious choice, as argued by Pulver with his *symbolism of space* or by Klages in his idea of *Leitbild*.

One approach comes from the German graphologist Robert Heiss (see Chapter Three) who proposed what he called the *rhythm of the structuring of space*. This rhythm offers indications on the subject's adaptability to the outside world. A casual, conventional, or passive spatial arrangement indicates that the subject surrenders to the environment (*hypo-evolved rhythm*). If instead there is a personal element in the structuring of space, where the writing interacts with the blank surface in deliberate, flexible, and active ways, without losing control, one can presume a good exchange between the individual and the environment (*accentuated rhythm*). When the opposite occurs, and there is discordance in the application of the writing to the page, the relationship between the individual and the environment is likewise disorderly (*disturbed rhythm*).

Another approach is Pulver's *symbolism of space*. According to this view, the margins give the best indications, by their size and degree of regularity. The secondary indicators are: position of signature and its distance from the text, ways of heading the page, date, address, and paragraph style.

A third approach consists of analytical observation of the graphic components in the context of the relationship between written text and its internal and external space (relationship between "blacks" and "whites"). This is the approach of Crépieux-Jamin, using those signs that relate mainly to the categories *Space* and *Continuity*.

"*Whites*" create distances and visual detachment from the context – in other words from the written text. In fact Pulver advised turning the writing round top to bottom, thus separating it from its content, in order to see better the play between whites and blacks. "*Whites*" can be rhythmical and harmonious with the "*blacks*" or they can mark disconnections, interruptions, or empty spaces. They symbolize the *unsaid*, reflection, irruptions of imagination, intuition, or the unconscious that can be either stimulating or disturbing. The *"blacks"* represent the voluntary or conscious explicit message, the willing or invasive and at times obsessive sense of commitment.

The relationship between whites and blacks immediately implicates more graphic categories. But the simultaneous study of each category, even if prompted by the aim of clear teaching, in itself restricts the visual perception. In effect, the written words and the "silences", the spaces between words and lines, between and within letters, determine precise *signs*. These fall not only under the category of Space (*aerated, compact, spaced, invasive*) but also Dimension (*dilated, wide, squeezed, narrow*), Continuity (*connected, grouped, unconnected, disconnected*), and Form (*ample, looped, closed, crenellated, open*).

In addition to the signs of the French school, we propose also to consider the Morettian idea of *"triple width"* which considers the global balance of space between letters and words and within the letter itself. This principle in itself partakes of many categories and is proof of a very articulated graphic synthesis.

Signs and interpretations (see Fig. 29)

The signs can be classified into two groups: signs which account for the quantitative relationship between whites and blacks (*Aerated – Spaced – Compact*), and signs which account for the qualitative relationship between whites and blacks (*Orderly – Disorderly – Tangled lines – Invasive – Typographic – Triple width*).

The signs *orderly, disorderly,* and *invasive* have already been considered in the evaluation of *harmony*, in particular the sign *orderly* which has hardly been listed in the manuals since Crépieux-Jamin, who described it according to criteria substantially similar to those of *harmony*. On the other hand we describe in the Lexicon the signs *disorderly* and *invasive* in the terms used by the Morettian school, which apply especially well to Italian writing. Concerning the sign *typographic*, we connect it to the symbolism of space and the structure of the margins.

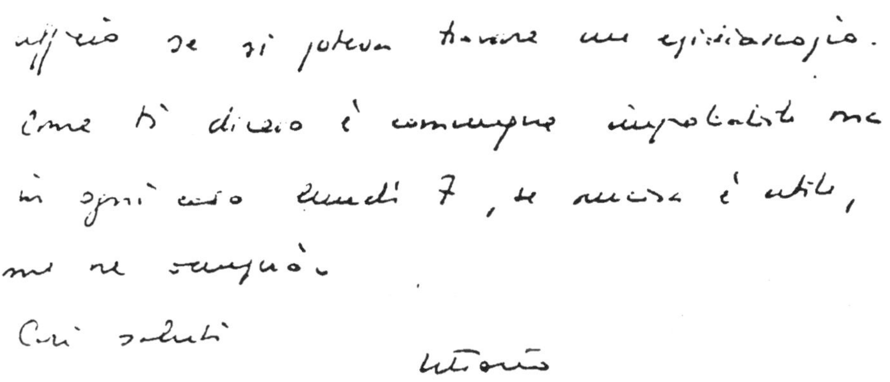

(a) Aerated – Orderly (40 year old male bank manager)

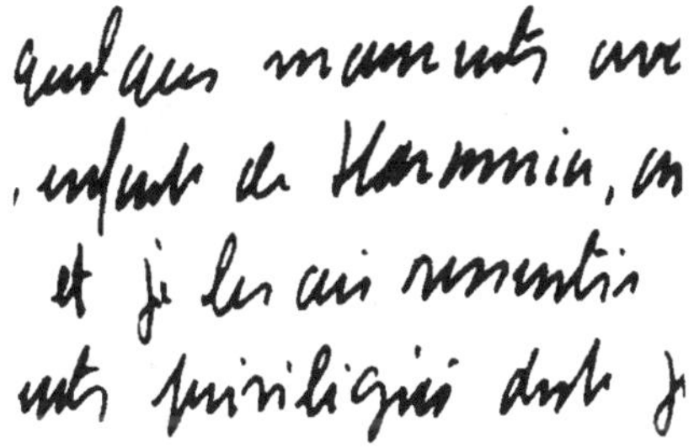

(b) Compact – Orderly
(36 year old female painter)

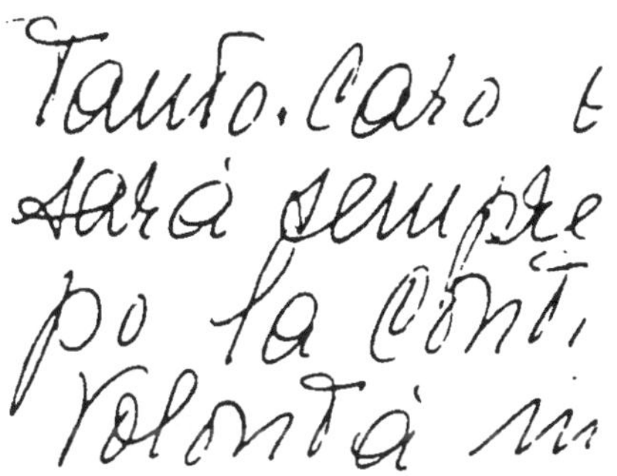

(c) Tangled lines – Invasive (Female 75)

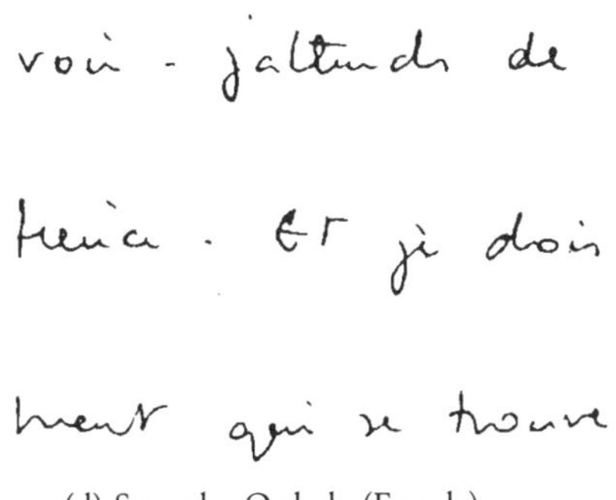

(d) Spaced – Orderly (Female)

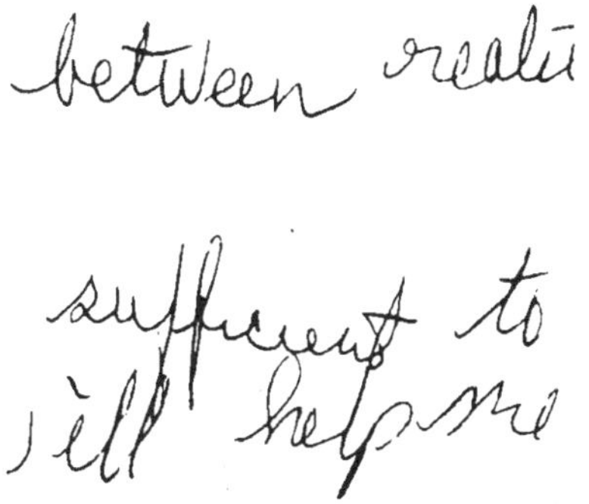

(e) Disorderly – Perturbed
rhythm of space (Female 65)

Figure 29
Organisation of space

Aerated writing is a highly qualitative sign. Ania Teillard describes it thus: "It is writing which allows breath, air, light, and spirit to enter." A correct and harmonious balance between the dark masses of the words and the silences of the whites is created, as entangled lines are by definition excluded. According to French cultural ideas, *aerated* writing produces well-defined indents and paragraphs, and often a *social margin*. It is therefore logical that this sign expresses a balanced adaptability with the environment and clarity in judgement and action.

The more prominent the whites are, the greater is the distance between the written and the unspoken message. Spaced words indicate reflection, which implies a distancing from the immediate context and, as Dr Gille-Maisani emphasized [105], brings "the capacity to restrain the flow of spontaneous associations and to weigh up decisions." The space between lines is chosen more consciously than spaces between words. Spaced lines imply therefore the intention of distancing oneself to reach a more detached and synthetic vision and organization.

When spaces between words and lines are both clearly marked in a writing, its interpretation depends on the *graphic environment*. The conceptual, emotional, and functional detachment that these spaces express can favour the faculty of abstraction and synthesis and consequently organization and concentration. However it can also lead to isolation, to fear of genuine involvement, and inhibition.

It is obvious that the positive aspect goes together with a sufficiently flexible and structured writing. Rigidity and looseness are the two extremes that generate a negative graphic configuration, and so the whites may express mental tension if placed in a rigid context, but in a weak and broken environment they are an indication of the most lax character. The psychological art of the graphologist consists in always weighing up the interactions that alone can provide a precise interpretation.

Irregularity further nuances interpretations. If whites appear suddenly and arrhythmically, they indicate the irruption of the unconscious and could be evidence of mental disturbance rather than a source of inspiration.

The opposite of spaced writing is *compact* writing, where the condensing or invading of space by the blacks tends to drive out the whites. This particularly affects spaces between lines and words and gives information on how reality is confronted. With this sign the message is urgent and prevails over the unspoken, the *breath* of which Ania Teillard spoke is no longer the protagonist. The effort is extended in the expression, in penetrating reality and possessing it. This is a pointer, on the positive side, to the subject's strong commitment to the environment, to a concentration of energy in a stable and solid manner. Compact writing must be compared with *squeezed* writing (squeezed letters) and with *narrow* writing (letters higher than they are wide) to better determine the real degree of compactness.

On the negative side, the impulse that constricts the whites, avoiding separation between words and lines, shows insufficient reflection and synthesis, and excessive influence by situations, by the unforeseen, by the other, without sufficient discernment. The degree of tension and pressure will also nuance interpretations. The presence of the signs *rigid, angular, heavy,* or their opposites *wavy, rounded, light* will give opposed meanings. In the first case compact writing confirms the subject's tendency to an unwavering conviction, but in the second case the subject's judgement and behaviour is easily influenced by others' ideas.

Triple width with regard to space shares the qualities of *aerated* writing, where *breath* passes through, and with regard to dimension it establishes a *proportional* synthesis: neither too full or too tall, nor too wide or squeezed.

IV. DIMENSION

Overall expansion or obvious constriction of stroke, compared to the basic school model and the cultural habits of the subject's country, determine signs which are grouped under the category *Dimension*. The size of the writing – and especially the size of the middle zone – is an element which must be considered right from the start in the *definition*, directly after evaluation of the graphic environment.

One must principally consider the basic sizes and dimensional relationships between the elements of writing. Two main points are, firstly, as regards the letter size: fullness of the middle zone and the development on the vertical axis of the upper and lower extensions, and whether looped or not. Secondly, free strokes must be examined, because if they are out of proportion it takes the writing into a "large" configuration, independently from the actual size of each letter. The present determination of measurement, following the scientific work of Ajuriaguerra, concerns specifically the *height* of the middle zone, also called the *i*-height, defined as "normal" at 2.5 mm. One must always however refer to national writing models, and the cultural and educational habits of the various social classes according to the historical moment.

According to Pulver, size of writing expresses the first type of social relationship between the I and the You. Large writing in which the *i*-height exceeds the norm, could be the expression of a spontaneous and simple impulse in accord with the environment, or of a compensatory reaction, reactive to the environment.

Both Klages and Pulver believed that fullness of dimension expresses an element of "pathos" which can range from spontaneous emotional participation in the other and in events, to the emphasis of the personality which proclaims and imposes its own emotional and imaginative parameters, its own projections or idealizations.

Large writing can evoke the biologic egocentric world of the child, as well as spiritual strength. It can express the closing of the self to reality or the subjective transformation of reality, which can turn into the cult of the personality, or the elevation of imaginative values and heroic identification. It could be a sign of protest, of the Ego with its grandiose ideas and enterprising dash, but also the vehemence of self-love and arrogance which obstructs objective criticism.

Experimental and statistical research on children with basic education has proved their tendency to write "large". The effort for them of muscular control produces a fuller stroke (see Chapter Ten). The same tendency is also found in the illiterate and sometimes in the aged, though elderly writing can be either small or large.

Small writing can stem from a weak biological impulse or from a sense of oppression, or a tendency to question the objective data of reality. Small writing together with sobriety shows concentration and modesty. But besides these aspects, Pulver said that small writing can be a consequence of "a perversion of the spontaneous impulses of power" weighed down with resentment and defeatism, and modesty in this case is only apparent. One can compare, for example, an overuse of exclamation marks which gives writing an invasive and verbose exuberance, or certain enlarged accents or vigorous *t*-crossings thrown forward and sharp-pointed, which if placed in the context of small letters take on such value that the basic criteria proper to small writing cannot be regarded as completely valid. They will be overturned by the authoritarianism and despotism revealed by these *t*-crossings. Some graphologists have mentioned "the tyrannical pride of small writing."

Signs and interpretations (see Fig. 30)

Fundamentally, size informs us on self-assurance. In adolescent writing it varies according to changing or conflicting conditions of security, but generally settles down in adulthood, taking on connotations relating to the individual's physiological or mental strength (see Chapter Three: Pulver). Signs of dimension can be put in groups relating to the structure of the graphic body.

1. Size of middle zone:
Large – Medium – Small

(Crépieux-Jamin only noted the signs *large* and *small*. We include another frequently used in practice, *medium*.) The middle zone is very important because it represents the "graphic body". When it appears well structured with a firm outline it indicates good psychophysical well-being. The middle zone is also a signifier of turmoil in the soul, and insecurities; above all we look for sudden size variations and problems of connection. It is here that the Ego manifests itself with its elation or depression, ego-centricity or altruism.

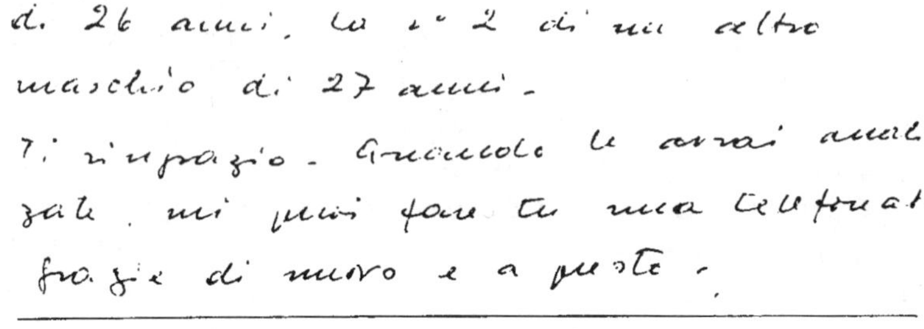

(a) Small to medium – Sober – Low (Female novelist, 45)

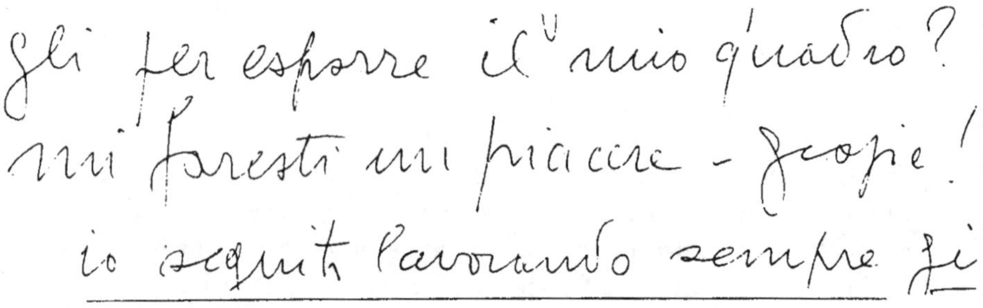

(b) Large – Full – Triple width (Male painter, 70)

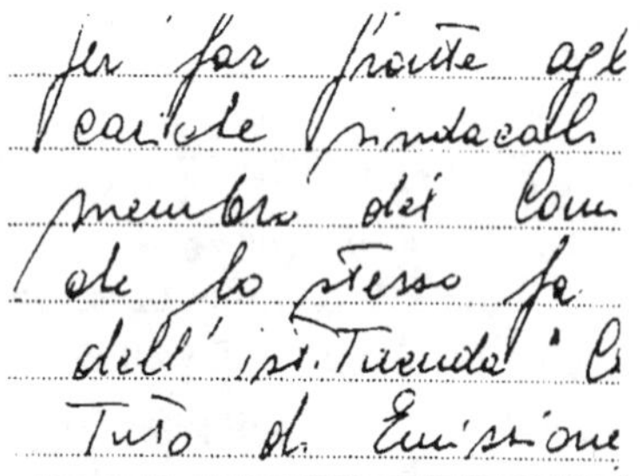

(c) Prolonged upward and downward –
Superelevated – Squeezed (Male, 40)

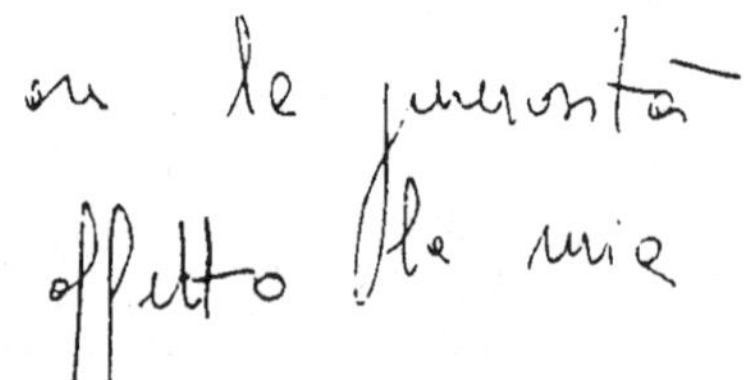

(d) Prolonged downward –
Narrow letters (Female, 30)

Figure 30
Dimension (30% reduction)

2. Proportion between zones and development on the vertical axis:
Low – Prolonged upward – Prolonged downward – Prolonged upward and downward – Superelevated

The extensions beyond the middle zone, above and below, have already been covered in treating the theory of Pulver. The notion of superelevation indicates that a graphomotor impulse heightens a letter or part of a letter, when it should only be situated in the middle zone. This is therefore an impulse coming from the zone of the Ego, which stretches and overexpands. Superelevations had already been observed by the first graphologists, in susceptible people, those with demanding self-pride and need for self-advancement.

3. Fullness of stroke and development on the horizontal axis:
Full – Narrow – Squeezed – Wide – Triple width

These signs concern *progression* of the graphic flow towards the right, as reflected in the development of the letter width (*narrow* to *full*), and the distance between letters and between words (*squeezed* to *wide*). These are notions well framed within the concept of "triple width".

Full writing contains exaggerations which contrast it with *sober* and *squeezed* writing, the stroke expands with impetus, generosity, euphoria, richness of imagination and participation. If the writing is moderate in its dimensions and proportions, balancing the *triple widths*, it approaches the sign *ample* in the category Form. In this case the interpretation privileges the positive aspects of this sign. If however the writing shows obvious irregularities, excessive or inflated thrusting movements, and gives free rein to exhibitionism, at times with hysterical impulses, we must see evidence of the poor trustworthiness of someone living in a fantasy world.

4. Course of stroke and general development:
Swords – Enlarging – Irregular – Sober

These signs describe the ways of regulation of the graphomotor impulse and are described in the Lexicon. See also Chapter Two, concept of *irregularity*.

V. DIRECTION

Crépieux-Jamin absorbed *Direction* and *Slant* into one category. He believed that the graphomotor movement imprinted a certain *direction* to the writing, in relation to the direction of the line (*horizontal, descending*, etc.), to the direction of single words (e.g. *galloping*), and to the axis of single letters (*vertical, leftward*, etc.), these aspects being independent from each other. The post-Jaminian French school, instead, preferred to classify under *Slant* those signs covering the direction of the axis of letters.

The direction of the line can be traced by linking the base of the letters from the beginning to the end of the line. In the same way the direction of a single word is seen by linking the base of each letter. Progressive or regressive aspects of direction take in *spatial symbolism*, with the significance accorded to left and right. The direction is called *progressive* when the movement goes towards the right and avoids returns to the left; when the opposite occurs it is called *regressive*. Even individual letters are involved in progressive or regressive tendencies, as well as tendencies to invert the gestural sequence to execute certain forms, so the category *Direction* also includes signs which deal with the outline of single letters and single traits.

It is important to bear in mind that direction varies with the mood of the moment and the type of document being written such as an official letter or notes. It also changes with content: love letter, condolence, reprimand, etc. In addition the piece could have been written under difficult circumstances, standing, in a cramped position, or with inadequate writing equipment.

Often direction mirrors the immediate state of mind, by which the flow of the lines reflects our enthusiasms and our depressions of the moment. It will always be better to base an interpretation on characteristics which show a high degree of constancy within the document under study, and if possible between different examples of the subject's writing. The graphologist needs to have all necessary documentation.

Direction can be considered from two viewpoints: a purely *graphomotor* aspect of the movements in the graphic flow and a *symbolic* aspect which derives from the comings and goings of the outline.

Graphomotor aspect

During early school years the rules in the exercise books encourage the horizontal direction of the line, so keeping to the model initially does not enable much distinction between the signs in this category. As soon as a child acquires graphic mastery and begins to write on unlined paper, how the lines slope can be observed and interpreted. A rigid direction on the line reveals an exaggerated internal tension in the child and consequently shows a great difficulty in natural and spontaneous development. In Ajuriaguerra's graphometric scale the *descending* line has been identified as an *infantile component*, a trait that statistically disappears with writing development between the ages of 6 and 11. Its presence can therefore be interpreted already in preadolescence. This condition must be related to pressure. If it is strong the combination demonstrates a highly confrontational attitude. If pressure is light it shows resignation and discouragement, increasing towards indifference if the form has signs of weakness.

Symbolic aspect

The symbolic structure of the written line from left to right represents the essence of being present in each of us, the advancement towards a goal, towards tomorrow, towards the other. While movement represents the impetus which pushes us forward, the way in which the line is encountered – with abandon, rigidity, or sloppiness – becomes a symbol of the relationship between our sensibility and the real world.

Signs and interpretations (see Figs 31 - 2)

We group together the signs in the two categories described above – graphomotor development and symbolic configuration – to convey better the *movement* of the *direction* grappling with the impetus that drives, represses, or upsets it. The writing model teaches us to position letters on the base line and to follow a horizontal progression. For an adult to write spontaneously on unlined paper, it is evident that the maintenance of such a progression along the line implies great self-control, whether conscious or unconscious. Through the graphic environment, the evaluation will be made as to whether this control is a systematic brake to a natural spontaneity, or if it simply shows the dictates of an interiorized educational rule. The evaluation of rigidity or fluidity at this point helps a correct interpretation.

Suzanne Bresard [46] grounds direction as an expression of *vital flow*. From her we adopt the evocative terms "trajectory" and "propulsive force" used magisterially in her celebrated analyses of Tolstoy, Nietzsche, Rodin, Balzac, Hemingway, and others. She identifies four types of movements as the directing principle of her method, based on the *psychology of movement*:

- *propulsive* to the right
- *regressive* to the left
- *looped ovals* in the middle zone
- *disconnection*: a type of suspended movement that the author interprets as "pauses inherent to the analytic reflex" or "loss of awareness about direction".

1. Trajectory of line and words:

Rising – Concave – Convex – Descending – Horizontal – Rigid – Wavy lines – Diving

Interiorized line of conduct and mood of the moment influence these trajectories. These signs do not present interpretative difficulties, once the criteria of spatial symbolism are assimilated. The sign *Diving* is treated in Dr Gille-Maisani's well-documented articles.

2. Development of outline forms:

Contrary – Progressive – Regressive – Backward – Slender – Twisted

In *contrary* writing the direction of some strokes (and consequently the form of some letters) proceeds in a contrary way to the "natural" writing model. Noted anomalies occur in conjunction with deviations in most categories and in particular *Continuity – Speed – Pressure*. Contrary *Form* is the result of one or more contrary directions, sometimes regarding the sense, sometimes the sequence. The stroke achieved in the opposite way to normal writing could represent a personalized form, but at the same time it indicates a tendency to go against the grain. In this view it could be the result of a creative, aesthetic, cultural element just as well as revealing a more or less conscious negativity, revolt, and polemic. It could therefore show a desire for emancipation or an undisciplined confrontational character. One must be aware in any case that the two could coexist. It is also important to check whether the contrary stroke is in some way in harmony with the whole or if instead it appears in an incoherent and discordant context.

Max Pulver says this particular stroke is one of the signs that can reveal lying because its movement implies a perversion of moral values, with a tendency to double dealing and deception. However, such a negative interpretation must be amply correlated by other graphic confirmation. In the psychology of the unconscious, the *contrary* stroke is frequently found in personalities having Freud's anal phase and in those people who have a paranoiac configuration. One must be very careful: ovals and *t*-crossings contrary to norm are in fact logical to a left-handed person and must not be interpreted in the above way.

The sign *backward,* introduced by Dr Paul Carton as *en recul* and adopted by Gille-Maisani, for whom it "constitutes an accentuated mode of the sign regressive", is interesting in the way in which it differentiates itself from regressive or leftward. The backward stroke is indeed a stroke of fear, of turning away, and not of withholding as regressive writing would be. As a type of reflex, the backward movement at times pervades the whole writing, and at times it is concentrated on the so-called free strokes such as the *t*-bars or final strokes.

For the signs *progressive* or *regressive* refer to Chapter Two, Section III as well as the Lexicon. The other signs are sufficiently explained in the Lexicon.

Twisted extensions, normally firm and vertical, are frequent in the prepubescent and herald the start of the physical changes typical to that age. They often remain during the adolescent phase as a statement of difficulty in adapting and identification. If persistent in adulthood, it is a sign of unresolved adolescent problems. If twisted verticals suddenly reappear in adult writing, it could indicate unease. This could range from temporary tiredness to circulatory or nervous malfunction. Twisted writing reveals emotional suffering, a lack of confidence, and distress.

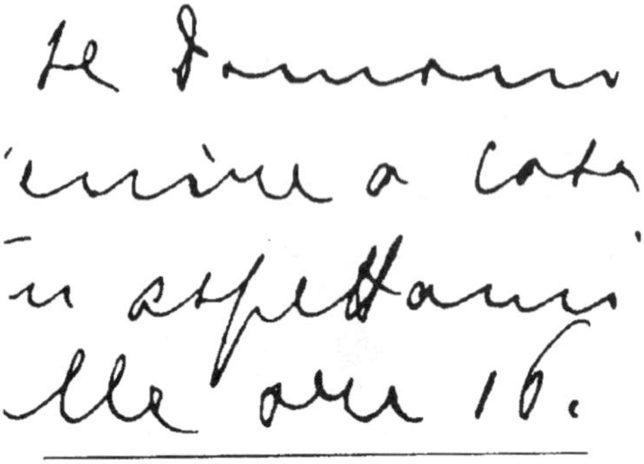

(a) Wavy lines – Progressive – Descending – Concave (Fr Moretti)

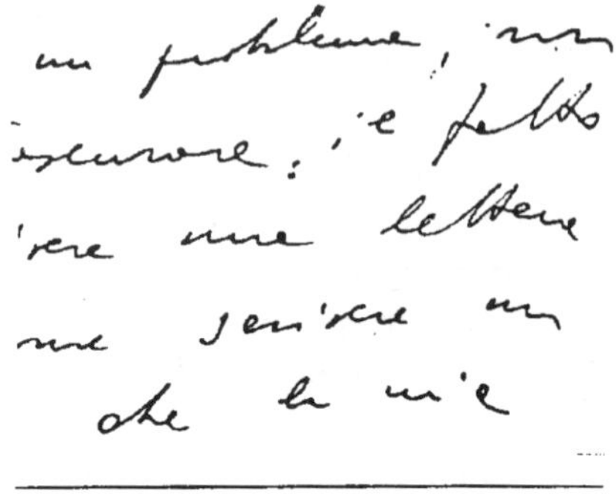

(b) Wavy lines – Progressive – Galloping – Diving (Female, 50)

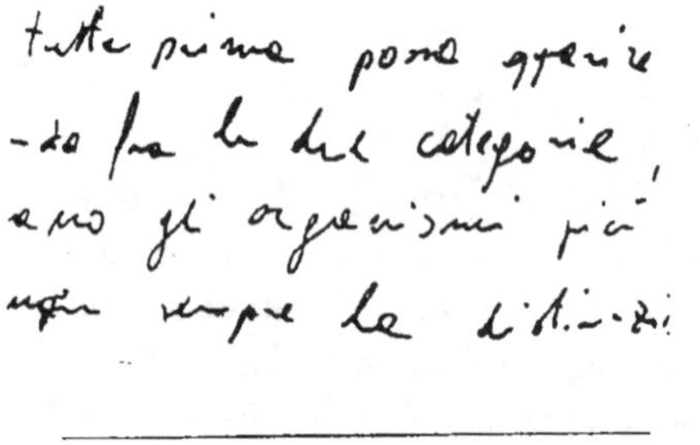

(c) Wavy lines – Galloping (Female, 30)

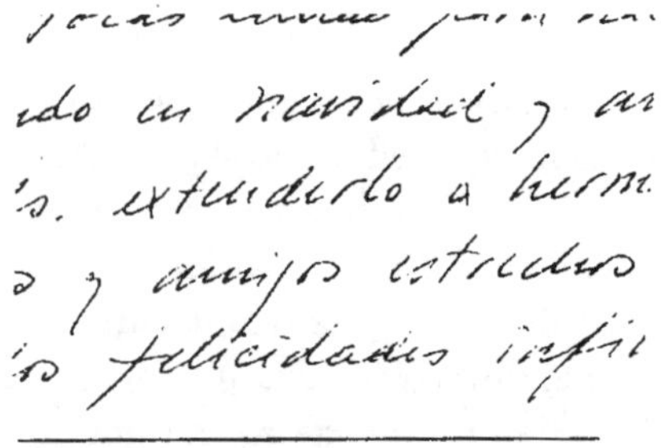

(d) Rigid – Horizontal (Male painter, 55)

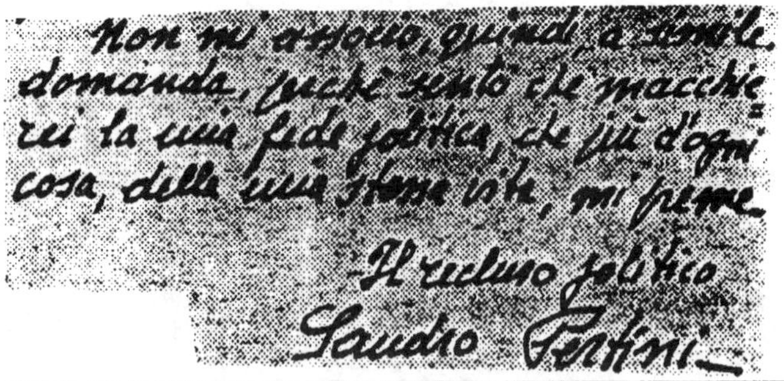

(e) Horizontal (Sandro Pertini, Italian President)

Figure 31
Direction

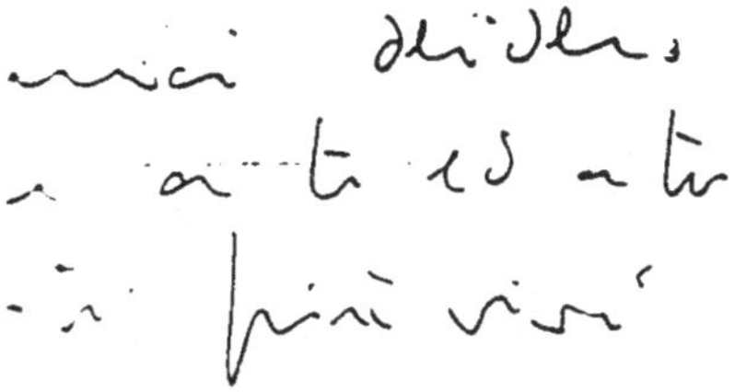

(a) Progressive (Female, 30)

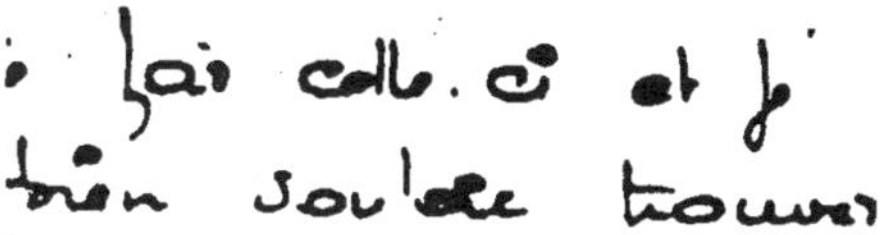

(b) Regressive

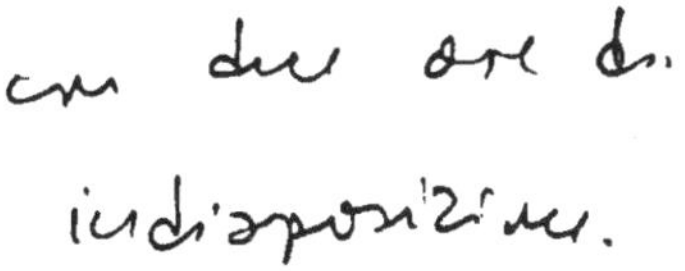

(c) Contrary

(d) Backward

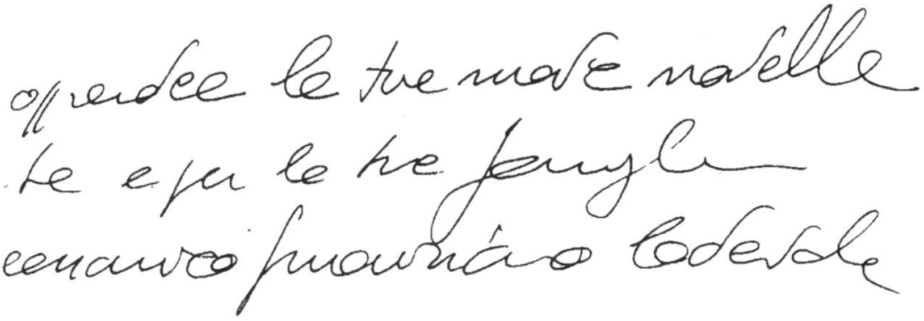

(e) Slender

Figure 32
Direction

VI. SLANT (OR INCLINATION)

In general the basic school model defines a particular slant, sometimes clearly enforced, more often only suggested for imitation by the teacher. At the moment the model is fairly free but in Europe the prevailing style is "vertical". On one hand slant is an automatic impulse and already in children soon becomes personalized. On the other, it is one of the writing elements over which an adult can exercise great control. Slant is easily imitated and can easily be altered to hide one's own writing style.

Slant refers to the orientation of the letter axis. To trace such axes one has to draw a line between the top and base of the letter. For greater precision in rounded or curved letters, the upper and lower tangents can be traced and the letter axis is the perpendicular to the two tangent points. The angle of the vertical axis can be measured with respect to the horizontal line starting from the right. Such an angle could vary from 20° (very slanted to the right) to 160° (very slanted to the left). *Vertical* writing forms an angle of around 90° with the base line; to the right of the vertical axis, *rightward slanted* or *inclined* writing forms an angle between 70° and 45°; under 45° the writing is *very slanted to the right*. To the left of the vertical extension, *leftward* writing forms an angle with the base line between 90° and 160°.

Signs and interpretations (see Fig. 33)

The axial orientation of the letters easily determines the three fundamental signs of inclination:

Leftward - Rightward slanted (often just called *Inclined*) - *Vertical*.

Excessive slant of over 45° becomes *very slanted to the right*. Irregularities also generate three other distinct signs rich in interpretations:

Heterocline - Irregular - Straightened.

In addition, two of Moretti's types, *Wavy* and *Twisted*, concerning the way in which the letter axes cross, are very interesting. To best understand

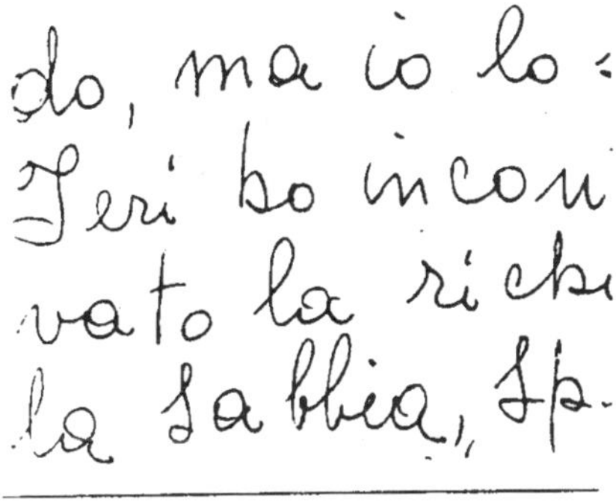

(a) Vertical

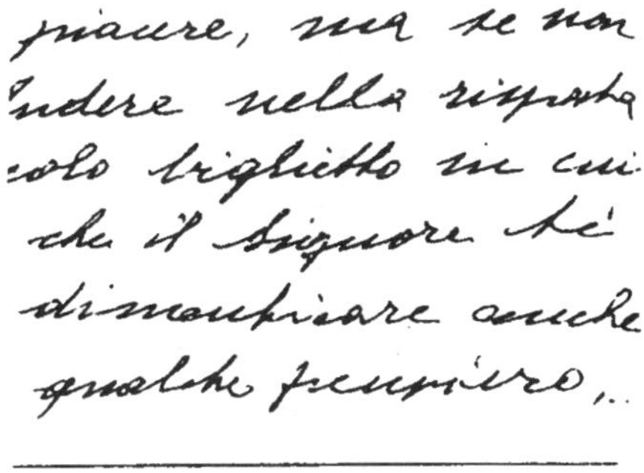

(b) Rightward slanted

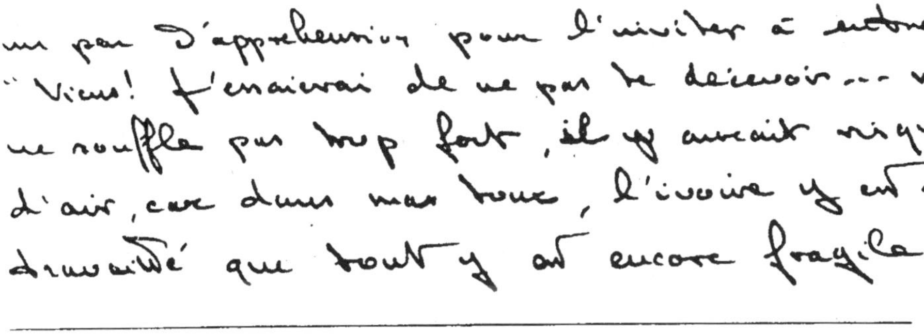

(c) Leftward

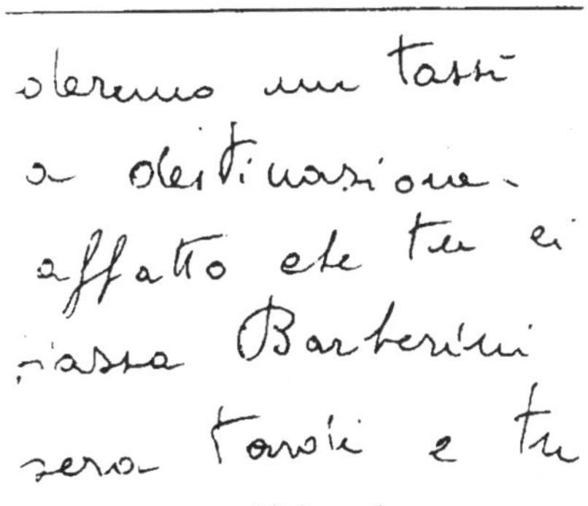

(d) Irregular

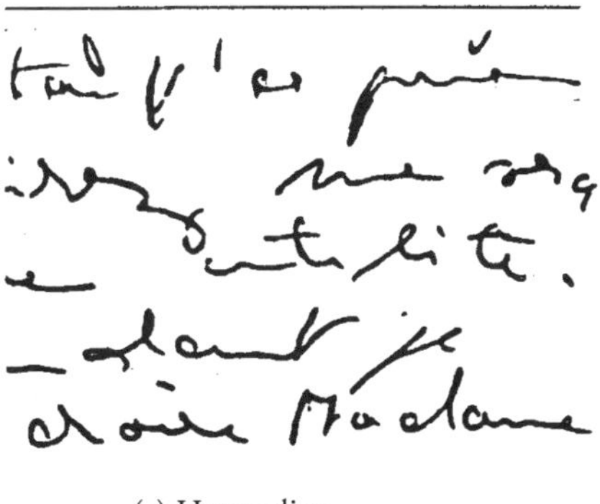

(e) Heterocline

Figure 33
Slant

them, it is advisable to consult Torbidoni and Zanin [230], as they are not so clearly treated in the French school. They are included in our Lexicon, on the understanding however that each sign must be framed within one's own methodology linked to a particular school.

In research carried out by the first graphologists, at a time when the school model clearly taught "slanted" writing, interpretations are in agreement. The neurophysiological control, implying a stroke kept around the vertical, reflects a tendency to self-control, while leaning towards the right gives greater freedom to the impulsive thrust of communication. If it is true that the impetus towards the right indicates sensibility towards the "you" and the "other", according to Pulver, it is also true that the quality of this sensibility is indicated by other parameters. It is necessary for example to evaluate if it is a tendency intrusive to the other or an altruistic affection. Quality of stroke, curved or angular outline, fullness or constriction, can completely alter interpretations.

Very slanted writing in its excessive impetus to the right can also speak of love or passion as well as hate and, in a context lacking strength, of impressionability and sometimes depression.

It will be important to look at other elements, such as rigidity or excessive regularity, that indicate inhibition or obsessive tendencies, or their opposite, sudden changes which mark *irregular* or *heterocline* writing in which uncertainty, indecision, and ambivalence erupt. A slight variability in the writing axis tells positively of an efficacious mental and emotional adaptability.

VII. CONTINUITY

Continuity more than any other category expresses what we can call the *graphic dynamic*. Whether a writing is small or large, inclined or leftward, light or heavy, the degree of graphic cohesion is the element which welds the relationship between thought and action, from which one can determine more or less the *rhythm*, which is the key element of graphic personalization.

Continuity therefore covers all the signs of graphic cohesion, of coordination or division, at various levels:
- general graphic configuration: homogeneity, monotony, shakiness
- connections between letters and sometimes between words
- fluidity between single strokes: pauses, sudden jumps, suspensions, retouching

Learning to write requires the child to be able to join together letters progressively without having to lift the writing instrument unnecessarily. At around the age of ten, children acquire a sufficient gestural flexibility that allows them to connect different letters into one group, a sign of intellectual development. However we shall see in Chapter Nine that motor or emotional difficulties can hinder normal graphic fluidity, without the slightest intellectual deficit.

"False connections" similar to adult "pick-ups" (where the pen is removed from the paper and then put down again in the same place) express typical childish difficulties which become interesting to interpret if they still exist in adulthood. A fluid *cursive movement* is rarely achieved before the age of eleven and for a long while a somewhat static appearance prevails. When a certain degree of movement takes over this is not always fluid but rather laboured. The basic school model and gestural logic teach a child to connect different letters and later insert elements which would otherwise break the flow: an accent or the dotting of the *i* or crossing the *t* for example. The writing model in Anglo-Saxon countries predicts some breaks or connections differently from the Latin model (see Chapter Eight).

During the course of adolescence the type and degree of connection take on a slowly developing configuration until it becomes personalized. Along with the rhythm of whites and blacks that figures predominantly in the management of space, we find that the elements of continuity differentiate one writing from another even when their forms are very alike.

Signs and interpretations (see Figs 34 - 37)

Signs of continuity can be put into three general groups:

1. Degree of graphic organization:
Unorganized – Organized – Disorganized

These three signs, perhaps little used today, are part of classic graphology and define the maturity and evolution of a handwriting, from the *unorganized* script of children and illiterates to the normal *organized* adult script. Illness or senility produces *disorganized* writing, which had previously been *organized*.

2. Type of connection:
Unconnected – Connected – Overconnected – Secondary connection – Grouped – Combined

These signs describe connection *par excellence*, in other words the links between letters. These are certainly influenced by basic writing models according to time and country and at the present moment seem to be very conditioned by cultural fashion, in particular during adolescence.

The fragmented appearance of *unconnected* (also called *disconnected*) writing refers to a broken *tempo*, caused by reflection or inhibition according to the situation. It is widely recognized even at a popular level that continuity of connection presupposes perseverance in ideas and action, according to an individual logic that could be more or less objective or clearly subjective.

In both unconnected and connected writing, the basic movement is the determining factor in judging the quality of graphic cohesion. With unconnected writing, there could be a subtle connection – more virtual than real – in space, in which the ideative impulse could appear. With connected writing, the continuity of the link might only reveal a mere automatic movement lacking any associative impulse. The keys to reading similarities and differences in writing are still rhythm and movement.

Connected writing in adults is easy to see. One must always consider if the connection is simply made according to the basic writing model; this could be the case in people of low to medium educational level. The evaluation of joined writing must consequently be adjusted. In children's writing, connections may hide some "pick-ups", as can be found sometimes in adolescents and even in adults.

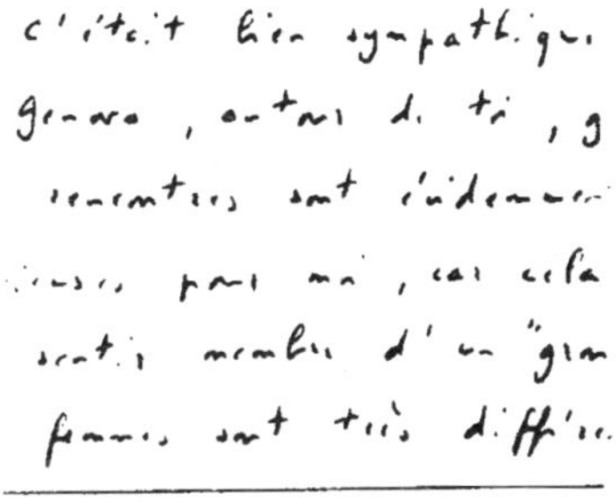

(a) Unconnected

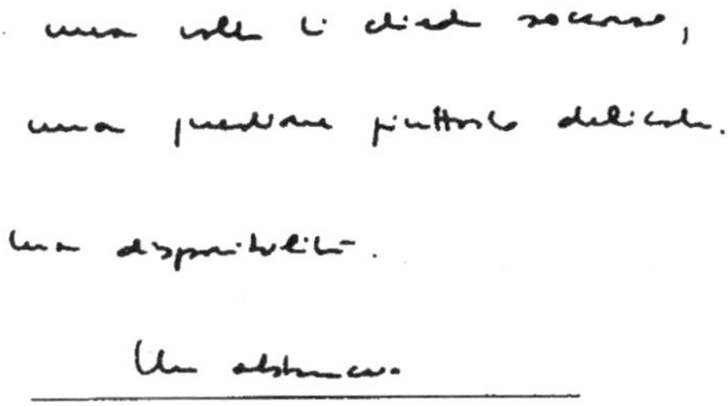

(b) Grouped

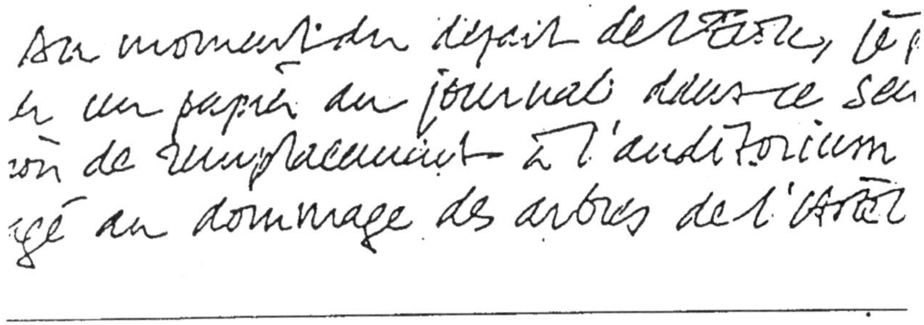

(c) Connected – Overconnected – Combined (Male architect, 38)

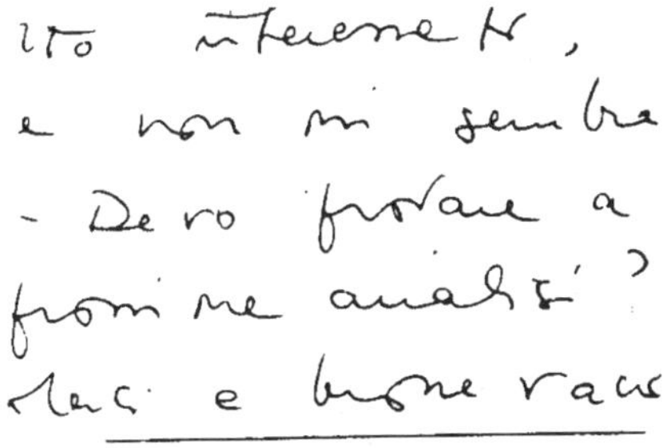

(d) Combined
(Female graphologist, 32)

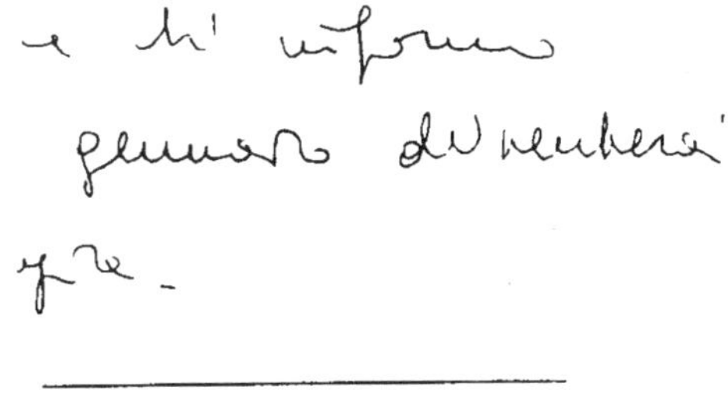

(e) Combined
(Female psychologist, 30)

Figure 34
Continuity

Static and dynamic disconnection

A sign always judged negatively in the history of graphology is *static disconnection*, which we want to reconsider. It involves judging whether there is a certain degree of dynamic movement which joins letters "virtually" to each other, or if the letters are placed in a static way, one next to the other.

The graphologist must take into consideration the growing number of adults and adolescents choosing a writing style in capitals or near to script, where the letters seem to be passive and barely show any imagination. We do not intend here to analyse psychological or sociocultural reasons for this phenomenon. But on the graphological level we must examine the dynamics of the stroke which cause these types of writing. By definition they correspond to two basic criteria: the first, structuring rhythm of form, is dominant in relation to movement (whatever the quality of the form may be), the second is the lack of connection between the letters.

"Form" dominant over "movement" indicates, according to German graphology, a tendency to follow a structuring imperative as a directing image, with more or less elasticity, firmness, or rigidity according to cases. Under this profile, the graphic gesture is therefore adjusted primarily by a constructive albeit constrictive force. The absence of connection between letters accentuates the control of movement over form.

Classic graphology as we have seen, viewed disconnection in a very negative way. Crépieux-Jamin [65] wrote: "Disconnected writing always reveals inhibition", and he identified it with slower activity and enfeeblement, "a sign of impoverished faculties". Describing the beautiful handwriting of the philosopher Bergson (Fig. 35) as "very harmonious and distinct, clear, sober, simple, and simplified", Crépieux-Jamin added, "it appears disconnected because the document in question is a copy." In actual fact it was the philosopher's normal writing.

Knowing Crépieux-Jamin's rigorous observations, we are surprised by such harsh judgement (and in the case of Bergson by such an error). One is tempted to think that the influence of the graphic model and its manner of continuity was at the time such that all writers with disconnected writing may probably have been considered as "handicapped in graphic connection". Crépieux-Jamin in effect rejected as "a fascinating illusion" Michon's interpretation which defined "juxtaposition of the letters without joining" as the primary sign of "pure intuition or faculty of conception and creation", giving the example of Chateaubriand's writing, well known to specialists. Today however we know that intuition can also be expressed through other graphic aspects.

The more recent observations of Pierre Faideau on "Disconnected, connected, punctuated writing" have allowed a re-evaluation of disconnected writing. Faideau distinguishes "static disconnection" from "dynamic disconnection", where the link is virtual, invisible, innate in space according to a progressive dynamic. Bergson's writing therefore becomes a prototype, with a positive meaning attached to its relations with the environment, and whose essential element becomes its radiant intuition.

The graphologist continues to find difficulty when faced with static disconnection where there is no precise evidence of a virtual link or of any link at all. In such an instance, the absence of connection and the static rhythm suggest their negative graphological connotations: inhibition and inability to adapt. Does Jaminian severity then fall anew on "static" disconnection?

A particularly interesting study by Hélène de Maublanc and Cookie Lami [164] tackles the problem of this type of writing, which is frequently found today. Their research distanced itself from the presumed intellectual inability to adapt or socio-emotional disadvantage attributed to this type of writing, starting from the observation of "static disconnected writing" by subjects who had studied at university and gained professional and social success. These studies happily show the value of investigating such apparently passive and defensive writings, and give proof of the inexhaustible opportunity for research which graphology always offers.

We have summarized the results in Table 14. As always the logic of gestural observation can guide our interpretation. Distance is established with the detachment of a letter from the following one, consequently the way in which detachment occurs indicates the meaning of the distance itself. One must also know the basic writing model of the writer as well as the sociocultural level (independent of writing ability).

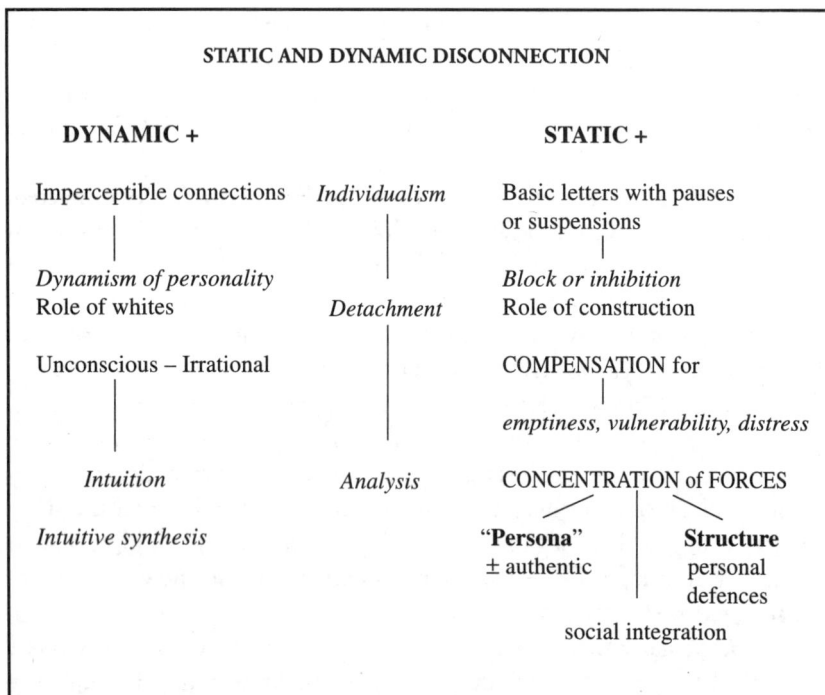

STATIC AND DYNAMIC DISCONNECTION

DYNAMIC +		**STATIC +**
Imperceptible connections	*Individualism*	Basic letters with pauses or suspensions
Dynamism of personality		*Block or inhibition*
Role of whites	*Detachment*	Role of construction
Unconscious – Irrational		COMPENSATION for
		emptiness, vulnerability, distress
Intuition	*Analysis*	CONCENTRATION of FORCES
Intuitive synthesis		**"Persona"** **Structure**
		± authentic personal defences
		social integration

Table 14

---

3. Degree or type of graphic cohesion:

(a) SPECIFIC COHESION:
Comfortable – Constant – Enlarging – Homogeneous – Hopping – Irregular – Nuancée – Swords

Signs in this category concern the cohesion between words, that is, the development of the graphic *continuum,* while the word unravels. These are described in the Lexicon and in general do not carry particular interpretative difficulties.

Irregular describes the variations on writing homogeneity, and for this reason Crépieux-Jamin classified this sign within continuity. But the sign in itself already represents a *directional synthesis* as it could show inhibition or dynamism. Irregularity, in other words, permeates writing and falls under several categories. For example, an *irregular* middle zone will be so defined for its variable height, width, and depth as well as for changes of inclination in the letter axis, or changes of pressure or form. Having ascertained the general significance, the Lexicon takes irregularity into consideration separately by category.

(b) ALTERNATING COHESION:
  Amended – Covering strokes – Disharmonious – False connections – Fragmented – Jerky – Punctured – Shaky – Suspended

The signs in this category are rich in nuances and interpretation, and are fundamental in considering the different disturbances that can upset the graphomotor dynamic. These signs not only indicate difficulties in gestural continuity but also describe alterations of the *stroke*. Graphopathology, in addition to the study of rhythm, principally examines these signs, which serve as pointers to incipient or actual organic illnesses, or to mental tension or full blown mental illness.

We take from Gille-Maisani the interesting notion of the sign *disharmonious*, a term that has forced us to translate the notions related to harmony by the terms "harmonious" and "inharmonious", reserving the term "disharmonious" to the sign illustrated by Gille-Maisani, which covers a psychiatric connotation.

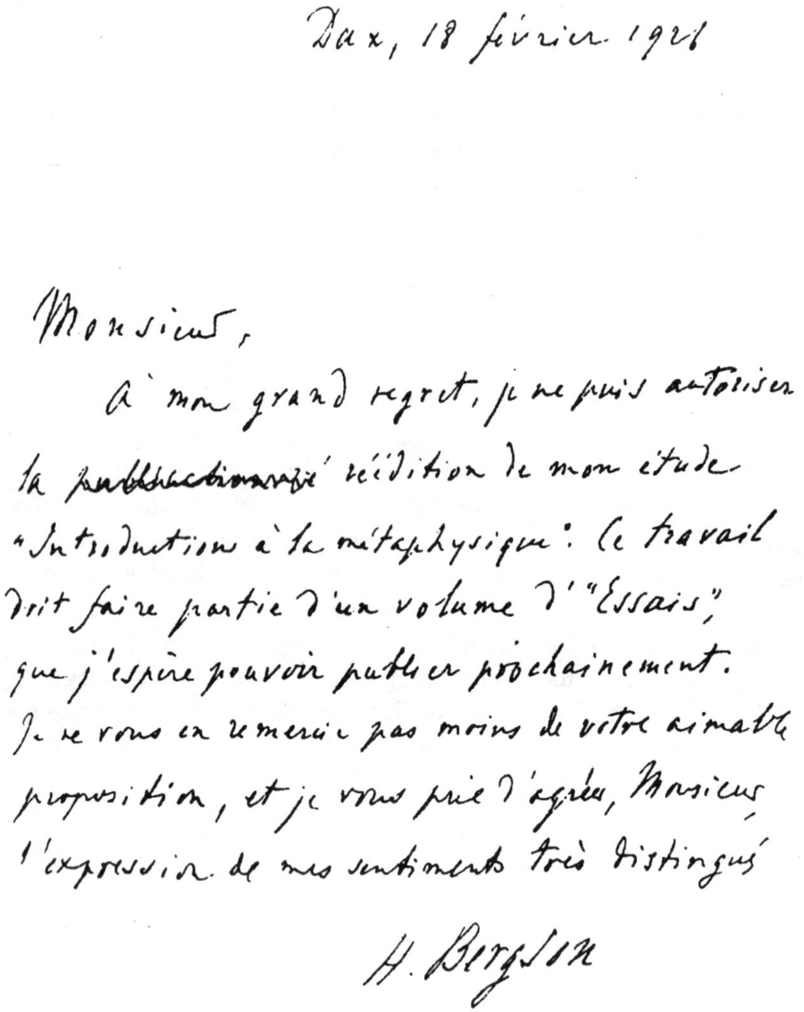

Dax, 18 février 1926

Monsieur,

À mon grand regret, je ne puis autoriser la publication réédition de mon étude « Introduction à la métaphysique ». Ce travail doit faire partie d'un volume d' « Essais », que j'espère pouvoir publier prochainement.

Je ne vous en remercie pas moins de votre aimable proposition, et je vous prie d'agréer, Monsieur, l'expression de mes sentiments très distingués

H. Bergson

Figure 35
Writing of the philosopher Henry Bergson:
Accentuated rhythm of space – Precise and light stroke – Dynamic disconnection

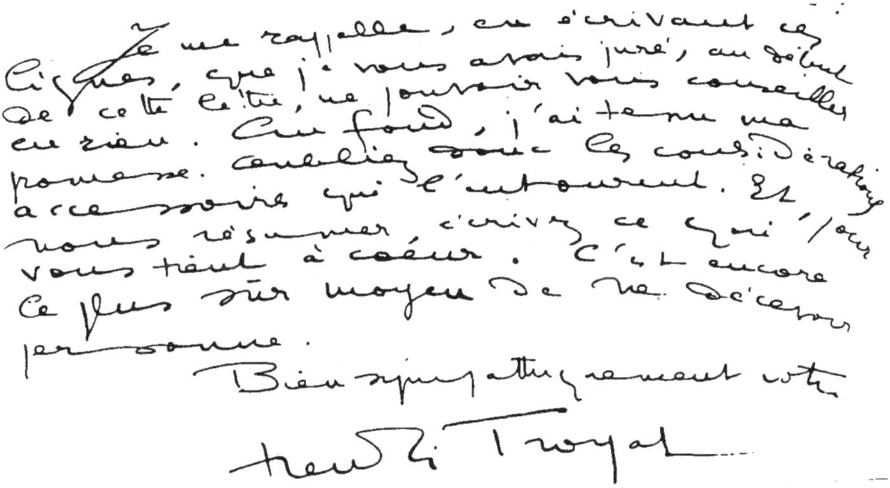

Je me rappelle, en écrivant ces
lignes, que je vous avais juré, au début
de cette lettre, ne pouvoir vous conseiller
en rien. Au fond, j'ai tenu ma
promesse. Oubliez donc les considérations
accessoires qui l'entourent. Et pour
vous résumer, écrivez ce qui vous
tient à cœur. C'est encore
le plus sûr moyen de ne décevoir
personne.
Bien sympathiquement votre
Henri Troyat

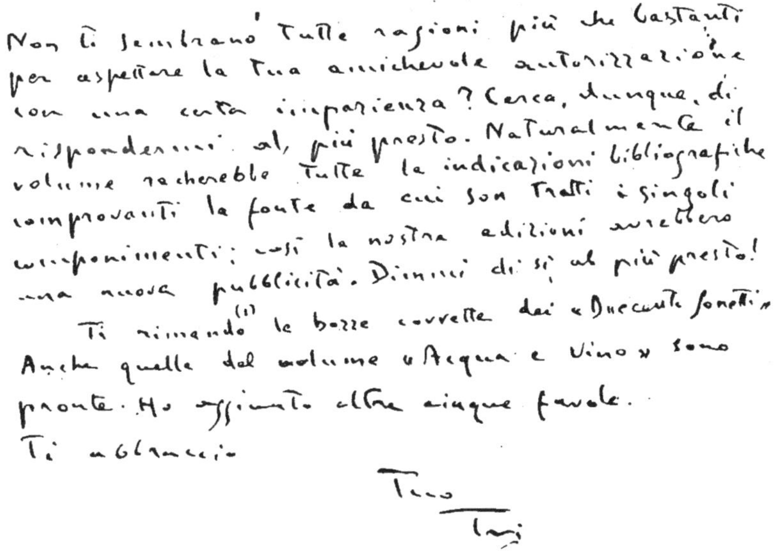

Non ti sembrano tutte ragioni più che bastanti
per aspettare la tua amichevole autorizzazione
con una certa impazienza? Cerca, dunque, di
rispondermi al più presto. Naturalmente il
volume recherebbe tutte le indicazioni bibliografiche
comprovanti la fonte da cui son tratti i singoli
componimenti; così la nostra edizione avrebbero
una nuova pubblicità. Dimmi di sì al più presto!
Ti rimando[1] le bozze corrette dei «Duecento sonetti»
Anche quelle del volume «Acqua e Vino» sono
pronte. Ho aggiunto altre cinque favole.
Ti abbraccio
Tuo
Tri

Figure 36 (reduced)
Continuity
(a) The writer Henry Troyat: Connected with gaps, Secondary connections
(b) The poet Trilussa (Carlo Alberto Salustri): Dynamic disconnection, Fragmented

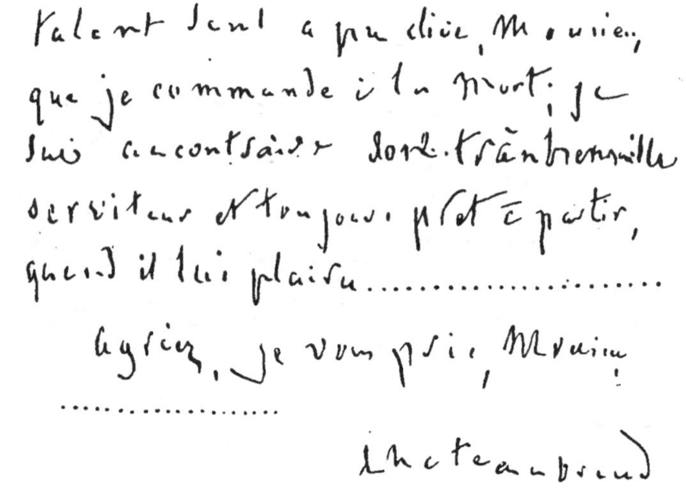

Valent seul a pu dire, Monsieur,
que je commande à la mort; je
suis au contraire son très humble
serviteur et toujours prêt à partir,
quand il lui plaira......................

Agréez, je vous prie, Monsieur
....

Chateaubriand

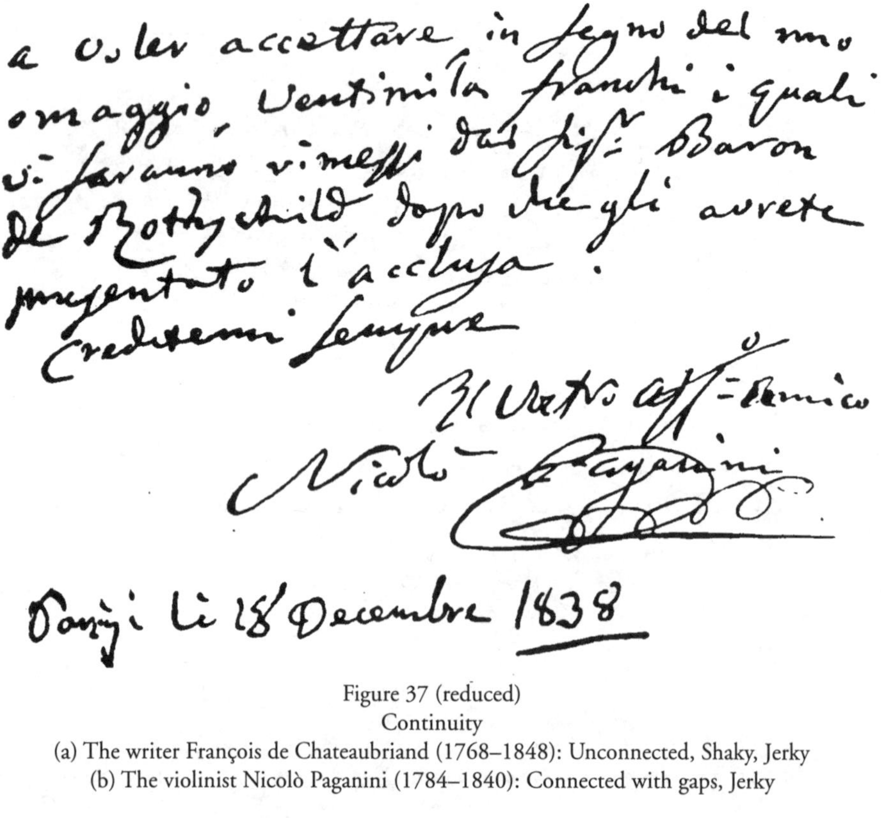

a voler accettare, in segno del mio
omaggio, ventimila franchi i quali
vi saranno rimessi dal Sig.r Baron
de Rothschild dopo che gli avrete
presentato l'acclusa.
Credetemi sempre

Il Vostro aff.mo amico
Nicolò Paganini

Parigi li 18 Decembre 1838

Figure 37 (reduced)
Continuity
(a) The writer François de Chateaubriand (1768–1848): Unconnected, Shaky, Jerky
(b) The violinist Nicolò Paganini (1784–1840): Connected with gaps, Jerky

VIII. SPEED

In learning to write, speed represents "the consequence of graphomotor maturity that allows the child to develop movements of writing and progression that correspond to the needs of the school years" (J. Peugeot [199]). In subsequent sections we shall examine how writing slowly builds its own sequences, during the formative years, organizing the relationship between graphic cohesion and rapidity, or how graphic homogeneity is neglected in favour of speed.

In the adult speed is the expression of the level of graphic dexterity achieved as a result of exercise, writing habit, and a person's profession. Subject to many variations according to the type of document and emotional state, speed is best considered over several documents. The speed at which a doctor writes prescriptions will not be the same as when writing a letter of condolence. There are cases when slowness can express a non-agile mind, or it can show inhibition, or a need for clarity, for diligence, or for acting scrupulously.

Ideally speed should be appreciated by observing the subject while writing. Even if some speed tests can supply an average measurement of time employed, the graphologist is mostly interested in catching sudden stops, jerks, suspensions, hesitations, or those gestures that writers sometimes trace in the air, completing numerous spirals before writing, perhaps extremely fast. It is a type of preparation, a slightly nervous and anxious reflex, which certainly influences an average speed.

Starting from the principle that rapidity is gained to the detriment of precision of form, and that complicated or regressive gestures generate less speed, some signs of speed and slowness can be listed (see Table 15). It is important to consult the sign "Slowed down" in the Lexicon, where we have described possible causes of obstacles to speed: gestures of inhibition, perfection, ornamentation, elaboration, conservation, unease, dissimulation, and psychosexual gestures.

Signs and interpretations (see Fig. 38)

The signs of speed can be divided into three categories:

1. Basic signs with measurable speed:
Accelerated - Precipitated - Poised - Rapid - Slow

2. Signs influencing the impetus of speed:
Animated - Carried away - Dynamic - Flying strokes

3. Signs influencing the control of the impetus of speed:
Controlled - Slowed down

Interpretation is principally tied to liveliness of reactions and the rhythm of activity. Often the partnership between emotion and exteriorized ideative agility causes fast writing and in this case it does not necessarily show an efficient activity, indeed it often expresses a state of excitability and restlessness. Intellectual stimulation and a search for depth are more often associated with poised writing, in which moments of reflection are more important than quick reactions. Pulver thought that a slow and affected writing could hide a cunning disposition.

SIGNS OF SPEED AND SLOWNESS	
SIGNS OF SPEED	**SIGNS OF SLOWNESS**
Irregularities of every type	Regular writing
Imprecise form	Precise form
Progressive writing	Regressive writing
Flying strokes, centrifugal	Interrupted strokes, centripetal
Garlanded	Angular and arcaded
Simplification, sobriety	Superstructure, lassos, paraphs
Connected writing, rightward slanted	Leftward writing
Precise stroke	Pasty stroke
Enlarging writing	Squeezed writing
Rising writing	Convex writing
Pressure in relief	Tapering pressure, spasms
Straight, short connections	Curved, long connections
Progressive left margin	Regressive left margin
Combined writing	Retracing strokes
Filiform	Loops
Finals thrusting, rising	Finals turned back
Dots on *i* and accents	Tremors, dents
placed to the right	Twisting, congestion

Table 15

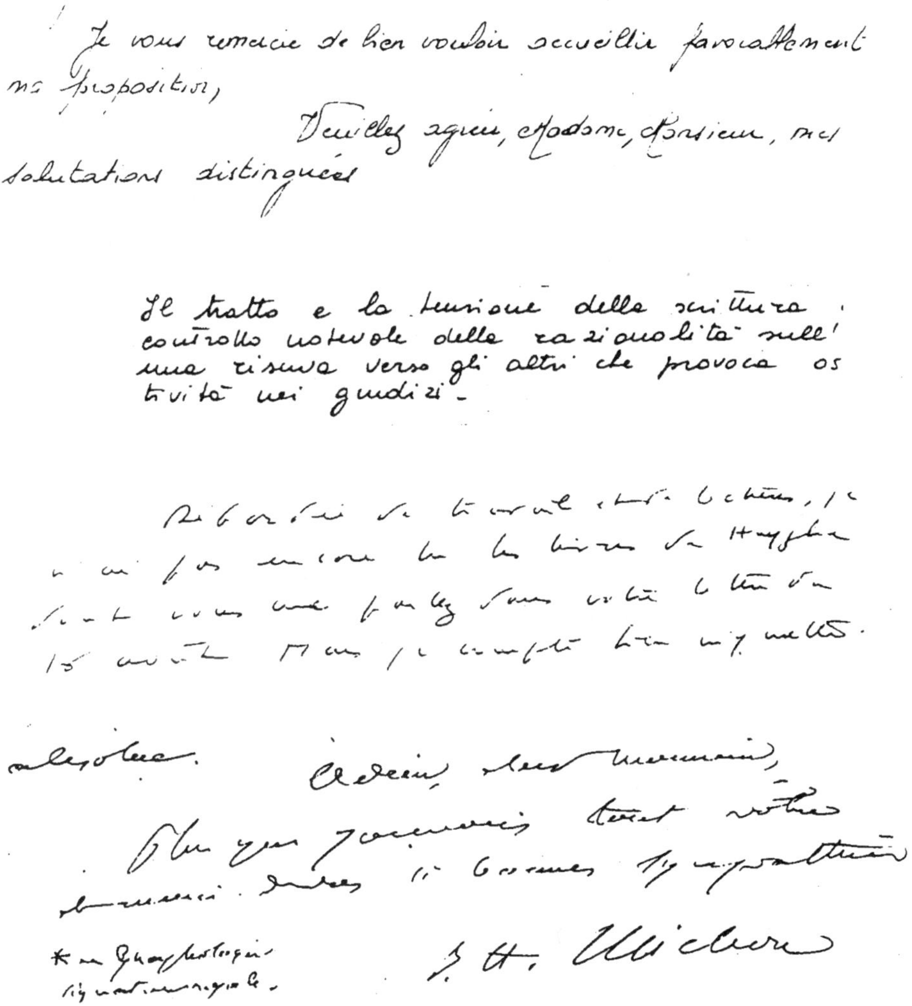
Je vous remercie de bien vouloir accueillir favorablement ma proposition,
Veuillez agréer, Madame, Monsieur, mes salutations distinguées

Il tratto e la tensione della scrittura controllo notevole della razionalità sull' una riserva verso gli altri che provoca ostività nei giudizi.

Figure 38 (reduced)
Speed
Slow/slowed down/poised – Accelerated – Rapid – Precipitated/flying strokes

IX. PRESSURE

Pressure expresses mental vitality and energy and must be one of the principal aspects studied to define a writing adequately. The authors of the French manual [200] began with the description of this category. In the present work, we prefer to follow the usual order, but we have devoted some space already to the notion of "stroke" in the description of graphic environment (see Chapter Three, Section IV). According to the above mentioned manual, "the stroke evokes in particular intrinsic qualities related to ink use: pasty, precise, etc." and these are qualities we consider essential for the correct evaluation of graphic environment. We therefore use the term *pressure* to encompass both *stroke* and *pressure* in the classical sense.

For Pulver, pressure corresponded to arterial pressure and reflected the mental and physiological variations in the stages of life: in puberty or menopause, as well as in phases of physical or mental disturbance, pressure alters. In older people the stroke sometimes becomes heavier and pastier and sometimes more precise, light, and less elastic. In cases of arteriosclerosis pressure loses differentiation in contrast, in other words shading disappears. Pressure is the principal pointer in the field of sexual behaviour and deviation. Handwriting of sexual criminals contains specific pressure anomalies.

Signs and interpretations (Figs 39 - 41)

In order to observe the pressure we must consider:

1. Basic weight of stroke:
Heavy – Light – Precise – Pasty

2. Quality of stroke:
Blurred – Firm – In relief – Pale – Thick – Thin – Velvety – Weak – Well-nourished

The quality of the sign *firm* lies at the divide between the influences that reinforce pressure and those that devitalize it.

The three signs *firm*, *in relief*, and *well-nourished* all indicate the presence of strong psychomotor energy. If they are reinforced with *large* and *angular* forms they proclaim great self-assurance, secure in opinion and action. When in addition the pressure is *heavy* we are dealing with fighters, the mythological type Mars. Such accentuated pressure is also found in the Jungian *Sensation* type.

The sign *in relief* in particular is worth observing, in the context of Pierre Faideau's analysis [92]. In former writing models it was the standard method, taught by applying heavier pressure on the descending stroke and lighter pressure on the upstroke. The graphic gesture that imparts energy more strongly on the descending stroke corresponds to the rhythm of expansion with which the gesture immerses itself to gain a deeper knowledge of things. This gesture of relief shows the total energy, the motor and unconscious reserves, indicating the vital potential. The lightening of the upstroke indicates a *conserving* instinct which allows the stroke to *free itself*. It indicates the capacity for detachment, judgement, loosening of tension.

3. Peculiarities of pressure:
Clubbed – Congested – Deviated – Sharp – Sharp-pointed – Smeary – Spasmodic – Spindle-shaped

In Ania Teillard's book *The Soul and Handwriting* [227], she presents several samples with anomalies of pressure that show sexual disorders.

Research by Oscar Venturini on the elderly [237], beyond collecting statistical material, summarized findings made by many authors on pressure in old people. "Weak" pressure is present in 68% of cases, "marked" in 31%, "irregular" in 22%, and "in relief" only in 4%.

The author states: "The tendency of pressure to decline reflects the writer's lack of vitality, weakening of instinct, and dulling of the senses. With irregular pressure, there is still tonal support, although often inconsistent. This reflects an untimely diffusion of shakiness in the tonal mechanism, caused not by 'willpower as domineering force' (Marchesan) nor by a strong Libido (Pulver), as one would be tempted to think for subjects whose writing otherwise appeared to be sufficiently sure and personal, and not caused solely by hyperemotivity (as interpreted by Moretti in assessing Thickened style II) but by a suffering of mental or physical origin and a general weakening in energy. According to Periot such shakiness is due to 'mental hesitation and periodic anxiety, systolic cardiac murmurs, renal pathologies, spasmodic dyspnoea in arteriosclerotics ...': according to Pulver these conditions derive from mental or physical disorders and in particular from circulation problems."

With regard to tremors, this condition deserves a treatise of its own with an in-depth study of the different types of tremors and their incidence in the most varied illnesses and cannot be enlarged upon here. We must however learn to distinguish tremors due to graphomotor difficulty (children, illiterates, disabled) from those due to pathologic disturbances, including tremors which appear to be imitative and false, which form yet another field of study by themselves.

According to research conducted by F. Lefebure of the Laboratory of Anthropobiometric Research of the Salpêtrière in Paris, the "stroke" is the key expression of impulsive needs, of our mental and bodily structures, and should be placed in the context of "rhythm", the expression of the individual dynamic. If rhythm permits a natural release of potential energy and its adequate use, there will be conformity between rhythm and stroke.

The choice of forms in turn could be either in harmony or in contradiction with the stroke. We cite a few eloquent examples:

- stroke well-nourished and thick + conventional forms + slow, hesitant rhythm: vital forces and impulses do not find a release in a positive activity.

- rapid, light, fragile stroke + wasted shapes with filiform tendency + taut rhythm: the tension of the rhythm supplies the mental energy to sustain the inadequacy of vital potential shown in the stroke.

- slightly pasty stroke with some precise strokes + controlled, regular, and flexible rhythm + small but well-shaped forms (i.e. balance of stroke/rhythm/form): general balance.

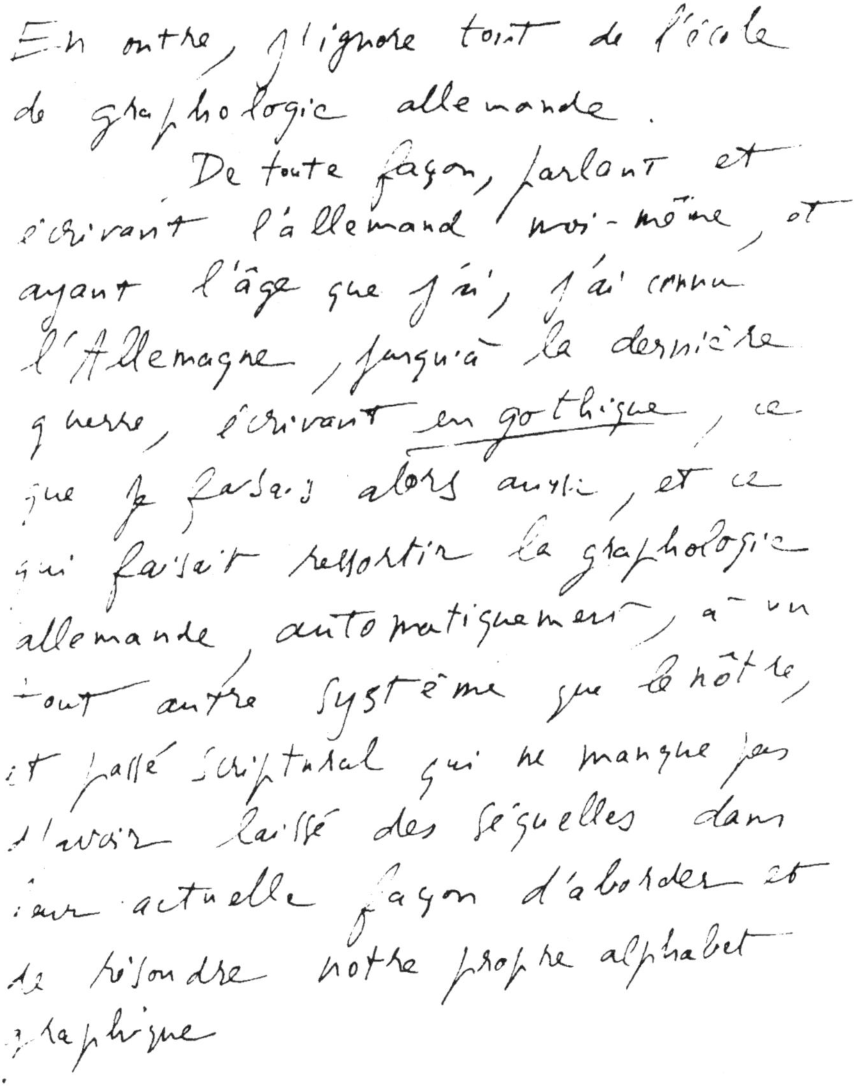

En outre, j'ignore tout de l'école de graphologie allemande.

De toute façon, parlant et écrivant l'allemand moi-même, et ayant l'âge que j'ai, j'ai connu l'Allemagne, jusqu'à la dernière guerre, écrivant en gothique, ce que je faisais alors aussi, et ce qui faisait ressortir la graphologie allemande, automatiquement, a un tout autre système que le nôtre, et passé scriptural qui ne manque pas d'avoir laissé des séquelles dans leur actuelle façon d'aborder et de résoudre notre propre alphabet graphique.

Figure 39 (reduced)
60 year old artist. Pressure: deviated, sharp-pointed, in relief, spasmodic

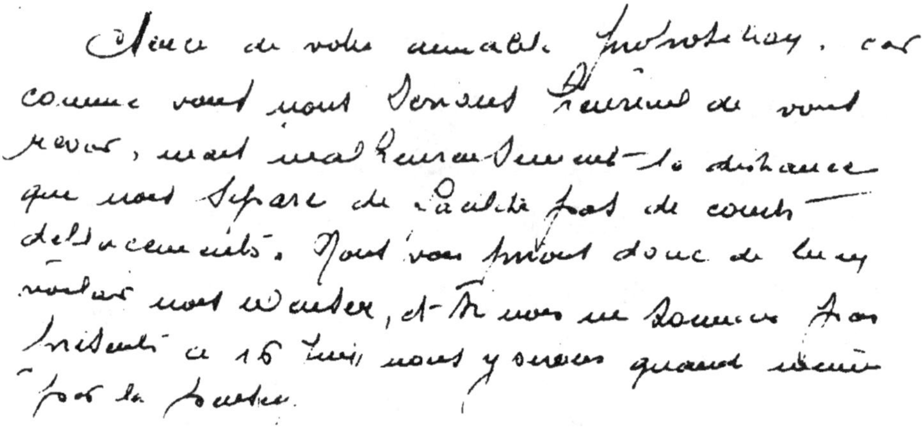

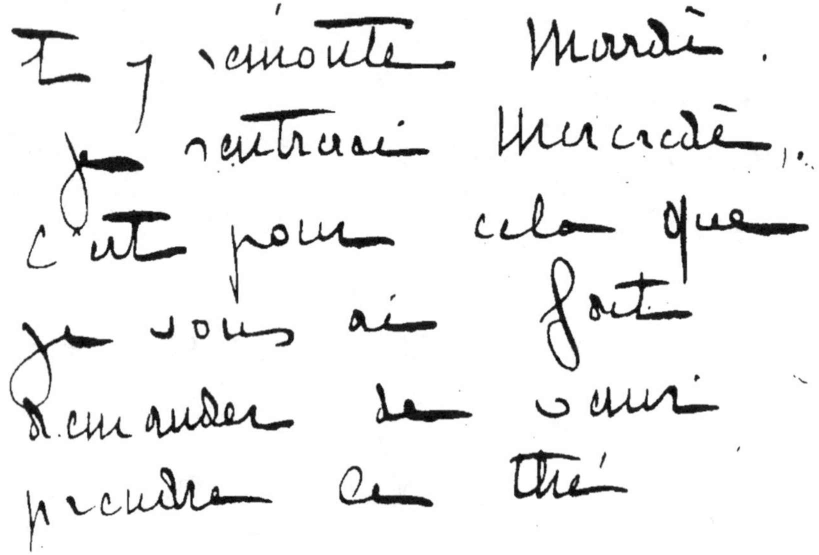

Figure 40
(a) Insurance clerk, 65 years old
Pressure: deviated, sharp-pointed, with hypertrophy of lower extensions
(b) 40 year old man (from one of Ania Teillard's courses)
Pressure: spasmodic, deviated, sharp-pointed, clubbed

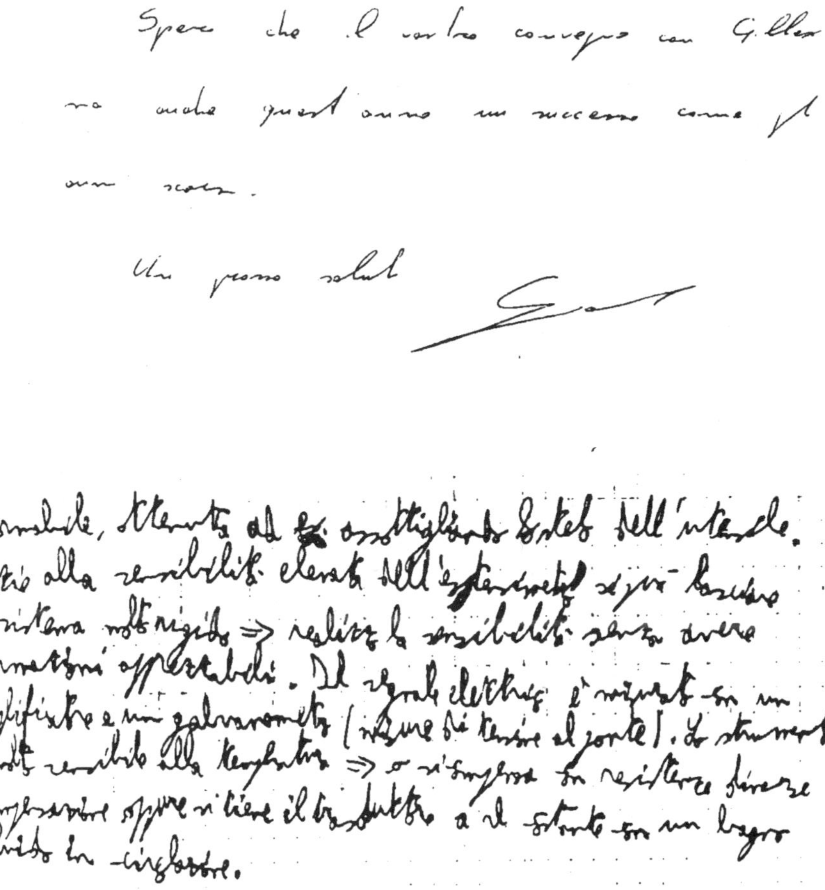

Figure 41
(a) Engineer, 27 years old
Pressure: light (blue pen), nuancée in a progressive and spaced context
(b) Mathematical genius, 28 years old (reduced)
Pressure: congested in a hopping and disharmonious context

X. FORM

For good teachings reasons, the study of the category Form can be reserved to the last: in effect, form constitutes the final selection resulting from the dynamic of all the graphic gestures. Attaining a "form" in fact involves the general management of space in which the form could be lost or impose itself powerfully, or modulate itself in either an original or conventional way.

Form engulfs space and time, in the fullness or otherwise of its curves (*ample* or *narrow*); it chooses its essential gestures, stretching vertically or horizontally (*simplified*), at other times giving itself to space (*open*, *crenellated*) as if suspended in time (*suspended, spaced*), or hides itself in the present (*closed, bow ties, looped ovals*).

Form is also shaped by *stroke*. Consistency, basic tension, dynamism, speed, stops, jerks, sudden acceleration, all play a part in the pressure of stroke which influences the form (*angular, filiform, tormented*, etc.). Form undergoes the deepest stresses: from the will to structure itself, to develop and yet restrain, to its ultimate lack of defence against sudden deterioration. It therefore simplifies or complicates itself, it controls or overreaches itself, it generates a desired (*acquired*) or affected (*artificial*) style.

Form also obeys the symbolism of the graphic field, while it can allusively elaborate itself symbolically in letters or in words, as boat, scythe, cross, knot, egg, etc. Signatures sometimes symbolize the job of the writer (pilots, mariners) and Ania Teillard [227] presents two examples in the chapter "Symbolism of Space", explaining: "Writing movements such as unfold in paraphs are the best indicators of our unconscious life."

In the graphic stroke *form* is observed not only in the whole letter but in the free gestures, loop, bar, stop, as well as in the connecting strokes, visible or virtual, on the level of the line or also suspended in space. The basic gestures in creating form are the *curve* and the *straight line*. From the curve come *garland, arcade*, and *filiform*, while from the straight line comes the *angle*. The teaching of writing consists in tracing curves and lines which together form writing. After the first difficulties the child usually settles for the rounded type of writing with a large middle zone. Plump forms are typically childish, the ovals are wider than high and overblown; their persistence in later years is a sign of emotional immaturity.

In the child the duality of Movement-Form will always be quickly significant. After the initial tension learning how to achieve forms, there comes a progressive integration of movement that supports the form and joins it to others, as an indicator of intellectual maturity. During pre-adolescence, after reaching the *calligraphic* phase (10–11 years), we see fresh troubles in the writing but also a striving for individualism focusing mostly on the choice of forms: fashions or fantasies which enrich the graphic outline. Sometimes, however, there are dominant disturbances in the psychosexual field that produce a graphic imbalance. Generally around 18 years writing assumes its adult profile, and the intellectual development and ideals of the writer will influence the choice of forms.

Form provides indications of self-realization, spirit, and individuality. As we have already seen, according to the German school (Heiss), the *rhythm of development of Form* distinguishes forms which come from *movement* (authenticity and individuality) and forms of *structure* (the need to imitate or represent). For Crépieux-Jamin sobriety of form is an indication of internal harmony and balance, and assumes a writing environment of good standard which excludes monotony or rigidity. Form is the ultimate goal of the graphic gesture, its achievement. More than any other writing category it follows our own taste and choice.

Signs and interpretations (Figs 42 - 47)

In order to have a full view of form, we shall present the signs here according to certain groupings, while in the Lexicon we shall find them again in alphabetical order. To classic Jaminian signs we shall add some taken from Dr Gille-Maisani and others from the Morettian school.

1. Form as calligraphic model

It is important to know the basic writing model of the subject and often the profession. A graphic designer or primary schoolteacher will be easily influenced by the habitual writing style used in their professions.

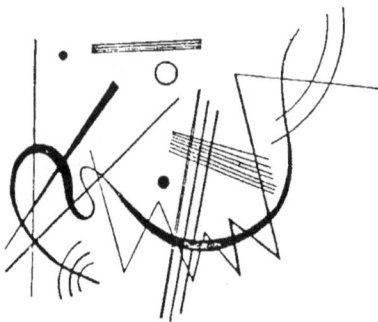

Figure 42
Writing and drawing by Kandinsky (reduced)

Fashion must be taken into consideration, especially when dealing with adolescent writing, and we must obviously be aware of the writing models in the country of origin. Certain signs are therefore the expression of a general model either taught or acquired:

Copy-book – Script – Typographic

Copy-book conforms to the writing model taught at school. This type is often used by primary schoolteachers and people who have not had much continuous education.

Interpretation of what is called *script*, a sort of small block lettering, is rather difficult, and requires other information such as country of origin, age, and profession. In some countries like Switzerland it is used as the school model. The English model too corresponds to the criteria for script, but with special connections between some letters (see Chapter Eight). Today it has become fashionable in schools in France and Italy, especially among pre-adolescent or adolescent males for clearer legibility. It therefore reflects a need for clarity or for security, but is also perhaps a sign of less emotional involvement.

In a personnel search carried out by the author in 1985 for warehouse assistants, out of the 15 applicants, half had written their replies with characters similar to script. It leads us to think that such writing represents a guarantee of legibility for many less educated people not in the habit of writing. None the less, this writing requires a certain amount of visual and motor ability. We have observed that it is used by people with a certain level of schooling and not by the illiterate, or immigrants. In consequence the interpretation can be directed in very different ways according to context.

Typographic writing reproduces printed letters and has a similar spatial arrangement to that of a printed page.

2. Form as qualitative calligraphic synthesis
The so-called qualitative signs focus on the global aspect of personality in either positive or negative sense and involve the whole of the graphic outline:

Acquired – Artificial – Complicated – Confused – Conventional – Inflated – Limpid –Simple – Simplified – Structural – Stylized – Systematic – Tormented

Artificial writing is often analysed in a negative way. Artifice in fact opposes simplicity and spontaneity, but it could also correspond to a need to seek originality, at times creative. It is important to distinguish *artificial* writing from *stylized* or *systematized*, which do not present particular difficulties and are described in the Lexicon. It must also be distinguished from *acquired* writing, which comes from a more or less voluntary control in order to "master" one's own graphomotor impulse and to make it conform to an interiorized image of self. The result however is always close to the sociocultural norms of the writer. We believe that it is an everyday occurrence now and provides a defence mechanism against anxiety and subconscious fears. It is also a way of recovering a sense of order in a confused world. For *acquired* writing in the full sense meant by Klages, see Chapter Three, Section II.

Artificial writing arises from various needs which often intertwine and expresses itself in complications, exaggeration, ornamentation, and the bizarre. The subconscious needs that it reveals can be different:

1. Need to stand out: desire for originality, individualism, snobbism, exhibitionism.
2. Need to structure oneself around an aesthetic, ethical, mystical, or mythical quest: through requirements of principle, behavioural rigidity, reaction against anxiety, or paranoiac social delirium.
3. Need to hide: through weakness, fear, childishness, passivity; through insincerity, simulation, mythomania, dual personality, imbalance.

It must be noted that *artificial* is different from the meaning of *altered* writing used in forensic graphology as the opposite of *spontaneous*. *Altered* means the concealment of one's own writing or the faking of someone else's.

Complicated writing could come from an aesthetic quest, either more or less successful, or from a desire to hide oneself, and in this case it is close to *artificial*. It could also belong to those with a disorderly personality (exhibitionist and hysterical). In past centuries certain complications were often habitual, especially in the signature and its paraphs. One must remember that people without much education may have a complicated writing through inexperience or by trying to reach a better standard.

Pulver maintained that writing is an unconscious design or structure. Unconscious designs have been studied by many graphologists. See Gille-Maisani [105] for problems concerning the history of writing and *structural* writing. Today it is rare, but structural writing was a prerogative of medieval manuscripts. The distinction between *structural* and certain forms of *artificial* writing is delicate because "all intermediate levels can be found between pleasant design and exaggerated fantasy", in Gille-Maisani's words.

Conventional writing is akin to *copy-book*. However, it is influenced by a model used in a particular environment, whether it is a fashion or conformism, rather than by the base model. It could also include *artificial* writing. It could also correspond to a rigid model imposed in childhood (as in *sacré coeur* writing), and does not exclude some positive aspects of writing.

The signs *confused*, *limpid*, *simple*, and *simplified*, do not require further explanations beyond those given in the Lexicon.

Because generally there are only negative explanations in manuals describing *inflated* writing, we need to examine the dynamic of the gesture of this sign before we interpret it. Obviously, enlarging ovals and loops can be, in certain cases, a sign of exhibitionism and vanity or at least the expression of impulses difficult to contain. One must not underestimate however the expansion, vitality, and enthusiasm which sometimes animate the basic gestures of such writing. The arrogant inventive imagination, even if exaggerated, can be the spring mechanism for a free and artistic personality.

Systematic writing has also been studied by Gille-Maisani. This is a type in which a particular gesture tends to unite all movements, which seem to come from one mould (e.g. looped arcades). This mechanism alters clarity and sometimes ends up as *artificial*.

Tormented writing is often the mark of a complicated and interesting personality even if full of anguish and tension. The agitation in tormented writing is often inbuilt, especially if the writing is small. The writer is under pressure from unremitting anxiety. This becomes accentuated with age if a creative balance is not achieved, which can take much hard struggle. The classic examples are Napoleon and Beethoven, especially in advanced age.

3. Form as modality of base or as connection

In this category of signs the "basic gesture" of form is obvious in both structural and dynamic aspects. For example *filiform* writing would indicate that the single letters *m* and *n* are written like a thread, or that the normal method of connection is threadlike.

> *Angular – Arcades – Filiform – Garlands – Graceful –*
> *Looped garlands – Round (or semi-round) – Undulate*

The Morettian school has focused on the distinction between *curve* and *angle* as the cardinal point of graphological observation. At present the school model teaches forms based on curves and straight lines. The curve helps smoothness and consequently speed of writing.

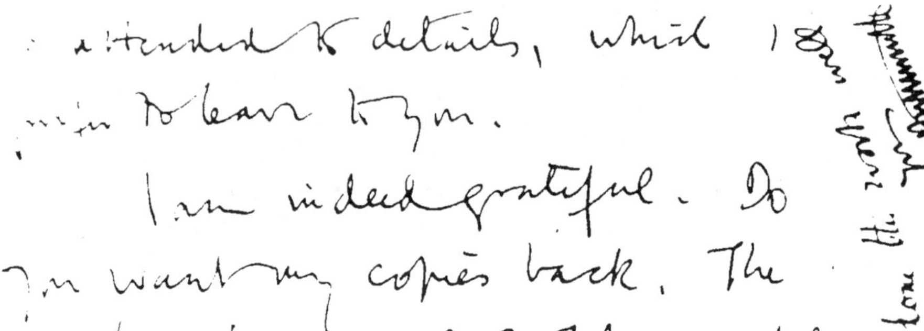

Figure 43
Writing of Donald W. Winnicott. Garlanded connections with velvety stroke

"Each angle needs an interruption of gesture, a pause, followed by a restarting of the graphic act" (Saudek [218]). The angle is necessary to give firmness and grit to writing. By reversing the page and observing the base line of the text, one can see if the impression of letters on the line is mainly angular or not.

In children, arcades and garlands are basic writing forms. Arcaded writing is maintained until the age of 12. In fact garlands can already be visible around 10 years. If transformation of *m* and *n* into garland forms is a sign of graphic evolution showing intellectual flexibility, the persistence beyond 12 of arcaded forms does not show the opposite. The child can maintain arcades for longer and sometimes forever for other reasons: application, conformism to the model, reserve, fear, closure, or even a sense of construction.

The *garland* is a direct product of the curve, with its form "festooned" or "cupped", symbolizing opening, receptivity, and also generous disposition. The garlanded form is seen mainly in the letters *m* and *n* and in connections, and in its maximum expression it confers a smoothness and flexible manner of writing in which the *triple width* of Moretti is located. However, interpretations will not be all the same, because sometimes another dominant could counteract the significance of the garland.

The garland must be placed in relation to tension and quality of stroke:

- with a *pasty* and *velvety* stroke: the meanings of openness, sociability, and heightened sentiment are strengthened and strong participation is found. Maximum *dedication* will be found in a flexible, pasty, and rightward slanted garland;
- with a *precise*, dry stroke: the tendency towards defensiveness, latent opposition, predominates, especially when the writing is slanted left.

If the garland gesture is accompanied by the "lasso" movement with its tendency to form loops, one has to assess these two aspects, and the context more than ever determines the interpretation. The serviceability of the garland easily transforms itself with the agility of the lasso into an egotistical configuration. Dr Gille-Maisani devoted an entire chapter to "looped writing" which he says "is more frequent in women – at least in Spain and France, but not in Germany."

HUGO Pratt

Morgan la Fée
è un personaggio delle leggende Arturi
secondo le leggende del ciclo Bretone, Morgan
nasconde suo fratello, il Re ARTÙ nell'isoli
di Avalon e insieme a Viviana
la sua allieva imprigiona il mago
Merlino nella foresta di Broceliande
in Bretagna – la leggenda vuole
che Oberon fosse suo figlio.

PUCK.
amico
di MORGAN
LA
FÉE
il suo
n.

CIRSIUM
LANCEOLATUM

Figure 44
Writing of Hugo Pratt (reduced)
Ample writing, triple width, widened garlands, and semi-angular arcades

BORIE hob'
par Ce... ies
HÉRAU'T

Chère Madame
Je suis bien affligé de ce qui est arrivé à votre fils et crains de ne pouvoir vous éclairer sinon négativement. Je n'ai jamais entendu parler de M. Vitry de Villagrand qui n'est pas de ma parenté, du moins à ma connaissance. Et non plus de Claude Léache.
Je vous saurai gré de me dire que tout cela a passé comme un mauvais rêve. Nous quittons Bollène, Saint-Pierre de Senos, à la fin de l'été pour cette vallée du Haut Languedoc
Que Dieu vous donne sa paix

Figure 45 (reduced)
Architectural writing of
Lanza del Vasto:
ethical-mystical stylization

Dr Gille-Maisani has also reintroduced the *undulate* type: "the interme-diate letters (*m*, *n*, *u*) are like the waves on a calm sea" (see table in [105]). We shall define it therefore as a connecting, continuous, nuanced, slightly loose movement, which replaces intermediate letters with flattened, progressive strokes, generally in open curves, which are close to the filiform stroke without actually reaching it. It is writing with a tendency to looped garlands, which comes from a progressive simplification and remains clear without its speed becoming too fast.

From the curved form the sign *graceful* derives. It was introduced by Solange Pellat and taken up by Gille-Maisani to underline the graceful aspect, sometimes benevolent, sometimes adulatory, of the profiles with wide curves at the beginning of words and especially at the beginning of paragraphs. They are less frequent in today's society, and if present they are certainly telling.

4. Filiform

Filiform must be treated fully. This sign alone is the opposite of almost all the other signs of form, being by definition more a thread or an outline than a form, in other words negation of form. Filiform gives information on the intellectual, emotional, and active capacities, as well as on deep psychic dynamics. It is a true and proper graphic style which influences many other signs belonging mainly to the following categories: Form, Continuity, and Speed.

In a study of filiform, N. Kergal and J. Pinon [118] asked whether filiform must be a choice, a liberation from the chains of form, or if it represents a constriction or incapacity to build structure, or again, if it represents a mark of ability or, on the contrary, of inexperience. Whilst it compromises clarity and legibility, in general filiform favours *movement*, which together with pressure confers strength to the filiform outline. On the whole the organization of space is irregular, with small margins, indicating difficulty in facing up to both self and others.

The authors defined the writer who uses filiform as "handicapped in the middle zone", that is, the zone of the self, of the lived, of consciousness of oneself and one's potential, as well as of affective and emotional tendencies. The way of thinking, acting, and loving in the subject with filiform writing is therefore founded upon the fragility of narcissism, vulnerability, uncertainty of one's own value, emotional insecurity, and ambivalence.

The authors distinguish various types of filiform. Pressure and movement will determine the prevailing type. The implicit dilemma in filiform will be more or less increased by irregularity. We now give the interpretations proposed by this research.

Firm attacking filiform

With dynamic movement and tension of stroke, with form drawn by speed in a progressive movement:

Quick thinking, mental curiosity, planning ability

Rational emotional life: "giving" to participate, but "keeping" to protect one's own security. Use of humour as safety valve

Few preconceptions but radical convictions

Need to influence

Defence against attack. Action for "being"

Competitive. Loves risk but reluctant to expose self to setback

Firm resistant filiform

Less thrust than attacking variety, but tension is more constant, space and movement more controlled, keeping to the base line, and stronger connections:

Importance of intellectual life: pragmatic concrete reasoning. Sense of utility and realism

Bases more on observation and experience than imagination

Honourable emotional life: acceptance of constrictions and traditions

Sense of tactics, enterprise with risk estimation and defence preparation. Tenacity at work, likes to be valued

Vibrant filiform

This movement is produced by subtle oscillations, differing pressure, well-organized space, childish components:

Very speculative intellectual life; refinement, sharpness, critical observation and mental curiosity, taste for paradox
Sensitivity but doubt, uncertainty, and solace in traditional rules
More self-regard than ambition; apparent shyness and coldness; defensive humour, irony, scepticism
Serious and conscientious activity but poor decision-making ability
Incessant internal arguments and prevarication
Often celibate, or late marriage

Watery filiform

Movement evoking water, undulating and widening outline, barely touching paper leaving a large part white. Soft but not weak stroke, pasty but with precise edges. Tendency to stop and start. Stable base line:

Irrational type with instinctive and diffuse perception rather than logical
Assimilation, original ideas, imagination, inspiration
Emotional vulnerability and immaturity, naïve
Difficulty in being understood, or in breaking out of loneliness
Extended relationship with mother
Strong bond to family grouping
Activity as a means of expression more than self-affirmation, undertaken with thoroughness to ensure real integration
Passive resistance
Need for harmony and conciliation
Artistic but little motivated to earning and competition
Attractively mysterious

Effervescent filiform

Slightly untidy movement with lengthened gestures. Irregular management of space, compact with many large spaces: very irregular outline, unstable base line. Little homogeneity of speed and pressure. Many childish components: "soldering points", letters touching, amendments, fat letters, badly formed loops, arcaded extensions, and fluctuating base line:

Alert intelligence, instinctive sensitivity

Little critical sense, little objectivity; quick enthusiasms but changeable; ideas and imagination but badly directed

Not interested in others but tries to be indispensable

Feeling of abandonment or isolation

Verbose, needing reassurance; emotional blackmail

Lack of organization and method

Activity with constant tension; hyperactive perfectionist, with tendency to fight off anxiety attacks

Complex tormented filiform

Several movements oppose and confront each other; often discordant and arrhythmic. Arrangement of space without any homogeneity: anarchic or rigid. Lack of elasticity of stroke: too heavy, with little difference, or scratchy, dry. Outline has a rapid appearance due to movement but is jerky, with collisions and alterations in progression. Irregular but inflexible base line:

Rapid conceptual intelligence, speculative, brilliant.

Judgement is altered by doubts and lack of proportion.

Contradiction between openness and enterprise.

Hypersensitivity and internal tension.

Instinctive insecurity towards self and others: reflection and analysis without any certainty. Finding solace in intransigent stance.

Tries to escape anxiety but disillusion through lack of realism and foresight. Able to excel in exceptional circumstances.

At a professional level able to find better solutions to own conflict.

Struggle between impulses and a tyrannical Superego. Sense of blame.

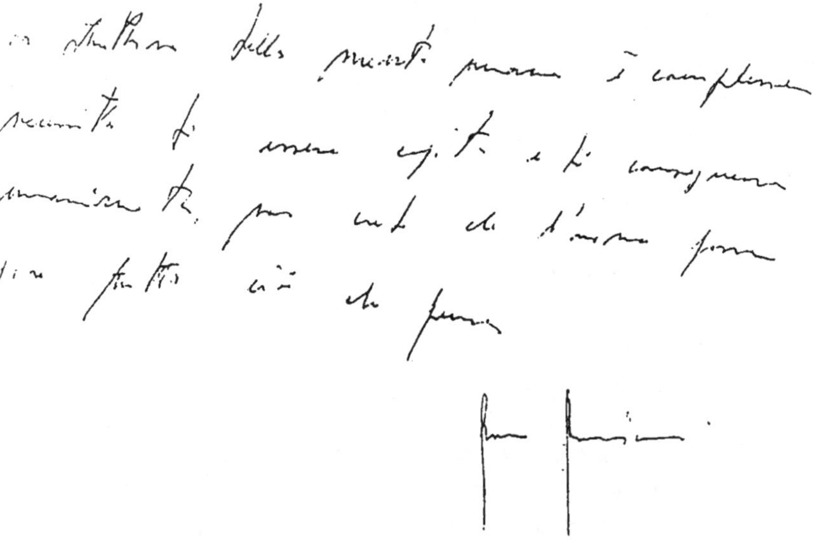

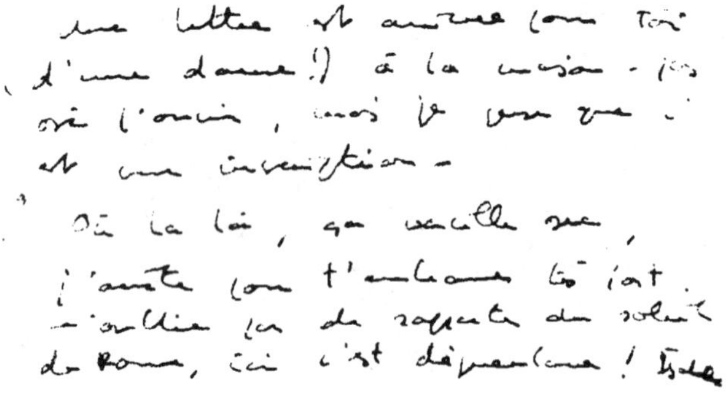

Figure 46
Filiform: (a) 40 year old male director
(b) 35 year old female psychologist (writing on a train)

5. Form and openness

Signs concern predominantly the form and the opening of the ovals of letters:

Ample – Bow ties – Closed – Crenellated – Flattened ovals –
Open – Ovoid – Round

The oval represents a cardinal element of the graphic structure, because it is a feature of the middle zone as well as the graphic synthesis of a *form* and of a *basic movement* – a form theoretically rounded and a movement which produces more or less fullness and determines the degree of closure of the oval.

In early schooling the letters *a* and *o*, known as "affective letters", have an extremely suggestive symbolic significance. In fact even before, at the scribble or doodle phase, the closed rounded form signals an evolution in the three year old that represents the child itself, the human form, the other, the mother. The graphomotor impulse pushing the adult either to enlarge or restrict these letters, to close them hermetically or leave them half open, determines a true personal graphic style, the mark of a precise writing identity.

One must evaluate whether enlargement represents a childish residue or if the writer wants to impose a style, as can often be the case for some plastic artists. Every type of closure generates a different graphic flow. In the study of false writings, within the area of forensic graphology, how the oval is closed is an important clue to identification. It is indispensable to know the teaching model of the country and the historical period. In Italy for example a certain type of *a* closure is regarded as normal, which in France is called bow ties or looped ovals (see Chapter Seven).

The notion of *flattened oval* or *ovoid* forms are very interesting. These terms coined by Suzanne Bresard are explained in the Lexicon, and also fully illustrated by Dr Gille-Maisani.

As an example of a writing with open ovals we show the beautiful writing of Federico Fellini (Fig. 47): comfortable and undulate with pasty stroke and a tendency to unconnected letters; often "o"s are open to the left, and "a"s high on the right. Both constitute a sign of exceptional receptivity, and also vulnerability, which is partly compensated for by the firmness of the verticals.

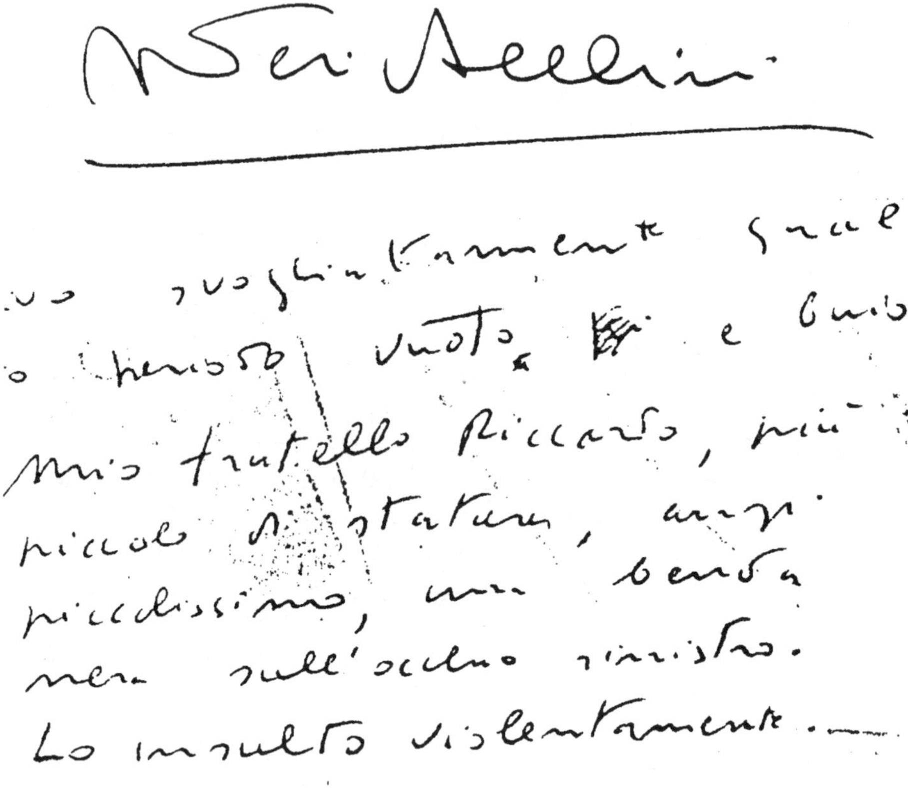

Figure 47
Writing of Federico Fellini (from the diary of Fellini's dreams)

Chapter Five

THE ANALYSIS OF WRITING

1. DOCUMENTATION

Before analysing any writing one needs to gather adequate documentation and make a brief evaluation of accessory elements: choice of instrument, and the type and format of the paper. Those who are especially keen to have their writing analysed often supply adequate material with great reluctance, which expresses their ambivalence between the desire and fear of being discovered. The request for a signed letter or several writings over time may extinguish their enthusiasm completely. They would however be ready to receive any "oracle" based on a few hurried lines written on unsuitable materials. The graphologist must overcome this mixture of superstition and fear by having as much documentation as possible, because of the high expectations of those requesting the analysis.

Necessary documentation

As a minimum sample a graphological analysis requires a written and signed letter on unlined paper, and above all it must be an original. A photocopy is regarded as a reserve but it is absolutely insufficient for an accurate result, seeing that it could be altered or manipulated. The Deontological Code speaks very clearly in this context. It is recommended that documentation be obtained written for various purposes and spanning many years. It is especially pertinent for the period of adolescence where one document is not sufficient. Writing development from 10 years onwards, even if it comes simply from exercise books, is required.

Choice of ink

Graphological literature has written much about the choice of ink and details are found in many books. We believe that today the problem is not very relevant, at least in Italy, where often the choice of instrument and colour of ink is mainly casual. In France where predominantly the fountain pen is used the choice of ink and nib is certainly significant. Subjects requiring analysis can at least be asked about their choices. Blue ink is supposed to have a sensory and communicative aspect whereas black reveals greater abstraction and cerebral capacity.

Choice of pen

Without doubt there are some who prefer a pen that glides on paper while others choose one with more resistance. The use of felt-tip pens becomes a stumbling block for the graphologist as it evens out the stroke, removing subtle pressure differences. In this case the graphologist must learn to recognize gradations of shading, at least where the felt-tip is not large – if this were the case one must ask the user if this particular type of instrument is always used by preference because then it acquires significance. If we think in terms of an artistic sensibility, it is clear that the choice of a large felt-tip pen, giving a pasty and almost heavy stroke, achieves the same sensory effect as a painter's brush. This can step over into gross sensuality, whose signs of lack of control will open up some worrying tendencies.

The ball-point pen or biro, however, allows good observation of differences in shading and the graphologist easily learns how to assess the strength or lightness of pressure. Sometimes it can be more tricky to differentiate between "precise" and "pasty" strokes. Often a photocopy of the original shows up better contrasts, while only the original will reveal the pressure of application.

Choice of paper

The choice of paper is well documented in graphology manuals and at one time it was critical in expressing and conveying real communication. Today the use of standard manufactured papers makes these previous considerations completely obsolete. Letter-writing papers still exist and their choice sometimes reflects cultural refinement or showy exuberance. Many young people choose "recycled" paper, often with faded or dark colours making legibility difficult. With a minimum of common sense the graphologist can consider all these aspects and their relative importance in the context of education, gender, and age.

Heading and envelope address

When observing headings we enter straightaway into the "graphic space" and therefore into the way in which the subject relates to others. One must therefore take into consideration the spatial relationships, and the margins, and evaluate what importance the heading has in relation to the following text. Cultural fashions and habits, and obviously the formal standard use for official or commercial letters, affect the analysis. In personnel selection, the graphologist certainly observes the degree of education, of respect or nonchalance, that comes from a clear, ordered, or otherwise untidy heading. In the same way, we can consider the position of the address on an envelope beyond its educated and formal aspect – legibility, dimension, and regular direction – applying Pulver's symbolism of right and left, high and low.

II. KEY ELEMENTS OF WRITING

Signature (Fig. 48)

According to Pulver, "The signature is the expression of the individual's existential quality." The small child is attracted by this mark which represents him and makes him similar to the parent, and reflects his unmistakable image. The adolescent tries many times to imprint his own identity with his name, which he often loves in an ambivalent way. Does he want to imitate or be different from the parent? Does he follow a fashion that surrounds him or does he try to differentiate himself from it? One must consider how the signature acquires its weight and recognition upon reaching official adulthood: identity papers, work applications, etc. are all signed. In the selection of personnel, evaluation of the signature is very important because it represents the professional identity of the subject.

Different elements are taken into consideration such as: dynamic configuration of the signature itself, structure and dynamics of the signature's relation to text, social and cultural customs of the country, graphic homogeneity, distance, etc. (see Table 16).

For example a signature could be described thus:
- position close to text (= 2 lines from text);
- larger than text (signature/text ratio = +2);
- central;
- legible with simplified tendency;
- vivacious and underlined; emphasizes surname.

SIGNATURE AND ITS RELATIONSHIPS WITH THE TEXT					
Lines from text	*Size ratio signat./text*	*Position*	*Style*	*Dynamic*	*Structure*
1	+1	Central	Normal	Vivacious	+ Surname
2	+2	Centre right	Legible	Static	+ Name
3	+3	Centre left	Illegible	Tense	+ Paraph
4	+4	Right	Abstract	Wide	Underlined
5	–2	Centre left	Initials	Heavy	Overlined
6	–3	Left	Symbolic	Light	Rolled up Rising Descending Horizontal

Table 16

It is very important to remember how much the interpretation of the signature varies according to context. The enlargement of the signature in certain cases shows up the conceited attitude of a person, in others it shields insecurity. Signatures prop the writer, act as armour for social or professional ambition, or compensate for a feeling of inferiority.

A whole treatise could be written on the role of the forged signature in the area of jurisprudence. By mentioning this we want to underline the fact that many graphologists have been able to understand better the essence of graphomotor gesture in the context of judicial verification, and so establish if such-and-such a gesture can be attributed or not to such-and-such a "hand". The signature or initials often show the basic gestures of the writer.

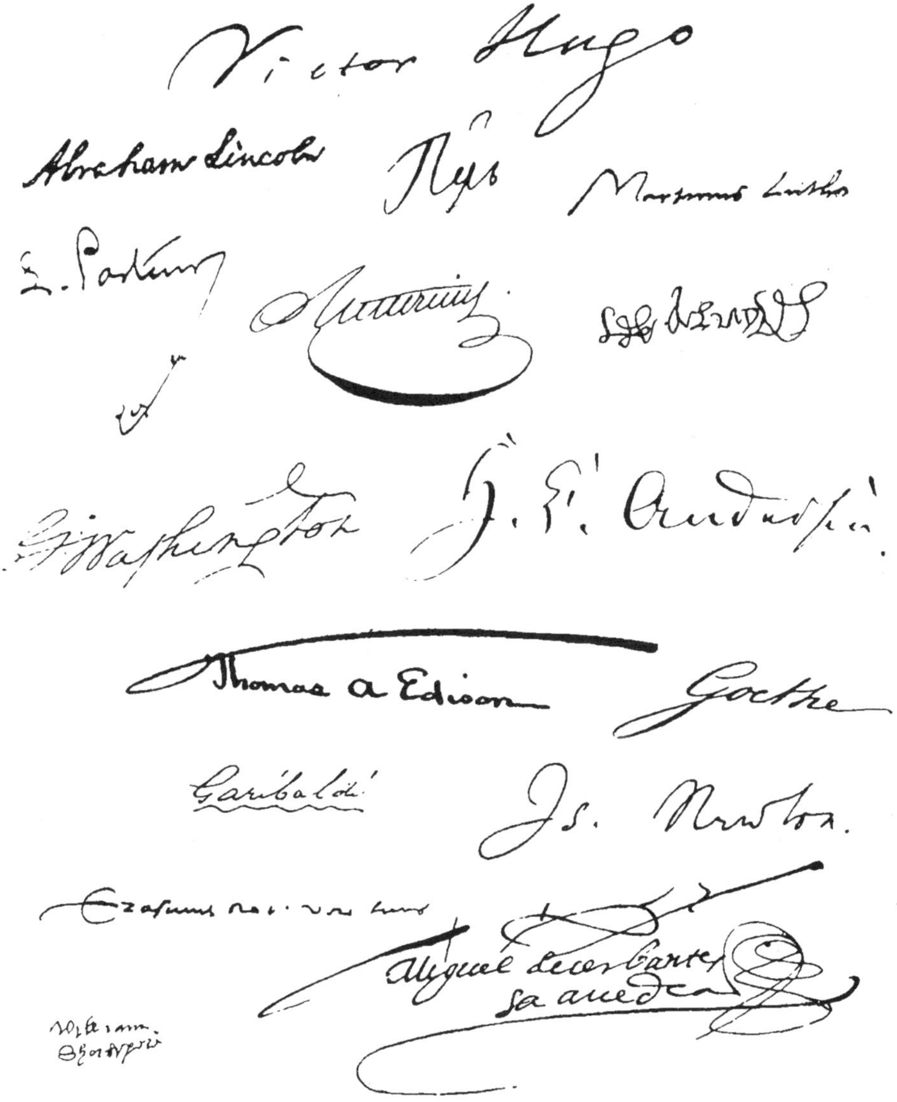

Figure 48
Some signatures over time (exact sizes unknown)
Victor Hugo, Lincoln, Tsar Peter the Great, Luther, Pasteur, Metternich, Henry VIII,
Washington, H. C. Andersen, Edison, Goethe, Garibaldi, Newton, Erasmus,
Shakespeare, Cervantes

Figure 49
The signature in art: Monet, Cézanne, Picasso

The signature in art is a unique mark, a certificate of authentication which encapsulates the artist's personality, whatever the art (Fig. 49). In the case of the plastic arts, it can evoke the art itself, giving it body with its recurring "basic sign" (Monet, Picasso). In some poets or musicians it can also share the artistic dynamic (Beethoven, D'Annunzio), whilst with others (Rimbaud, Cézanne) it turns away from all this as if the art were joined as a possibility of saving sublimation. This subject requires a specific treatment itself, and for this reason we shall not linger further.

Free signs and typical-gesture (Fig. 50)

The first graphologists had been very attracted to the "free signs" such as the *t*-crossing, accents, punctuation. In reality, each free gesture is framed in the context of the graphic categories, principally direction and pressure, and must be interpreted in its graphic context. Let us remember one of Crépieux-Jamin's "basic principles": there are no particular signs independent from the overall writing movement: there are only general signs, in different ways.

None the less we must pay attention to the free signs when they take on a very different dynamic from the context. This is the case with pointed, large, and therefore aggressive commas, which are dissonant in a controlled context, or with discordant and spasmodic *t*-bars, to the point where they strongly condition the overall evaluation and indicate extreme and marked character aspects. However, even in such cases these signs still share in the standard graphic categories, and we feel that one must resist the temptation to interpret any small signs in isolation because this risks the spreading of errors and a superficial evaluation.

The small sign must only be emphasized when it takes on the value of *typical-gesture*. Moretti's "fleeting signs" and "curls" (which extend the usual range of "free signs", see Chapter Three, Section III) are grouped by category in a very organic way and represent therefore a substantial visual writing dynamic. In practice Morettian "curls" are true and proper signs in the Jaminian sense and they too correspond to the notion of typical-gesture.

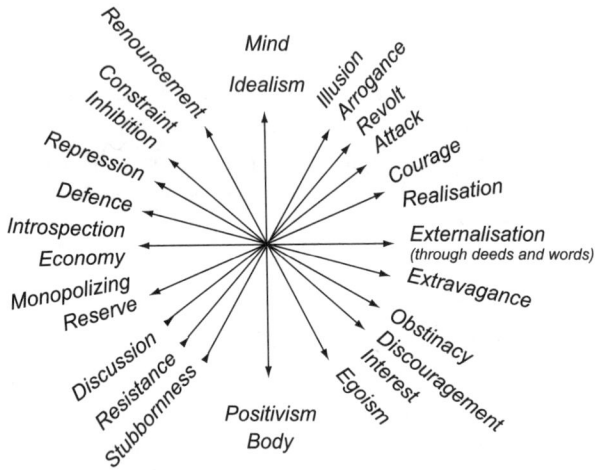

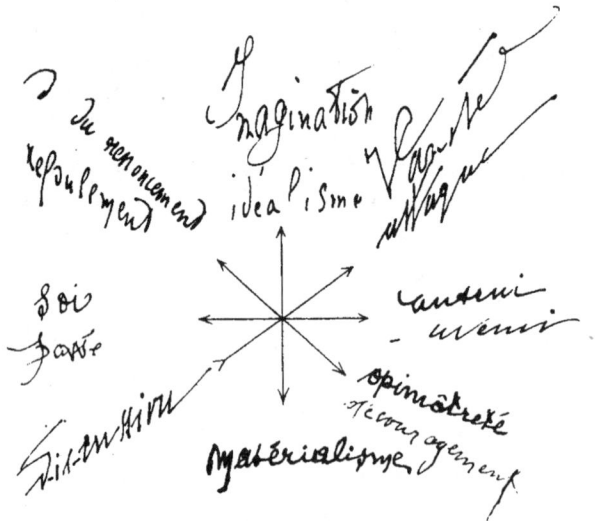

Figure 50
Typical-gesture: Saint-Morand's compass [217, p. 90]
"Gesture rises to the sky or falls to earth. It goes towards the other or gathers into itself.
It goes forwards or backwards."

The brilliant graphologist Hélène de Saint-Morand, greatly admired by Gille-Maisani, insisted strongly on this notion. Typical-gesture denotes a graphic sign which assumes a dominant role within the writing. It imposes and repeats itself, weakening other graphic aspects and establishing in itself a sort of "directional synthesis", to take up one of Gille-Maisani's ideas, but sometimes it creates a real antithesis to the rest of writing.

We shall look here at a few of these typical-gestures which produce such a peculiar tone, sometimes in keeping with the writing but at other times strident or disturbing in the context of the whole. Even in this latter case their significance is equivocal and needs to be treated in context. They can either save or sink a writing.

- *Free gestures*: *t*-bars, accents, excessively large punctuation, with systematic reinforced pressure, or at the opposite end graceful and fleeting
- *Triangular lower extensions*
- *Bow ties or loops in ovals*: opening and closing, systematic looping
- *Very accentuated gestures in the opposite direction*
- *Abnormally full gestures*
- *Components "outside normality"* (Gobineau): disproportion between one part of the letter and the letter itself, exaggeration or atrophy of free signs or capital letters

Opening and closing of the ovals (Fig. 51)

This is a very valued distinctive sign in forensic graphology. It appears that the way in which ovals, principally *o* and *a*, are drawn and their degree of closure, is particular to each person and difficult to imitate with the same ease. Although it may vary, this mannerism tends to recur throughout a writing.

The *direction* of the gesture forming the oval needs to be taken into consideration, where it starts, and the position and manner of closure.

(a) *anticlockwise* direction (conforming to the basic model): starting at the left, right, above, or below; position of closure: at the start, or elsewhere.

(b) *clockwise* direction (*not* conforming to the basic model): starting at the left, right, above, or below; position of closure: at the start, or elsewhere.

The formation of ovals can also occur with one or more bow ties or loops.

Three situations should be considered closely because they raise questions: the clockwise direction, the lower closure, and the use of bow ties or loops, especially if they occur systematically and not occasionally and if they add up between them. They can be treated as concealing signs, especially in a slow or slowed down writing without any justifiable reason. However one needs to ensure that the subject is not left-handed, because in this case a clockwise direction is completely logical.

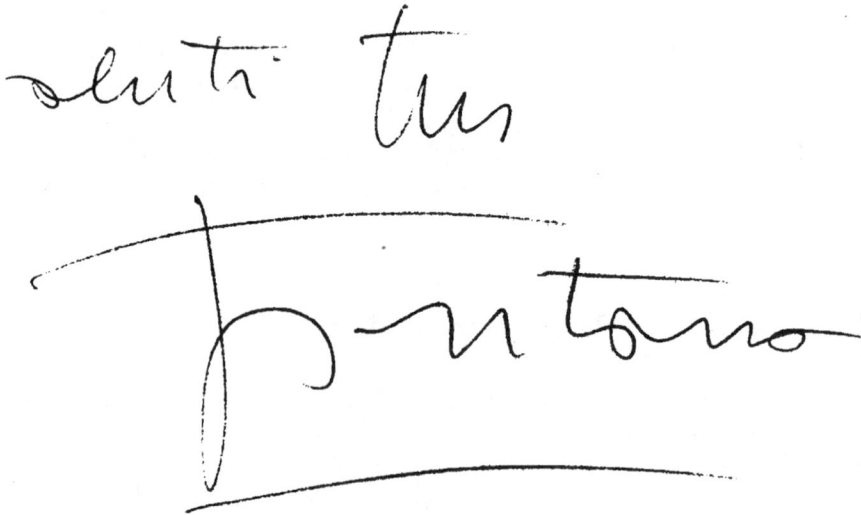

Figure 51 (reduced)
Direction of forming ovals

The writing model for *a* in comparison to that for *o* expects a supplementary movement: a downstroke follows the oval and so greatly distances the starting position of the oval from its ending (see Chapter Seven on the difference between the French and Italian writing models).

Concerning ovals open at the top, see *crenellated* writing; for completely closed ovals, *closed* writing; for tied up ovals, *bow ties* or *looped ovals*.

III. TECHNICAL STUDY OF WRITING

Concept of organization

Modern French graphology establishes the criterion of *organization*, in other words the correspondence between the academic level of the writer and his writing level. One needs to know therefore the educational history of the subject to compare, in practice, the writing level with the norms, by sex, age, and upbringing.

Observation of graphic environment

Observe the writing, looking at the whole of the script. See if writing circulates between lines and words, evaluating the spacing, the whites, the blacks, tonality, retouching, basic gesture, typical-gesture. Stop at details and return to the whole, the global view. Pick out relationships and connections, the development of outline, trajectories, crossings, impetus, returns, pauses. Immerse oneself in the graphic environment.

Technical definition

The technical definition of any writing has four parts. The *first* is the evaluation of the graphic environment, which we do through a spontaneous observation as described above, and then set in more precise technical terms. The *second* consists in listing the graphic *signs* in hierarchical order, that is by order of importance with respect to the context and graphic environment. To graphic signs we add the free gestures: initial and final strokes, *t*-crossings, accents, and we evaluate the margins and the position, form, and size of the signature in relation to text. The *third* consists in grouping the observed signs into *graphic syndromes*, according to a logic which comes from the writing itself. The *fourth* consists of a correlation with the principal psychological theories, such as Freudian psychosexual stages, defence mechanisms, Jung's psychological types, Kleinian positions, or other typologies (Hippocratic, mythologic, Szondian, psychobiological, according to the graphologist's choice).

The graphological profile

Whether one wants to draw up a brief attitudinal profile or a psychological personality analysis it is necessary to study the writing in depth. The difference is found in the way the result is expressed. The way and the style in which the presentation of the report is communicated takes on great importance. One needs to know to whom the report should be addressed: employer, psychologist, to the person in question, to a third party having the right to ask for this analysis, or to the editor of a publication.

The style of the report is defined by simple common sense in each case. The employer must understand in straightforward and descriptive terms the attitudes of the person who intends to take up a particular position or given role. The psychologist instead will be given in psychological terms the configuration of the subject's personality and problems. It is important to consider the social and cultural level of the subject if addressing the person directly. One must be tactful and polite, proposing solutions or possibilities while avoiding value judgements, and never abusing one's power.

With a third party there can sometimes be a delicate problem in finding the reason for the requested analysis and to weigh up whether it is for the purpose of placating their own anxiety, or for improper use. Many mothers who ask for analysis of their children are themselves very anxious. If they can be persuaded to tell their offspring what they are doing, it is often noticed that children as well as adolescents will collaborate willingly.

If it is for a publication, the profile will have to be brief but clear on the technical side without being too joky. We put forward in Tables 17–19 some guidelines for the graphological profile. The analysis does not list qualities or defects. The art is to present the elements in complete sentences in an elegant style, bringing alive the subjects' personality and the underlying dynamic of their motivations.

CHARACTER TRAITS: I. INTELLECTUAL

- *Mental organization*
  - clarity, order, method
  - confusion, rigidity
- *Concentration*
  - reflection, attention, vivacity, precision, memory
  - distraction, time wasting, routine
- *Judgement and estimation*
  - objectivity, rationality, rapidity, assurance
  - subjectivity, ingenuity, slowness, haste, insecurity
- *Reasoning*
  - analytical, synthetic, logical-deductive
  - categoric, stubborn
- *Critical spirit*
  - mental acuteness, perspicacity
  - contradictory spirit, polemic
- *Imagination*
  - realistic, concrete, utopian, sensory
  - fanciful, unrealistic, delirious
- *Broadness of mind*
  - common sense, open, intuitive, versatile
  - narrow-minded, prejudiced, closed
- *Ability to see*
  - global vision, essence, detail
  - superficiality, negligence

Types of intelligence:
concrete – abstract – meditative – intuitive – imaginative – inventive – creative

Table 17
Profile guide

CHARACTER TRAITS: II. BEHAVIOUR

- *Self-assurance*
  - assurance, optimism, enthusiasm
  - insecurity, unscrupulousness, sway, restlessness
  - inferiority complex, depression, distress, excitability
- *Self-image*
  - simplicity, modesty, distinction, self-respect, boldness
  - affectation, vanity, pretension, pride, presumption
- *Emotional life*
  - internalized, externalized, stability of moods
  - quick reactions, diffidence, panic
  - hypermotivation, instability, coldness, apathy
- *Self-control*
  - prudent, reserved, measured
  - impulsive, irritable, violent
- *Feelings*
  - fellow feeling, charitable, receptive, understanding
  - sensitive, dedicated, generous, prodigal, altruistic
  - tactless, without understanding, selfish, mean
  - passionate, jealous, envious, brutal
- *Sociability*
  - adaptable, sociable, flexible, able
  - rigid, intransigent, opportunist
- *Politeness*
  - polite, discreet, reserved
  - impolite, insolent, indiscreet, gossipy, slavish
- *Moral sense*
  - intellectual probity, honesty, ethical, sincere, spontaneous
  - hypocrisy, ambiguity, baseness, deceit, pretence

Table 18
Profile guide

CHARACTER TRAITS: III. WORK

- *Activity rhythm*
  - fast, calm, constant
  - mechanical, inconstant, slow
- *Will*
  - willingness, tenacity, perseverance
  - stubbornness
- *Dynamism*
  - initiative, decision, enterprise, foresight
  - hesitation, inadequacy in situations, apathy
- *Method*
  - organization, order, precision, accuracy
  - rigidity, negligence
- *Sense of responsibility*
  - sense of duty, professional conscientiousness, scrupulousness, reliability
  - avoiding responsibility, superficiality, unreliability
- *Ambition*
  - wish to achieve, to lead, to stand out
  - conceit, yearning for power

Tastes and motivations:
  - for active life, sedentary, stable, varied, on the move
  - working for short or long periods, casual, with moves
  - for activity as manager, large company enterprise, for risk
  - for a disciplined life, military, police, financial official
  - for earnings, possessions, power, abuse of power

Aptitudes:
  - intellectual, humanitarian, technical, artistic, scientific, administrative
  - commercial, accounting, public relations, sociological, communication
  - manual, artisanal, ecological, sporting, military, voluntary service

Table 19
Profile guide

IV. GRAPHOLOGICAL PROFILES

Charles Darwin (Fig. 52)
Summary profile

A great pioneer of modern scientific thinking, Charles Darwin displays a totally harmonious writing: contained, aerated, with flexible impetus, aesthetic but without ostentation. Only the signature is witness to his professional ambition. The writing expresses the clarity and the search for objectivity as the prime motive for incessant activity, proof of which is his rapid and rhythmic graphic impetus. The *space* plays almost a better part than the words: *whites,* that is the graphic silence, symbolize the unconscious and the distance from the context. Intuition frees itself and the strength of the whole embraces the most courageous ideas.

What has been gathered is further deepened by critical reflection and passed through the sieve of truth (precision of *outline, wide spaces* between words, pressure *in relief, angular arcades*), while the fertility of ideas and their associative and creative flow is made urgent (*thrusting* movement with the upper zone predominant).

The wide distance between words and lines could also symbolize the scientist's isolation in his ivory tower. All the more when the irregular middle zone, which is sometimes squashed, indicates an injured and easily resentful sensibility. These aspects are however compensated by the vital thrust and the need to participate concretely (*movement* which dominates *form*, inclined to the right, firm *pressure*). Even the *t*-crossings, long, centrifugal, and pointed, which scan the writing like combative antennae, aim peremptorily towards the realization of ideas. No longer modest or discreet, they represent a true Darwin *typical-gesture.* This reveals his intellectual enthusiasm, which helped him greatly to confront his internal doubts (there is a depressive tendency in his graphic signs), when his disturbing theories caused sharp polemic.

In Darwin, mental clarity and intellectual independence have combined with his need for isolation, to push him to leave, to run away from himself, to break away from structures, in order to build new visions of the world.

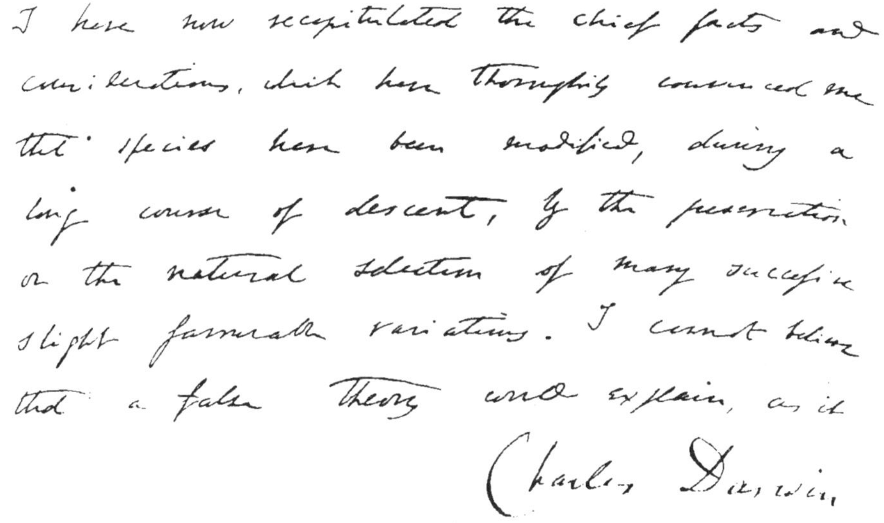

Figure 52
Charles Darwin's writing (from Saudek [218])

We now discuss two analyses undertaken several years ago, the first based on criteria at that time in force for the French diploma. It includes therefore two methods which are now no longer taught: the so-called Hippocratic (or Galenic) *temperaments* and Le Senne's *characterology*. We are aware that in modern psychology the use of such methods is entirely obsolete. However, having been used for many years, we must recognize that they have contributed significantly in deepening understanding of character traits. They will therefore be mentioned briefly.

Claudio (Fig. 53)

Aged 45, married, four children. Finance director of a large company. He had asked for an illustrated analysis for teaching purposes, with technical details.

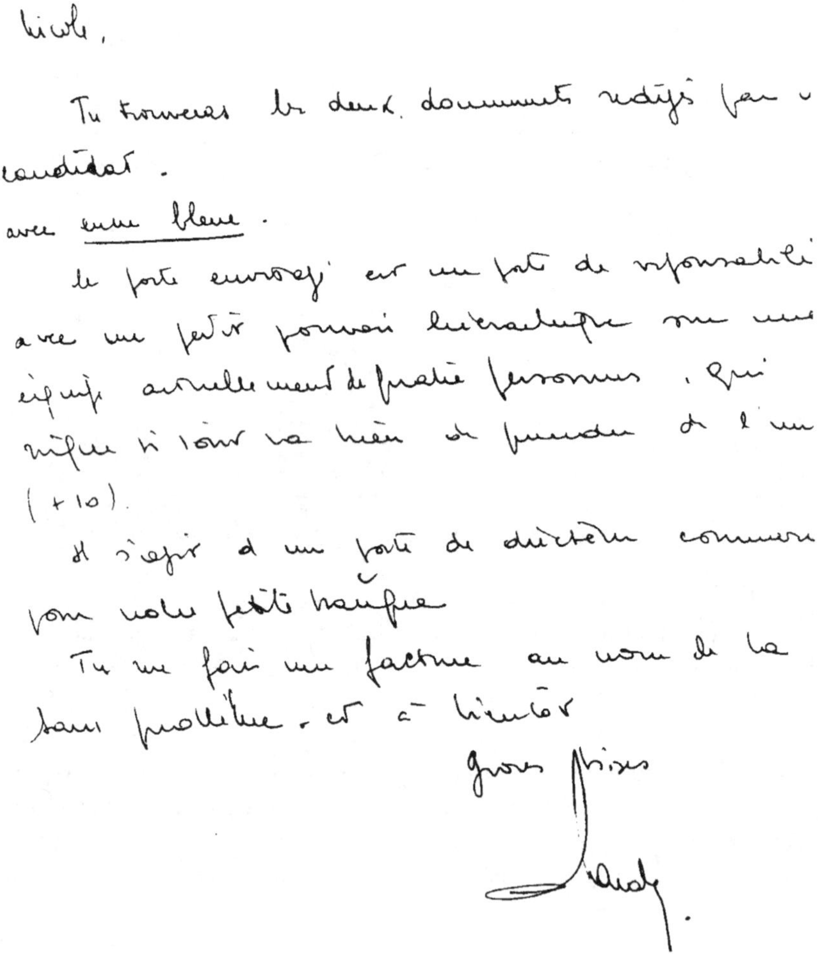

Nicole,

Tu trouveras les deux documents rédigés par u
candidat.
avec encre bleue.
Le poste envisagé est un poste de responsabili
avec un petit pouvoir hiérarchique sur une
équipe actuellement de quatre personnes. Qui
risque si tout va bien de prendre de l'am
(+10).
Il s'agit d'un poste de directeur commerci
pour notre petite banque
Tu me fais une facture au nom de la
sans problème. et à bientôt
Gros bisous
Claudio.

Figure 53 (reduced)
Claudio's writing (one of four documents provided for the analysis)

A. GLOBAL APPROACH TO THE GRAPHIC ENVIRONMENT

1. *General impression of writing* (optional)
   Smooth, vibrant writing permeated with tension. Overall very "variegated" (nuancée).

2. *Harmony* (according to Crépieux-Jamin)
   Average +: homogeneous overall notwithstanding the signature's superelevation; lacking some clarity.

3. *Formlevel* (Klages)
   Average +: individual and vibrant rhythm. Contrasts between freedom and control. A certain warmth.

4. *Relationship between Form and Movement* (succinct observation)
   Fundamental balance between Form and Movement is interrupted sometimes by certain complications.

B. HIERARCHICAL DEFINITION
(List of signs from the essential to the least significant)

- Small size with irregular dimension and slightly squashed middle zone
- Wavy with arcaded connection
- Aerated
- Lefward and irregular
- Widening with narrowing
- Irregular pressure: well-nourished with firm verticals, congestion, small spasms
- Moirée
- Connected and grouped with some lapses
- Simplified with combinations
- Accelerated with slowing down
- Hegar: Light ±   Pasty ±   Curved   Rapid ±
- Progressive gestures, others regressive
- Unnecessary strokes under *p, f, q*
- Left margin regular
- Social margin

- Signature:
        larger than text, to the right
        superelevation penetrating text
        initial capital letter low and oval-shaped
        centripetal final gesture, extended. Firm and heavy
- Short connections, short endings, clubbed
- Crossing of *t* : firm, flying strokes, pointed, clubbed
- Heavy accentuation, both high and low
- Full stops as dashes

C. GRAPHIC SYNDROMES

1. Small, wavy, aerated, irregular, progressive, simplified: *clear and organized mind, flexible thinking, receptive and intuitive, intellectual sensibility, objective and thoughtful judgement.*

2. Wavy, widened, pasty stroke, connected: *sociable, communicative, sensitive to environment, diplomatic.*

3. Pasty and light stroke, leftward slant, irregular, regressive gestures, full stops as small dashes, middle zone slightly flattened, short or clubbed endings, suspensions: *diffidence, caution, selectivity, injured sensibility, anxiety.*

4. Firm verticals, progressive and combined gestures, *t*-crossings flying and pointed: *firmness of opinion; intellectual, enterprising, and creative activity.*

5. Signature superelevated with upper extensions, final stroke heavy and centripetal, firm verticals, *t*-crossings high with arch in space, regular left margin: *self-esteem, assertiveness, ambition, authority, important role of Superego and Ideal of the Ego.*

6. Pasty and slightly slow stroke, congestion, deviations: *sensual, taste for a quiet and comfortable life, dreamy.*

D. PSYCHOLOGICAL AND TYPOLOGICAL APPROACHES

Hippocrates: Lymphatic – Bilious/Sanguine – Nervous

Hegar: Light ±   Pasty ±   Curved   Rapid ±

Le Senne: EnAS to EAS (at the intellectual level). Sentimental/
passionate – wide field of conscience

Freud: Marked by anal stage. Phallic signature. Overcompensation for inferiority complex. Superego, Ideal of the Ego

Jung: Thinking – Sensation – Intuition (thinking extrovert –
sensation introvert). Not lacking in sentiment but injured,
more archaic. Anima

Analysis of writing according to Hippocrates

Good overall temperamental balance. A basic *lymphatic* temperament (homogeneity, leftward slant, wavy, curved and filiform connections, pasty and semi-rapid stroke): receptive and reflective, thoughtful in action, patient, controlled mind, together with sensory disposition. The other three temperaments, even if less conspicuous at first glance, overlap and respond to this base, making the character profile more complex.

An immediate contrast is given by the *bilious* influence (firm verticals, flying strokes, direct initial forms, restrained clubbed finals, firm, flying, or pointed *t*-crossings). Onto the placid base of the lymphatic, the motor element gives a dynamic input: the engagement of the will, the stimulation of ambition, authority. Tempered with the reflective aspect of the lymphatic, this allows creative initiative and shakes the nonchalant and habitual basic nature.

The *sanguine* element is more difficult to see; there are some inflated round ovals and some with lower loops, in contrast to the middle zone with its "squashed" tendency. Also the upper extensions shoot directly out, culminating with such yearning in the signature. The most revealing sanguine elements are the small "unnecessary" strokes under some *p*, *f*, and *q*. Sometimes they are made rectilinear by the vivacity of the movement but in general they are "u" curves open towards the right. In spatial symbolism they are added "unnecessarily" under vertical letters which symbolize assertion and enter the zone of the unconscious; they will therefore have to be placed in relation to deep aspects of personality (see Freud, below). From the dynamic point of view this small curved gesture is full, written from left to right, open to the right, and restrained by a clubbed pressure as in the finals. To sum up, fullness and roundness, spasms, and "useless" strokes, indicate the restraining aspect of the sanguine temperament.

Constantly present even if discreet in its manifestation, the *nervous* element is like a "vibration". Small irregularities (slant, pressure, continuity: widening and tightening, squashing and contortions in the middle zone, impaired ovals, jerks) confirm the underlying nervous tendency. The contribution of the "cerebral" (precise, rapid, and pointed strokes) produces a mobile, critical, and perspicacious intelligence. The "sensitive" aspect, through which a latent anxiety emerges, also shows up secret sensory difficulties which the lymphatic keeps under control at a conscious level.

Analysis of writing according to Le Senne

Emotive

Emotive dominance (nervous irregularities, flying strokes), often internalized (lymphatic aspects, spasms, squashed ovals, suspensions); the result is a muted anxiety. Emotivity is exteriorized mainly on the plane of thinking and intellectual activity (flying strokes in the upper zone, accents high and heavy).

Active

Average activity (reasonably fast and progressive writing but some slowing down and regressive strokes), but good coordination between thinking and action (sober, wavy, filiform tendency, reasonably connected and combined, with a flexible outline). There is rhythm, firm support, vertical and horizontal, indicating self-mastery and decision-making ability. The active tendency comes mostly from the balance between objective thinking and personal motivations (large superelevation in the signature), giving the writing a potent and vital impulse.

Primary and secondary response

Some *primary* elements: flying strokes in the upper zone: therefore lively and immediate reactions on the plane of ideas. But restraints, squashing of the middle zone, pasty stroke, congestions, a controlled spatial arrangement, and a leftward tendency, indicate *secondary* response. Received or perceived impressions do not resolve themselves immediately and reactions are often delayed, or postponed. Impressions are persistent and the present is connected to the past in a vital cohesion. Secondary response sustains activity in a persevering rhythm, it leads to efficient organization and a life of generally fixed habits. It points to interiorized emotivity, which can sometimes give a phlegmatic external appearance (so-called crypto-emotivity).

Analysis of writing according to Jung

Presence of the four mental functions. Dominant: Thinking and Sensation. Dialectic between introversion and extroversion.

Principal function: Thinking

It is the most controlled function of consciousness: small writing, rounded, simplified and sober, combined, wavy, prolonged upper extensions. Thinking expresses itself here in an equilibrium between extroversion and introversion, with extroversion rather the stronger. This is not speculative thinking turned in on itself, but thinking that generates combative ideas and incites action: flying strokes pointed in the upper zone, widening, prolonged finals, controlled margins.

Secondary function: Sensation

This function sustains the thinking, which is not then purely abstract but is also concrete and sensory. Hence receptivity to impressions, to images, to sensuality: pasty stroke, congestions, supported by the baseline. Sensation seems to express itself more in the introvert manner: intimate sensory world, a little indifferent, satisfaction of his own sensations and impressions.

Third function: Intuition

This function brings an influx of "irrationality" and a quick perception of what is possible: combined, nuanced stroke, whites, flying strokes in upper zone.

Fourth function: Sentiment

The following signs are present: width of words, curved connections, warm stroke but also tightening, squashed, leftward tendencies, regressive angles. Sentiment is in part slightly inhibited or otherwise subjected to unconscious ambivalence, adjusted at the conscious level by the mind and by the desire to adapt. This could result in slightly childish sentimental attitudes.

Analysis of writing according to Freud

The general writing movement, restrained, inhibited, fluid, and comfortable, signifies contrasts in the deep personality.

A feeling of inferiority (squashing in the middle zone, suspensions, twisting) is partly compensated by a very strong self-respect aiming at personal achievement, which favours good social adaptability without seeking excessive power. It is also compensated by excessive scruples or by an anxiety for perfection (precise and heavy accents, retouching), which does not exclude a persistent latent anxiety in the unconscious.

The small and slightly congested middle zone indicates, in this context, persistence in the *anal* phase, without excessive fixation to the phase (writing is not compact, closed, angular, or pointed). Problems of emotional adjustment, however, have arisen in the psychosexual development during this stage, a stage of ambivalence towards oneself (self-esteem, shame, and guilt combined) and towards others (both sensual and hostile love; dialectic between giving and possessing, between domination and submission).

Aggressive tendencies unleash themselves in relation to ideas. The stating of thoughts and opinions is combative and bold. At the emotional level, on the contrary, aggression short-circuits (some narrowing with small angular returns, flattened ovals). One can deduce masochistic tendencies and feelings of blame (flattening, retouching, heavy accenting).

The signature is extremely eloquent: it is similar to the text in the middle zone but the straight and superelevated extension of the second letter following the initial flattened oval, is a symbolic representation of subconscious tendencies. Flattened and foetal appearance of the initial: anxious search for reassurance; followed immediately by a superelevation which rises as a virile aspiration, phallic and creative, but which is also an expression of the Superego and of a powerful Ideal of the Ego: Father seen as ideal image. This confirms the first impression from the writing: order, homogeneity, large upper margin, social margins, tall capital letters, superelevations, and signature: i.e. a significant Superego. There are acquired demands, prohibitions, and moral judgements which form a sort of nucleus of the personality.

With the Ego (middle zone) there are conflicts, frustrations, and inhibitions. The Superego has been all the more developed to see dangers: conflicts with the Id (lower zone of instinctive impulses, of the unconscious: with "unnecessary" strokes). These strokes in this sensory context seem to indicate attraction towards a sensual world which floats between experiencing, prohibiting, and imagining it, like small self-sufficient islands which do not intend to disturb the life of the rational Ego.

On the other hand, latent anxiety, the nervous/sensitive aspect tied to the introverted sensuality and to anality, predisposes to psychosomatic functional disturbance, which is the result of a sense of guilt tied to the conflict between the Superego and Id and to the Oedipal conflict. The general structure of the personality denotes a slightly obsessive tendency. Social adaptability does not suffer but the structure of the Ego becomes vulnerable in difficult situations.

GRAPHIC PROFILE

The writer presents himself as someone who has reached a certain balance and has learnt to live exceptionally well with the interior weaknesses. Acknowledging his own vulnerability, motivated to fulfil himself but at the same time maintain a pleasant way of life, keeping to social norms, he has succeeded in reconciling his intellectual and interior needs by adopting a *savoir-faire* attitude.

His mental life is a continuous stimulation. His refined and receptive intelligence, characterized by a continuous reference to the concrete, is also fed by considerable intuition. An inventive imagination nourishes the perception of reality without distorting it, supporting the association of ideas and favouring ingenious solutions to complicated problems.

The mind is clear and lucid, critical and attentive to detail. Aims and purpose are always clearly perceived. There is a synthesis between immediate rational perception and long-term prospects. This presumes a continuous play between observation of the moment, the integration of past experience, and the choice of operations to be carried out to fulfil objectives. This mental elasticity comes not only from rational and conceptual aspects of intelligence, but also from an extremely subtle sensibility which is open to others and to the world around.

Reflection is important; it integrates sensitive feelings with reasoned judgement of situations. This encourages not only forward thinking and a practical sense, patience and a methodical spirit, but also interior dreaming and a calm resignation to habits.

In contrast to this receptivity, on the plane of ideas there is a lively and combative dynamism. The taste for argument, criticism, or irony, with a touch of sarcasm, leads to discussions and the defence of his own opinions. This sometimes becomes overexited and compensates for internal vulnerability, altering the objective perception of the opinions of others with a wish to dominate in the world of ideas.

If the mental assurance along with a general behavioural discretion denotes a natural adjustment at a social level, it is also an indication of a need to be valued.

At the unconscious level there is a conflict between emotional dependence and desire for independence; between a slightly egocentric and childish search for protection and a more altruistic aspiration, more active and virile. There is conflict also between attachment to the past and ambition for future achievement of a highly idealized nature. From this come alternating needs for security and avoidance of disagreements or discord, and for challenging himself.

A latent anxiety, which springs from these conflicts already present since early childhood, acts negatively on his emotional life, and often generates an internal malaise of self-regarding contemplation and a slightly guilty wish to run away to an imaginary place. All these problems are in daily life overcome with ease. A natural, simple and unostentatious modesty, reserve, and restraint, allied with a lively sociability, attracts sympathy.

Relationships are warm, diplomatic, more selective than appearance implies. There is always a certain restraint, a slight distance, a diffidence in showing his own feelings. When this distance is overcome and when ties are created that arise out of shared views on life and thinking, they produce deep and lasting friendship. In relationships there is also a desire for seduction, not without a competitive need for respect, the aim of which is to recreate a reassuring circle. The sensual side of his personality also seeks comfort and ease, aesthetic enjoyment, and a general atmosphere of sensitivity and well-being.

His personality achieves, through the diversity of his capabilities and his constant intelligent and realistic reference to context, a good maturity and a balance of conciliation and a high moral and ethical sense.

In active and professional life, the rhythm of work can be regular and sustained, with an eye to a long-term target. In organization and method, a very adaptable disposition, without excess rigidity, produces a capacity for coordination and adjustment to unforeseen circumstances which shows complete professional mastery. In the same field, the taste for exchange and tolerant and subtle cooperation widens the scope for action and stimulates the creative spirit.

His dynamism in action does not rest on an excessive impulse of temperament but upon the skill of mastering his own strengths. This is a mastery based on reflection, foresight, and the acquiring of information which together eliminate risk or sudden hasty initiatives. Intelligence, willpower, spirit of synthesis, and mental agility, as well as ambition, make him suited to a director's role. The sense of authority, that is, competent authority and not authoritarianism, creates a natural superiority, reassuring for subordinates. Professional knowledge of the most opportune decisions, and how to simplify problems, ensures the efficiency of professional action.

This is a rich personality who is also complicated and vulnerable. Beyond professional life, there is a need to preserve a protected lifestyle, away from stress, with various simple sensations, divided between nature, sport, reading, or music, for example. Family life represents an important emotional haven.

Gabriella (Fig. 54 - *see overleaf*)

Writer and art critic, aged 45. Profile at her own request for reasons of self-analysis.

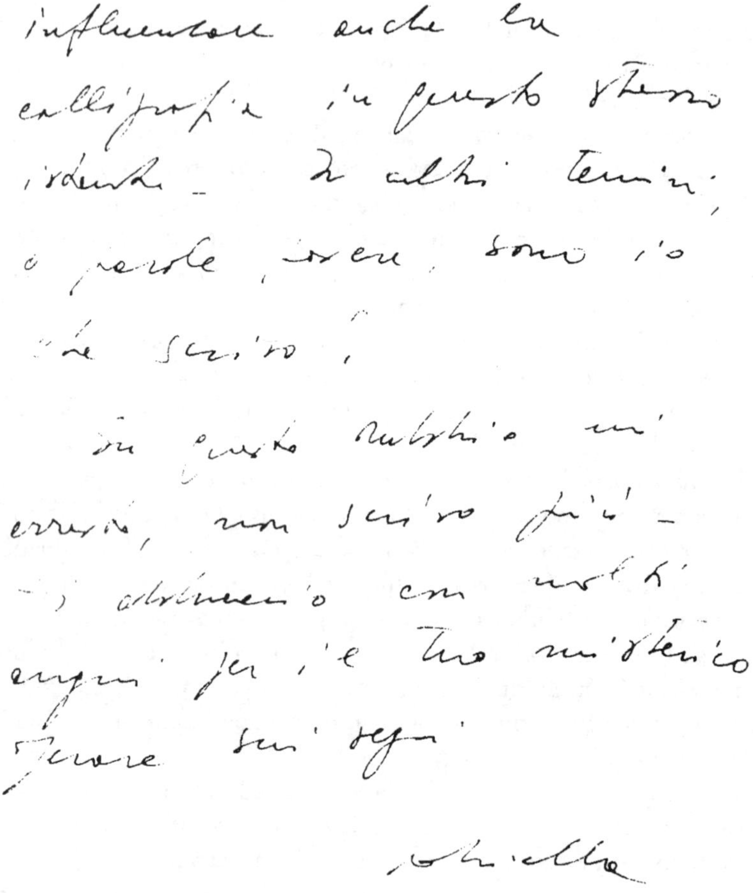

Figure 54

GRAPHIC PROFILE

The rhythm of this vivacious and discreet writing evokes the flow of a mountain stream which rushes between barren rocks, then widens into meanders which irrigate dry fields – and so nourishes a sunny space of the imagination. The high cultural level produces a delicate nonconformist spirit, which does not run on preconceived lines, but leaves itself open to the unexpected.

The agility and flexibility to adapt favours a practical and technically efficient intelligence. But the intrinsic quality of the intelligence is located above all in the conceptual and abstract. From this area the creative ability takes form and life. The life of the mind is maintained by an imagination which is sometimes contained and also repressed, at other times it is coloured by a utopian elevation which encourages audacious impulses in which internal fantasies can become a lived fulfilment. Even more than imagination, it is intellectual sensitivity that feeds the mental life. This subtle and receptive sensibility allows an exceptional mobility of ideas, sensations, and perceptions, which pattern themselves by instinctive reflection.

This is not the reflection that matures through laboured analysis but the reflection that comes from an internal radiating intuition. The synthesis between sensitivity and intuition produces clarity of mind and judgement, always ready for the point in question, because the antennae of refined sensitivity do not lead to rigid or limited evaluations.

On the other hand a basic insecurity does not permit personal affirmation at any price. "*Rien n'est jamais acquis*" (nothing is ever acquired) could be a motor for continuous renewal, even if anxiety and suffering are part of the game.

The capacity for critical penetration is notable. It is carried out with a very personal and carefree impulse involving a certain irrationality. The mental ingenuity, the sense of complexity, and the ability to find choices with subtlety and discernment denote intellectual organization of the highest quality.

If the intellectual and intuitive life remains in the forefront, it would be artificial to divide it from the emotional plane. Her emotional life is particularly complex and thinking assumes a reassuring role. The intellectual filter acts as a defence mechanism. There is no doubt that at the emotional level contradictions abound. This is a personality who expresses a need to communicate, but this impulse also springs from an internal solitude. On the one hand arise projects, investment in the future, but on the other there is a depressive tendency and the constant struggle for renewal.

One suspects that the internal struggle is continuous, between the attraction of an intimate, meditated realization, so subtle that it slips away partly from the control of the concrete, and a tendency to resignation. The failure in self-esteem must be compensated by a significant internalizing of spiritual values, which shroud interior suffering.

Intellectualizing avoids, in the case of grievous conflicts, a regression to the most archaic state of primary narcissism, which is marked by an emotional frustration and by an unrequited eagerness, and therefore by a form of resigned and depressive contact. A defence mechanism provides shelter from this danger and allows the Ego to integrate the conflicts and impulsive energies. In such a way a possible re-evaluation of self comes through intellectual mediation. It is therefore the quality of mental life that permits a self-awareness sufficient to combat internal vulnerability.

The dialectic between extroversion and introversion takes on the same defensive significance. It means that deep introversion, a quality of subtle inward regard, is not prey to an underlying negative resignation, and uses extroversion as a compensatory force. From this, the seeking of social contact, the impulse for communication, is not only a simple act of voluntary enterprise but is also a reactive process. Communication can take on unpredictable and surprising attitudes, blocking or reacting with intellectual combativeness, or aggression. But at the subconscious level, it is above all a defence mechanism against the anxiety of playing an internal chess game in the most intimate subjective world: susceptibility becomes extremely vulnerable, the sense of guilt waits in ambush, and the demands of the self can become persecutory.

A balance is regained through idealistic and humanitarian values. Strength of thinking, enthusiasm for ideas or ideals, and the capacity to verbalize emotions are aids to understanding and transcending the self. Critical and conceptual, as also poetical, expression develops: literary poetical expression is favoured by synthetic thinking, more intuitive than logical, and by the hidden desire for conscious exteriorizing of her own mental processes.

At the social level, self-assurance is only achieved through a sense of competence. She has a deep inability to assert herself and stand out through inauthentic tasks and superficial actions. Withdrawal rather than superficiality is her choice. Sociability, even if spontaneous, is founded on mental affinity or on intellectual curiosity and not upon the need for social relationship at all cost. There could be a tendency to social climbing, but this is understood as a danger, as it certainly would be, because of the overwhelming need for collective and dynamic participation in her overall balance.

Thus fervour for action linked to a free and easy mental agility stimulates the vital impulse like an everlasting spark. Thinking and action are intimately connected through the subtle motivation of *fulfilment through being*. The active drive is not therefore fuelled by the affirmation of an overflowing vitality: on the contrary her vitality is by nature delicate and needs to be conserved.

On the emotional plane there is tension and subconscious anxiety. Sentiments are not experienced with full feeling and serenity. They cause fear; they are childish, unformed, eager, and transient. These traits confer to this character a slightly elusive personality. There is an ethereal detachment from strong sensual impulse.

From the first, the mother image has been experienced in a very ambivalent way, with an intense desire for dependence and safety as well as a feeling of neglect and frustration. In consequence this has created a painful self-image which has been re-valued only by intellectual maturity. It seems that the father figure has not played an efficacious role, but has only been an ideal, abstract image, not a strong figure to lean on for reassurance.

She has gained control over herself through the power of intuitive thinking and by renouncing material and immediate gratification, resulting in a disinterested giving of the self. Hence a purpose fixed towards the future, the present being "too narrow", always savoured as part of an unfolding project. But her emotional life is also characterized by the risk of excessive giving of the self; her emotion being neither giving nor taking is more likely to be exposed to "masochistic" risk. Certainly an attitude of "escape" in intellectual engagement has been a healthy defence mechanism, given the balance reached, without sacrificing sensitivity, without bitterness or fancies of domination.

In conclusion, the vibration and intensity of this graphic rhythm reveals an original touch of creativity, thanks to the balance reached between the need to be faithful to the internal self and the wish to share the tensions of exterior renewal.

PART III

EVOLUTION OF WRITING

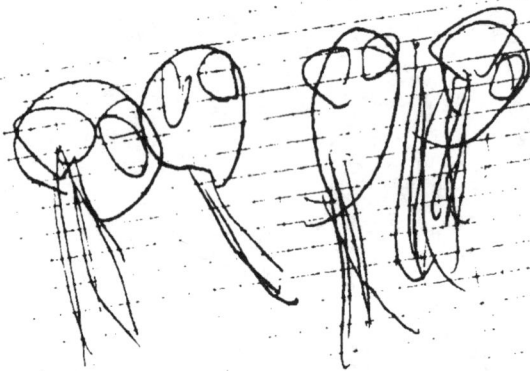

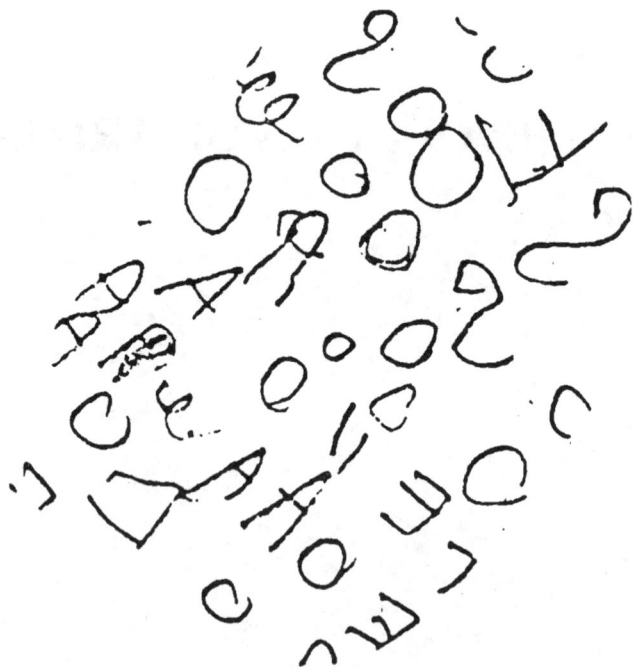

mi la vere porta sempre la felicità
dei bambini, ed anche alle vei miei di!

Chapter Six

FROM GRAPHIC GESTURE
TO TEACHING MODELS

I. THE STAGE OF THE SCRIBBLE AND
THE MAGIC OF THE SKETCH

If one watches a small boy holding a writing implement of chalk or pencil while dragging it over any surface, wall, floor, or sheet of paper, we can see his astonished delight that his gesture has left behind an outline, a record of his passing and of his will. Who does not remember those scribbles by children during the war, when paper was rare, which invaded walls, doors, and shutters in the homes of tolerant grandparents, or pressed into earth or sand their imaginative charge! In today's society, a small child can find large sheets of paper readily available at nursery school or at home, with a supply of coloured pencils or bright felt-tips whose use is a real visual delight.

It would seem that even at nine months a toddler can already begin to scribble. Although this has actually been found by research it is hard to know whether the subjects are precocious toddlers or simply a group who have been able to benefit from materials near at hand and consequently stimulated by the environment. In fact often the pencil goes into the mouth at this stage and any possible trace on a surface is rather casual and indifferent to the child, who is largely concerned with placing any material or object into the mouth. The child needs to reach the stage of eye and motor coordination before a simple motor gesture produced by the hand and the whole body, which leaves a mark, can acquire the status of graphic production.

When toddlers of one or two years of age engage in play-work, we see that they often feel an intense pleasure, linked to their current emotional state. Some children participate cheerfully in this activity, others angrily, or at least with an attention which is more or less loaded with latent aggression and sometimes anxiety. Others can show a form of indifferent passivity, or a worrying state of automatism. Even though the child's gesture is not well coordinated it is already *expressive* and when it produces an outline, this is the moment when the child feels the visual pleasure so exciting. According to the process of *feedback* – when the effect is retroactive on the cause— the eye's satisfaction acts therefore on the motor gesture of the hand. This gives the child the incentive to reproduce the gesture-outline. The eye and hand interaction which is preliminary to the act of writing is thus instilled.

However it is not only the two isolated functions of vision and motor control, but the whole tonic function of the child's body which is implicated in this process. It is now that the psychoemotional state plays a part in finding a balance between muscular *tension* and *relaxation*, between the static balance and the dynamic balance necessary to undertake the gesture. At the same time, motor control of the hand develops and little by little the exercise produces a more controlled gesture.

II. FROM THE SCRIBBLE TO HANDWRITING

The first scribbles are in general outlined with a circular motion. Previously the child may have covered large surfaces with delicate traces of simple strokes which sometimes end in a small knot or curved gesture. After the age of three, at nursery school, the child expresses participation or inhibition, not only in the realization of motor gesture, of *design*, but also in relation to the *graphic space* (Figs 55, 56).

The graphic space is not in fact a simple platform but represents a layer of communication which deals with action, struggle, or simple participation.

Figure 55 (*see opposite page*)
Elena, 3 years old (reduced by 70%)
This nursery school scribble with vivacious colours and a free and wide stroke, with rounded forms, reveals the sociable behaviour and adaptability of this little girl. The large space of the paper is completely filled; the stroke is flexible and firm; the movement's sequences occur without any jerks or agitation even though they are different and repetitive.

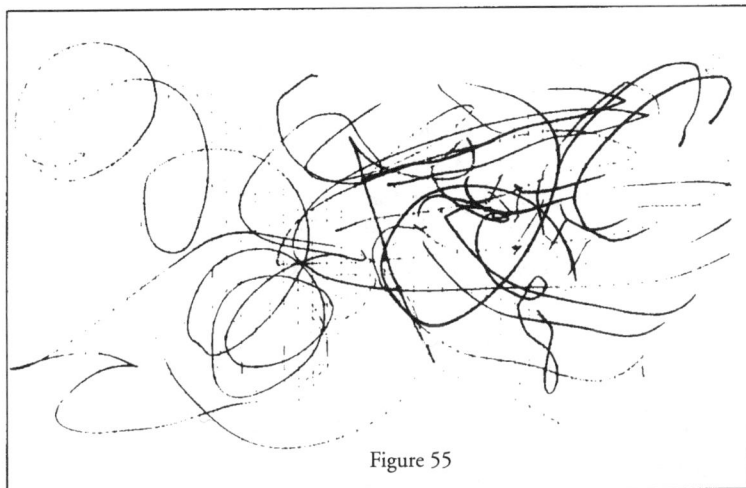
Figure 55

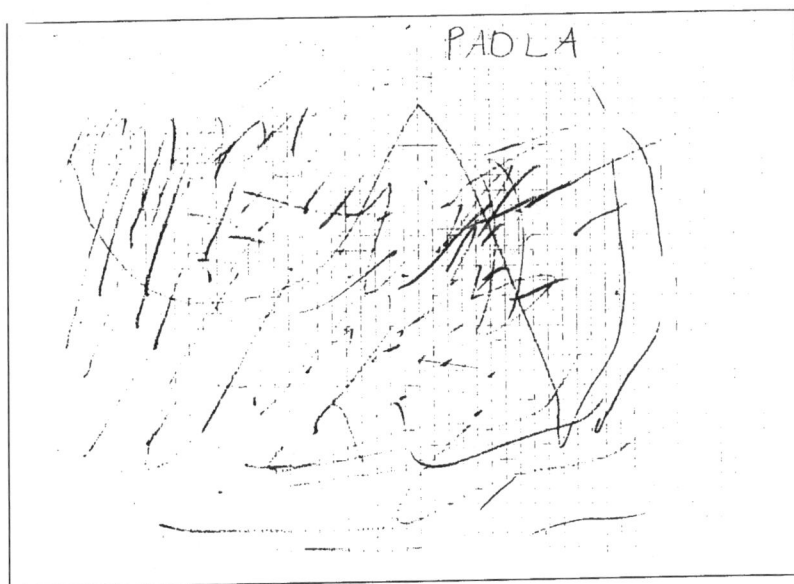
Figure 56
Paola, 3 years old (reduced by 70%)
The scribble has a less expansive profile than Elena's. There are few curves and movements are broken up, signs of less sociability and involvement. However there is no strong aggression as in some other scribbles where the crossing of furious strokes denotes a choleric mood in the child, even if momentary.

Many children who do not want to leave home find themselves totally inhibited at nursery if placed in front of a sheet of paper or blackboard for their own use. They only draw weak strokes, whereas others colour ten or more pages with wide and spontaneous strokes. If the teaching methods are satisfactory, such inhibition must attract attention particularly if it persists for some time, because it reveals difficulties in adapting which could have repercussions on future school progress.

At the motor level, scribbles are in general impulsive and the child uses the right or left hand indifferently. The particular use of one hand is not defined with precision before the age of five or so. Whichever of the two hands the child uses, the starting point of the outline is the axis of the paper and this corresponds to the projection onto the graphic space of the plane of symmetry of the body. Starting from this axis, the right hand produces movements to the right and the left hand towards the left of the paper. The consequent outlines are in reality produced by the arm movement at shoulder level. At this point different types of movements occur: one around the vertical axis which starts movements going to the right or the left, and the other around the horizontal axis, which generates movements towards the top and bottom. The circular movement comes from the coordination of movements around the two axes. In addition to these movements produced by the position of the arm, there are more specialized ones due to the rotation of the hand around the wrist which allow rounded and looped gestures. But we shall not linger on these technical descriptions, which require special knowledge which is not the field of the graphologist.

With these new graphomotor capacities, and following precise stages, the child evolves rapidly in writing ability. Towards the age of two years the child acquires the notions of *vertical* and *horizontal*. He begins to take notice of his own image in the mirror, to explore his own body and identify singly its various parts: hence his own *body schema* is structured.

Between two and three years, one can see some particular forms take shape in the scribbles of the child, showing a determined stroke, and thus they express emotional, sensory, and cognitive attitudes. Extraordinary drawings of *little people* begin to appear which have inspired countless contemporary artists, finding in them the primordial figurative essence which is common to each civilization termed "primitive" in anthropology (Fig. 57).

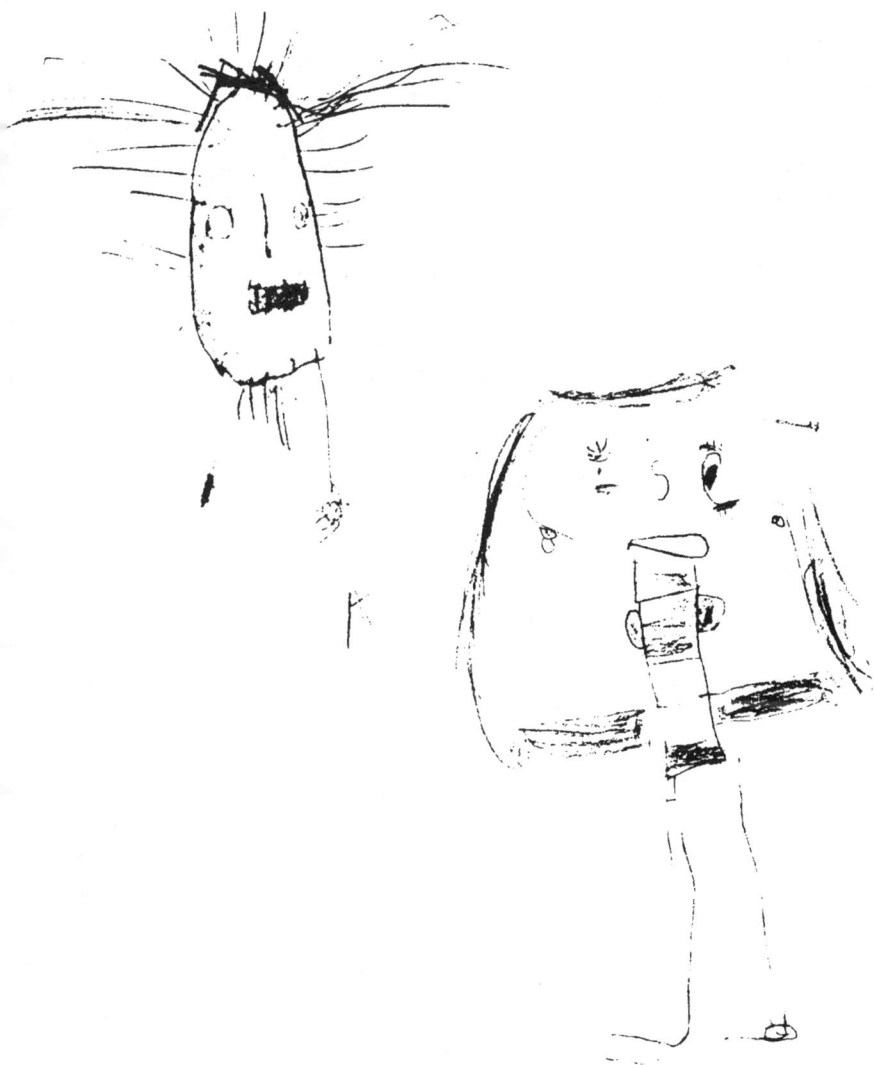

Figure 57 (reduced)
Elena 3 years old: sketch of the *little person*.
5 years old: drawing of *little person*, practically a self-portrait with many
details and variation in colours. It denotes an agile and quick mind

In our present society children are very stimulated by the school and home environment, by many illustrated books, by educational games, and therefore often in spontaneous drawings they sketch some letters of the alphabet, not without pride! Towards the age of four they can close a curve (even if it was already possible at an embryonic level, it now reaches a stage where there is a greater motor control and intention). At five the child is able to copy a *square* and to draw the *little person* type. This is an important stage which has inspired many psychological studies, in particular the Goodenough Test.

From this moment the child draws, and the imagery can be studied at various levels. On the purely graphic plane are the management of space, quality and energy of the stroke, and formal and structural intentions; at the conceptual level, type of narrative, sequence of images, persons, things, which makes us ask what the child wants to represent. Lastly, on the creative-expressive level are freedom, exuberance, inhibition, dullness, repetition, stereotype, and so on. In this case it is necessary to watch the child discreetly while drawing. It is possible to evaluate what is called *latent time*, that is the psychological space with which the child tends to distance the drawing-work from the act of drawing. It is also possible to evaluate the child's initial impulse and the fluctuations of mood during the various stages of the drawings.

When a graphologist analyses the writing of a child first starting school, it is important to be able to examine many scribbles and drawings previous to or contemporary with the writing.

One often notices that the child even before learning to write traces an outline of letters (Fig. 58), imitating the adult writing style whose important role is recognized unconsciously. This is also the age when the child pretends to read the newspaper, inventing a syllabic language in a very happy way. At six years of age the child is able to copy a *rhomboid* shape and acquires the notion of diagonal direction, with an understanding of distances, proportions, and details. Intellectual evolution turns towards the capability of abstraction. This period is the socializing stage, when the child begins primary schooling.

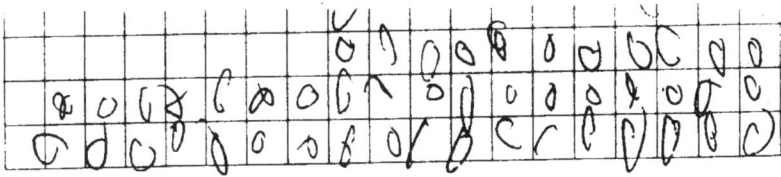

Figure 58
Giulia, 3 years 6 months: outline of letters

The child draws with great enthusiasm, and at the age of seven drawing and play are synonymous. Drawing touches the apex of the expressive impulse. This exuberance will progressively diminish, often to the great disappointment of parents who see their child as a future artist (Fig. 59). According to our observations, children after the age of ten who still have a strong motivation for drawing express a fairly stable attitude in this direction and perhaps an artistic predisposition. Unfortunately, in children where a strong original and independent imagination predominates, drawing lessons at school tend to discourage creative spontaneity, concentrating on more technical results.

Dysgraphic children often show outstanding flair in free drawing (Fig. 60) even if they have great difficulty in the spatial layout of their writing or with the shapes of letters. They can certainly express themselves when they are free from the tight restrictions of space, line, and form. Not least, their drawings are generally evidence of the difficulties they encounter in achieving a flexible and well coordinated gestural sequence. Their movements are more broken, more angular, and proceed with jerky strokes.

We shall return to the evolution of children's writing, but first we need to study problems related to the basic writing model, for the best use of the method proposed in this book. We therefore continue with a comparison between the Italian and French school models.

Figure 59 (reduced)
Elvira,
drawing at
8 years old

Figure 60 (reduced)
Fabrizio,
left-handed and
dysgraphic,
drawing at
8 years old

Chapter Seven

ITALIAN AND FRENCH
SCHOOL MODELS

By the age of six, school begins to represent the central reference point of the child's social world. A new discipline substitutes application for play, and freedom of movement is replaced with sitting still. Each child will react in a different way, according to maturity, not only motor and intellectual maturity but also emotional. These three areas of maturation, and the problems connected with them, assume a major role in dyslexia and dysgraphia, as we shall explain in later chapters.

We will consider now in detail two school models of writing which we can document with precision, the Italian and French, and compare them. We shall also have a quick look at the other main European models. Table 20 shows the difference between the letters in the English, Latin, and German models.

Because the Italian and French (Latin) models are very close it is important to pick out the differences, in writing and in culture. These subtleties can sometimes lead to diverging interpretations. Moreover, the data we present is very fluid as it can vary according to schools or reforms in school systems. These models are in any case basic models drawn from the majority of the adults and young whom we have analysed. For future generations, they could change.

I. CURRENT MODEL ALPHABETS

Because of their Latin origin the form of letters in the two alphabets is similar. They can however show some variations with regard to capital letters, which in Italy presents a significant regressive development, and

ENGLAND	FRANCE	ITALY	GERMANY

Table 20
Comparisons between European writing models

regarding the shape of the letter *z* which in the lower zone of the French model is looped. It is also important to observe some particular details which only concern the *Italian* model:

- the presence of an *initial stroke* in front of ovals;
- the presence of a *final stroke* to the letter *o*;
- the formative movement of the letter *a* which begins and ends to the *left*.

This last characteristic plays a particular role when one is required to evaluate and interpret the graphic signs to do with the opening or closing of ovals, these aspects being for example connected to signs of insincerity in adult writing.

Formative movements and typical-gesture: the ovals

The simple observation of the formative movement of the *ovals*, which involves starting *from the left* in the Italian model, and *from the right* in the French model, is already charged with implications. We shall see that the *logic* of this movement determines variable and even different evaluations and interpretations regarding important notions such as, for example, those of *regression* and of *closed* writing.

The letter "a"

This letter is made essentially by an *oval* and a small vertical stroke. In the two countries under examination, the achievement in writing these two elements together shows good graphomotor evolution. But, according to where the initial *point of attachment* is, the forms produced take on differing characteristics: *looped*, *rounded*, or *closed*, which are not always revealed at first sight.

We do not wish to focus attention here onto a small detail, but rather to follow the logical development of the writing gesture viewed from the *psychology of movement* – to take up again Suzanne Bresard's principle – and attempt to elucidate the linguistic aspect.

Linguistic value of the letter "a"

Some aspects linked to the linguistic-cultural value of the letter *a* can assume an important role in acquiring the gestural agility required by its formative movement. In Italian the letter *a* is frequent as a *word ending* and is used twice as much as in French, where the letter *e* is the most frequent word ending. Graphology has also taught us that this letter symbolizes the emotions, as is shown in the formative movement, in the ovoid and even foetal shape of this letter.

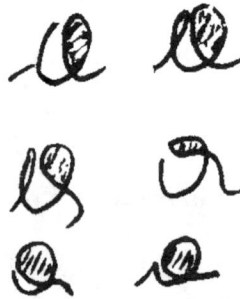

Figure 61
The letter *a* at the end
of a word in Italian

There is no doubt that the letter *a* in Italy has a feminine echo, given that it corresponds to the ending of the majority of female names as well as the singular feminine article, pronouns, adjectives, and past participles. The *a* is also pregnant with symbolism for its presence in words of affection: *mamma, papà, nonna*. From the first moments at school, the Italian child becomes involved in the linguistic and cultural value of this letter, which results in what we can call a *typical-gesture effect* of the *a*. The Italian child reaches more quickly than the French a graphic agility that allows this letter to be formed at one go, without lifting the pen, especially at the end of a word. At times the *a* quickly acquires a typical movement which incorporates a *final hook*, which is not found in French writing. This hook takes on the gestural function of release which establishes an exquisitely Italian typical-gesture.

We shall see in studying *graphometric scales* that one must not automatically mistake the all-in-one writing of the letter *a* for a sign of graphic evolution, instead the focus must be on the typical-gesture effect described before. Furthermore the formative movement beginning at the left determines more easily, in adult writing, rounded and regressive strokes, which will have to be evaluated differently in the two languages.

The letter "o"

The formative movement of the letter *o* in Italian involves the same variants already met for the letter *a*. At the same time, from the linguistic point of view, the *o* takes on a *masculine* connotation.

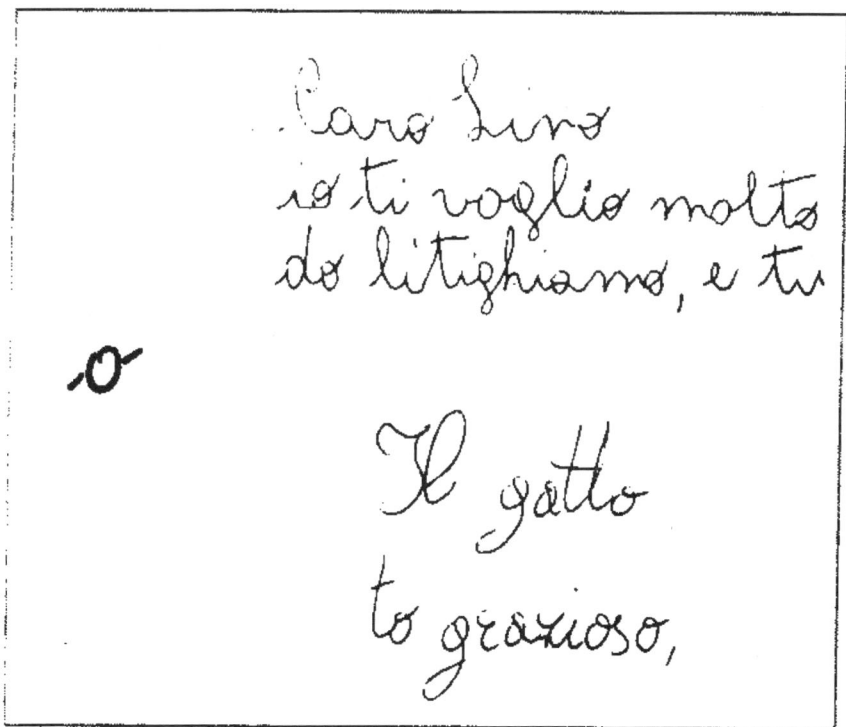

Figure 62
The letter *o* at the end of a word in Italian

In addition to the *initial stroke* found in front of all the ovals, this letter is characterized by a *final stroke* above and to the right of the letter, in a diagonal direction and in general centrifugal. This element is unique in the whole of the alphabet and is typically Italian, only very rarely found in France. We know that the diagonal centrifugal gesture takes on a symbolic value of attack, of combativeness, and often aggression. One needs to take into consideration this gesture when it no longer represents an infantile mode, but rather a deliberate graphic choice.

Other ovals

The formative movements of the ovals in the letters *d*, *g*, and *q* follow the same logic as in the letter *a*. The *initial stroke* in front of all the ovals, only found in the Italian model, has been the subject of statistical research.

All these differences have lead us to conduct research for Arigraf [33] to identify the consequences of the use of *graphometric scales* in the evaluation of infantile components, which will be the topic of later chapters.

Capital letters

We notice that in the Italian model, the capital letters *D*, *P*, and *R* enlarge to the left, all the more so because the size of the capital letters is greater in Italy than in France, due to wider line spacing.

The letter "z"

In France the shape of this letter has retained the lower extension as had been used in Italy before the 1950s.

In addition to the letter *z* the French alphabet has two more letters than Italian with a lower extension, *j* and *y*. The study of the development of the lower extensions is therefore more rewarding in the French language, from which many observations and interpretations can be drawn.

II. SCHOOL EXERCISE BOOKS

Just by thumbing through some pages of Italian and French exercise books we can pick out a completely different atmosphere (Fig. 63). Without taking into consideration the variables of whether the writing is tidy or untidy, with ability or difficulty in motor writing skills, we can identify a spontaneous, ample, cheerful, and ornate appearance in the Italian samples. The French examples on the other hand are more structured, restricted, and austere. At the formal level there are also several differences to consider, principally concerning the standard exercise books with their system of lining and spacing. In Italy, in elementary school there are different types of smaller and larger exercise books used according to subject and classes.

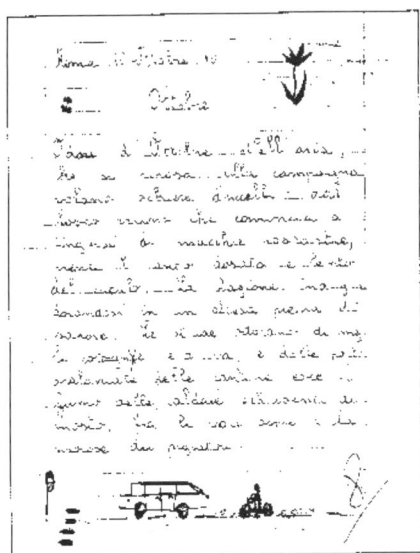

Figure 63
Left: Elvira – 8 years 9 months old, 4a elementary school. Page from an Italian exercise book with small coloured drawings inserted

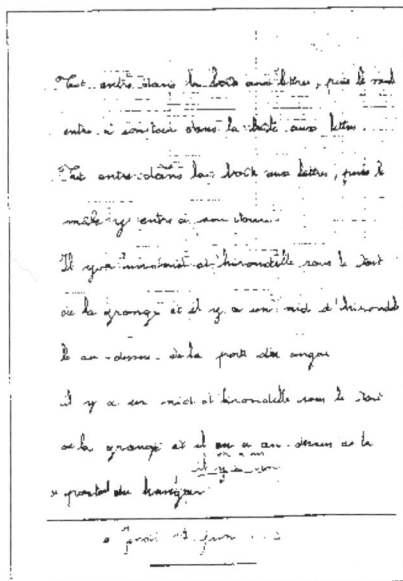

Right: Philippe – 8 years 6 months old, 3a elementary school. Page from a French school book. Note the diversity of the margins

In France exercise books are always identical, with the exception of those in large format for specific subjects such as science and drawing. In Italy today there is an increasing trend towards using larger format books.

The page of the exercise book and its margins (Table 21)

The page of an Italian small format exercise book is slightly smaller than the French page. The upper and lower margins are similar in both countries while the lateral margins differ greatly. In Italy the left margin is of only 15mm against the 27mm and sometimes 40mm in France. In Italy the right margin is the same as the left, whereas this does not exist in France. The Italian pupil therefore learns to place his writing between two narrow lateral margins, which become even narrower the thicker the book. The French pupil instead becomes used to a wide left margin, while he can extend to the extreme right edge of the paper, as there is no margin to stop him.

It is obvious therefore that interpretations on margin symbolism and management of space in the two countries must be on the whole considered differently. This is especially important when dealing with adolescents and young people chosen for professional selection, and also adults who have not pursued further education, and are tied only to the experience of study in their own country.

Line height

The Italian child in the first year of elementary school learns to write within extremely wide spaces. He is given a space of 5mm in height for the middle zone and a space of 7mm to develop the upper and lower extensions. Capital letters can extend to 12mm high, and if they have a lower extension they reach a total height of 19mm, the same height as the lower-case letter *f*. The French child, on the contrary, has to use small spaces, with 2mm for the middle zone, while the extensions of the *d* and *t* do not go beyond 4mm. The looped extensions are no more than 6mm, the lower extensions descend only 4mm, and capital letters have no particular fullness.

The basic model does not alter in France during the school years. But in Italy at 3a elementary level the middle zone reduces to 3mm. A complete change takes place at the beginning of 4a: books are then simply lined at an interval of 1cm and there is therefore no further guide for the development of the respective zones. In addition in Italy there is also another type of book only used for arithmetic which has squares which vary from 5mm for the first classes to 3mm from the 3a elementary class. So there is a succession of changing spaces within and between lines.

A recent Italian reform in the 1990s introduced exercise books of bigger format which seem to be preferred by teachers. The margins of these are larger (from 15 to 20mm), but the system of lines remains the same. In the nursery and elementary classes exercise books are used with large 1cm squares.

COMPARISON BETWEEN THE ITALIAN AND FRENCH EXERCISE BOOK MODELS (UP TO THE 1990s)
(measurements in mm)

	ITALY	FRANCE
PAGE SIZE		
- width	147	168
- height	202	220
- upper margin	20	20/27
- lower margin	15	12
- left margin	15	27/40
- right margin	15	absent

DEVELOPMENT OF ZONES AND LINES	1a and 2a elementary	3a elementary	Throughout school
- middle zone	5	3	2
- upper extensions	+7	+7	+2: *d, t* +4: *loops*
- lower extensions	+7	+7	+4
- upper and lower extensions	+19	+17	+6/8
- capital letters	+12	+12	+6

From 4a elementary:
simple 8mm spaced lines   No changes

Arithmetic books:
5mm squares, then 3mm from year 3a

Table 21

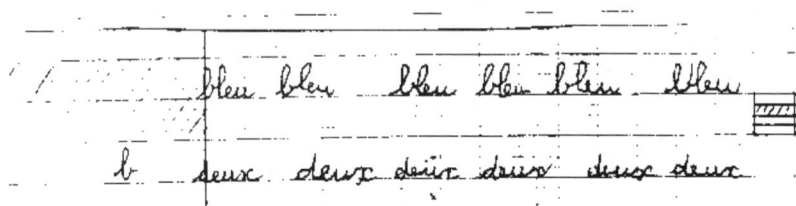

Figure 64 (reduced)
Above: French exercise book lines and margins.
Successive examples below (Italian): lines and margins in 1a elementary school;
in 2a and 4a elementary school; arithmetic book

III. PSYCHOLOGICAL CONSEQUENCES

Which psychological reactions to the various models of exercise books and lines should we expect? The Italian child can develop a greater gestural fullness than the French child, and according to Ajuriaguerra's research, this would confirm the spontaneous tendency of the child to write large. It reflects the Italian school demands which are more flexible in Italy than in France.

However, the frequent changes of exercise books in elementary classes, as well as the disappearance of the spaces for the various zones of writing when the child is around the age of nine, seem to generate in Italy a more chaotic graphic development. The French child reaches, around the age of ten, a more stable graphomotor level. This fact has been checked during the course of the research mentioned before. The Italian child retains more jerky gestures and tremors, or letters running into each other.

On the spatial writing level it would seem that the Italian child must show a constant capacity to adapt, while the French child follows more rigid and established rules. Because there is no doubt that the overall elementary school life is much more demanding in France than in Italy, both in teaching and discipline, we must conclude that a constriction or graphic inhibition (small and narrow writing, for example) takes on much more relevance in Italy, and an exuberant full writing takes on a greater significance in France. So we can see the importance of knowing fully the starting point of the basic model.

In this chapter we have followed the development of the graphic gesture when it faces *space* – established by lines and margins – to accomplish a codified *form*: letter, stop, or accent. These are all observations which leave out any graphological interpretation.

Many interpretations of children's writing, from the beginnings of graphology to the present day, are abstracted from studies carried out on adult writing. It is therefore necessary to know in depth the basic method and then apply it in a special way to the study of writing during childhood. So we will first examine the other main European calligraphic models, then we will deepen our study of children's writing.

Figure 65
Elena: 1a elementary school in central Rome.
Despite a more rigid teacher than most, one can see the free and cheerful appearance
of a page from her exercise book

Chapter Eight

ENGLISH AND GERMAN
SCHOOL MODELS

I. GENERAL CONSIDERATIONS

We do not expect to supply a full explanation of the various European models in this short chapter. Instead the purpose is to identify quickly the major differences in foreign writings that we may encounter for analysis. We shall exclude the American Palmer model which is not much used in Europe. This method requires an in-depth study of North American cultural values.

Within a comparative frame of English, French, Italian, and German alphabetical letters, we show the major differences between letter forms, according to the school models (see Table 20). Some differences are immediately noticed. The initial stroke on the ovals is very obvious in three countries, but do not exist in the French model. The direct joining of a letter without the initial support can be traced back to the typically French psychological tendency of going directly to the essential. Seen from the same viewpoint, French writing places great value on sobriety. We also see that the beginning and closure of the oval to the left is noticeable only in Italian writing, as already mentioned in the previous chapter.

The script writing model

Script writing is taught in England, Switzerland, Luxemburg, and was also taught experimentally in France in a few middle schools after 1945. Already before the 1940s for special headings script was used in France in place of English style, because, according to Richard Berger [22], "*script* writing is considered more legible and better looking than *English* writing."

In comparison with typographic characters the lower-case script has simplified outlines "reduced to simple geometric forms: circles, semicircles, and vertical, horizontal, and diagonal lines. Only a few essential loops are kept (taken from *English* writing)" (Berger [22]).

One can see (Fig. 66) that in *script* the body of most letters is written within a square, the exceptions being *i*, *l*, and *t* that increase in height, *m* and *w* which are twice as wide than high, and *c*, *r*, and *s* which are written in a rectangle. In addition, the middle body height is identical to that of the upper and lower extensions. The loops of *f*, *g*, and *y* are formed by a semicircle also developed within a square.

When learning script, the letters are not connected. Today, script is not in itself a writing model, but reflects printed characters that the student can see every day.

Hulliger writing, created by a professor from Basel, has been adopted in Switzerland for writing in German (Fig. 66). Its principles have influenced other European teaching reforms: geometric letter base, downstrokes formed with precision.

II. THE ANGLO-SAXON WRITING MODEL

Anglo-Saxon writings that the graphologist may encounter are mostly British or North American. These handwritings come from two different school models: *Simple Modern Hand* and *Palmer*. Around 75% of Americans have used the Palmer model and 25% Simple Modern Hand; the latter is the model for most British people. As already mentioned we will not be dealing with the American Palmer model, except for some comparisons.

In Britain as well as the United States, there are also two other types of so-called "English writing": *Formal Italic Hand* and *Chancery Cursive*. Both are taught in special calligraphy courses, to the point that some people have two distinct styles of handwriting, according to the type of correspondence. One is the school model and the other is based on *calligraphy*. It is important that the graphologist is fully informed before interpreting a subject's writing.

Un agneau se désaltérait

En une heure nous arrivâmes à cette ville si re-
nommée. Elle est toute de marbre et elle est grande trois fois comme Paris. Toute la ville n'est

Figure 66(a) Model of *script* writing (from Berger [22])

Rot ist die Liebe, rot ist das Blut,
Rot ist der Satan in seiner Wut.

Der Hoffnung Grün erquicke dich,
Der Liebe Rot entzücke dich,
Der Treue Blau beglücke dich,

Figure 66(b) *Hulliger* writing model

Returning to the basic school model in Britain and Northern Ireland, we see a completely different graphic configuration to the Latin style. According to the graphologist Odile Ellison [90], the fact of living on an island, of having been explorers spreading their customs world-wide, and of being Protestant, has perhaps given the British a particular grounding which is reflected in their psychology and cultural habits, as well as in their writing models.

Simple Modern Hand

Simple Modern Hand, the current school model, developed from a *script* base, but with a slight inclination, and so the letters are formed within a parallelogram. The initial teaching model is without any connections between letters.

GENERAL GRAPHIC CHARACTERISTICS (Fig. 67)

Sobriety of graphic form and structure distinguishes the English model, which often creates a "stylized" appearance. From the psychological point of view this corresponds to the English mentality of self-control, which tends to hide one's own problems in order to project a "sublimated" external image (a term coined by the graphologist Renna Nezos [181]). The *precise stroke* also present in this model points to the sense of autonomy and independence of the British population. The general characteristics are summarized in Table 22.

TYPES OF CONNECTIONS

A few rules governing connection between letters are entirely specific to the English model and must be known by non-English graphologists to avoid giving the wrong judgement. We cite the main ones.

Angularity of the connecting diagonals

The diagonal strokes between letters or parts of letters, or some endings of letters, form an angle of 45°. This recurrent angularity gives a structured aspect to English writing.

ANGLO-SAXON WRITING MODEL

Spatial Aspects
- adequate but scarce whites – text is not compact
- structured blacks
- few margins either to the left or right
- little space between lines but lines are not tangled
- horizontal lines
- horizontal signature, placed on the right

Form and Signature
- simple capital letters, of typographic style
- upper and lower extensions without loops
- lower extensions do not come back over the line
- angular terminal profile of letters *r, v, w*
- letter *s*: *typographic* at the beginning of word or after a break; *calligraphic* if connected to previous letter
- filiform is rare
- simple signature, legible, same style as the text

Stroke
- precise; neat outlines

Connections
- connected, but absence of certain specific connections
- overconnected

Table 22

Absence of particular connections

There is no connection: between letters *r, t, v, w* and a following *e*; between *t* and a following *h*; between *x* and the following letter.

Given that the lower extensions do not come back over the line and remain open without loops, the connection between the lower extension of a letter and the following letter does not occur, with the sole exception of the letter *z* which can have a lower extension returning up to the line.

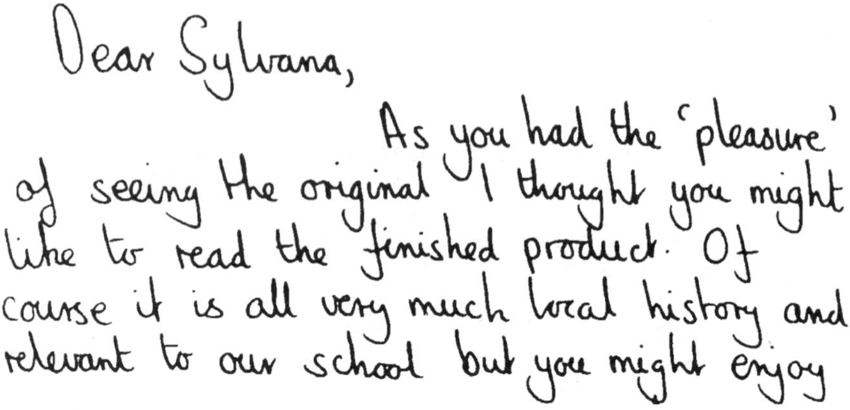

Dear Sylvana,

As you had the 'pleasure' of seeing the original I thought you might like to read the finished product. Of course it is all very much local history and relevant to our school but you might enjoy

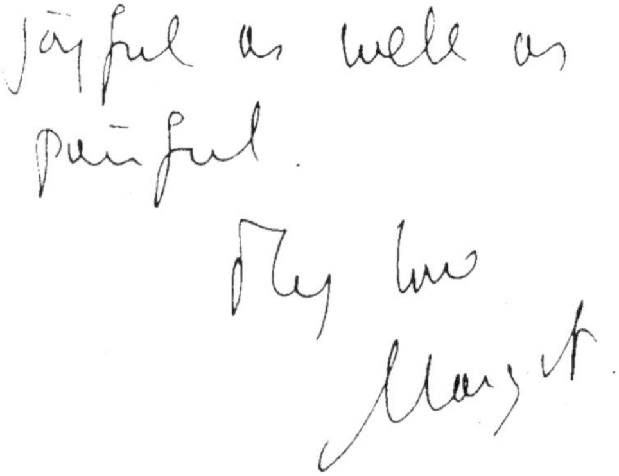

joyful as well as painful.

My love
Margit.

Figure 67
English writings:
(a) and (b) female;
(c) Laurence Olivier's writing

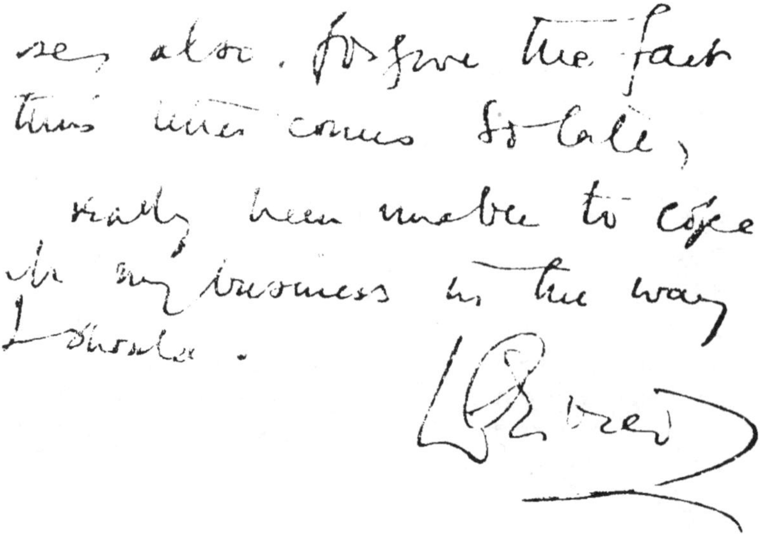

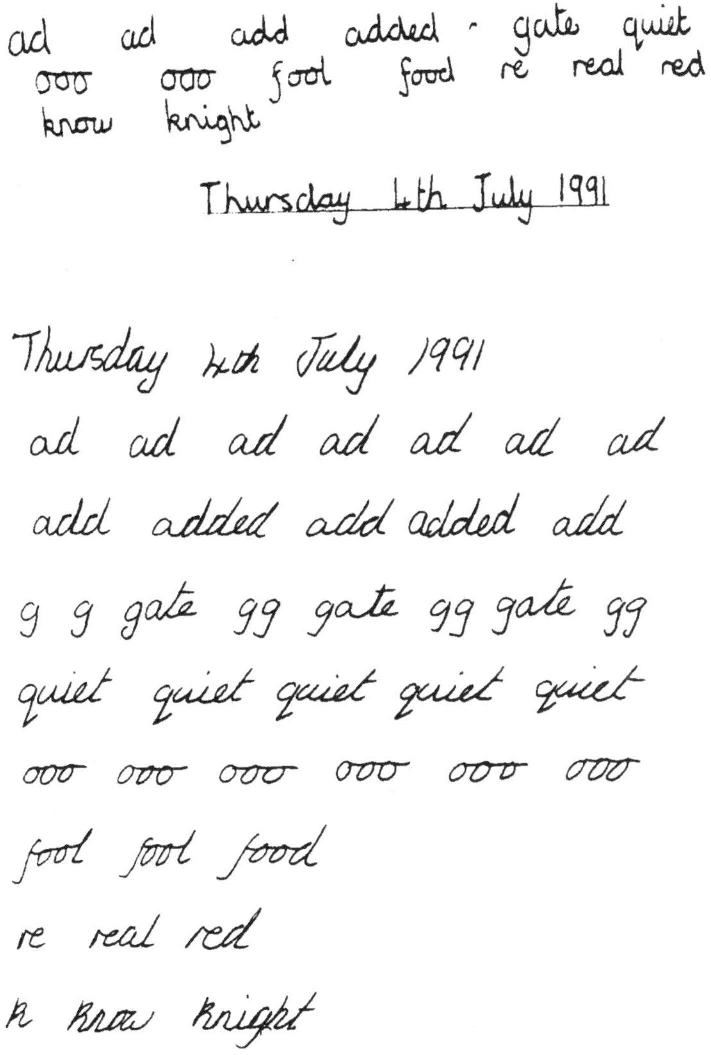

ad   ad   add   added - gate   quiet
ooo   ooo   fool   food   re   real   red
know   knight

Thursday 4th July 1991

Thursday 4th July 1991
ad ad ad ad ad ad ad
add added add added add
g g gate gg gate gg gate gg
quiet quiet quiet quiet quiet
ooo ooo ooo ooo ooo ooo
fool fool food
re real red
n know knight

Figure 68
English children's writing (reduced)

Given that the *b* and the *p* are formed in a typographic style, no connection with the following letter occurs, with the exception of "double letters", in which case the first is connected to the previous letter and the second to the following one.

Special type of connection

There are in addition other types of letter connections typical to the English or Irish model: for example the *t*-crossing is often connected to the following letter.

Overconnections (Fig. 27)

A typical characteristic of English writing, especially in fast and agitated writing, is the long connection of the final strokes of a word to the beginning of the following word:

- the word ending extends to start the next word;
- the *t*-crossing sometimes runs along the entire word and the space between the next one, and indeed sometimes beyond two words;
- the *y* ending shoots a prolonged extension from the lower zone to connect with the next word.

In these cases it is therefore the "movement" that prevails and the connections are in general able and flexible, expressing the ease of associated thought. All these hyperconnections are found in both sexes, and in all ages. They are prevalent in high society, in the writing of artists, politicians, lawyers, with a creative connotation. And even if they can show a paradoxical spirit, they do not signify the hyperlogic of a pathological type.

THE ENGLISH "I"

"The way in which the unique capital letter 'I' is written reveals the *Self/ Ego* of the person, the image of oneself and the sense of the subject's self-esteem. It also supplies indications of the way in which he wants to be seen by others", says Odile Ellison [90], who also conveys other interpretations of an English author concerning the symbolism of the "I", formed from a vertical axis and two horizontal strokes which close it.

According to this symbolism the stroke placed on the top represents the "father" and the lower one the "mother", the earth. According to whether or not the vertical is connected with these segments, problems relating to identification can be deduced.

III. THE GERMAN SCHOOL MODEL

With some variations, the German school model extends to the following other countries: Austria, German-speaking Switzerland, Liechtenstein, Luxemburg. In the history of Germany the lack of unity has favoured local development, with a conflict between central power and the regions. Modern Germany proper, as a Federal Republic, is comprised of *Länder* (largely self-governing regions) and the central federal organs of power. This decentralization implies a hierarchical structure, with decisions being taken at every level.

With the reunification of Germany in 1990, Berlin once again became the seat of the central government and parliament, which is now increasing its powers at the expense of the regions. However, each *Land* has its own authority regarding civil and criminal jurisdiction, public works, and police, and in particular has total autonomy in the running of education and cultural affairs.

The schools

The teaching of education is managed by the *Länder* but all examinations are valid throughout the whole country. There is no lay teaching and no division between State and Church. Catholic or Protestant religious teaching is mandatory up to the age of 14. There are few private schools and they are usually residential and very expensive.

Since 1968 schools have been arranged into Kindergarten, from 3 to 6 years, private, not compulsory, paid according to income, and Elementary school, from 4/6 to 10 years, only attended in the morning. Many subjects are taught, and in each class there is one main teacher (class teacher) and individual teachers for each subject.

At the beginning of school there are six weeks of preparatory time using sound games with rhymes and syllables, visual games like cutting words, uniting them or finding the same letters in different forms. Children play at learning typing or printing. The teacher can freely decide the reading method but in general the synthetic global system is used. At the end of elementary school, future educational direction is based on the teacher's evaluation in collaboration with the parents.

Socio-psychological aspect

Some spatial-temporal German perceptions differ from Latin ones. The German time system is much more planned, closed, and inflexible than the Latin, everything is managed rigorously and goals are not rushed. Spatial perception is much more closed. In France for example office doors are kept open whereas in Germany they are shut. This is reflected also in the retail market, where the aim is accumulation: the object must last and be of good quality. The German shopper buys more through anxiety for security than for pure pleasure.

In working and managerial life there is a weakness in grasping quickly new ideas and prospects. Against the spontaneous Latin *feeling* the German sets precise and full technical information. The German does not accept intrusion in an established space-time environment and loses ability to extrapolate, but gains in long-term security. Products are marketed on lasting quality, and with this type of perspective, research and development demands high investment. Consequently, even if further education diplomas are not numerous, middle-level technical diplomas abound.

Between the ages of 15 and 18 60% of young people follow a professional foundation course financed by companies with contributions from federal subsidies, and only 40% follow full-time education. The training of the young focuses therefore on professional apprenticeship and students are already part of the managerial life, future workers tutored by skilled operatives. Personnel representatives take part in companies' strategic decision-making.

School model

At the moment the school model is similar to the Latin model, although it still feels slightly "Gothic", which for a long time has characterized the German writing style. Table 23 gathers the principal characteristics of this model and Fig. 69 shows some children's writing.

GERMAN SCHOOL MODEL

Spatial aspects
- small margins either left or right
- little interline space, but it is not compacted

Form and Signature
- important middle zone
- simple capital letters
- a few script forms: *f, m, n, r, s, t*
- often the letter h is badly shaped
- filiform is rare
- general rhythm
- simple signature, typographic in style

Stroke
- precise

Connections
- connected, but absence of certain specific connections
- overconnected

Table 23

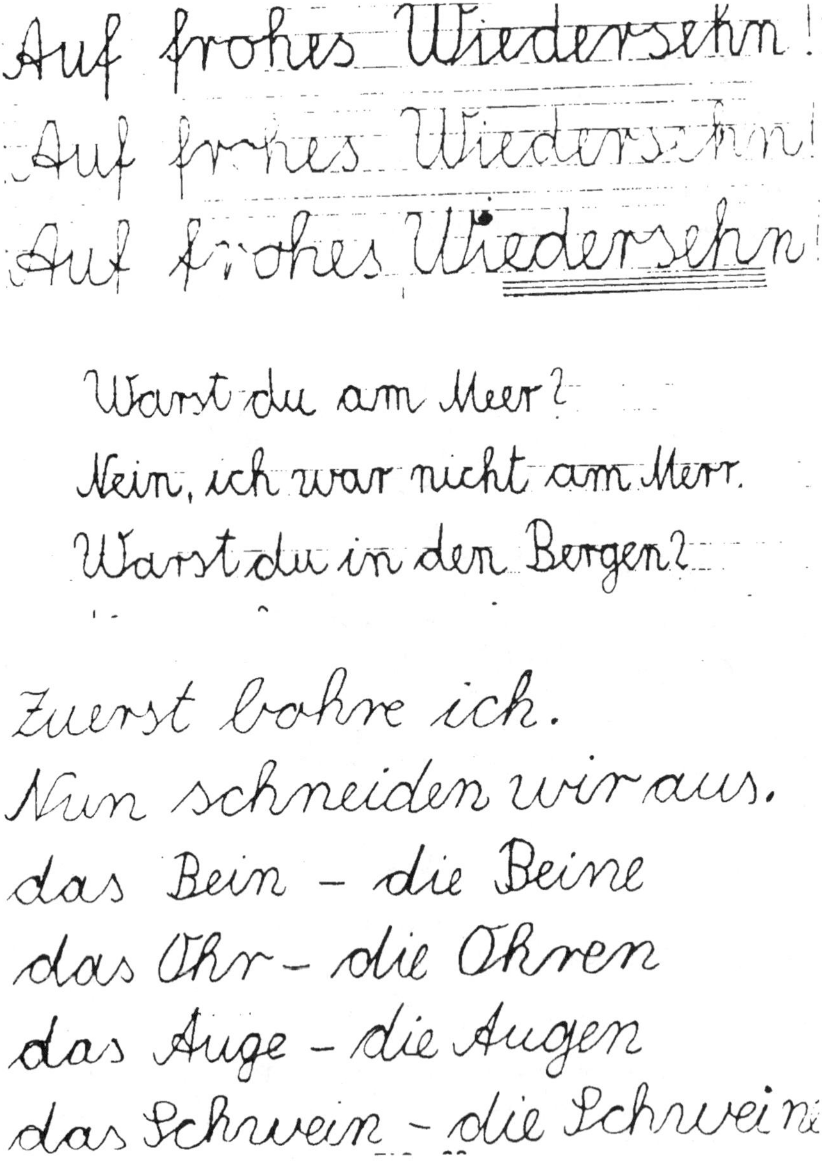

Auf frohes Wiedersehn!
Auf frohes Wiedersehn!
Auf frohes Wiedersehn!

Warst du am Meer?
Nein, ich war nicht am Meer.
Warst du in den Bergen?

Zuerst bohre ich.
Nun schneiden wir aus.
das Bein – die Beine
das Ohr – die Ohren
das Auge – die Augen
das Schwein – die Schweine

Figure 69
German children's writing

Modern Gothic style (Fig. 70)

Even though it has almost disappeared, the German Gothic style has certainly given a stamp to the German model, not least in the collective subconscious. Regular, angular, and rightward slanted, Gothic writing seems to offer, at first sight, a profile of the typical nineteenth-century German. A more detailed comparative examination reveals clear differences, but it does require a certain amount of knowledge of such writing.

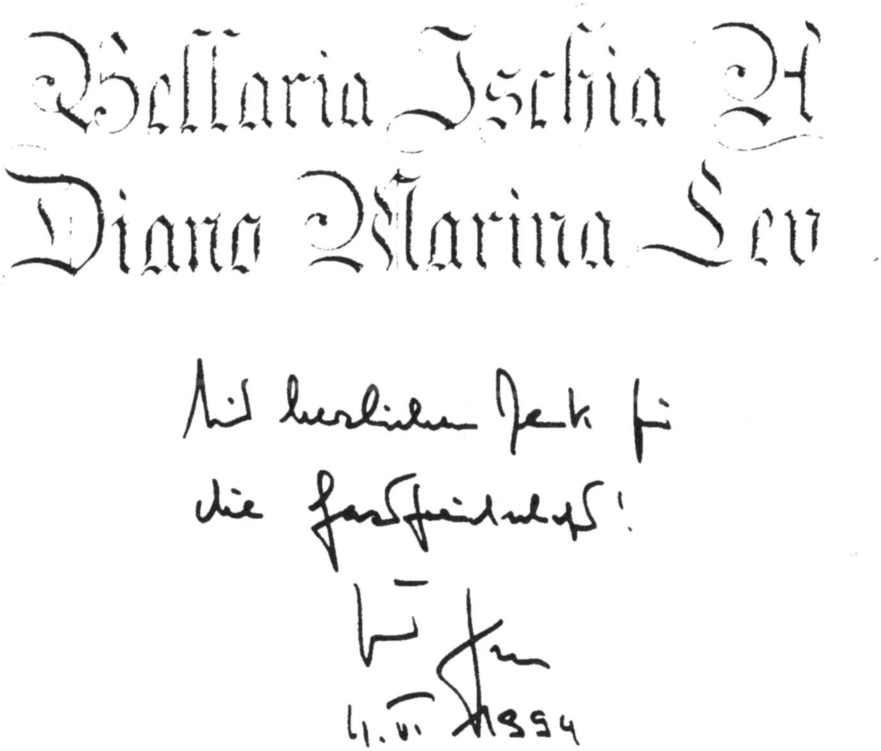

Figure 70
(a) Modern Gothic model
(b) Helmut Kohl (from *Angewandte Graphologie und Persönlichkeits-Diagnostik*, 1994)

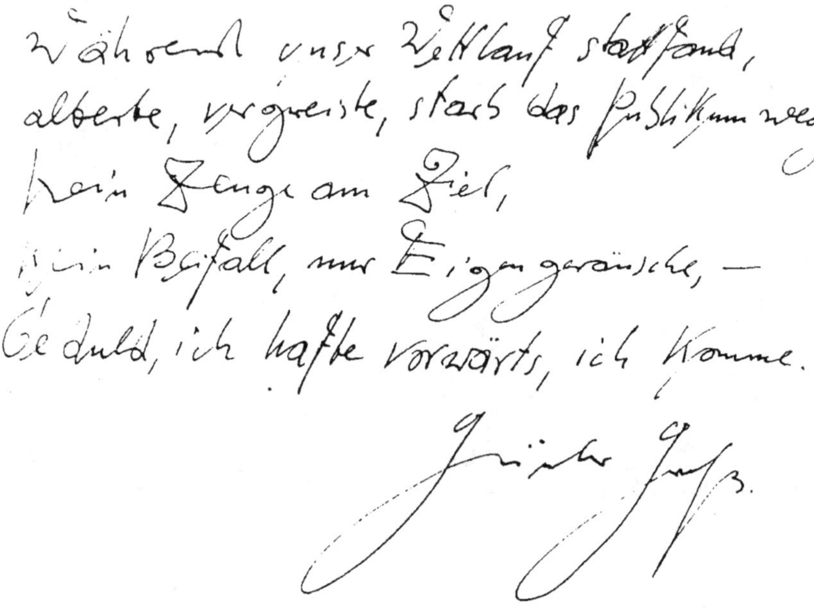

Während unser Wettlauf stattfand,
alberte, vergreiste, starb das Publikum weg
kein Zeuge am Ziel,
kein Beifall, nur Eigengeräusche, —
Geduld, ich hafte vorwärts, ich komme.

Günther Grass.

Figure 70
(c) Günther Grass

Chapter Nine

EVOLUTION OF WRITING AT ELEMENTARY SCHOOL

With this chapter we return more specifically to the schooling in Latin countries, although the basics of motor and graphic evolution are found in every writing model. Children beginning to write respond simultaneously to differing demands and must consequently: master their own gesture to achieve a stroke, a form; place their own gesture in a determined space; establish the relation and succession of various strokes to compose a word; and then structure a line and the spacing between the lines.

Writing instruments used today such as biro, fountain pen, or felt-tip allow the child a greater ease in controlling writing, and at the same time make it personal in comparison to times when nibs dipped into an inkwell were used. Until the 1950s in fact, little research focused on children's handwriting, which seemed in the main to have a uniform and dry aspect. Crépieux-Jamin himself considered this writing *unorganized*, and considered that it reflected only instability and ignorance. He had however observed that no child's writing was like another's and that all children confronted the act of writing with their own reactions according to their attention span, care, motor ability, memory, and capacity for abstraction. He regarded as "nonsense" the excessive variations in letter height found in children's writing after the age of eight and considered it a sign of mental deficiency. Thanks to scientific research on dyslexia and dysgraphia today such interpretations are no longer accepted.

Research by J. de Ajuriaguerra and his team on *graphometric scales* has established the existence of three major phases in the growth of writing from the earliest learning stage up to adulthood: *precalligraphic, calligraphic,* and *postcalligraphic*. The *calligraphic* phase represents the goal of learning in conformity with the model, and is generally reached fully around 11 years, after which, notwithstanding adolescent upheavals, a writing keeps an unalterable individuality.

But even before reaching the identification of these three phases, the researchers examined all additional factors contributing to the development of the *graphic act*, which we briefly illustrate now.

I. FACTORS FOR THE EVOLUTION OF WRITING

There are two determinant factors for the evolution of writing: *practice* and *motor development*.

Practice

Practice starts at the scribbling stage and progresses to the simulation of writing and finally to real writing, and perfects itself with the habit of writing in maturity. Up to around the age of six graphic gestures and play are synonymous, and the stroke is freely placed on the surface, but things alter radically at the start of school, where the *graphic act* undergoes a series of constrictions intended to regulate its spontaneity.

These principally involve, on the technical side, a compulsory choice of writing surface and instrument, to be held in a particular way. On the postural and therefore psychological side, sitting still for long periods is expected, often with the paper at an incline, with the consequent positions of body, shoulders, elbows, hands, and fingers, in other words a mixture of positions that for some children are extremely difficult. Lastly, at the intellectual level is also imposed a symbolic system, a writing model (implicitly an *ideal writing*, easily acceptable by some but an unreachable target for others), a respect for order and legibility in exercise books, and a respect for spelling which, especially in France, may represent an anxiety factor.

Motor development

Motor control evolves with practice but it demands a complex neurophysical maturity, and more specifically as explained by Ajuriaguerra depends on: the maturation of the nervous system reinforced by motor exercise; general psychomotor development allowing coordinated movement; motor development of the hands and fingers.

Together with exercise and motor maturity, writing growth is also influenced by the child's development, not only at the intellectual level but also on the social and emotional level. We shall see how much these latter aspects may often be determinant factors in attaining simple and harmonious graphic performance. The graphologist who analyses a child's writing must bear in mind this sentence by Ajuriaguerra: "The whole writing growth between 6 and 12 years reflects the dynamic contradictions between growth factors which inculcate its movement, and constrictions which direct, channel, guide it, and sometimes push in the wrong way."

So the graphologist will not be content with only technical observation of the moment, but in the overall picture will bear in mind the scholastic as well as the psychological aspects which have influenced graphomotor development. The analysis will be therefore more sensitive and more appropriate to each case.

The evolution of children's writing at school, where the child is subjected to intensive daily application, is divided into three phases, now universally accepted.

II. THE THREE PHASES OF WRITING EVOLUTION

Precalligraphic phase (Figs 71-3)

This phase lasts from around five to eight years old. The child controls strokes poorly and the writing shows a lack of outline firmness, with bent and trembling downstrokes and angular and messy curves and ovals. The inability to achieve a flexible cursive flow produces wrong or awkward joins between letters or parts of letters, and continuous variation in slant and pressure. Also the child cannot place the writing into the spatial logic of a page, and one sees words which dance on the line and lines which veer in many directions.

Within these parameters we notice however how two children beginning the first class of elementary school – of average intelligence and with no neurophysical disturbance – can react in such different ways to the act of writing and in their socio-emotional adaptability to school life (Figs 72-3).

Calligraphic phase (Figs 74–5)

In this phase, around eight to nine years of age, writing acquires flexibility, gestural awkwardness disappears, and already we can notice significant individual differences. Principal graphic characteristics are better spatial control (margins and alignment), a more homogeneous and flexible stroke, some easy connections between letters, and also a few simplifications.

According to the French school the period around 10 years of age is considered the *golden age* of writing. The schoolchild has mastered the rules and makes effective but not rigid application of them. Writing reflects a stage of balance and adjustment to norms. This phase in Italy seems much more volatile, and the "sensible" French manner around 10 years old is not often found, probably because of the changes in line model as well as less discipline in the Italian schools. We will return to this subject in the next chapter, on *graphometry*.

Above all, in every country the *calligraphic phase* demonstrates the ability to master the cursive movement through an easy and flexible gestural manner, after having absorbed the given basic model. If the principal writing characteristics in this phase do not show up, causes must be looked for: *dysgraphia*, *dyslexia*, *mental deficiency*? It is not enough to focus on the signs of a simple lack of application but on signs that reveal a specific disturbance, and this study requires a great deal of training and specific preparation by the graphologist.

Writing in this *calligraphic phase*, says Ajuriaguerra, "shows a certain graphic mastery; it has adapted to a certain level of demand and shows a determined level of evolution." When the analysis of an adolescent and post-adolescent writing is made, it will therefore be very useful to take into consideration the writing level previously achieved, to know how the writing has undergone changes, and which ones.

Hardly has this balance at the calligraphic phase been reached, when pre-adolescence brings new problems. The child enters middle school with the difficulties associated with a change of school, of teachers, and often of friends. All of this contributes to an upset in writing, which becomes an important psychological pointer of this particular period. Ajuriaguerra confirms that between 12 and 16 years "crisis is the general rule in subjects who stay at school."

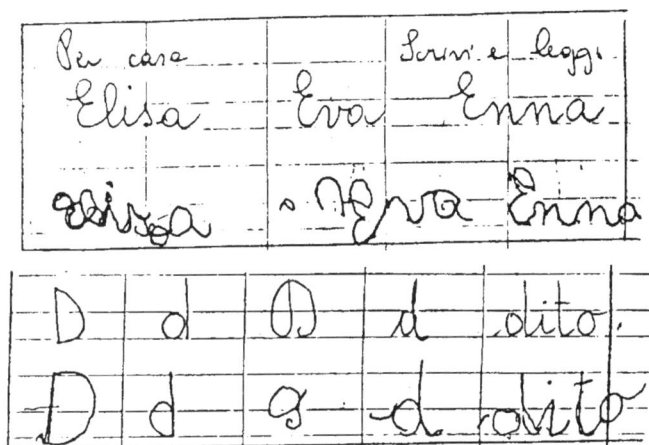

Figure 71
Sofia – 1a elementary experimental school, 1987. Precalligraphic phase.
Above, at 5 years 9 months: learning various types of writing. There is no teaching of how letters should be traced.
Below, at 6 years 5 months: she forms ovals in the opposite way to normal, in other words clockwise. Her ample stroke is somewhat untidy and impulsive, however some letters show by contrast a significant graphico-ideative dexterity (*a* in *dettato*, *g* in *Giugno*). A certain restlessness emerges, incompatible with the school rhythm, despite the intellectual vivacity.

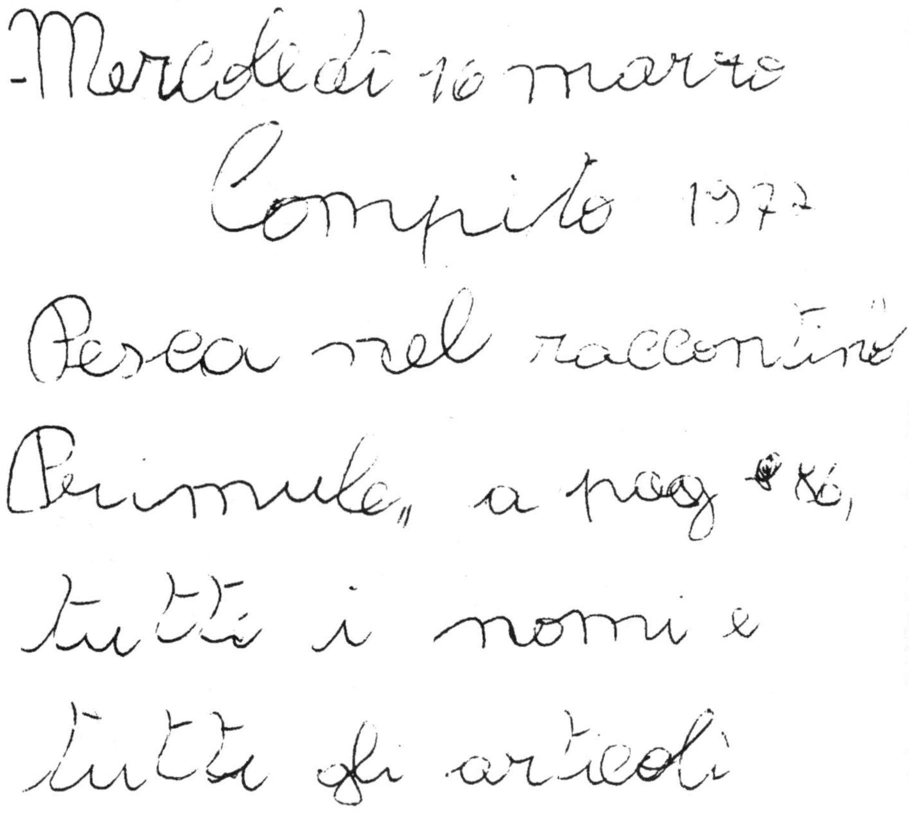

Figure 72
Elena – 7 years old, 1a elementary school. Precalligraphic phase.
The girl presents a normal profile for her age. She does not have particular motor difficulties. There are bent downstrokes, though the gesture is controlled and supple (see the word *tutti*), the long downstrokes of the *M* are slightly shaky, and some curves are still flattened (see the *m* in *nomi*). Some letter connections are not well formed (in *tutti* and between *rc* of *Mercoledì*), others are very comfortable especially in joining *o* to the following letter (-*coledì, continuo, nomi*). The slant is not very stable, it oscillates around the vertical, and the pressure is not always even, sometimes it becomes weaker (*raccontino*). There is no difficulty in following the line but there are oscillations in certain letters of words. Elena is well adapted to her environment.

Figure 73
Fabrizio – 7 years old, 1a elementary school, left-handed. Precalligraphic phase.
The boy shows at first glance a typical profile of graphomotor difficulties. He is unable to
control the placing of writing in a space, the size of letters, or the flexibility of connection
between the letters. This is a case of *dysgraphia*. In this sensitive and vulnerable child
difficulties of motor ability and of adaptability to school run round in a vicious circle.

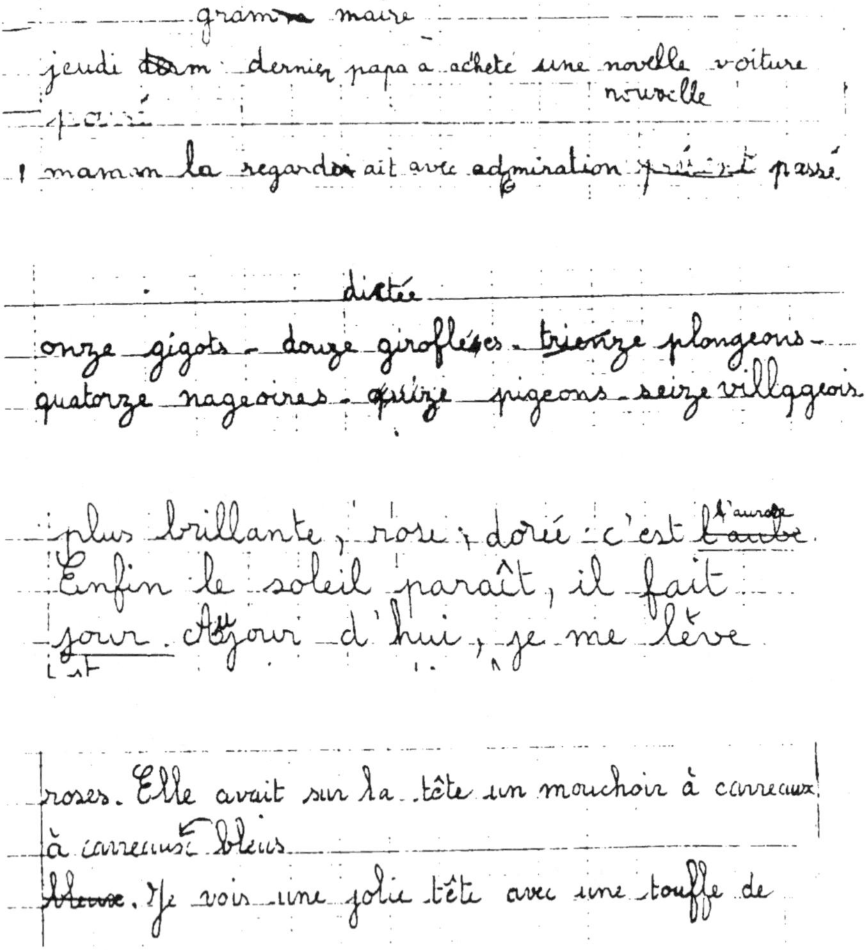

grammaire

jeudi derm dernier papa à acheté une nouvelle voiture
nouvelle

maman la regardait avec admiration passé passé

dictée

onze gigots - douze giroflées - treize plongeons -
quatorze nageoires - quinze pigeons - seize villageois.

plus brillante, rose, doré : c'est l'aurore
Enfin le soleil paraît, il fait
jour. Aujourd'hui, je me lève

roses. Elle avait sur la tête un mouchoir à carreaux
à carreaux bleus
bleus. Je vois une jolie tête avec une touffe de

Figure 74
Phases of writing development. Nathalie
(a) 7 years 6 months, 2a elementary school, precalligraphic phase
(b) 8 years 5 months, 3a elementary school, beginning of calligraphic phase
(c) 9 years 4 months, 4a elementary school, September
(d) 10 years, 4a elementary school, June, calligraphic phase
In (c) one can see a flexible and comfortable gesture along with a certain fullness of form. In (d) a greater inhibition appears, with the first typical pubescent twisted extensions. One needs to check that they are not imitated from another pupil, but when they are authentic they show a certain anxiety and insecurity, well seen in the tightening of the loops of *l*, *f*, and *e*.

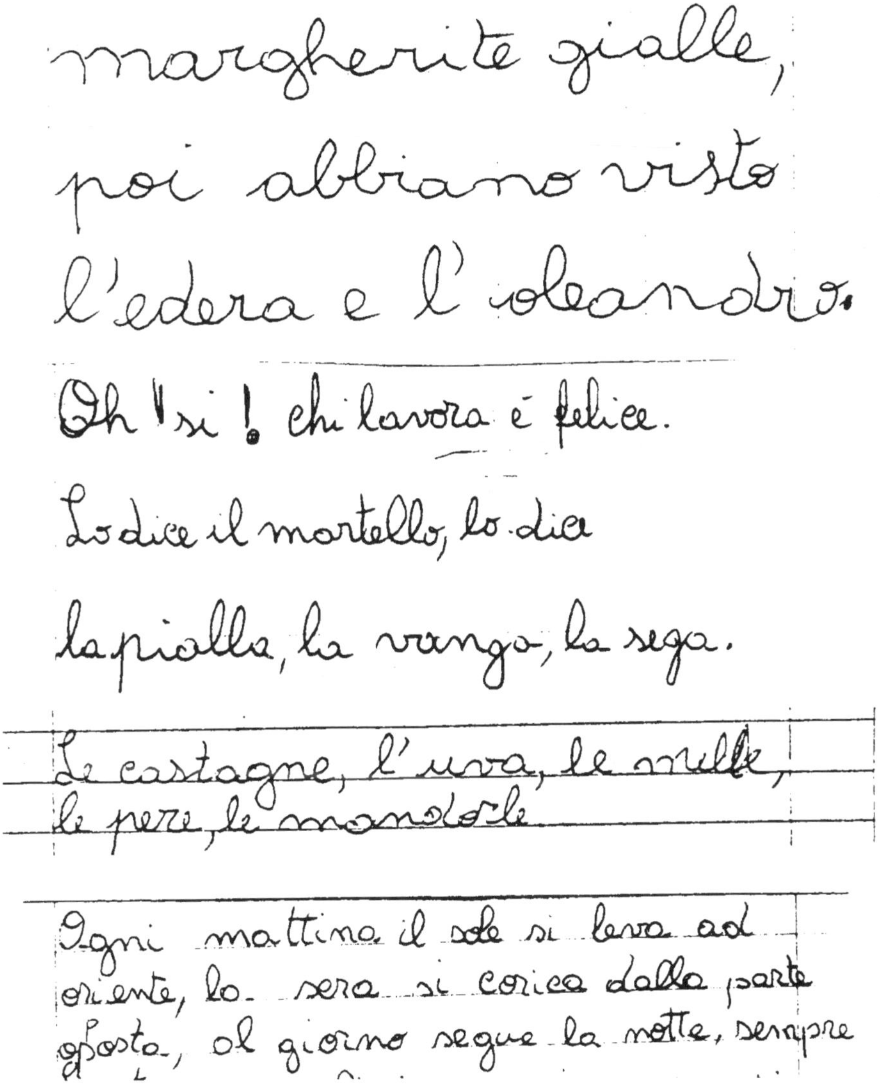

margherite gialle,

poi abbiano visto

l'edera e l' oleandro.

Oh ! si ! chi lavora è felice.

Lo dice il martello, lo dia

la pialla, la vanga, la sega.

Le castagne, l' uva, le mele,
le pere, le mandorle

Ogni mattina il sole si leva ad
oriente, la sera si corica dalla parte
opposta, ol giorno segue la notte, sempre

Figure 75

Phases of writing development. Elena

(a) 7 years 6 months, 2a elementary school, precalligraphic phase
(b) 8 years 4 months, 3a elementary school, beginning of calligraphic phase
(c) 8 years 9 months, 4a elementary school, September
(d) 9 years 8 months, 5a elementary school, September

Compare this with Nathalie at the same age: differences in line direction and line spacing. Observe Elena's evolution from year 1 of elementary school (Fig. 72).

Postcalligraphic phase

This phase stretches from adolescence to adulthood. It is characterized by flexibility, mastery of space, ease and individuality of connections, and simplification of forms. Cultural factors unique to each country appear, which we have covered in earlier chapters. This phase will not be illustrated here as it will be treated again in Chapter Eleven concerning pre-adolescence and adolescence.

III. THE FOUR TYPES OF CHILDREN'S WRITING COMPONENTS

Ajuriaguerra identified four types of components of children's writing, based on graphometric study and observation of the phases in the growth of writing. These components are not limited solely to items on the graphometric scales –which are indications of the growth of writing and diminish with age – but they include all aspects of writing, for example *pressure* which does not present an evolution in growth, but is an individual variable.

Components of motor incapacity

These witness the difficulties in sustaining and guiding the graphic instrument in an adequate way to coordinate the cursive movement. The following graphic aspects can be grouped together in this category:

- lack of firmness of outline: curving or trembling verticals, flattened curves;
- difficulties in gesture coordination: soldering, false connections, jerks, and mingling letters;
- difficulties of structuring of space: wandering lines, irregular line spaces.

Components of effort

Show the tense and subjected attitude of the child in front of schoolwork. The continuous effort leads to muscular fatigue, then symptoms similar to motor incapacity, for example *tremors*, though the reason is different. If these components are of sufficient strength, they generate an anxiety that could lead to rejection of school. In addition they show slowness or perfectionism and consequently a slower assimilation. Revealing graphic aspects could be:

- the *squashed* stroke seen in the flattening of ovals in the middle zone;
- (stopping and) restarting, retouching;
- heavy pressure, tremors;
- rigidity of page layout, direction of lines, slanting of letters;
- perfection of forms.

Components of economy

These tend to disregard precision and diligence whether graphic or psychological. They reveal a conflictual state of the child who chooses a defence mechanism to avoid difficulties and argument. This is not a solution approved by educational authorities and usually generates other problems. These components mostly concern form:

- unfinished letters, atrophied or badly formed through carelessness; badly closed ovals;
- scarce fullness of first and last letters of words:
- development of extensions and loops.

Calligraphic components

Are those acquired in the *calligraphic phase* and presume that the three previous component types have been experienced and are under control. In practice the child masters the writing instrument, arranges space logically, and appears comfortable, flexible, homogeneous, and precise in graphic stroke, having acquired the sequences of muscular synergy necessary for cursive movement. In addition there are already certain aspects of a personalized writing style, and in particular the choice of forms with some adapted simplifications, without negligence.

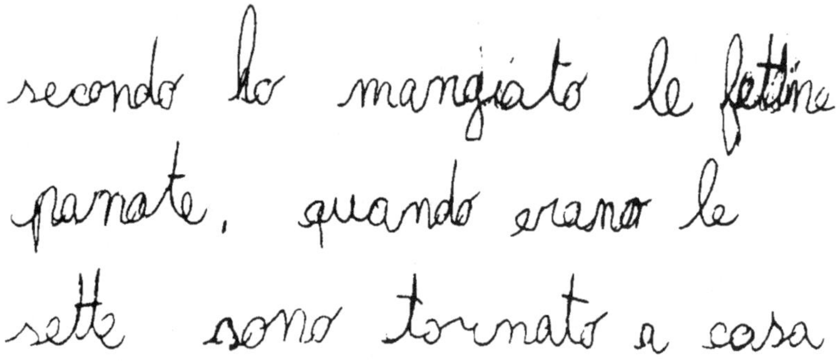

Figure 76
Children's writing components
Mauro –3a elementary school: *components of motor incapacity* (flattened curves) and *components of effort* (very heavy pressure, restarting, retouching)

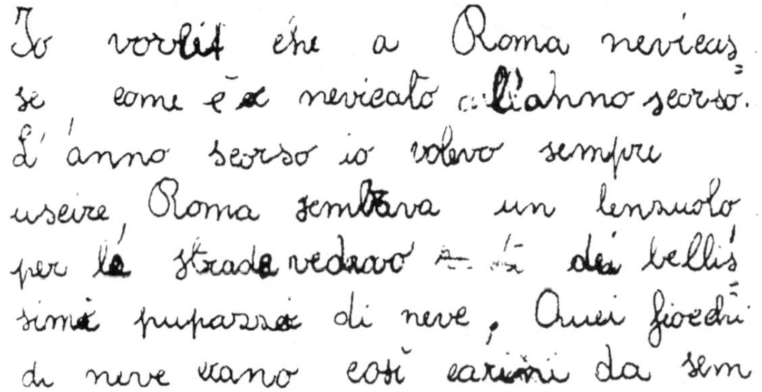

Figure 77
Children's writing components
Lisa – 9 years 3 months, 4a elementary school: *components of effort* (heavy pressure, retouching, crossing out, restarting). The anxiety level is high; when it lowers, the girl presents a much more fluid writing and her schoolwork improves.

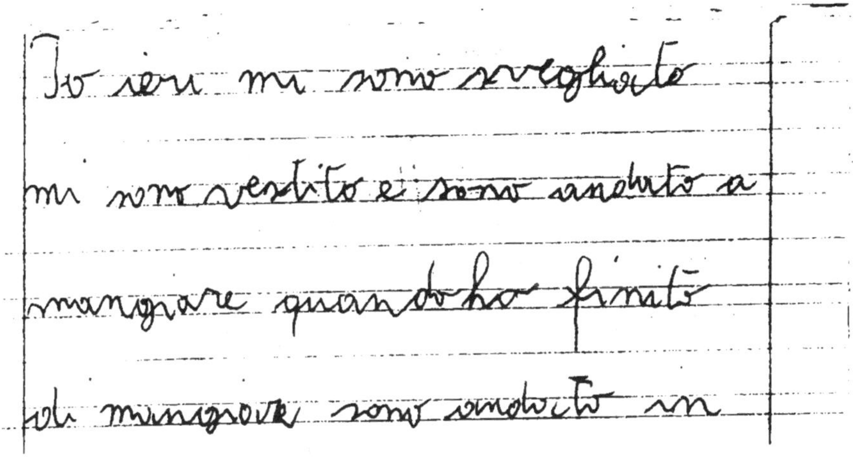

Figure 78
Children's writing components

Dario – 9 years, 3a elementary school: *components of economy* (badly closed ovals, atrophied
  g, high dots on *i*, imprecisions, flying *t*-crossings. The boy tends to shirk duty,
  but intuitively knows how to get through.

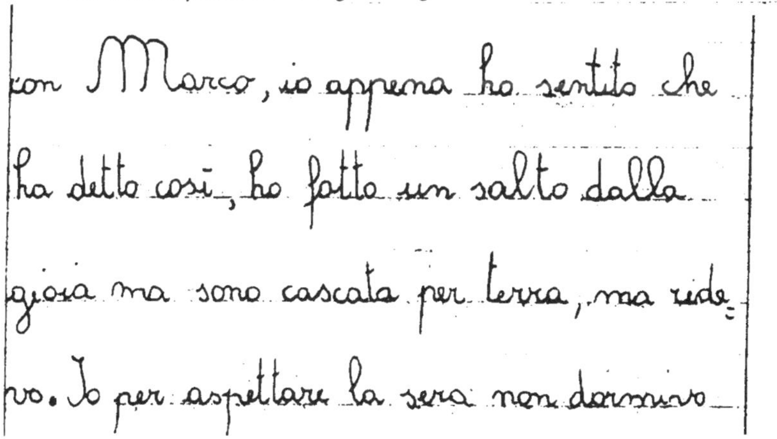

Figure 79
Children's writing components

Claudia – 9 years 3 months, 4a elementary school. Total mastery of *calligraphic components*.
  The following year in 5a elementary school her writing will no doubt become
  more individual, but for now capital letters, *p*, and the *t*-crossings are still school
  type.

IV. APPLICATION OF
CRÉPIEUX-JAMIN'S CATEGORIES

It has become clear over the previous sections that the difficulties met by the child while controlling the writing instrument and accomplishing the coordination and progression of the outline in a given space, occur mainly in the Jaminian categories *management of space, direction*, and *continuity*. The signs related to these categories are therefore of special value for the interpretation of children's writing.

Management of space

The child is obviously influenced by the schoolbook models with their margins, lines, and interlines. If the child writes on unlined paper, he is practically lost in space and as a rule does not leave margins at the top or to the left. It is necessary therefore to look at the exercise books as well as spontaneous writing on unlined paper. On the other hand a margin on the left needs interpretation. One can also take into account the child's tendency to space lines and words or to invade space, filling it in a compact, untidy way, or systemically rigid.

Direction

As a result of difficulties for the child to direct the stroke in space it is clear that the direction of the line will show uncertainty and fluctuations. A wavy line must not therefore be interpreted, because it corresponds to the usual childish awkward writing outline. But exceptional cases can be interpreted, for example a rigid line which reveals tension and probably a block in the child's free expression. Particular attention should be paid to *descending* writing (see Chapter Ten).

Continuity

It must be interpreted according to the writing phase corresponding to the subject's age; then, excluding graphomotor difficulties normal in the evolutionary phases, one will be able to observe a certain graphomotor *style*. Such style corresponds to the excessive presence of components of motor incapacity, or else of economy of effort. Lastly the fluidity or restriction of the stroke will be evaluated according to graphometric parameters.

In summary, when motor difficulties disappear and firmness of outline is gained as well as acceleration, not only as general speed but, according to Ajuriaguerra, as "progressive differentiation of graphic *rhythm*, in the most exact sense of the word", then writing develops towards individuality even before prepubescent troubles begin to upset the balance reached around the age of 11. "The entire history of writing growth is that of the building of true and individual *spatio-temporal graphic structures*."

With this final statement Ajuriaguerra, who was not a graphologist but an experimental psychologist, confirms for us that writing is a spatio-temporal activity generating its own *rhythm*. The child of 10 to 11 years old has acquired graphomotor control together with an individual rhythm, and so begins secondary school. We shall now examine the graphometric research associated with Ajuriaguerra.

Chapter Ten

GRAPHOMETRY AND
THE EVOLUTION OF WRITING

We now consider the important scientific research conducted by the psychiatrist J. de Ajuriaguerra, who, continuing Hélène de Gobineau's studies, undertook an enormous statistical study without any graphological preconceptions, based solely on the observation of writing [4]. Although he worked with an entire team, his name is the one now associated with graphometric studies and we speak of Ajuriaguerra's *graphometry*. More recently Jacqueline Peugeot [199] added her own original contribution to Ajuriaguerra's work, after years of research in a medical-psychological-teaching environment.

Ajuriaguerra's team established an inventory of writing aspects which define the *early development of writing*, by ascertaining that "the act of writing is a motor action and the gesture is therefore the result of such an act", a very simple as well as basic principle. The purpose of researchers has therefore been to perfect a *scale* of graphic components to account for the *growth* of writing within its framework of freedom and constriction. These components were drawn solely from analytical observation of children's handwriting, without any *a priori* criteria linked to "quality" of writing.

The opportunity of having at one's disposal a laboratory of experimental psychology with a team of researchers for many years, has allowed the development of a vast statistical study, which we now summarize.

I. THE BASIS OF AJURIAGUERRA'S GRAPHOMETRY

The sample of study

Researchers drew from a random sample of 700 children in French elementary schools, eliminating only extremely anomalous cases, with a roughly equal number of boys and girls at every class level. They were then grouped together in six-month age bands from 6 to 11 years old. The sample included different types of school (private/selective, state/normal) each divided into three educational levels.

The chosen candidates were given a writing test under the same conditions.

Calculation of the graphometric scales

The researchers identified which writing characteristics always present in children tended to disappear with age and were statistically absent in adult writing. They therefore selected those components which by their progressive disappearance reveal writing evolution, the *graphomotor level* reached, in other words the *genesis* of writing.

In all, 30 *components* of children's writing, called *items*, that tend to diminish with age were taken into consideration. They were grouped on a scale called *scale E* (E for "*enfant*", in French) and we shall keep the same letter. Components were also divided into two *sub-scales* according to how they provide information mainly on difficulties of shaping *forms* (items *EF*) or on *motor* difficulties (items *EM*). There are 14 items of *form EF* (F1 to F14) and 16 *motor* items *EM* (M15 to M30) (see Table 24).

The graphologist must be well trained to evaluate the presence or not of the items and above all to quantify them appropriately. Following Ajuriaguerra, each item can be evaluated on a three-point system: 1 for an overwhelming presence of the item according to established criteria; 0.5 for the simple presence; 0 for its absence. 0 represents therefore a sign of writing evolution, whereas 1 shows the heavy presence of a children's component.

The system of weighting

Having established the point for each item's presence, we must weight it according to its degree of persistence over the time considered by the scale, that is between 6 and 11 years of age. It is easy to see that a children's component still present, for example, in 76% of cases at 11 years of age (see item M26: *fluctuating lines*) has less significance for writing evolution than a component only present in 4% of cases at 11 years (see item M21: *tremors*). *Tremors* therefore tell us much more on the *graphomotor level* reached, or better still *not* reached.

The *index of weighting* is calculated as follows. For each item, Ajuriaguerra indicated its frequency by percentage at every age for boys, girls, and the combined total. A calculation can then be made of the difference between the sums of the frequencies at the extremes of the age range, that is:

(frequency at 6 years + frequency at 7) – (frequency at 10 years + frequency at 11)

In this way a certain *index* is obtained on the basis of which the *weighting coefficient* is established: if the index is higher than 80, the coefficient is 3; between 40 and 79, the coefficient is 2; less than 39, the coefficient is 1. In Table 24 the numbers to the right of each item represent the coefficient of weighting by which the points attributed to the item must be multiplied.

Therefore items with a weighting coefficient of 1 are items of *weak discriminatory genetic force*, given that they are present with little difference at every age. Those with coefficient 2 are said to be of *average discriminatory genetic force*, while those of coefficient 3 have *maximum discriminatory genetic force*, indicating that with age they should disappear, so if they are still present they carry a heavy weight in the diagnosis of writing evolution.

Here are a few examples:

Item **F2** (*plump* writing) is present in 91% of cases at 6 years, and 81% at 7 years; it is still present in 84% of cases at 10 years, and 70% at 11 years. The calculation for the *index* is:

$$(91 + 81) - (84 + 70) = 172 - 154 = 18$$

The index of 18 corresponds to a weighting coefficient of 1, and therefore with *weak discriminatory genetic force*. Its presence, in effect, does not show great differences between the various ages.

Item **F4** (*large* writing) is present in 87% of cases at 6 years, and 73% at 7 years, and in 54% of cases at 10 years, and 42% at 11 years. The calculation is as follows:

$$(87 + 73) - (54 + 42) = 160 - 96 = 64$$

The index of 64 corresponds to a weighting coefficient of 2, and therefore an *average discriminatory genetic force*. Still often present at 11 years, it does however diminish greatly in comparison to F2, for example.

Item **M21** (*tremors*) is present in 81% of cases at 6 years, and 58% at 7 years, whereas it is present in only 11% of cases at 10 years, and 4% at 11 years. The calculation is therefore:

$$(81 + 58) - (11 + 4) = 139 - 15 = 124$$

The index of 124 corresponds to a weighting coefficient of 3, therefore a *maximum discriminatory genetic power*. In effect, it tends to disappear by the age of 11, so its persistence will therefore be particularly significant.

Determination of graphomotor age

Having established the point for each item and multiplying it by its weighting coefficient, the total E ($EF + EM$) and the ratio $EF : EM$ is also determined. Each overall total must then be compared with those corresponding to the age *norms*. It is therefore essential to know the exact age of the child, to the month. The *graphomotor age* of the subject will correspond to the age at which the total E is found on this scale.

The methodology appears complex, but in reality it is above all detailed and requires time and attention. To absorb it, it is advisable to practice it according to the established criteria. The comparison has only a *statistical* value, afterwards one must evaluate the reasons why the age norms may not have been followed and understand which types of children's components influence a possible higher or lower level in comparison to the norms.

GRAPHOMETRIC SCALE FOR CHILDREN (6–11 YEARS)

Name	Sex	Class	Left-handed
Date of birth	Age	School	Other
Exam date	EF norms	EM	EF/EM > 0.75

F1	writing on the surface	2	M15	lower extensions in stages	3
F2	plump writing	1	M16	amended letters	3
F3	lack of movement	2	M17	dirty overall appearance	3
F4	large writing	2	M18	curved extensions	1
F5	*m*, *n* as school model	2	M19	dented ovals	3
F6	*t*-bars as school model	1	M20	poorly formed loops	2
F7	*p* as school model	1	M21	tremors	3
F8	*a* in two parts	3	M22	weak strokes	2
F9	*d-g-q* in two parts	2	M23	jerks	2
F10	capitals as school model	3	M24	mingling letters	2
F11	false connections	3	M25	broken baselines	2
F12	soldering	1	M26	wavy baselines	1
F13	irregular line spaces	3	M27	descending lines	1
F14	zones poorly differentiated	2	M28	words dancing on the line	2
			M29	irregular size	3
			M30	irregular slant	1

TOTAL EF   TOTAL EM

TOTAL E (EF+EM)   RATIO EF : EM

Proposed adjustments for Italian writing based on ARIGRAF research (not to be systematically applied but to be determined case by case):

(a) If F4 = 0: up to age 9 weighting coefficient = 1, after 9 years = 2
(b) If F8 = 0, and F9 = 1 or 0.5: F8 changes to 0.5
(c) M19/M21/M29: have a weighting coefficient of 2 instead of 3
(d) M23: has a weighting coefficient of 1 instead of 2
(e) For M24: after 8 years 6 months mingling letters must be considered rather than the Morettian type Touching

Table 24

Comparison between levels *EF* and *EM*

Ajuriaguerra noticed that the two component types *EF* and *EM* do not have the same evolution. Both in boys and girls *EM* items evolve much more quickly than *EF* items. When the ratio *EF* : *EM* is less than 0.75 it is obviously an anomaly which needs to be addressed. Such a ratio indicates the excessive presence of items *EM* and on the whole, it presumes motor problems. We must therefore apply the *scale of dysgraphia* which will be covered later in Chapter Twelve.

If by contrast, the *EF* total is much higher than the *EM* one must assume a probable intellectual insufficiency, which could also come from emotional problems, inhibitions, anxiety, etc.

By examining each item in its statistical evolution and its degree of presence in a particular age, or sex, the scales can give much information. Comparing the *EF* and *EM* totals to each other as well as to the statistical norms, and lastly evaluating the total *E* always as regards the statistical norms, will give results.

The 30 children's components or items

We return to Ajuriaguerra's book [4] for precise statistics regarding age and sex in relation to the frequency of items, and not least for the explanations and the exhaustive writing illustrations which supplied the author with the scoring system. His frequency tables for the 30 components, the six-monthly age groups, and the educational levels have also been used by J. Peugeot [199], who shows the practical use of these elements within an overall vision of children's various problems.

We list here in Table 25, as a guide, the sums of *EF*, *EM*, and the total *E* for a school of average educational level (Ajuriaguerra level Q2), for each six-month age group, for both boys and girls. "Average educational level" is that of a good state school. The statistics in fact vary for some well-known private schools (Q1), or for less qualified institutions (Q3).

STATISTICAL SCORES FOR BOYS: AVERAGE EDUCATIONAL LEVEL										
Age 6	6.6	7	7.6	8	8,6	9	9.6	10	10.6	11
EF 26	24	22	19	17	15	13.5	14	15	12	9
EM 30	22	17.5	15.5	13.5	11.5	10	9.5	9	8	6.5
E 55	47	39	34	29	27	25	24	23	19	16

STATISTICAL SCORES FOR GIRLS: AVERAGE EDUCATIONAL LEVEL										
Age 6	6.6	7	7.6	8	8.6	9	9.6	10	10,6	11
EF 23	20.5	18	16	14.5	13.5	13	13	12.5	10.5	9
EM 23.5	18.5	15	13	11.5	10	8.5	8.5	8	6	4.5
E 48	40	33	30	27	24	21	20	19	16	13

Table 25

It is obvious that the statistical results are only a guide and must not be rigidly interpreted. These results are extremely useful however in reflecting upon a number of characteristics. As further points for reflection we suggest some examples:

- The fact that item F14 (poorly differentiated zones) disappears totally by the age of 11 statistically, must attract particular attention. This appears, albeit with a lower weighting coefficient, in the scale of dysgraphia. In a case where it may not refer to dysgraphia, very probably it refers to a cognitive or pathological disturbance.

- Observing the frequency of the individual 30 components (see next section) the *regression* that occurs between 9 and 10 years can be seen. In other words before the golden stage of writing, the graphomotor level regresses. We can perhaps place this fact in relation to prepubescent disturbances, often noted at this stage: restlessness in boys, fantasies and mythomania in girls.

- Whereas F11 (false connections) has statistically disappeared in girls by age 11, it is still present in 21% of boys of the same age.

- Note in Table 24 the values to be changed with respect to the Italian writing model.

- One needs to distinguish item M24 (mingling letters) from the Morettian type: Touching.

II. DESCRIPTION AND FREQUENCY
OF THE 30 CHILDREN'S ITEMS

Items *EF*

F1: Writing on the surface
Writing of shaky appearance: crooked extensions and flattened curves
Frequency: 100% 6–7 years, 94% 8–9, 87% 10, 68% 11
Absence of firm extensions and of flexible curves: .... 1 pt
Absence of firm extensions but some flexible curves: .... 0.5 pt
Presence of firm extensions and flexible curves: .... 0 pt

F2: Plump writing
Overblown and widened appearance of ovals and loops; this is taken into consideration only if F1 is present
Frequency: 91% 6 years, 81% 7, 69% 8–9, 84% 10, 70% 11
Plump writing in all zones: .... 1 pt
Slightly in all zones or distinctly in one zone: .... 0.5 pt
Not present: .... 0 pt

F3: Lack of movement
This concerns the difficulty in making cursive movement; letters tend to be placed next to each other (without connections)
Frequency: 100% 6–7 years, 94% 8, 86% 9, 92% 10, 68% 11
Many separated letters or false connections: .... 1 pt
Some connections but without true progression: .... 0.5 pt
Hint of cursive movement, some simplifications: .... 0 pt

F4: Large writing
The standard for the height of the middle zone is 2.5mm; draw on tracing paper two grids: A = 2.5 mm, B = 3.5 mm
Frequency: 87% 6 years, 73% 7, 59% 8, 48% 9, 54% 10, 42% 11
Over half the middle zones go beyond grid B, or all reach the limit of grid B: 1 pt
Over half the middle zones go beyond grid A, but are included in grid B: ..... 0.5 pt
Nearly all the middle zones are included in grid A: .... 0 pt

F5: *m* and *n* as base model
The school model expects an upper rounded arcade and downstrokes fixed between them
Frequency: 92% 6 years, 85% 7, 75% 8, 74% 9, 70% 10, 61% 11
Nearly all *m* and *n* are of the school model: .... 1 pt
Some personal touches: garlanded, or with downstrokes separated
   (by movement or awkwardness): .... 0.5 pt
The majority are personalized: .... 0 pt

F6: *t*-bars as base model
The school model expects a small crossing placed precisely high on the stem, without cutting it
Frequency: 76% 6 years, 71% 7, 62% 8, 51% 9, 48% 10, 33% 11
Awkward execution and erroneous positioning: .... 1 pt
School model form and position: .... 0.5 pt
At least half are personalized: by connection, slant, or distance from the stem. 0 pt

F7: *p* as base model
The school model is arcaded with a lower extension
Frequency: 96% 6–7 years, 95% 8, 89% 9, 85% 10, 78% 11
All are carried out in two movements: .... 1 pt
School model form: .... 0.5 pt
They are personalized and often progressive to the right: .... 0 pt

F8: *a* in two parts
The *a* is carried out in two movements: oval and small descending stroke connecting to the next letter
Frequency: 78% 6 years, 57% 7, 34% 8, 30% 9, 33% 10, 20% 11
All are written in two movements (lifting of the pen, sometimes camouflaged by soldering): .... 1 pt
At least half are carried out in two movements: .... 0.5 pt
Almost never carried out in two movements: .... 0 pt

F9: *d-g-q* in two parts
These letters are carried out in two movements: oval and downstroke
Frequency: 86% 6 years, 67% 7, 62% 8, 53% 9, 62% 10, 45% 11
All are carried out in two movements (lifting of pen, sometimes camouflaged by soldering): .... 1 pt
At least half are carried out in two movements: .... 0.5 pt
Almost never carried out in two movements: .... 0 pt

F10: Capitals as base model
Consider both awkward forms and the pure school model forms
Frequency: 91% 6 years, 82% 7, 57% 8, 46% 9, 42% 10, 34% 11
Each capital letter is awkward and of school model form: .... 1 pt
Capital letters are only slightly awkward and of school model form: .... 0.5 pt
They are well formed with a certain amount of personalization: .... 0 pt

F11: False connections
The child connects letters by stopping and then restarting the connecting stroke
Frequency: 79% 6 years, 66% 7, 46% 8, 27% 9, 30% 10, 11% 11
10 examples or more in 30 words: .... 1 pt
5–9 examples: .... 0.5 pt
0–4 examples: .... 0 pt

F12: Soldering
The following letter is pushed back to touch the end stroke of the previous letter
Frequency: 52% 6 years, 41% 7, 36% 8, 30% 9, 29% 10,26% 11

10 examples in the first 30 words:	1 pt
4–9 examples:	0.5 pt
0–3 examples:	0 pt

F13: Irregular line spaces
The space at the beginning of the lines must be considered and not the variability of spacing along the text
Frequency: 73% 6 years, 58% 7, 35% 8, 17% 9, 14% 10, 14% 11

All the spaces at the beginning of the line are irregular:	1 pt
At least two spaces are identical even if they are not together:	0.5 pt
Spaces are regular:	0 pt

F14: Zones poorly differentiated
There is no proportion between the three zones: one can invade another
Frequency: 37% 6 years, 22% 7, 12% 8, 3% 9, 2% 10, 0% 11

Some cases in different words:	1 pt
1 or 2 cases:	0.5 pt
No obvious case:	0 pt

Items *EM*

M15: Lower extensions in stages
Not to be confused with twisting
Frequency: 62% 6 years, 34% 7, 12% 8, 8% 9, 12% 10, 2% 11

3 or more cases:	1 pt
1 case only:	0.5 pt
None at all:	0 pt

M16: Amended letters
letters or parts of letters are retouched; excludes spelling corrections
Frequency: 66% 6 years, 68% 7, 64% 8, 41% 9, 32% 10, 20% 11

At least 2 obvious cases:	1 pt
At least 1 obvious case:	0.5 pt
None:	0 pt

M17: Dirty overall appearance
A generally neglected, imprecise, and pasty aspect
Frequency: 53% 6 years, 55% 7, 30% 8, 18% 9, 12% 10, 4% 11

Overall very dirty and clumsy:	1 pt
Dirty appearance when observing details:	0.5 pt
Clean overall:	0 pt

M18: Curved extensions
Verticals of d, t, p, q show some deviations
Frequency: 55% 6 years, 48% 7, 41% 8, 50% 9, 53% 10, 39% 11
More than half are curving: .... 1 pt
Some are obvious or are all are slight: .... 0.5 pt
No case at all or rarely: .... 0 pt

M19: Dented ovals
Rounded letters are badly formed with illogical angles
Frequency: 69% 6 years, 40% 7, 14% 8, 3% 9, 8% 10 2% 11
Nearly all rounded letters are dented: .... 1 pt
Half are dented: .... 0.5 pt
None or rarely: .... 0 pt

M20: Poorly formed loops
The edges of the loops are not rounded but present small angles, constriction, and flattening
Frequency: 73% 6 years, 68% 7, 59% 8, 63% 9, 52% 10, 45% 11
At least two-thirds are obvious cases: .... 1 pt
Some obvious cases or all slightly so: .... 0.5 pt
None: .... 0 pt

M21: Tremors
These are seen with a magnifying glass: from slight oscillations to large irregular deviations
Frequency: 81% 6 years, 58% 7, 23% 8, 9% 9, 11% 10, 4% 11
Nearly all verticals in the three zones have tremors: .... 1 pt
Some obvious cases or all slightly so: .... 0.5 pt
None: .... 0 pt

M22: Weak outline
The overall outline is badly managed in relation to space, the stroke is graceful, letters are badly structured
Frequency: 46% 6 years, 21% 7, 10% 8, 3% 9, 3% 10, 0% 11
Overall entirely vacillating: .... 1 pt
Overall slightly vacillating: .... 0.5 pt
No occurrence: .... 0 pt

M23: Jerks
Progression occurs with jerky angularity or too long connections
Frequency: 40% 6years, 35% 7, 19% 8, 13% 9, 15% 10, 20% 11
At least 3 obvious cases: .... 1 pt
1 or 2 obvious cases, or all slightly jerky: .... 0.5 pt
No obvious case: .... 0 pt

M24: Collisions
Letters or parts of letters seem to collide (see the Morettian type Touching)
Frequency: 65% 6 years, 60% 7, 51% 8, 44% 9, 38% 10, 24% 11
Some extremely obvious cases: .... 1 pt
1 or 2 obvious cases or slightly overall: .... 0.5 pt
None: .... 0 pt

M25: Broken baselines
The line shows a sharp angularity (the curving line must be excluded)
Frequency: 29% 6 years, 13% 7, 6% 8, 2% 9, 2% 10, 0% 11
At least one broken line: .... 1 pt
At least a hint of angularity in one or more lines: .... 0.5 pt
None: .... 0 pt

M26: Wavy baselines
The line undulates without any sudden deviations
Frequency: 90% 6 years, 94% 7, 90% 8, 85% 9, 88% 10, 76% 11
All the lines are wavy: .... 1 pt
2 or 3 lines are wavy: .... 0.5 pt
Well maintained lines, or slight waviness: .... 0 pt

M27: Descending lines
Lines descend in a constant way. Look at the opposite side of the text and use
a grid with a line descending at 6° to the horizontal
Frequency: 31% 6 years, 19% 7, 22% 8, 23% 9, 12% 10, 9% 11
The angle is equal to or higher than 6°: .... 1 pt
The angle is less than 6°: .... 0.5 pt
The lines are horizontal or rising: .... 0 pt

M28: Words dancing on the line
The base of a word is not straight but wavy. Look at the long words. Not to be
confused with M26 which concerns the whole line
Frequency: 95% 6, 91% 7, 83% 8, 75% 9, 68% 10, 49% 11
All the words dance on the line: .... 1 pt
Only some words do not have a horizontal base: .... 0.5 pt
Nearly all words have a horizontal base: .... 0 pt

M29: Irregular size
Look at the height variation in the middle zone
Frequency: 92% 6 years, 85% 7, 64% 8, 47% 9, 47% 10, 20% 11
At least 3 long words vary in middle zone height by more than 2:1: .... 1 pt
Frequent variations but less than 2:1: .... 0.5 pt
Slight irregularity in size: .... 0 pt

M30: Irregular slant
Look at the variation to the right and left of the letters' axis
Frequency: 83% 6 years, 79% 7, 71% 8, 77% 9, 70% 10, 58% 11
Very slanted (less than 30°) .... 1 pt
Slanted between 30° and 90° .... 0.5 pt
Vetical .... 0 pt

III. PHYSIOLOGY OF WRITING MOVEMENTS

At the age of 5, said Ajuriaguerra, the child learning to write has already been through various phases in prehensile evolution, indispensable prerequisites for the acquisition of writing ability. "*The act of writing depends not only on the pressure of the thumb and index finger on the instrument and on the middle finger, but also on a half-leaning position of the wrist and its possibility of progression.*"

Callewaert [51] has identified in the muscles of the hand those that allow writing with dexterity (function of inscription), those that reinforce the hand (function of support), and those that affect the synergetic fixation of the hand (function of fixation). "*The components of motor control which affect the graphic movement are: the tone, the strength, the positioning of the movements, and speed.*"

In the graphic act, tone implies adequate positioning of the head and torso, and the maturation which must generate a relationship between the tone of the torso and that of the limbs; otherwise, a stiffening of the posture can be seen. Strength depends not only on muscle power but also on the reduction of unproductive movements.

We limit ourselves to these small considerations seeing that the physiology of movements, as of underlying cerebral mechanisms, is a complex subject for specialists.

Chapter Eleven

TOWARDS ACQUIRING
WRITING RHYTHM

In this chapter we will deal with the evolution of writing from the age of 11, by which time, theoretically, the basic graphomotor level is acquired. In these teenage years young people go through secondary and further education, or take their first steps in paid employment.

The development of writing passes clearly through an adolescent age, a study which requires a separate treatise. Here our only intention is to identify the phases and obstacles caused by adolescent difficulties, not to give an exhaustive account. We will cover *elementary writing* in the following chapter, in other words the writing of people who have acquired the rudiments of school learning but lack the capability for practical or intellectual training.

We have commented upon various adolescent problems at several graphology conventions. In a report to the convention held at Foggia in 1993 which focused on adolescent personality difficulties, we insisted upon the aspect of *permanent adolescence*, to which we still adhere. Later we shall say something more about this, but here we want above all to trace how in adolescence the graphic gesture frees itself from the period of childhood. Table 26 is a guide to the study of this important period.

I. PREADOLESCENCE AND WRITING DIFFICULTIES

As we have already seen in Chapter Nine, having reached the graphic mastery of the *calligraphic phase* the pupil then faces the preadolescent age, with all its difficulties connected to physical and glandular changes. It must be understood that in our present Western society prepubescent symptoms present themselves ever earlier. We therefore have to be particularly cautious in evaluating writing disturbances between the ages of 8 and 11 and avoid attributing them erroneously to dysgraphia or mental problems, because they can simply reveal precocious prepubescent processes. The best way is to do a longitudinal study: obtain evidence for the graphic development of the child up to the age in question and check how and when the disturbance occurred, eliminating the more or less transitory causes connected with family upsets.

In general the expert graphologist can already observe preadolescent writing disturbances at the start of middle school. It may however be difficult to obtain writing from the last year of elementary school (age 11) which is sure proof of the previous graphomotor level achieved. The graphologist's greatest difficulty consists in distinguishing possible signs of preadolescent unease present in writings which have kept to the school models.

Even if the adolescent "crisis" is normal, as stated by Ajuriaguerra, between 12 and 16 years for those who continue their schooling, it is not always visible in writing. Writing of good appearance typical of the depressed or anorexics is proof of this. Once again the graphologist must resort to longitudinal study, and to obtain an accurate evaluation, integrate it with graphic tests: the tree test, the human figure, the person, the family, for example, all tests which can be presented as a game and do not place the subject in an artificial situation.

We shall focus therefore in this section on the principal graphic signs of preadolescent unease common more or less to all young people, leaving aside the more serious cases which are often part of a larger problem.

Graphic evolution in middle school (11–14 years)

During middle school and often between classes 1 and 2 there appears to be a certain amount of graphic upheaval. The graphologist is rarely able to view young people's writing on unlined white paper because, outside school exercise books, they do not write much. The letters to grandparents of former times have been substituted by telephone calls. It is not thought opportune to focus too much attention on a young person, by asking for a special performance. There is an exception however when we have the chance to enter a classroom to give everyone some tests, of which one would be a "letter to a friend", which pupils are always willing to do.

THE DEVELOPING YEARS FROM AGE 11 ONWARD

Information required:
Age – sex – left-handedness – school level – sociocultural environment – family environment – position and role in the family nucleus: age of siblings – type of family life and life outside it – extracurricular activities

Materials
Recent: signed letter on unlined paper – page from exercise book – notes
Past: exercise book pages from age 8 upwards – short letters and drawings
If possible: parents' handwriting – possibly of siblings

Graphological examination

A. *PREADOLESCENCE* : around 12–14 years

1. *Graphomotor level*
Establish the graphomotor age reached around 11 years – observe the actual persistence of items E and the presence of components of autonomy

2. *Jaminian categories*
Space management – direction – continuity: evaluation and interpretation still similar to that for children's writing
Pressure – dimension – slant: evaluation and interpretation close to that for adult writing
Form: this lies at the heart of the term "development"

B. *ADOLESCENCE* : normally over 14 years

1. *Graphomotor level*: observation of items E still present

2. *Study of graphic signs*: evolution of categories in relation to statistical results; classic graphological study, taking account of transitional adolescence and of fashions seen in specific groups

3. *Longitudinal study*: graphological development from elementary school onwards

4. *Comparison with statistical results on adolescents* (European): Tables 28–9

5. *Synthesis of observations and psychological study*: prognosis of evolution; educational and/or professional direction; possibly advice to parents

Table 26

Most of the time, then, we can only study the middle school exercise books, and as already mentioned we also look for at least one exercise book from the fifth year of elementary school. The principal signs we look for are those of a progressive general disorder:
- arbitrary spatial organization, absent or invasive margins, writing either too compact or too spaced;
- fluctuating line direction;
- continuous alterations in letter slant;
- irregular pressure with spasms;
- jerky letter connections, or the opposite, mingling letters;
- sometimes more accentuated regressive signs: leftward movements, narrow letters, narrow spaces between letters and between lines.

Finally we must evaluate the graphomotor level reached:
- presence of "children's" components, referring to Ajuriaguerra's scales;
- presence of components of "autonomy", that is to say signs of graphic evolution: simplifications, combinations, balance between whites and blacks, firmness of stroke.

"Alarm signals" of Ursula Avé-Lallemant

The German Ursula Avé-Lallemant has contributed to the study and prediction of problems in the teenage years [12]. In a brief report in his recent book [69], Pacifico Cristofanelli writes that the German longitudinal research begun in 1969 is coming to fruition. This study is examining about 2000 writings of children and adolescents. Some "alarm signals" have been identified which, even if they were already known by graphologists, are gathered in a clear way into the plan of this study and can therefore provide a useful working tool for a consultant graphologist. In addition they have the merit of referring to almost any graphic environment. As Cristofanelli says: "the identified alarm signals are independent of education, language, and graphic model."

They concern various graphic categories such as space, form, movement, and stroke, and for each type of signal educational advice is offered. In Table 27 we give a summary of these signals, with slight category changes. Obviously the more signals present together the more they are reinforced, and each must be addressed according to its degree of intensity and its permanence over time. They must also be considered in relation to the development period, some being "normal" in the prepubescent or pubescent phase. In our graphological practice we have noticed that changes in space and stroke, when they are accentuated, give most cause for concern. Oddities and anomalies in the distribution of whites and blacks, sharp contrasts between looseness and constriction, uncertain, retouched, and "dirty" stroke, are all signals of great unease. We have also found in youngsters who have been sexually molested some morphological hypertrophy, with extremely full loops in the lower zone, denoting an abnormal sensory impulse.

The educational interest is clear, and once these signals are identified, the graphologist can easily deduce psychological consequences, make a prognosis on scholastic achievement, and not least offer suitable advice, from the need to calm tension and fears to the investigation of causes of possible physiological weakness. One can then avert the risk of mistaking inhibition and insecurity for inability to study when faced with a poor school output, and avoid for the pupil a vicious circle of frustration and intellectual loss. Low attention span, insecurity, loneliness, can be read in a different light.

PRINCIPAL "ALARM SIGNALS" OF THE DEVELOPING YEARS
(After Ursula Avé-Lallemant and Pacifico Cristofanelli)

Excess of:

Spacing	between words, gaps, chimneys, islands
Confusion	tangled lines, collisions between strokes, tumultuous movement, mangled forms
Rigidity	systematic regularity, overstructured space, tension, angular joins, stiffened movement, narrow letters
Relaxation	insufficient tension

Disturbances of:

Movement	lack of elasticity, blocked endings, fractures, mingling
Stroke	covering, retouched, pasty/imprecise, fragmented
Form	meandering connections

Table 27

Pupils' choice of studies

Silvio Lena [142] undertook various statistical checks on the presence of graphic components in the formative period from 11 years, and paid particular attention to problems of scholastic aptitude. In the conclusion to his book the author offers very useful suggestions for graphological consultation regarding school studies. The graphologist must know what various schools and professions have to offer. He must identify the interests and aspirations of each pupil and relate them to real ability, and together reach a wide-ranging evaluation, focusing on the possibility of attainment, without rigidity and taking into consideration changes in interest which can happen. "It would therefore be opportune to postpone the choice [of academic direction] until after the first two years of upper school, when there is clearly a greater stability of interests."

In Fig. 80 we show Paola's writing who consulted us at 17 years of age in a period of great psychological upheaval. Her writing at 9–10 may seem at first sight childish. However, graphometric examination identifies a higher evolutionary level than the average for her age. A clear change is noticeable from 13 years, when the studious girl shows signs of being very demanding on herself, to 15 years when a passionate character sparks up, receptive to many interests, with idealistic hints, emotional excitement, the obstinacy of her own subjective logic, all symptoms of intense adolescent conflict; at the end of which the girl becomes prey to depressive episodes.

In Fig. 81, we see the changes in the writing of Dario, who is ambidextrous, from 9 to 13 years. In this case too, we see that single snapshots of his writing do not show the picture which emerges after longitudinal study. We have to realize that the unexpected impetuosity which emerges at 13 years (bottom), is painted onto a nervous, insecure, and very sensitive temperament. We need to determine whether this aggression could be a constructive stimulus or whether it risks generating a sense of blame and consequent discouragement and depression.

These two examples simply show that adolescent problems are tied to psychological and existential conflict more important for them than their choice of academic direction. Often at age 14 they feel attracted to every-thing and to nothing in particular, and the important thing is to restore a little clarity to allow them to make choices, the least wrong ones possible.

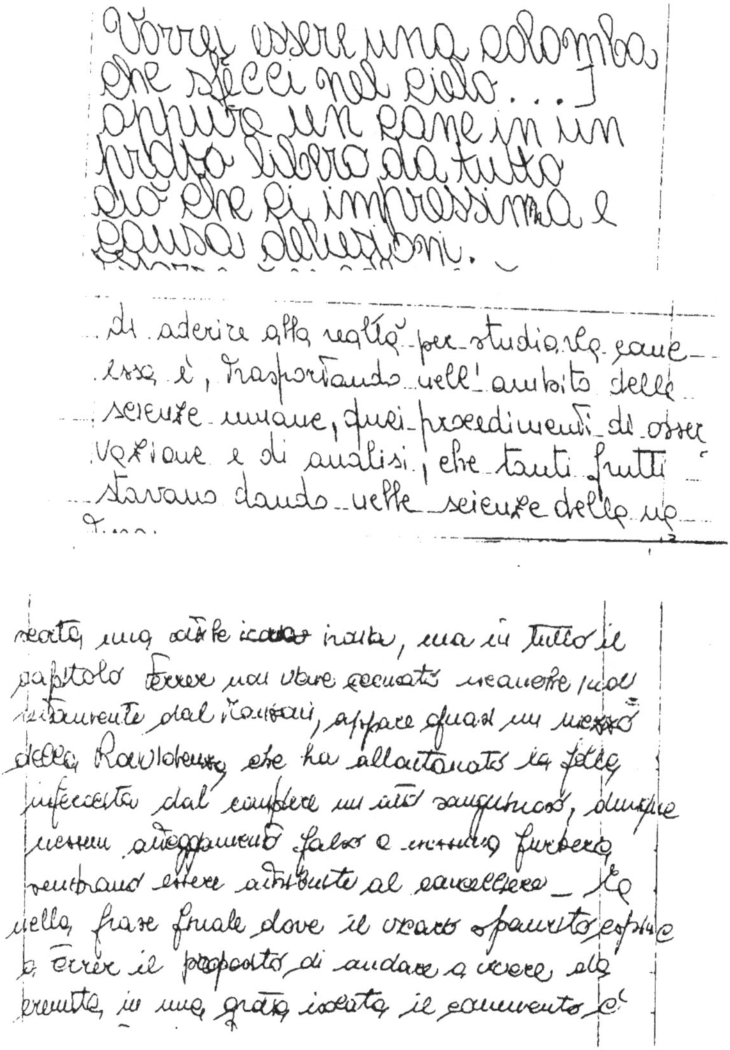

Figure 80 (reduced)
Paola's writing: 10 years old in elementary class 5,
13 years in middle school class 3, and 15 years in upper school

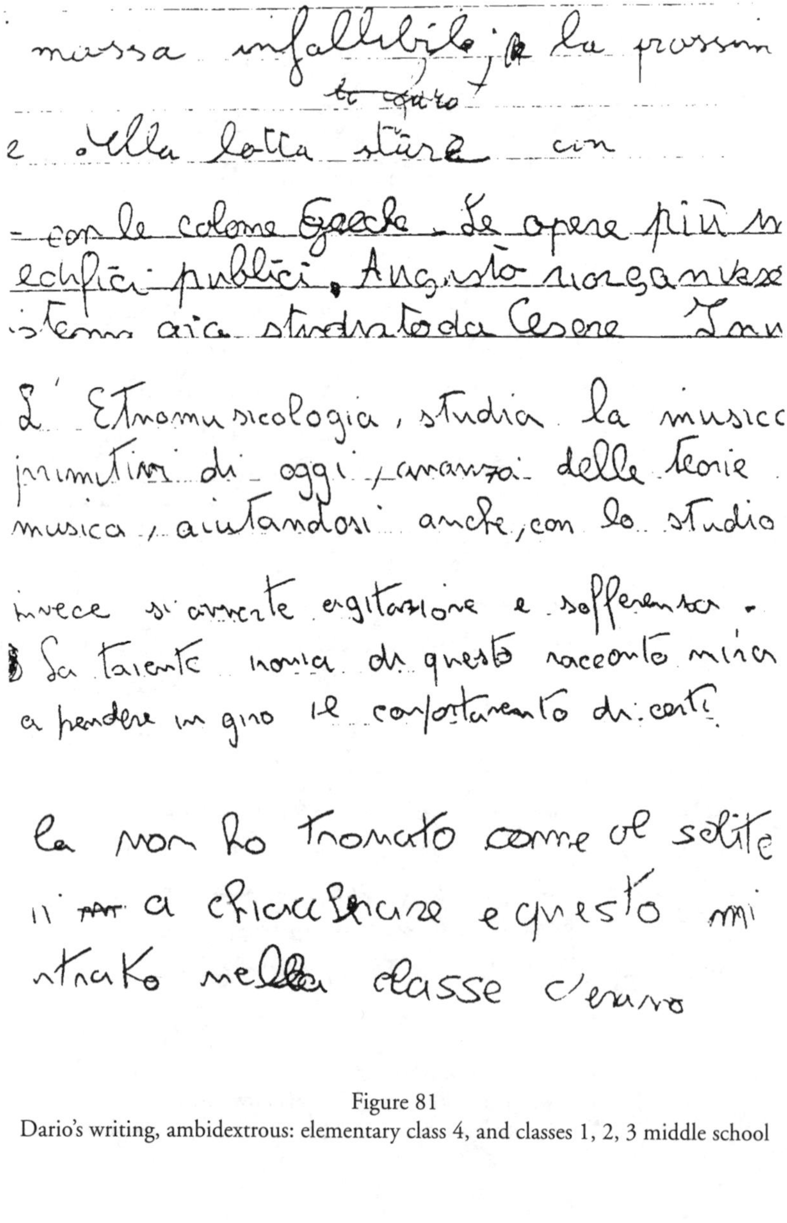

Figure 81
Dario's writing, ambidextrous: elementary class 4, and classes 1, 2, 3 middle school

II. ADOLESCENCE

The concept of "graphic evolution" in adolescence does not have much value. In general, graphomotor dexterity has already been acquired. However, a personal graphic rhythm has not clearly developed. Writing changes according to the moment's mood, to fashion, to the most varied influences, among which are some more deleterious linked with asocial behaviour.

Research conducted by the Société Française de Graphologie at European level, summarized by Arlette Lombard [223], focusing principally on the communication of adolescents in the last class of secondary school, in France a year earlier than in Italy (in other words at age 17), has produced interesting results. The principal graphic aspects in adolescence are already close to adult writing, as can be extracted from statistical data.

Graphic aspects of no significance compared with adult writing

Some characteristics present in the majority of adolescent writing cannot be regarded as significant in relation to adult writing:

Irregular dimension, direction, and pressure
Light pressure
Absence of margins
Grouped writing
Vertical direction

Graphic aspects of some significance compared with adult writing

For a résumé of graphic signs which, in adolescent writing, take on a greater *positive* (less negative), or more *negative* (less positive) value, or different values, as regards adult writing, see Tables 28 and 29.

Adolescent unease

While not intending to expound on the biological development of adolescence here, we will focus attention on the unease that erupts.

Sometimes we are able to anticipate this condition through the examination of writing, or, when we can only confirm its presence, we can advance a prognosis.

ADOLESCENT WRITING:
SIGNS AND EVALUATION DIFFERENCES
COMPARED TO ADULT WRITING

more positive (+)   *more negative* (–)   *same value*
very positive (+ +)   *less positive* (+ –)
less negative (– +)

+ + in relief   – filiform   large
    firm   angular   small
    aerated   thin stroke
    distributed rhythm
    mastered and easy movement

– + controlled   + – slanted
    leftward   line maintenance
    "persona"   pasty
    poised   precise
    irregular slant   disconnected
    disconnected
    connected
    spaced

Note: "disconnected" is placed in two columns, because it covers a less negative value as regards *relation with others and activity*, but also a less positive value for *intuition and analytic thought*.

Table 28

ADOLESCENT WRITING: CATEGORIES

Evaluation differences compared to adult writing

Space   *arrhythmic whites/blacks*: normal
absence of margins: not obviously a sign of extroversion or activity but of inability to organize

Inclination *leftward*: defensive
variable: changeable moods rather than ambivalence

Direction   *rigid line*: sign of tension with dispersion of energy

Continuity *grouping* is almost always illogical and casual
connected writing is often barely flexible, denoting inhibition = adherence to taught regulations and mind without logic
disconnected writing: a search for autonomy and also of adaptability (for clarity); it is not therefore only a sign of analysis and intuition
meandering connections: compensatory effort to instability
frequent *suspensions, collisions, jerks,* and *twists*
hesitant tendency: obstructions, interruptions, markings

Form   *angular*: with an elevated graphic level, sign of firmness; with average level, tension and opposition; often reactive hypersensitivity, difficulty in adapting
heavy and static garlands: impressionable, dependent
arcaded: conformity to model, closure, search for protection
filiform does not indicate adaptability or capacity for disengagement but a tendency to avoid commitment, escape (rare in Italian adolescents)
"persona" writing expresses adaptability to conventions and fashions; it is therefore more positive than that of adults

Pressure   *pasty*: resistance to affection and to circumstances, passive affection
precise: defence

Movement *poised*: the value is positive because it indicates a mastery of movement

Significant frequency of Morettian signs
(see statistical study by A. R. Guaitoli [111])

Large space between letters + curved: *lack of resistance – passive adaptability*
Excessively large letters: *lack of concentration, superficiality – easily influenced*
Touching: *anxiety* (could be from stimulus to do better)

Table 29

The great generation conflicts that once occurred no longer happen. Adolescents are in general happier now in comparison to previous times, being more independent in movement and initiative. They are, however, more dependent at the psychological level because they are given less responsibility. The present adolescent reality is therefore dual. On the one hand Elena Manetti [160] notes: "the model proposed by the media is above all that of the physically beautiful, sporty, and socially disengaged, perfect products of a society itself adolescent, whose technological and consumerist reality gives rise to needs rather than to duties." On the other hand we find young people who are disenchanted and afflicted by boredom which often nurses a latent aggression.

Key points

Bear in mind these fundamental aspects of adolescence:
- adolescence as a window on society and its own unease;
- identity crisis and ambivalence;
- depressive threat;
- aggression and self-aggression;
- acting out and delinquent behaviour.

We draw from Anna Rita Guaitoli [111] some statistical data concerning identity crisis and the severe unease that it causes. This data was compiled by ISTAT (1994–6) in Italy:
- *anorexia*: 10% of population between 13 and 26 years (connected to bulimia)
- *suicide* (1980–90): 11% increase in boys; 17% reduction in girls; greater attempted suicides in girls (ratio 5:1); but in actual suicides boys outnumber girls 3:1. Under the age of 21 suicide is the second highest cause of death after traffic deaths.

For a concrete example of adolescent graphology, let us return to Paola's writing, already seen in Fig. 80. We show in Fig. 82 her writing at age 17, and not least her third tree, or "dream" tree, which she drew with great detail in an hour, whereas her first two trees had been drawn extremely quickly with a very light pressure. This dream tree symbolizes the girl's imaginary vision of the world, grappling with a sense of the real burden of disappointment.

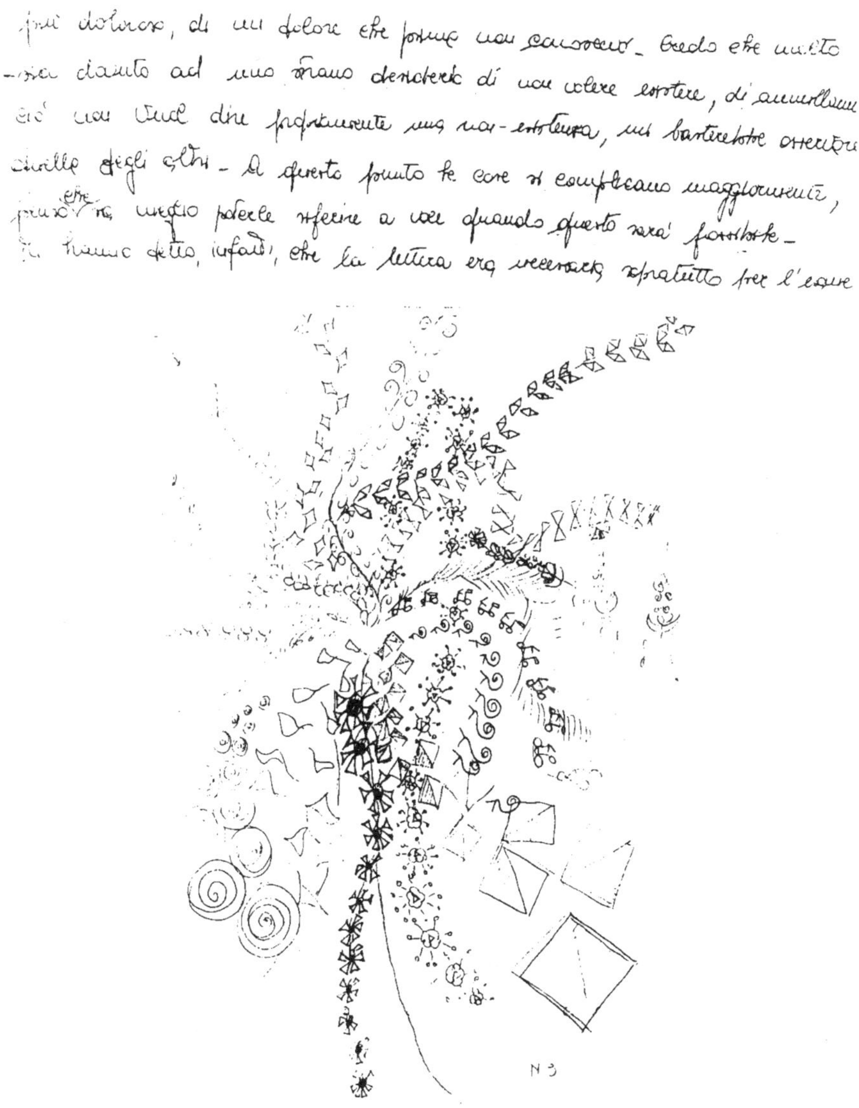
più doloroso, di un dolore che forse non conoscevo. Credo che molto
sia dovuto ad uno strano desiderio di non volere esistere, di annullarmi
ciò non vuol dire propriamente una non-esistenza, ma
quella degli altri. A questo punto le cose si complicano maggiormente,
penso che sia meglio poterle riferire a voce quando questo sarà possibile.
Mi hanno detto, infatti, che la lettera era necessaria soprattutto per l'
N 3

Figure 82 (reduced)
Paola's writing at 17 years with the tree test (third "dream" tree)

It is important to emphasize that only through a longitudinal examination, returning right back to her early writing, were we able to pick out
the various contrasting aspects of her character. Judging by the writing at
age 17 alone, the overall problems could not be put into historical
perspective. For reasons of discretion we cannot report details of her life
and the weighty difficulties which have dogged her for a long time. We can
only mention that she went against her own bent of artistic and literary
preference to establish herself quickly in scientific research work with notable
success. Although it has been a challenge, her strong willpower and
intelligence have brought about a positive result.

Rhythm of writing

Towards the age of 18, theoretically, a personalized writing rhythm is reached
as we free ourselves from the constrictions of school. In Italy, university
courses do not include written work, whereas in France they usually do, so
often an individual style is not perfected in Italy, and the originality of
writing does not improve, with the exception of those young people who
like writing anyway.

Often the graphologist must be satisfied with short examples or notes,
and it is not unusual for young people to mention that they have not
written for "a long time", because there is no need to do so or because they
use a computer. Others instead are inveterate scribblers and fill diaries and
notebooks with thoughts and stories, but rarely write anything such as
letters with a presentable page layout, which for us could be a source of
much information.

Adolescents at the end of the century

Generation trends move fast, and we have noticed that during the last 30
years, every five years or so a global change has occurred in the adolescent
group. These trends have ranged from a political and almost revolutionary
commitment, to an almost complete lack of interest in these subjects and
a shift to individualism.

The dangers linked to drug use and more recently to illnesses like AIDS
create an underlying lack of control. In addition problems of unemployment

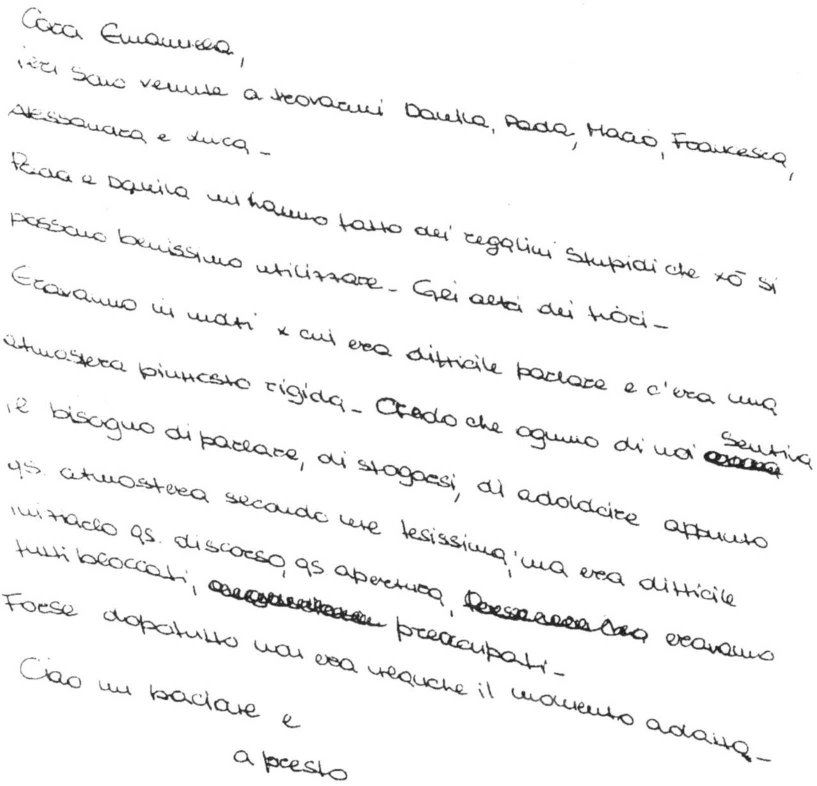
Cara Emanuela,
ieri sono venute a trovarmi Daniela, Paola, Mario, Francesca,
Alessandra e Luca -
Paola e Daniela mi hanno fatto dei regalini stupidi che xō si
possono benissimo utilizzare - Gli altri dei fiori -
Eravamo in molti x cui era difficile parlare e c'era una
atmosfera piuttosto rigida - Credo che ognuno di noi sentiva
il bisogno di parlare, di sfogarsi, di addolcire appunto
qs. atmosfera secondo me tesissima; ma era difficile
iniziando qs. discorso, qs. apertura, eravamo
tutti bloccati, preoccupati -
Forse dopotutto non era neanche il momento adatto -
Ciao un bacione e
a presto

Figure 83 (reduced)
Savina's writing at age 16: descending with crowded letters; adolescent crisis and depression

after an adolescence full of interests, yearning, and hope, provoke a dangerous post-adolescent state where young people between 25 and 30 years pass from precarious work to disappointment and often depression.

In France the children of immigrants (Magrebi, African, Asian, etc.) who have often become French, form a high percentage in state schools, where acute and particular problems arise. These young people live between two different cultures, at home and at school, with permanent conflict,

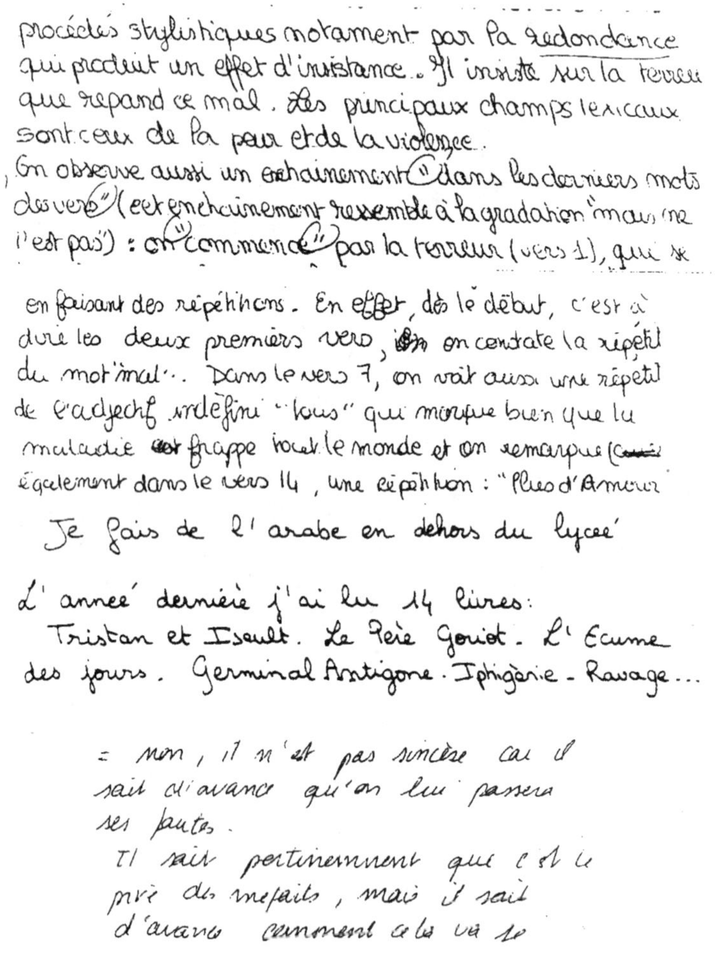

procédés stylistiques notamment par la redondance
qui produit un effet d'insistance. Il insiste sur la terreur
que répand ce mal. Les principaux champs lexicaux
sont ceux de la peur et de la violence.
, On observe aussi un enchaînement dans les derniers mots
des vers (cet enchaînement ressemble à la gradation mais ne
l'est pas) : on commence par la terreur (vers 1), qui se

en faisant des répétitions. En effet, dès le début, c'est à
dire les deux premiers vers, on constate la répétit
du mot "mal". Dans le vers 7, on voit aussi une répétit
de l'adjectif indéfini "tous" qui montre bien que la
maladie frappe tout le monde et on remarque (
également dans le vers 14, une répétition : "Plus d'Amour

Je fais de l' arabe en dehors du lycée

L' année dernière j'ai lu 14 livres :
   Tristan et Iseult. Le Père Goriot. L' Écume
des jours. Germinal Antigone. Iphigénie - Ravage...

   = Non, il n'est pas sincère car il
   sait d'avance qu'on lui passera
   ses fautes.
      Il sait pertinemment que c'est le
   prix des méfaits, mais il sait
   d'avance comment cela va se

Figure 84 (reduced)
16 year olds of Arab origin well integrated in the same class, in the scientific stream
(a) and (b) Girls, studious, reserved, with excellent school results
(c) Girl: strong character, passionate, independent, with little academic discipline
(d) Boy: vivacious, childish, lazy, kind but also prickly

often with parents intolerant towards cultural customs in the adopted country. This results in "problem" classes, a great challenge to teachers when they are face to face with sometimes very aggressive adolescents. In Fig. 84 we show the writing of adolescents in the 1990s of Magrebi origin who were well integrated into French schools (other problem samples are not included for reasons of discretion).

III. POST-ADOLESCENT PERIOD

The period of post-adolescence, which sometimes seems to go on for ever, has to be taken seriously in today's world, because the most prominent affliction, as already mentioned, is caused by unemployment. In a communication to a conference of the Italian Institute of Graphology of Trieste in 1994, we proposed the topic "*Post-adolescence: suffering and compensation*", to indicate that this period presents a serious problem, not only at an individual level but also socially, and we could add that it is a problem of our age.

In our capacity as consultant for companies, we know how difficult it is to evaluate the attitudes of these "adults by date of birth". They not only appear immature and insecure, but also are often split between their intellectual capacity – which is considerable and is formed by an excellent educational curriculum – and their inadequacy in social and emotional adaptability. Research conducted by Arigraf relating specifically to immaturity [35], pointed to a number of principal compensatory mechanisms adopted to face reality by persons around 30, mainly men, with very strong immature tendencies, mechanisms such as narcissism and assertive defence of their role.

Regarding the suffering provoked by a malaise which the young person cannot face unless at the cost of excessive compensatory effort, we mention some accounts from our communication. Leaving aside the excessive self-abuse common in a certain group of youth at the present time, such as drug addiction, anorexia, or casual violence, we concentrate on cases where the problems are more hidden but can be the cause of unforeseen behaviour.

The time of major risk definitely coincides with the young leaving their protected environment, after school for those who do not go on to higher education, or after university for the rest (who will then be in the post-adolescent period). Around the age of 25 the young leave the world of studies in which they have travelled with the attitude of "I will do that later" and now have to enter the "I want to do" stage. At this point the shock of reality occurs, and an identity crisis often happens due to the uncertainty of knowing what to do as an individual. It is made worse if there are problems concerning the family, emotions, or relationships, often with added feelings of loneliness. Not to find work, or to find something devoid of satisfaction or interest, is often the end result of years of intensive study and hopefulness.

In addition to bewilderment about their own limitations, the young often witness the family's disappointment. Parents have lived their own projections onto their children and the family balance which has settled around everyone waiting on the student now collapses. This occurs independently from the internal family dynamics, such as good or bad communication, identifications more or less established, a mother image more or less overpowering, and not least the various processes of idealizing children by the parents themselves.

The young person will then develop defensive methods of behaviour in order to avoid desperation. The most frequent are rationalization or intellectualization to an obsessive degree, a rationalization with a tendency to pragmatism and excessive narcissism, flight into actions or into a secondary activity pursued with steadfastness, such as a creative or sporting hobby, or yet again dreamy or self-justifying brooding with goals postponed. Graphologists can now consult longitudinal writing for help in identifying the unease and the efficacy or not of the defence mechanisms, as well as advising possible methods of recovery.

In France, where unemployment among the abundantly qualified young in the late 1990s took by surprise a thoroughly structured French society, creating a strong sense of unease and revolt, a research method called "balance of competence" has arisen. In this practice, other work possibilities are explored, not strictly connected with the student's completed studies, encouraging other areas of development in the hope of finding alternative work, and above all to rekindle hope in these often despondent and depressed subjects.

IV. ELEMENTARY WRITING

Writings by the uneducated, or by subjects with little practical use for writing who may not be entirely lacking in education or culture, have always interested and intrigued the graphologist. These are conceptually the opposite of "evolved" writings. In France, where there are many immigrant workers of uncertain socio-cultural status, it is not unusual for a company to submit to a graphologist a selection from applicants for the position of lorry driver, for example, or for a factory worker. These candidates often have a low educational level. (It is also obvious that other immigrants possess educated writing. In the selections it is not unusual to find an Asian or African engineer. Often their writing shows a graphic rhythm whose imprint is recognized by an experienced graphologist.) According to statistical research conducted by Dr Villard [244] it seems that elementary writing reflects a "mental" age of about 12 years. The great majority of these subjects have manual jobs or similar. We want therefore to find a method to approach this so-called *elementary* writing, in the light of research known to us and according to the basic principles of stroke which we have discussed.

Graphic level (Table 30)

Elementary writings can be classified according to three different graphic levels based on the schooling of the subject.

DISORGANIZED GRAPHIC LEVEL

The first level belongs to people who have not had any schooling. Such people are just as intelligent, practical, and efficient as others and at times also have a type of cultural perception which can be very surprising given that they are almost illiterate and have only managed to acquire the rudiments of reading and writing. This level is rare in our industrialized society, and mainly covers a few elderly people in underdeveloped rural areas, but it is also found in young immigrant workers as already mentioned.

The act of writing cannot be judged with certainty by the usual graphological criteria. Neither the space on the paper nor the writing instrument represents for them any choice, their attention is focused upon the approximate reproduction of a rudimentary form by a poorly controlled stroke. An obvious untidiness, with some mistakes or on the contrary an excessive application will only reflect their difficulty in writing and lack of practice.

ELEMENTARY WRITING: GRAPHIC LEVELS

1. *Disorganized graphic level*
   Disorganization of space – awkward forms – lack of outline coordination – rigid stroke = Nearly illiterate

2. *School writing level*
   Structured management of space – school writing forms – coordinated outline – reasonably flexible stroke = Basic minimum schooling

3. *Post-calligraphic level*
   Organized management of space – individualized school forms – simplifications and combinations – differentiated, personalized stroke = Schooling up to minimum leaving age and maintenance of the habit of writing

---

Table 30

School writing level

The second level is reached by people with basic schooling, even though they might not have attended school frequently. Writing could be linked totally to the basic model taught, gestural mastery can vary and depends on practice and individual application. Some respect for form is an essential characteristic of this level.

According to Crépieux-Jamin, from the beginning of learning the process of graphic individualism is already innate. In his time, attention by children to writing was pushed hard, with enforced calligraphic exercises. Nevertheless, he states that at the age of 6 the writing style differentiates itself, and as proof of what he called "the failure of the most tyrannical of writing styles", reproduces "two lines of calligraphy and spelling homework from a class of 31 boys between the ages of 11 and 13, of the same social background and intellectual development. Despite these similar conditions conducive to uniformity, every one had his own style" (Fig. 85). In our time the range of individual variation has widened considerably. Therefore if this second graphic level of development has been reached, the subject can be placed across a number of graphological criteria, which will be explained later.

Post-calligraphic level

Those who have attended school until the age of 11 or 13 reach the post-calligraphic level. They remain faithful to the basic model but the flexibility and personalization of the forms gives their writing a certain rhythm. Adults in this group have frequently maintained the habit of writing either for personal or professional purposes, business, accountancy, etc. Their signature in particular evokes their graphic ability; it retains a typical appearance that reflects on the one hand a lack of education and on the other the will to individualism.

These three types of writing are, then, considered "elementary" and in most cases we deal with those in the second or third level. However, handwriting which may appear of the school type is not to be considered "elementary" when the subject has a high level of education. If the educational or social level is not known, any diagnosis runs the risk of

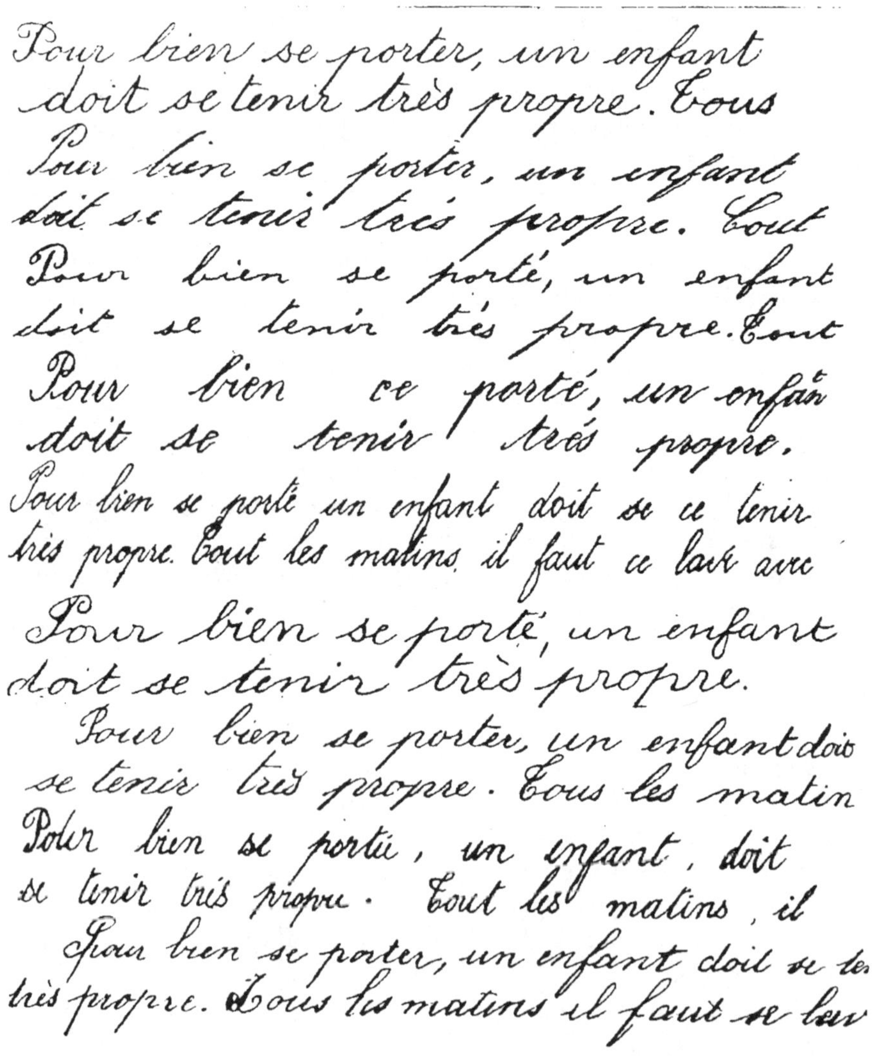

Pour bien se porter, un enfant doit se tenir très propre. Tous

Pour bien se porter, un enfant doit se tenir très propre. Tout

Pour bien se porté, un enfant doit se tenir très propre. Tout

Pour bien ce porté, un enfant doit se tenir très propre.

Pour bien se porté un enfant doit se ce tenir très propre. Tout les matins il faut ce lavé avec

Pour bien se porté, un enfant doit se tenir très propre.

Pour bien se porter, un enfant doit se tenir très propre. Tous les matin

Pour bien se porté, un enfant, doit se tenir très propre. Tout les matins, il

Pour bien se porter, un enfant doit se te très propre. Tous les matins il faut se lav

Figure 85
From Crépieux-Jamin: "the failure of the most tyrannical of writing styles"

being mistaken. Suzanne Bresard urges caution, when we notice that the writings of a factory worker and an engineer are sometimes very close.

We can consider that elementary writings reach the graphomotor agility of the calligraphic phase of 10 and 11 year olds as described by Ajuriaguerra, and may extend to the post-calligraphic phase, in cases where practice has been kept up. Subjects who have started work early do not appear to be exposed to the difficulties and doubts found in the writing of adolescents who enter further education. Writing is more of a useful act for them than an expressive means or a search for graphic identity.

Even in these cases though the psychophysical process at the heart of the graphic gesture puts into play complicated neuromuscular and cerebral interactions, and each writer projects himself in his own graphic gesture. We have to be careful above all that we do not link awkward writing with manual inability. We know for example that extremely able people have very awkward writing, and conversely, subjects with an elementary and awkward writing can carry out manual work with extreme dexterity. The disability of "hesitant" writing should not prejudice against technical ability. See, for example, the writing of an audio-visual technician (Fig. 86).

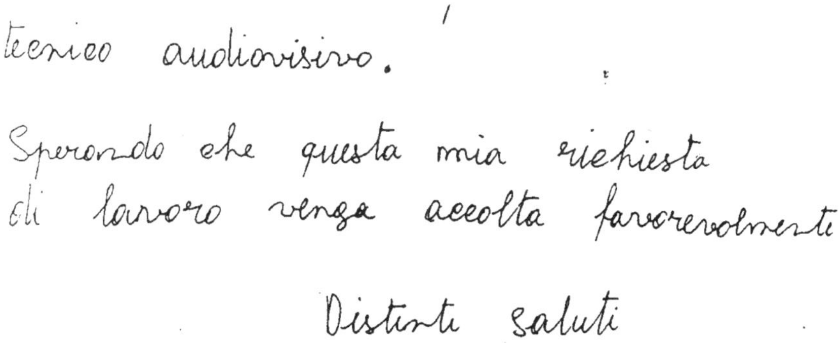

Figure 86 (reduced)
Audio-visual technician's writing, age 25
As an "unchanging specific" we can pick out the comfortably written ovals which, with the broad connections, indicate a sociable nature and need for communication

The "unchanging specific"

This interesting notion was outlined by the psychiatrist and graphologist Dr Claude Villard [243]. Dr Villard starts with Georg Meyer's well-known principle (1900), already mentioned in Chapter Three concerning the German School: "a graphic property is much more difficult to produce the less it belong to the imagery expressive of the will. The result of this is that the most *instinctive* graphic properties are never *acquired*: weak pressure, width, slant, degree of connection, double curve, garlands, fullness of form, progressive writing, small differences in length, reinforcement of the upper length, lack of organization, irregularity, speed."

The author of elementary writing is very careful at *reproducing* his writing and therefore shows a great conscious will, so the more unconscious properties are obviously less frequent. The presence of unconscious properties on the other hand will be extremely revealing.

The *unchanging specific* consists of a "factor of specific constancy" and is part of the most *instinctive* graphic properties. Dr Villard proposed therefore the following rule: "When an elementary writing presents a dominant *unchanging specific*, the significance of the latter will have greater weight the less the writing is evolved, on condition that the *unchanging specific* is restored to the category of instinctual graphic properties." Dr Villard adds: "In elementary writing, the unconscious 'comes out' less well. So when it does appear, it is decisive." The *unchanging specific* is closely linked to Saint-Morand's "typical gesture" and Moretti's "fleeting gesture".

We must evaluate the significance of this aspect according to its structure and basic form (curve, angle, arch …); manner of writing (jerky, impulsive, spasmodic …); participating or conditioned manner; stroke (final and initial profiles, punctuation, accentuation …). This aspect will supply a key to the reading of personality, going far beyond the significance of the small sign.

We have been dealing here with elementary writings not conditioned by particular neuropsychological difficulties; for these we need to consider problems related to disability. We close this short chapter with a few examples.

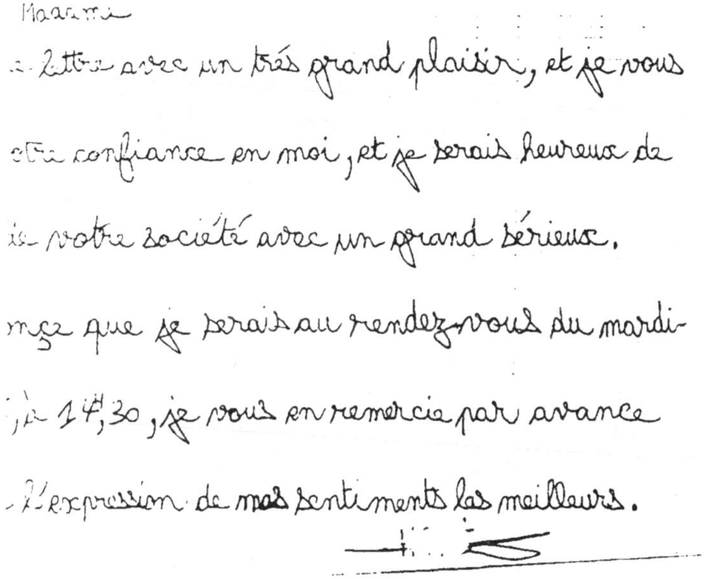
Madame
lettre avec un très grand plaisir, et je vous
otre confiance en moi, et je serais heureux de
ie votre société avec un grand sérieux.
mez que je serais au rendez-vous du mardi-
à 14,30, je vous en remercie par avance
l'expression de mes sentiments les meilleurs.

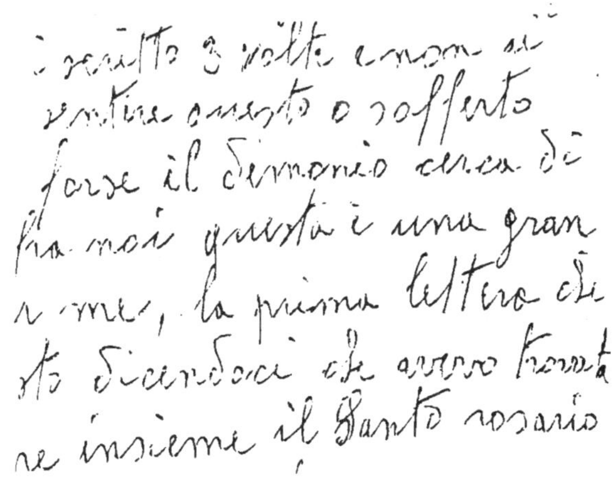
scritto 3 volte e non si
sentire questo o sofferto
forse il demonio cerca di
noi questa è una gran
me, la prima lettera di
dicendoci che avevo trovato
insieme il Santo rosario

Figure 87 (reduced)

(a) Worker of foreign origin: the triangle of the lower extensions with an extremely precise stroke indicates seriousness and commitment, but also a difficult character

(b) A practically illiterate woman: fluid writing with strokes towards north-east, rather excitable

Chapter Twelve

DIFFICULTIES IN WRITING

We shall now concentrate on the special difficulties which impede the acquiring of a fluid writing rhythm. We will not, however, be looking at *degenerative* writing due to organic illnesses or senility: cases from arteriosclerosis to Parkinson's disease and other illnesses. To study these conditions requires a vast case history and statistical evidence. We can only mention here Venturini's interesting research [237] in which he links various graphological signs to specific senile pathologies, and Renato Perrella's in-depth examination on the ability of the author of a handwritten will to understand and intend [196]. Among other publications concerning "tremors" in writing for judicial purposes is that by Bravo and Tarantino [45].

I. DYSGRAPHIA

We need to return, in our view, to Ajuriaguerra's researches because they constitute a basic scientific study whose truth cannot be ignored. When there are no intellectual or physical reasons why a child cannot achieve a normal writing performance, we call this condition *dysgraphia*. This is the case even if there are motor difficulties, as these are not necessarily the reasons for the disorder. Emotional or adaptability problems are often the source of children's pathologies, and in particular of dysgraphia. According to Ajuriaguerra, there are three major typical components in the pathology of dysgraphia:

- lack of page organization;
- awkwardness;
- errors of form and proportion.

Following a statistical survey on two similar groups of 55 children with dysgraphia and 55 without, Ajuriaguerra selected 25 items present in dysgraphia, of which 11 already belong to *Scale E*, but whose weighting coefficient could change. He therefore proposed a *Scale of Dysgraphia* with items listed from 1 to 25. To distinguish them from items *EF/EM* we shall call them D1–D25 (see Table 31).

SCALE OF DYSGRAPHIA

		Coefficient
Defective page organization		
D1 Overall dirty appearance	(M17)	1
D2 Broken baselines	(M25)	2
D3 Wavy baselines	(M26)	2
D4 Descending lines	(M27)	1
D5 Squeezed words		2
D6 Irregular space between words		1
D7 No margins		1
Awkwardness		
D8 Altered stroke		2
D9 Retouched letters	(M16)	2
D10 Pasty loops		1
D11 *m, n, i, u* with curved downstrokes		1
D12 *m, n, v, u* with angles		1
D13 False connections	(F11)	2
D14 Collages	(F12)	1
D15 Collisions	(M24)	3
D16 Jerks	(M23)	2
D17 Flying end strokes		2
D18 Irregular size	(M29)	2
D19 Poorly differentiated zones	(F14)	1
D20 Atrophied letters		2
Errors of form or proportion		
D21 Letters too structured or too weak		2
D22 Inadequate forms		1
D23 Writing too small or too large		2
D24 Zones out of proportion		2
D25 Writing either too wide or too narrow		1
		TOTAL:

DEGREE OF DYSGRAPHIA:
TYPE OF DYSGRAPHIA:

Table 31

II. TYPES OF DYSGRAPHIA

Ajuriaguerra identified five different groups of dysgraphic subjects, with each group presenting a similar graphic aspect with the same anomalies: *rigid, weak, impulsive, awkward, slow and precise.*

GROUP 1: **Rigid** (= tension across whole graphic syndrome) 12 items

1   Contracted overall
2   Middle zone letters taller than wide
3   External loops longer than wide
4   Angular (basic letters and connections)
5   Arches of *m*, *n* with acute angle (D12)
6   Squeezed lines (space less than two lower-case letters)
7   Squeezed letters (D5)
8   Very slanted writing
9   Numerous collisions (M24)
10 Retouched letters (M16)
11 Wide stroke and too heavy
12 Relatively constant slant

Always present in the first group are items 4 and 5; and in order of frequency 8, 2, 7, 1, 9, 12; the others are less frequent.

GROUP 2: **Weak** (= relaxed and careless across whole graphic syndrome) 11 items

1   Small writing
2   Hardly any development in the upper and lower zones
3   Floating movement
4   Rounded and sprawling, fat writing
5   Letters weak and a little imprecise
6   Descending lines (M27)
7   Words dancing on line (M28)
8   Many collisions (M24)
9   Atrophied letters (D20)
10 Irregular slant (M30)
11 Irregular size (M29)

Always present in the second group are items 3, 8, 11; and in order of frequency 7, 5, 9, 2, 1, 10.

GROUP 3: **Impulsive** (across whole graphic syndrome) 11 items

1   Impression of haste
2   Movement with a dynamic tendency
3   Numerous jerks (M23)
4   Wavy baselines (M26)
5   Inadequate page layout
6   Flying finals and accents (D17)
7   Connections either evolved or childish
8   Alternation of curves and acute angles
9   Alternation of tension and relaxation
10 Numerous retouchings (M16)
11 Strong irregularity of size (M29)

Always present in Group 3 are items 1, 2, 3; and in order of frequency 5, 11, 10, 7.

GROUP 4: **Awkward** (= graphomotor difficulties across whole graphic
          syndrome) 11 items

1   Overall awkward, badly formed
2   Surface writing, plump (F1–2)
3   Appalling quality of stroke
4   Insufficient margins and spaces
5   Outsized or atrophied writing
6   Childish connections (F11–12)
7   Strong irregularity of size (M29)
8   Words dancing on line (M28)
9   Arrhythmia of white spaces
10 High score on *EM* scale
11 Zones out of proportion (D24)

Always present in the fourth group are items 7 and 10; and very frequent 1, 9, 2, 8, 5.

GROUP 5: **Slow and precise** (= uniformity across whole graphic syndrome) 10 items

1   Studied page layout
2   Base line stable
3   Homogeneous spaces between words and lines
4   Lack of movement (F3)
5   Vertical writing
6   Surface writing (F1)
7   Precise and clear letters
8   Regular arcades in *m*, *n*
9   Reasonably constant slant
10 Reasonably constant size

Always present in the fifth group are items 3, 4, 6, 8, 9; and very frequent 2, 7, 10.

Observations

- Group 5 is often seen in a pure state.
- Groups 1, 2, and 3 are nearly always associated with other groups.
- Groups 3 and 5 are mutually exclusive.
- Group 4 is always associated with one or more groups. This is one of the key elements of dysgraphia. It may then be more appropriate to think of just four groups, with Awkwardness common to all, most of the time.
- The character type identified by belonging to a particular group directs the method of re-education.

Comparing normal children to those with dysgraphia, Ajuriaguerra finds the following difficulties:

- *positional difficulties*: hand, fingers, paper
- *tonic difficulties:* arm, shoulder, wrist, fingers
- *defective movements*: lack of finger movements
- *painful phenomena*: cramp, that is muscle contraction at the shoulder, lower arm, fingers, or other tonic variations; if speed is required; forced breaks in graphic tests. Often in slow writing with consequential school difficulties; badly coordinated movements, jerks, shaking, blocks; sweating; instability of posture or in holding the instrument; dislike of writing and panic.

In Fig. 88 we present the case of a French adolescent, very intelligent and sensitive, very good in scientific subjects but inhibited on the expressive plane especially in writing and spelling. Unfortunately he is not suited to experimental studies in chemistry and physics, because he trembles and often breaks the equipment. His writing certainly presents signs of basic dysgraphia and possibly dyslexia: psychological help with graphomotor re-education should be given. He can pursue normal sporting activities, for example play table tennis, and so is capable of coordination.

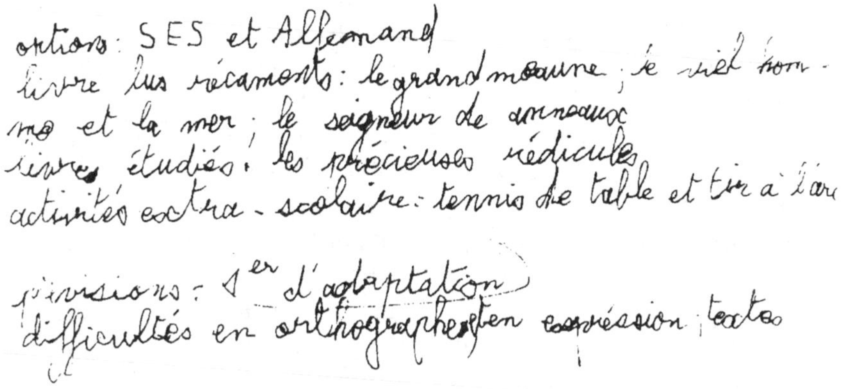

Figure 88
Thierry, 16 years old: excessively awkward writing

III. PSYCHOGENIC DYSGRAPHIA AND SCHOOLING

We present here a number of extracts from one of our papers on "cognitive and behavioural style and pathologies of the dysgraphic personality" [34a].

CASE 1
Boy aged 11 – elementary class 5 – "Rigid" group (Fig. 89a)

The basic syndrome of the Rigid clinical type is well represented. We find angles at the base of letters and in letter connections, also in the arches of *m* and *n*. The middle zone is taller than it is wide; in addition the pressure of the writing instrument is very strong, leaving impressions on the back of the paper. This fact alone, along with retouching, reinforces the signs of tension and anxiety.

At the behavioural level, we can deduce a strong repressed aggression. This is borne out by the crossing out of a word with heavy and repeated strokes. However, on a more positive note, we see that the words are not excessively squashed and a certain type of rhythm between the blacks (writing) and whites (blanks) emerges, which presages a reflective and critical ability. Sometimes several letters are connected in succession, indicating a capacity for logical thought.

From the emotional point of view, feelings and a vivacious sensitivity are obvious, but inhibited, susceptible, touchy, as borne out by the cramped middle zone, where letters are higher than they are wide, and also irregular in height. It is evident that the poor emotional expansiveness and probably lack of love from which this boy suffers predisposes him to a closed, diffident, insecure attitude and creates within him permanent conflict. However, his graphic rhythm is retained, making him strong enough to make progress, if helped to stretch himself, at the educational level.

Scale E shows an EF score of 7, indicating a higher than average intellectual level in comparison to others of the same age (at age 11 we find $EF = 8$ in Q1 schools), while the EM score of 16.5 indicates a motor level of around 9 years (at 9 years and 6 months we find EM 14.5 in Q3 schools). The score of 13.5 on the scale confirms the dysgraphia. The children's graphic components which determine this low level of motor skill are those which essentially concern basic rigidity: narrow letters – constant verticality – angles, to which is added the symptom of tension, an incisive and heavy stroke. We can therefore deduce that this boy's dysgraphia is not due to real motor difficulties but instead to a deep state of anxiety whose reasons must be sought, whether in the individual or in the family dynamic. The anxiety in this case creates an interiorized state of hypersensitivity with possible so-called "catastrophic" reactions, with a fear of not controlling situations.

On the basis of Ajuriaguerra's observations drawn from his work on the re-education of writing, we suggest that the teacher could take on the re-education role in this particular case. The teacher must instil the child with self-esteem as he is unable to withstand being reprimanded. The teacher needs to value him by attaching little weight to possible difficulties that he may have at school such as aggressive outbursts, and so ease his defensive tension. The child is not at all passive, his will can therefore be used as a lever to modify his mode of perception based on emotional apprehension, thereby turning to advantage his substantial vital energies.

CASE 2
Boy aged 9 years 5 months – elementary class 4 – "Weak" group (Fig. 89b)

A totally different graphic profile comes from the "Weak" group, which is the largest in our sample. Typical of the group, this handwriting shows a "sloppy" outlook, but it is not overall neglected, with its flowing, floating movement and tendency to rounded forms. The scale of dysgraphia gives a score of 15 and defines it as dysgraphia by "convention".

On each line it is noticeable that there are one or more words rubbed out and rewritten above, which demonstrates the boy's uncertainty and insecurity. We also see that there are some extended oblique *final strokes*, lacking firmness, indicating impulsive ambitious aspirations more than will. This weak context does not favour intellectual energies, he has a restless lack of attention, feeble concentration, and a rather unstable but passive mind. He is certainly difficult to motivate unless his good intention is used as a lever, as he is easily influenced and gregarious, which is proper to his lymphatic temperament.

There is no pathological state here but only a weak character, with childish emotions and a stunted graphomotor development. This is essentially identified through the uncertainty of spatial organization and the contrast between the nearly compulsive rubbings out (which do not easily appear on photocopies), and the flying strokes as releases of tension, within an overall indecisive and ambivalent tendency.

The pressure is very uneven, and in particular the high i-dots are distinctly heavy, confirming a state of anxiety subject to "nonchalance", prevalent in weak and inattentive children who are unconsciously highlighting their inadequacy. The writing style will be further weakened, not through lack of intelligence, but through lack of concentration, a changeable, wandering inattention, and a scatter-brain mind that does not grasp the essential of problems.

The boy risks being easily influenced and must be firmly controlled, but to develop the emotional level he also needs to be reassured. His self-image is full of doubt. More than anything else, he will need emotional balance and security to permit him to develop his potential. In this case too we are not concerned with graphomotor re-education, but rather looking for an emotional, protective, yet also guiding source of comfort. In the next few years the risks of being easily led, of weakness in resisting influences, must be held in check.

The "Weak" group, according to French researchers, is distinguished by a "floating" movement, numerous "collisions" between letters, size irregularities, loose and imprecise letters dancing on the line. However, having seen the Italian model much more than the French, we find that in Italy there is a slightly different graphic configuration, with full letters and strokes which stretch along the horizontal axis in a very weak manner.

In this group are found the *components of economy* (which are part of the four types of children's components identified by Ajuriaguerra), which tend to neglect both graphic and psychological precision and engagement. They reveal in the child a conflictual state, which sets up a defence mechanism that allows him to shirk difficulties and to escape conflict. The "weak" dysgraphic is certainly a child who is easily tired and becomes discouraged if not continually supported. However, escapism cannot be a solution approved by educational authorities, instead it ends up causing further problems.

CASE 3
Boy aged 9 years 5 months – elementary class 5 – "Insecure" group (Fig. 90a)

This is difficult to classify within Ajuriaguerra's categories, even if the neglected style, with weak forms and a floating movement, is close to the "Weak" group. But graphologists can adapt certain aspects. In this case we propose to call such writing "*insecure*", indicating a different graphomotor aspect from the group "Awkward". The aspect of psychological confusion, which this writing at first sight evokes by its broken down appearance, deserves closer scrutiny.

Scale *E* reveals a normal intellectual level (items *EF*) but the graphomotor level *EM* is only equal to the norm for the age of 8, almost two years late. The dysgraphia scale shows a very high score due, above all, to errors in structure and proportion (weak control in the middle zone, microscopic

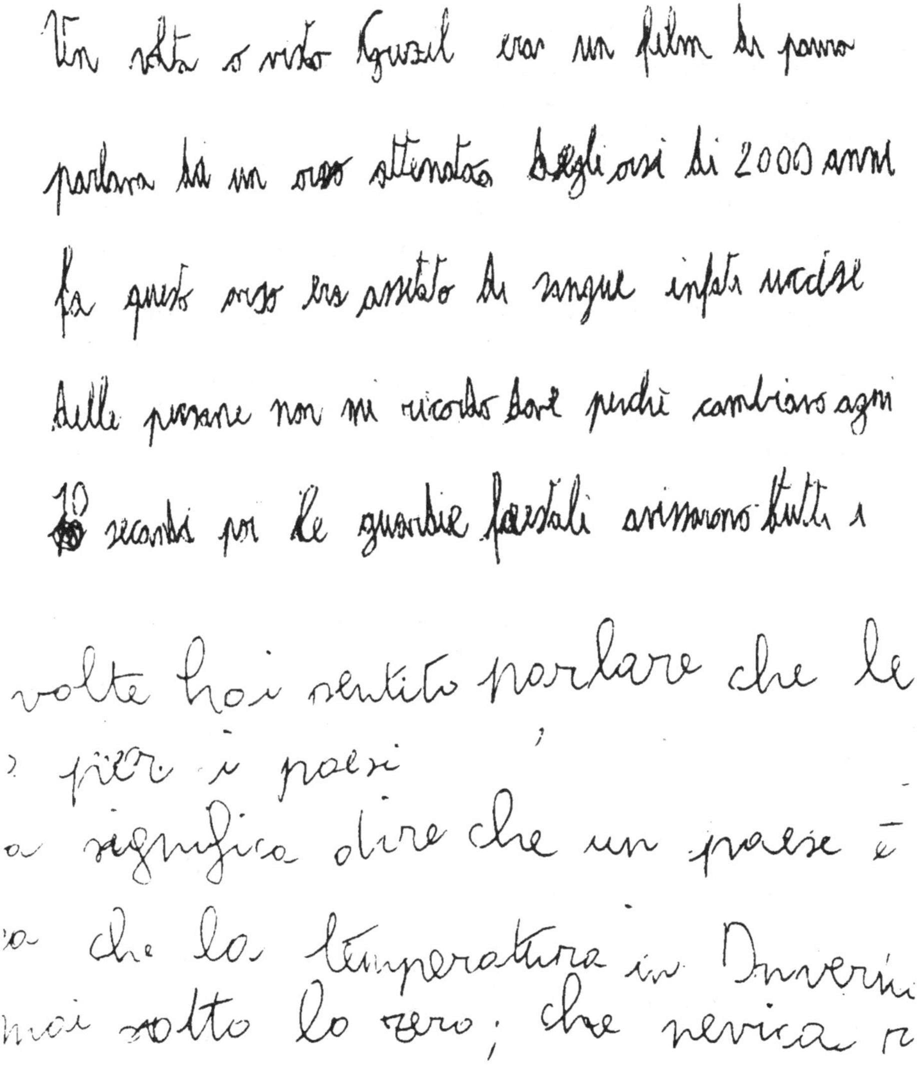

Un volta o visto Guzzil era un film di paura
parlava da un orso attentato degli ossi di 2000 anni
fa questo orso era assetato di sangue infatti uccise
delle persone non mi ricordo dove perché cambiano ogni
10 secondi per le guardie forestali avvisarono tutti a

volte hoi sentito parlare che le
? pier i paesi
a significa dire che un paese è
a che la temperatura in Inverni
noi sotto lo zero; che nevica r

Figure 89
(a) Dysgraphia, Rigid group: boy aged 11 years
(b) Dysgraphia, Weak group: boy aged 9 years 5 months

letters with sudden hypertrophy: *r, i,* sometimes *a* for example). The pressure is light, which reflects hypersensitivity and nervous fragility, while the atrophied lower extensions confirm insecurity, and the irregularity of size confirms emotional swings.

The style then suggests an intuitive boy, refined and sensitive but with difficulties in structuring his own thoughts, with fleeting attention, given to dreaming more than concrete reasoning, prey to fantasies, and in consequence indecisive and restless. A vicious circle is created between a dreaming mind and an almost pathologic impressionability and sensitivity. In our view there are deep underlying reasons for the dysgraphia, and the graphologist must advise psychological intervention given the risks of depression and even destruction. We also note that the boy has been educated too fast, at least a year ahead of his age group, and this has certainly not been helpful.

Case 4
Boy aged 8 years 4 months – elementary class 3 – "Impulsive" group (Fig. 90b)

The group of *Impulsives* shows a tendency to a dynamic and sudden movement with a jerky and badly controlled writing progression, and an inadequate page layout. This impulsiveness could either be stimulating or destabilizing. The instability that could follow may lead to insufficient development at school through lack of application and steadfastness allied to impatience, in other words an overall excitability. The child bores easily and is always searching for new and different stimulation. He is not interested in school commitments unless he becomes the leader or is the best in the class, and this is very difficult given his writing problems. Even for this group, dysgraphia prevents a sufficient writing speed and in consequence progress at school is hampered. Within this group we find

Figure 90 (*see opposite page* ☛)
(a) Dysgraphia, Insecure group: boy 9 years 5 months, class 5 elementary school
(b) Dysgraphia, Impulsive group: boy 8 years 4 months

Pan

Momenti di gloria

La prima [illegible] diceva che l'autrice aveva
una varietà di colori però gli mancavano i
[illegible] per il sangue, per le lacrime, invece
per tutte le [illegible] [illegible] che esistono al
mondo, invece aveva l'arancio per la

Vincita in piscina
Un giorno in
piscina (della scuola)
mi sono divertito
perché ho vinto

young boys with mild neurological problems which are difficult to diagnose precisely. According to Wallon, however, they can be noticed by "postural defects".

The unstable child, according to Ajuriaguerra, is rooted in "ambivalent and restless action" and "hungry for movement". Above all he "suffers from being poorly tolerated, poorly loved, poorly directed, which leads him to react in the opposite way, either aggressively or passively." In other words the unstable impulsive child readily presents personality disorders and often, according to Ajuriaguerra, "uses dysgraphia to oppose both the school and family environment." Psychotherapy is therefore thought to be necessary.

Not all impulsives reach this state of instability. For some, an appropriate graphic re-education instilling a greater calm and reassurance could be sufficient. We shall now illustrate such a case. (Except for this case, we have avoided cases of boys only aged 8 attending elementary class 3, because it is not always possible to distinguish motor difficulties linked to that age, from those specifically linked to dysgraphia.)

The results of the graphometric test were: *EF* scale, good intellectual level in relation to age (ovals written without lifting the pen), while the *EM* scale identifies a motor level normally linked to age 7. The dysgraphia scale shows a score of 16.5, confirming the dysgraphia noticed at first glance.

What is interesting in this writing is a dexterity which could be defined as "motor creative", where the boy avoids lifting the pen in forming ovals, by a movement (against the norm) in a clockwise direction, in sharp contrast to a graphic progression that occurs "in jerks". There remains the doubt that he might be left-handed, though the teacher did not say so.

Reasons why we can classify him within the impulsive range are the dynamic and decisive stroke with some flying final strokes. The contrast that we have pointed out certainly indicates conflict – if it may be said – between can and want, his real motor abilities not being at the level of his creativity. He therefore risks losing nerve and failing at both the intellectual and behavioural level. Graphotherapy is advised, with its related relaxation techniques and appropriate exercises to alleviate the child's lack of graphomotor rhythm.

IV. LEARNING AND BEHAVIOURAL DISORDERS

We will not enter into the vast case history of severe learning disorders, which is more the field of medical-psycho-pedagogical research. We present instead the cases of some children in elementary school for whom psychological or re-educational support might have been a lifeline, as often it is the teacher alone who must face up to these difficulties.

A case of dyslexia

At heart dyslexia is a reading disorder, with a tendency to letter inversion, confusing *p* with *b*, *t* with *d*, or to lengthening sounds. In practice dyslexia extends to a general disorder of learning and behaviour. Attention is vague, there is often a short-term memory, writing itself though not necessarily dysgraphic shows signs of abnormalities: inversions, repetitions of letters/ sounds, confused spelling. In these conditions school development becomes rapidly deficient. Various re-educational exercises can be started, but often parents do not want to admit the need for a neurological consultation, preferring to blame the child's indolence for bad school results.

Fig. 91 shows the case of a boy with excellent motor abilities – confirmed by the absolutely normal outcome of his tree test – but incapable of the minimum school performance. Well-behaved and passive, he takes part in school life without being involved on either the sensory or mental plane.

A case of epilepsy

Fig. 92 shows a sample of micro writing by a girl under medication for epilepsy and whose inclusion at school poses severe problems due to unpredictable and aggressive behaviour. The writing indicates that there is no lack of intellectual capabilities, but her self-image, as confirmed by her tree, is miserable. Due to complicated and dramatic family circumstances, the girl is in contact with too much of "adult" life for her age. She is also extremely lonely and is searching for attention and affection. Her relationship with the other children is not good and the teacher's effort to gain empathy from other parents to her problems has been particularly fruitless. This girl tends to attach herself morbidly to any adults who give her attention. (It must be remembered that aggression and excessive affection are often inherent to the pathology of epilepsy.)

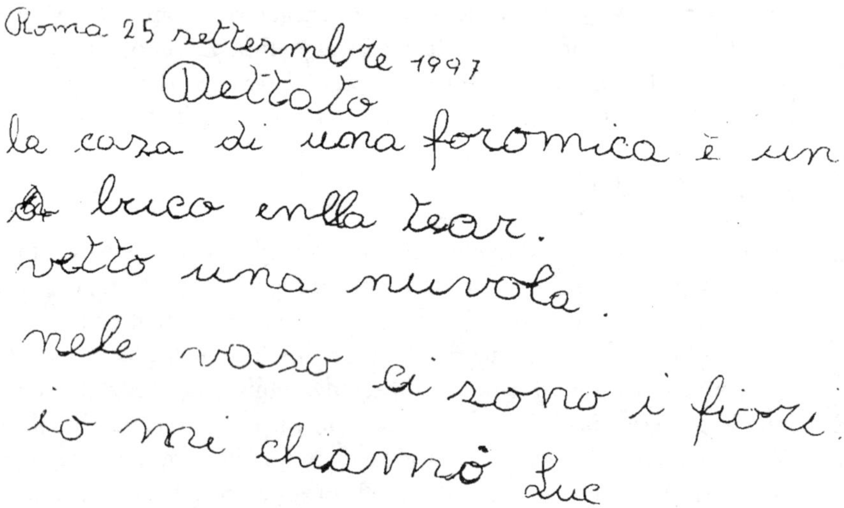

Figure 91 (reduced)
Luciano, 8 years, dyslexia and learning difficulties

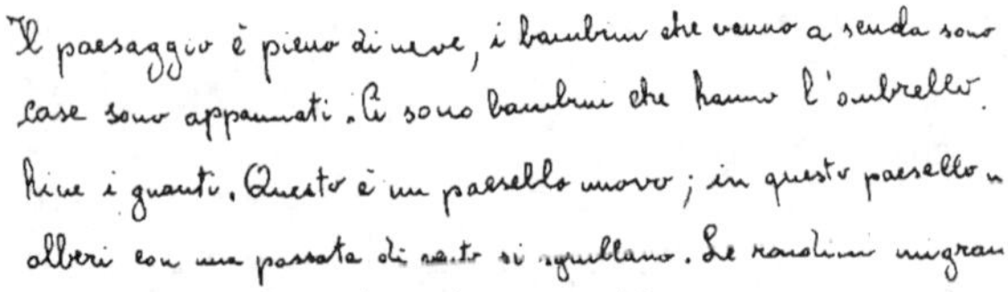

Figure 92 (reduced)
Marta, 10 years, epilepsy and behavioural disorders
(writing and tree both on one large page)

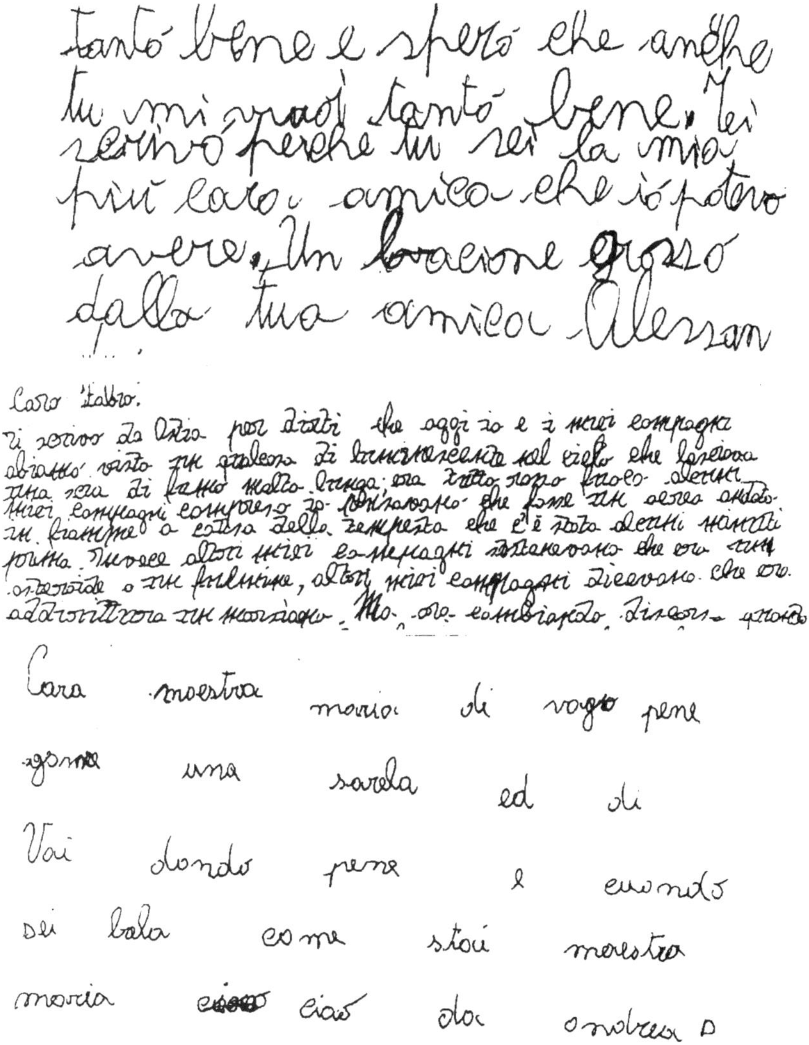

Figure 93 (reduced)

(a) Alessandra: 8 years 7 months, hysterical tendency, poorly valued by mother

(b) Sergio: 10 years 6 months, strong psychosomatic disorders, quarrelsome, proud

(c) Valerio: 11 years 5 months, very aggressive, mistreated as a young child; the excessive spacing is an "alarm signal": aggression seems reactive and not established but there is a risk of schizoid pathology

If we look at the writing of three boys from a school on the outskirts of Rome, we see that they pose a problem of inclusion to the teacher as a result of family upset (Fig. 93).

V. MENTAL HANDICAP, WRITING, AND SCHOOLING

A graphologist needs to be included in the medical and psychotherapeutic team for a delicate approach to mental handicap. Graphologists' roles in control, support, and prognostic help can be very useful. Often they are invited to assist in the case of children with difficulties at school, who have trouble with the *formal* thinking of Piaget. Through their writing we can identify the level of anguish, inhibition, and sometimes depression, or the opposite, impulsiveness and aggression.

MENTAL INSUFFICIENCY				
	Profound	Severe	Moderate	Light	Limited
IQ	≤ 25	≤ 40	≤55	≤ 70	≤ 85
MENTAL AGE	2–3		6–7		
RECOGNITION	Primary school			During school	
AUTONOMY	Little: Eating Cleanliness	Retarded motor dev. Some social freedom		No academic success but after school activities possible	
LANGUAGE	Almost none	No syntax or reading		No bad anomalies	
THINKING		Hardly working		No capacity of *formal thought*	
ALTERATIONS	Physical and neurological; epileptic crises			Rare somatic problems	
	SCHOOLING	IMPOSSIBLE		Low socio-cultural conditions	

Table 32 (Taken from our article [36])

In Table 32 we sum up the development according to the handicap term "mental insufficiency", which concerns between 1.5% and 5.5% of the population according to data taken from Ajuriaguerra and Marcelli [5] and in Figs 94 and 95 we present some written examples of mental handicap.

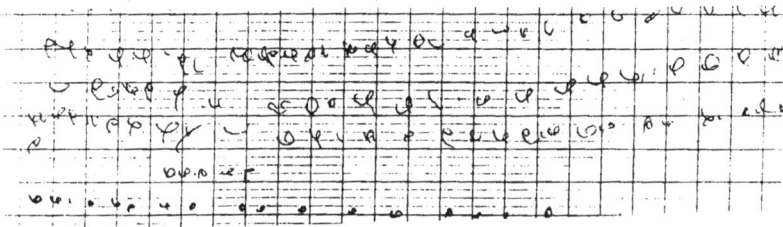

Figure 94 (reduced)
(a) Paulette, 16: "insufficient mental average", epileptic with character difficulties
(b) Pierre, 19: IQ = 50, "insufficient mental average", personality disorders
(c) Sonia, 19: "insufficient mental average", neonatal encephalopathy, personality disorders

Figure 95
Enrico, 10 years, hemiplegic from birth

PART IV

PSYCHOLOGY
AND
GRAPHOLOGY

Chapter Thirteen

PERSONALITY THEORY
AND THE FREUDIAN SCHOOL

A book on graphology cannot include all aspects of psychology or psychoanalysis, it can only offer a selection to help ground already established graphological connections, or those that might later be suggested. The psychology expositions are therefore only a guide for graphology students, who must deepen their knowledge of the named authors.

Before discussing the relationship between psychology and graphology, we give a brief introduction on the development of psychology and scientific graphology and their interaction from the nineteenth century to the present day. We then describe in Section II the principal aspects of Freudian theory and the graphological correlations which have been established. In Section III we introduce the perspective of Jean Bergeret, who, having perfectly assimilated Freudian concepts, suggests re-reading them according to a structural point of view, which today is at the heart of French psychopathology. We will also attempt to establish a basis for further graphological correlation with certain aspects of Kleinian theory in Section IV, a prospect we have already outlined in a paper to the Congress of Jerusalem in 1987.

I. INTRODUCTION

Birth of psychology

The term psychology seems to have been used first by the naturalist and philosopher Charles Bonnet in 1754 to designate a "science of the spirits", from the Greek *psychê* "soul, breath" and *logos* "word, discussion". A major impetus had already been given by Descartes (1596–1650): his theory of body and soul dualism had opened up empirical and experimental research on the mechanics of the body and the locus of mental functions. His doctrine of "innate ideas" had encouraged significant developments, even if only in opposition to his theory.

In 1834 the adjective "psychological" occurs in Boiste's *Dizionario universale della lingua francese*, at the time when psychology had detached itself from metaphysics and so from philosophy, and had emerged as a discipline in its own right. At this point psychology underwent a rapid evolution, based upon three principal currents: positivist philosophy, materialism, and empiricism.

In France the *positivism* of Auguste Comte between 1830 and 1854 exchanged introspection for the study of observable and provable phenomena, whether biological, social, or behavioural. *Materialism* favoured physiological processes as the basis of mental functions. On this subject we note the French research conducted by Bell and Magendie (1811–12) on the nervous physiology and the experimental research by Weber and Fechner in Germany (around 1860) on psychophysical laws of sensation. We mention also Helmholtz's research on mechanisms of perception and transmission of the nervous flow. Later in Leipzig, in 1879, Wundt established the first laboratory and first specialist journal, which gave an academic status to experimental psychology.

Finally the English *empirical* school recognized Locke (1632–1704) as its founder for demonstrating that "ideas" are the product of learning and custom, and all knowledge derives from empirical experience. His theses were taken up and expanded later by Berkeley, Hume, Hartley, and James and John Stuart Mill.

Around the middle of the nineteenth century the basis for an experimental psychology along scientific methods was, then, well established. According to Fraisse and Piaget [93] three European centres developed their own theories and practices: "In Germany experimental psychology grew from the meeting of philosophical ideas and psycho-physiological problems; English psychology is based on the evolutionist input and the debates that it provoked, while French philosophy is based on psycho-pathology interpreted by philosophers."

By the beginning of the twentieth century psychopathology, from Ribot's original ideas to Freud's psychoanalysis and Jaspers' phenomenological approach, contributed much to the development of psychology.

To the associationist doctrines that dissolve the mental functions into one elementary unity (psychological atomism) belong *holistic* concepts (from the Greek "whole, complete") which consider the totality of the organism different from the sum of its parts. This vision has been taken up within the medical world by the neurologist Hughlings Jakson, to elaborate his theory on hierarchic levels in the nervous system.

Above all, however, it was the school of *Gestalt psychology* or *psychology of form* founded in Berlin by Wertheimer, Koffka, and Köhler that radically revised in an original manner the principles of perception, and by extension those of cerebral organization. For *Gestalt* psychologists, perception is organized spontaneously according to an overall vision, on the basic principle that a *collection* cannot be reduced to the *sum* of its parts, but constitutes a *whole*, which presents a type of dynamic structure inherent to the interaction between the parts. In the same way, learning, intelligence, or the laws of mental function are viewed according to the psychology of form. Learning by means of intuition (*insight*) is then the basis of a new type of teaching.

Other developments have enriched this new discipline: *clinical* psychology, which builds on previous medical or educational experiences to work out methods of rehabilitation or re-education; *psychometry* and the statistical researches from Galton to Spearman or Binet which confirm a possibility for scientific validation; and *genetic* psychology from Stanley Hall to Watson, followed later by Piaget's *behaviourism*.

Birth of scientific graphology

Until the end of the nineteenth century, scientific graphology did not appear to have strong links with the psychology of the time. The cultural background of the Abbé Michon was essentially theological and philosophical. All the same Michon was an integral part of Victor Hugo's century and absorbed the enthusiasm of the Romantic movement. He had certainly been charged by the current of positivism as well, but he went beyond the purely associationist influence which dominated the psychological thought of the period.

It was only at the beginning of the twentieth century that psychology and graphology were linked in a more obvious way, starting in France. The experimental psychologist Alfred Binet in 1905 offered his own contribution to turn what he termed "*a nascent art*" into the scientific destiny of "*a future art*", undertaking work on statistical validation, as already mentioned in the first chapter, beside the contribution of Crépieux-Jamin, who seems to have allied himself to the German Gestalt psychology.

It was from the meeting of these ideas that Jaminian graphological theory was born. From a structural and Gestalt basis, Crépieux-Jamin was able in 1910 to acquit Dreyfus in the course of his judicial rehabilitation after ten years of hard labour in Guyana, by showing the similarities and differences between Dreyfus's writing and that of the true culprit and traitor, Esterhazy.

In the 1920s the doctor and psychologist Pierre Janet, one of the most authoritative figures in French psychology, paid particular attention to graphology. At the International Congress of Graphology organized by the Paris Graphological Society in 1928, which Janet attended as guest of honour, he declared that psychology could not be directly applied for graphology's immediate use, but rather that graphological science was "one of a variety of psychological studies, and worked on its own to represent facts, observations, and hypotheses", elements which must be compared with observations obtained by other means. At the same Congress, Crépieux-Jamin emphasized the importance of "starting with the study of the writing and not the psychology."

We should now focus essentially upon the graphologist, whose quality of research and ethical care, allied to technical, psychological, and cultural preparation, are guarantees of the development and progress of this science. However, even though graphology regards itself as an autonomous discipline, it develops within an interdisciplinary concept, and in particular its affinity with psychology directs its evolution.

Following the advent of psychoanalysis at the end of the nineteenth century, the notion of depth psychology has always been of great importance for psychologists. The new psychiatric directions of the 1920s, when the work of Bleuler, Kretschmer, Rorschach, and Jung appeared, as well as

Freud's reworking of the psychoanalytic theories of the Ego and Id in 1923, have prepared a fertile ground for graphologists to further their psychological investigation.

Around 1930 two Middle European graphologists, Ania Teillard and Max Pulver, integrated the notions of depth psychology to their graphological vision, as we mentioned in the first chapter. They did not propose new graphological theories but, having assimilated the psychoanalytic conceptions of Freud, Jung, and Adler, both departed from the solid base of the French and German graphological schools to propose a different *level* of character and personality interpretation, a level based on the deep dynamic of the personality, and taking into consideration the dimension of the unconscious and its mechanisms. Today such an approach is defined as a *"psychodynamic perspective"*. For more than sixty years the graphopsychological basis perfected by these two authors has been used, completed, and checked by generations of graphologists, without many substantial changes.

II. SIGMUND FREUD AND PSYCHOANALYSIS

Sigmund Freud, eldest child of a Jewish family in Vienna, was a brilliant student, and became a doctor of neuropathology in 1885 at the age of 29. After a stay in Paris where he attended Charcot's courses on hysteria, he pursued further studies on nervous illnesses on his return to Vienna, making use of electrotherapy and hypnosis. A second journey, to the psychiatrists and neurologists Liébault and Berheim at Nancy, put him into contact with post-hypnotic suggestion techniques. In 1895 Freud together with Breuer published *Studies on Hysteria* in which the famous case of "Anna O" is recounted. This period represented a decisive moment in Freud's life, when he structured his analytical method through the technique of "free associations". This is also when his last daughter Anna – who later became one of the most eminent psychiatrists of the century – was born and when his father died. From this moment, Freud deepened his hypotheses and observations by the process of *self-analysis*.

Beginning with his observations on hysteria and the cathartic effect of the crisis which allows us to recover the infantile trauma, Freud perfected his *psychoanalytical method*. This theory is based on the relationship between *conscious* and *unconscious* through *free associations*, the analysis of *dreams*, and the study of *transference*. Freud then proposed a *theory of personality* grounded on its *genesis* (interaction between hereditary and environmental factors), its *structure* (with its three instances: *Id*, *Ego*, *Superego*), and its *dynamic* (adaptation and use of mental energy or *Libido*).

According to Freudian theory, four key parameters guide the formation of personality: the *object relationship*, *psychosexual development*, the *identification process*, and the principal *defence mechanisms* which it brings on (*repression, projection, sublimation* …).

Instances: topical and dynamic concepts

According to the *topical* principle, which Freud reworked around 1920–3, three *instances* or systems structure a personality: the Id, Ego, and Superego.

The *Id* is a sort of reservoir of the libido and mental energy in general. Its contents are unconscious, hereditary, and innate, or acquired and repressed. Freud chose a neuter pronoun to indicate this system (*id* in Latin), to indicate that its organization is defined only in opposition to that of the Ego.

The *Ego* is the system which controls reality. Its independence, however, is restricted because in its essential task of mediation it faces on one side the pressures and impulsive overflows of the Id, and on the other the repression and prohibitions of the Superego. The Ego on the one hand develops from the Id and on the other hand structures itself through successive identification processes. It uses various *defence mechanisms*, which after Freud would be extensively described by Anna Freud and Melanie Klein.

"In its relation to the Id," says Freud, "the Ego can be compared to the horse rider who must control the greater strength of the horse, with the difference that the rider controls the horse by his own strength, whereas the Ego does it with borrowed strength … the Ego generally translates into action the will of the Id as if it were its own will."

The *Superego* is built on the internalization of repressive forces in which the moral conscience and feelings of guilt grapple with the Ego, as well as through various other identification processes.

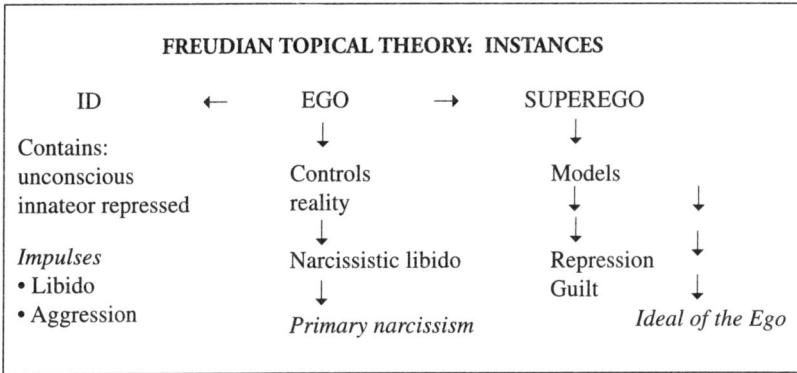

FREUDIAN TOPICAL THEORY: INSTANCES		
ID ← EGO → SUPEREGO		
Contains:	↓	↓
unconscious	Controls	Models
innateor repressed	reality	↓
	↓	↓
Impulses	Narcissistic libido	Repression
• Libido	↓	Guilt
• Aggression	*Primary narcissism*	*Ideal of the Ego*

Table 33

According to Lagache [125], the Superego corresponds to authority and the *Ideal of the Ego* to the way in which the subject must conform to come up to the expectations of authority. The *Ideal of the Ego* results from the convergence of narcissism (the idealization of the Ego) and identifications with parents or their substitutes and with collective ideals. The *Ideal Ego* (a different term) relates to an ideal of narcissistic omnipotence built on the model of childish narcissism, which according to Freud is a condition that the subject attempts to recapture. For Lacan the Ideal Ego is an essentially narcissistic formation with origins in the mirror phase and belongs to the imaginary dimension.

According to Lagache the Ideal Ego contains sadomasochistic tones, among which is the negation of the other relative to one's own affirmation. We quote finally Lagache's summary: "The *Ideal of the Ego* corresponds to what the individual must be to react to the demands of the *Superego*. The *Ideal Ego*, with which it is often confused, relates to what the subject expects of himself, to react to the demands of a childish illusion of omnipotence and to primary identification to an all-powerful parent."

Object relation

It is important to understand this principle well because according to different psychoanalytical theories it leads to different standpoints. The term *object* is in current use in the language of psychoanalysis either by itself or contained in various expressions: *choice of object, loss of object, love object, object relation, good object, partial object, transitional object*.

In Freud the *object* is defined as the *contingent* means whereby desires are satisfied. The *object relation* is therefore structured according to the relational intensity or to privations experienced in the course of psychosexual development, and connected therefore to gratification (or lack of it) of the impulses, these being linked to their bodily source. The *object* is that "*with which and through which*" the impulse can reach its intent. Thus for the unweaned child, a very precise object, the mother's breast or its substitute – adapted to being taken in, devoured – could be the basis of a so-called *oral relationship*. A relationship based on the means of incorporation will establish itself with the world at a real level and at an imaginary level, and, according to circumstances, could remain either more or less fixed or could evolve.

The *object relation* is the first manifestation of a dialectic interrelation. From the first *object*, the mother in a broad sense, it starts from the first partial or fragmented representations of objects, as well as from *parts* of the subject, to evolve into a relation in two directions: auto-eroticism, and the *anaclytic* relation, a relation of dependence. The latter occurs through experiencing the *absence* of the object and the traumas so caused. In contemporary psychoanalysis a *typical object* is located for each type of relation: *oral, anal, phallic, Oedipal,* according to stages in psychosexual development.

During a course of psychoanalysis a *transfer* mechanism occurs when an emotional relation to a childhood object – generally the parents – is transferred to another object or person, in this case the analyst. Within the context of such a clinical situation, this mechanism is controlled and represents the focal point of the therapy.

Mental development (Table 34)

For Freud mental life is governed by certain basic principles. The *Constancy Principle* tends to maintain within the mental apparatus an amount of stimulation at the lowest and the most constant level possible. This involves the satisfaction of "unloading" impulses but it also involves defending oneself against excesses of excitability. From this another principle derives, the *Pleasure Principle*, which aims to avoid sorrow and tension.

The *Reality Principle* safeguards adequate regulation of the *Pleasure Principle*, by developing conscious functions adaptive to reality, such as attention, memory, judgement. Parallel with the development of the Reality Principle – and in direct dialogue with the Pleasure Principle – mental energy flows in two ways, one more instinctual (*Primary Process*), the other (*Secondary Process*) more controlled.

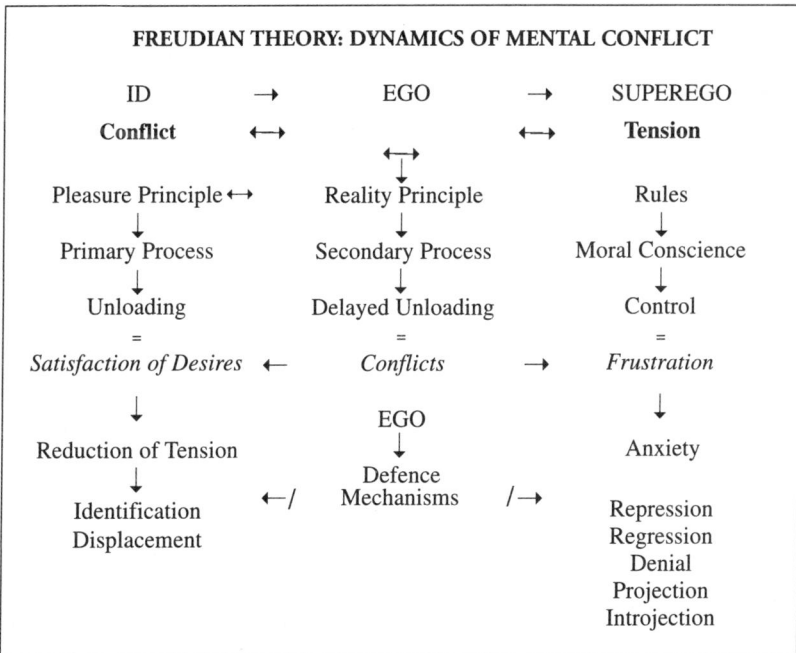

FREUDIAN THEORY: DYNAMICS OF MENTAL CONFLICT

ID →	EGO →	SUPEREGO
Conflict ←→	←→	**Tension**
	←→↓	
Pleasure Principle ←→	Reality Principle	Rules
↓	↓	↓
Primary Process	Secondary Process	Moral Conscience
↓	↓	↓
Unloading	Delayed Unloading	Control
=	=	=
Satisfaction of Desires ←	*Conflicts* →	*Frustration*
↓	EGO	↓
Reduction of Tension	↓	Anxiety
↓	Defence	
Identification ←/	Mechanisms /→	Repression
Displacement		Regression
		Denial
		Projection
		Introjection

Table 34

PRIMARY PROCESS – SECONDARY PROCESS

Freud called the two operating modes of the mental apparatus *primary process* and *secondary process*. In contrast to each other, the first expresses the free flow of mental energy, while the second signals the Ego's moderating intervention. In the *primary process* the mental function tends to escape from the control of reality to attain the intoxication of the desires. In the *secondary process* the Ego inhibits the Id by trying to delay satisfaction – even if not always successful. The eloquent imagery proposed by Freud evokes the immaturity of the "horse" in the primary process, the maturity of the "rider" in the secondary process, and that of the "judge" who impersonates the dictates of the Superego.

IMPULSES

Psychoanalytical theory has established a theory of *impulses*, defining them as energetic and motor drives that carry the body towards a goal. *Drive, source, object,* and *goal* are the terms used in this theory. The impulse according to Freud represents "*a concept bordering between psyche and soma.*" The *source* of the impulse is a state of excitement or tension in one of the body's organs: it is therefore somatic. The impulse's *goal* is the suppression of such excitement or tension, while its *object* is the way in which satisfaction is obtained. This *object* could be a real person, or it could be partly real or imaginary.

The impulse is therefore found at the boundary between the biological, the organic, and the mental. Freud set out two impulse theories: the first following his discoveries on *narcissism* (1911–14) and later a second, which draws a distinction between *life impulse* and *death impulse*.

LIBIDO

Freud called the general energy of sexual impulses *Libido*. This is a constant quantity that finds an object either in the self (*narcissistic libido*) or in an external object (*objective libido*). The love that a person devotes to the self is subtracted from the external objects and viceversa. For example in a state of illness, of weariness, or in the case of melancholic depression, part of the libido withdraws from the external world to concentrate on the Ego. The maturation of the body determines the development of the impulses, and during life's course, from infancy to old age, precise phases or *impulsive stages* succeed each other.

PHASES AND EROGENOUS ZONES (Tables 35–7)

Various areas in the body give sexual excitement. They are called *erogenous zones* and according to Freud "they constitute from the beginning of psychosexual development the elective points of exchange with the environment, and in a special way they solicit remedies and therefore arousal from the mother." (See Freud's *Three Reports on Childhood Sexuality*.)

ORAL PHASE		
Erogenous zone from birth	*MOUTH*	up to 2 years old
1. *Passive oral* Symbiosis + will to live, to receive	Sucking → Primary narcissism Autoeroticism	up to 6 months old Emotional greed + anxiety of being eaten
2. *Active oral* *or sado-oral* Aggression + Self-assurance	Biting → Teething Ambivalence: love/hate Narcissism	7 months, to weaning Demands + Frustration, sado-masochism
DEFENCE MECHANISMS		
Introjection – Projection – Denial – Fixation		
CHARACTER Active/passive dependence Dissatisfaction – frustration Emotional greed – curiosity for everything Exacerbated desires Emotional demands Pathology: *Hysteria*		

Table 35

ANAL PHASE		
Erogenous zone from 1	→ *ANUS*	up to 3 or 4 years
Arousal: evacuation possession	Sadism giving, retaining, holding	destructive elimination adult opposition
	Emotional ambivalence Bisexuality Establishment of Superego	
Aggression	Anxiety	sense of guilt, shame

SENSORY AND MOTOR DEVELOPMENT
Walking – Exploring – Taking – Holding – Destroying

COGNITIVE DEVELOPMENT
Reflection – Judgement – Firm motor functions – Achieving independence

LANGUAGE AND SYMBOLIC DEVELOPMENT
Magic of the "word" – Naming things – Role of "no"

DEFENCE MECHANISMS
Reactive formation – Denial – Isolation – Fixation

CHARACTER
Obstinacy – refusal – greed
Domination/submission
Dissatisfaction – aggression
Fanatical – active – sad

Pathology: *Obsessive neuroses – sadomasochism*

Table 36

For Freud sexuality is therefore a complex totality, that takes part in a series of excitations and activity already present in infancy, which will return later in normal adult sexual love. The libido develops along successive *phases*, each being under the dominance of a particular erogenous zone and under the influence of a specific object relation. In children these phases are: the *oral, anal, phallic,* and *genital.*

PHALLIC PHASE		
	→	
Erogenous zone from 3	*GENITALIA*	up to 5 years Masturbation
Urethral pleasure: passing water, retention	Mastery	Fantasy Sense of guilt
DEFENCE MECHANISMS Reactive formation – Identification		
OEDIPAL CONFLICT Identity problems – Attachment to past – Hesitation – Difficulty in engaging – Identification with maternal image		
CHARACTER Exhibitionism/voyeurism Ambition/disdain Psychological virility Initiative for doing/creating things by oneself		
Pathology Male: *Virile pride – aggression or block* Female: *Attracting attention from men, leaving them the initiative: fixation*		

Table 37

THE OEDIPAL CONFLICT

We quote the words of Daniel Lagache [125] on the dynamics of psychosexual development. "In the boy, the positive *Oedipus complex* consists of the fact that while intensifying his love for the mother, he feels a conflict between his love for the father (based on identification with the father) and hatred against the father (based upon the father's privileges which are forbidden to him). The anguish of castration leads him to renounce exclusive possession of the mother. One speaks of the negative *Oedipus complex* when the mother is seen as an obstacle to love for the father. In the girl, the advance towards the father is more complex because of her disappointments in her relationship with the mother, particularly in noticing the lack of the penis; *penis envy* is replaced by the desire to have a baby with the father."

Under the pressure of cultural values, after the age of six this impulse calms down, but returns in puberty. At that period limited impulses resurface (oral, anal, sadomasochistic, exhibitionist) which have not been overcome in previous phases; these tend to integrate themselves in the *genital* phase, the last step towards adult sexuality. Fixations or regressions to an earlier phase are the source of several pathologies. The Oedipal conflict, the latent stage, then puberty, are the steps to future psychosexual development, following completion of the various phases.

PROCESS OF IDENTIFICATION

Laplanche and Pontalis's encyclopedia of psychoanalysis [128] states: "The concept of identification gradually assumed centre stage in Freud's work, which makes it, more than just one psychological mechanism among many, the process by which the human subject is formed." The entry continues: "personalities are formed, and differ, by a series of identifications." The term identification has already entered common vocabulary, above all in the sense of "self-identity". In addition we have all observed a child's tendency to absorb aspects of another person and to become confused with characters or roles. We shall find this term again in the study of defence mechanisms, in its more precise psychoanalytical meaning.

PRINCIPAL DEFENCE MECHANISMS

The principal defence mechanisms according to Anna Freud are: *repression – regression – reactive formation – isolation – retroactive annulment – projection – introspection – reflection on oneself – conversion to the opposite – sublimation.* Melanie Klein added *projective identification*, whose precise definition we shall see in Section IV later, together with its graphological correlations.

Psychological conflict

Psychological conflict can generate neurotic and psychotic mechanisms. The following chapter will explain further the various pathologies arising from such conflict, always considered in a psychodynamic context without entering into possible genetic origins. We shall now proffer some basic definitions of such mechanisms.

Neurosis

Neurosis shows up a personality disorder without disturbing the mental synthesis or conscious faculties. The subject recognizes the condition and is not cut off from reality. In psychoanalysis, neurosis is a psychological disorder whose symptoms are symbolic expressions of a psychological conflict, which generally stems from the subject's childhood. The intrapsychic conflict is situated between the *Ego* and the *Id* and more precisely between the impulses of the *Id* and reality and between the *Id* and the *Superego*. The conflict causes *anxiety*. The subject suffers from this condition and is unable to face certain situations and to create new solutions to overcome the difficulties. Unresolved aspects prevent the subject from reaching maturity and adult responsibility.

The defence mechanisms struggle against these impulses and against anxiety, resulting in *neurotic symptoms* which are mostly a compromise between *desire* and *defence*. The Freudian approach distinguishes two types of neurosis: *psychoneurosis* or pure neurosis whose conflict originates in infancy (*hysteria, obsessive neurosis, phobic neurosis*) and *current neurosis* (today called *psychosomatic affection*), where the conflict does not arise in infancy but in the present, and whose symptoms do not have a mental significance and therefore are not confronted by the Ego's defence mechanisms (*anxiety, psychasthenia, neurasthenia, hypochondria,* and the *neuroses of existence – abandonment, reversal, fate, family*).

Psychosis

Psychosis is a personality disorder with alterations in mental and rational synthesis. The subject is unaware of his disorder and is *separated* from reality. The conflict is situated between the Id and reality. The subject lacks any *object organization*: the Ego has not been structured across the developmental phases *oral, anal,* and *phallic*. According to Freud, the psychotic is incapable of having a relationship with real persons and reaches states of depersonalization, division, unreality. Examples of psychosis are: *manic depression, delirious paranoia, schizophrenia*.

The origin of psychosis according to different authors

For Freud, a reduction of resources and the dominance of narcissistic libido over the objective libido is an essential characteristic of psychosis. Margaret Mahler sees a "symbiotic psychosis" that corresponds to a regression from the phase of separation-identification to the symbiotic phase.

Winnicott speaks of a "transitional area" during the period of separation from the mother, at the boundary between oral eroticism and the true object relationship. The *primary maternal preoccupation* creates in the child a feeling of omnipotence, the illusion of creating the world that surrounds it. This experience of *illusion* is quickly followed by *disillusion*. The child adapts by establishing a *transitional area*. If this double process does not occur, a *false self* is created, running the risk of a psychosis developing at the moment when the self should be structuring itself.

Frances Tustin, with a predominantly Kleinian approach, describes the premature break in the mother-son relationship as a "break in bodily continuity", which could be the origin of the child's psychotic behaviour. Melanie Klein, in contrast to Freud, advanced the phases of libidinal development into the first six months of life. She maintained that the suckling child already possesses a primitive Ego, able to experience anxiety and to set up defence systems which could form the basis for a psychosis. In Section IV below we examine her theory more thoroughly.

Graphological correspondences

The graphological correspondences in this chapter apply to so-called "adult" writings. It is obvious that the presence of a well-structured *Ego*, able to face reality and reasonably free of fixations in the pre-genital phases, could be clearly discerned in writing. Such an appearance is independent from the cultural and intellectual level of the writer, and the identifying graphological criteria are therefore independent from the *Formlevel*.

The criteria proposed in Table 38 show the capacity of adaptability and autonomy of the Ego, good self-assurance, and adequate social motivations. They therefore express attachment to the *principle of reality*, that is, a solid Ego. It is therefore the middle zone that mostly identifies the structure of the Ego, and it is rightly called the *zone of the Ego*. It represents the psychophysical health of the Ego, in other words the manifest personality and behaviour.

The characteristics listed in Table 39 clearly betray difficulties in adjustment, lack of autonomy, dependency or detachment or fixations, and hence an insufficient link to objective reality and a vulnerable Ego. Some aspects of pressure, which escape from conscious control – such as spasmodic pressure – are expressions of the *primary process*, a process which is barely regulated by the intervention of the Ego.

GRAPHOLOGICAL CORRESPONDENCES

Criteria for a structured Ego

Middle zone:	well structured with ample ovals, neither inflated nor puffy, clear forms, without artificiality; flexible with alternating rhythm of curves and angles
External space:	harmonious, aerated, proportionate margins; rational positioning of signature
Internal space:	balance between blacks and whites, structured words, triple width
Base line:	flexible, no rigidity or excessive waviness
Letter slant:	flexible around the vertical
Firm pressure:	on the verticals, well-nourished stroke, neither too pasty nor too precise, with neat edges

Table 38

GRAPHOLOGICAL CORRESPONDENCES

Criteria for a weak Ego

Squashed middle zone:	reduced height, tending to flatten on the line, often with congestion; too angular or too slack
Ovals and loops overblown in a childish manner	
Graphic flow proceeds in jerks	
External space:	untidy, invaded margins, tangled lines; or rigidity; signature too close or too far from text, or positioned in an absurd way
Internal space:	unexpected gaps, words out of focus and badly structured; overall appearance too compact; words too structured
Pressure:	spasmodic

Table 39

The presence of a well-structured Superego is noted through psychological deduction rather than by single signs. Stiffness in page layout, however, denotes a strong Superego, and other graphic characteristics allow an evaluation of whether such an aspect is supportive or crushing: angularity and dryness of stroke make it more alarming. In addition the play between the Ideal of the Ego and the Ideal Ego engenders complex dynamics.

It is not therefore tracing of signs that defines these various instances but rather focusing on the psychological dynamic which underpins them, and which allows us to ascertain their presence and psychodynamic role. See the examples in Figs 97–9 and the related discussion for some of the dynamics connected to these instances.

We give a summary in Table 40 of the principal graphological signs that mark strong correspondence (and sometime *fixation*) to a particular phase of psychosexual development. We present a number of examples in Fig. 96.

GRAPHOLOGICAL CORRESPONDENCES
Oral phase
Invaded space, rounded writing, childish, widened
Large middle zone, letters full, puffy, rounded, foetal
Passive oral: little movement, pasty or dry stroke, slack speed
Active oral: irregularity of movement, pointed endings, stroke pasty or precise, dry, spasmodic, twisted letters
Anal phase
Compact space, structured, rigid/neglected, dirty
Squeezed writing, movement hardly flowing with jerks and stops
Middle zone small, irregular, pointed, closed
Pasty and smeary pressure
Connections: connected or disconnected (rarely grouped)
Angular forms, pointed, with hooks
Reactive formation: compact space, writing light, grey, colourless, precise
Phallic phase
Space freely taken up
Large, extended writing, big capital letters
Firm stroke and movement
Oedipal conflict
Space and movement emphasize the left; scarce movement
Diminishing left margin, variable slant
Signature different to text, rounded forms, full
Large middle zone: nourished and velvety, or dry and light

Table 40

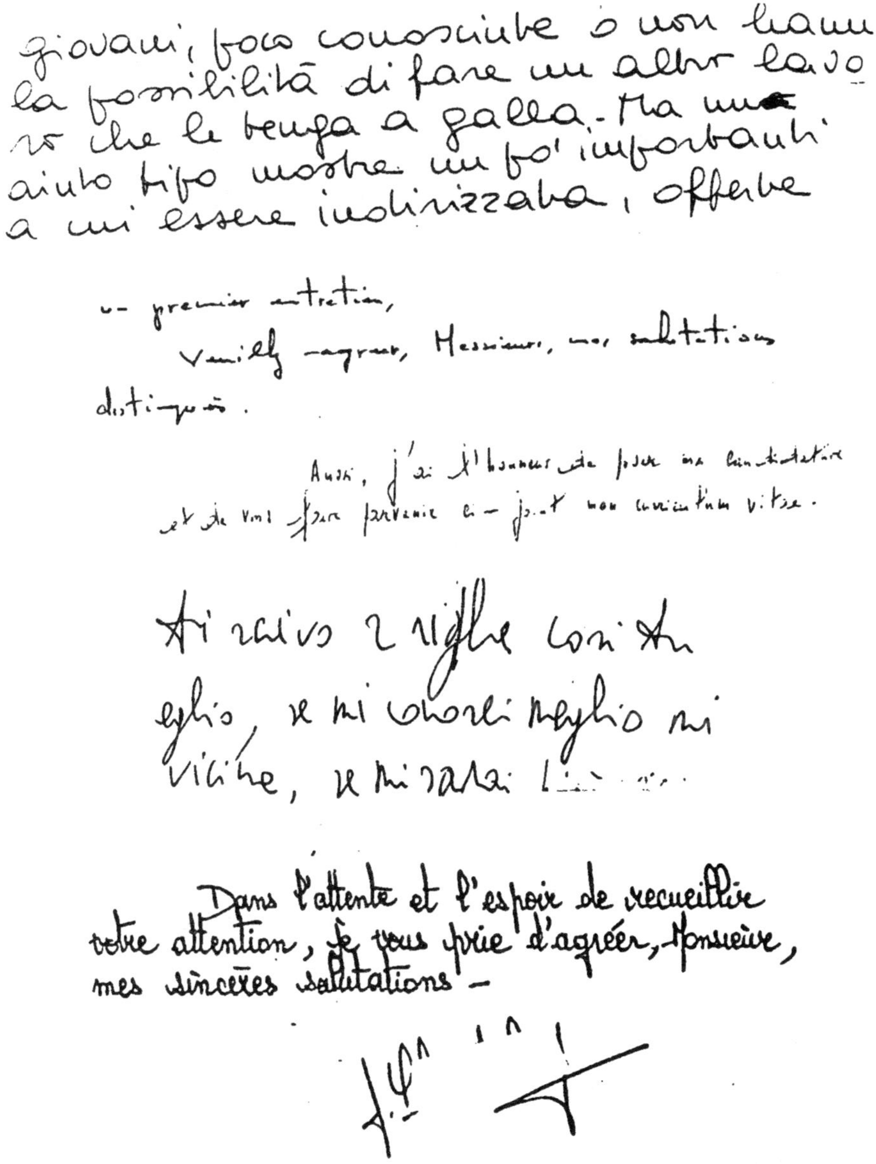

Figure 96 (reduced)
Writing samples marked by the oral, anal, and phallic stages

III. THE THEORY OF JEAN BERGERET

Theoretical foundations

The theory of the French psychiatrist Bergeret [23] seems the best one at the present time to define how personality types are classified, in their normal and pathological aspects, following both a psychogenetic and a psychoanalytic perspective.

If the psychotherapist, in the relationship with the patient, has the freedom to move outside the classification frame, respecting the subject's complicated mental constellation, as well as the subtle transfer relation, it is nevertheless clear that any transmissible information must depend on theories which imply classification criteria and value scales. Likewise, psychopathological graphology needs to make greater use of the terminology common to dynamic psychiatry and to psychoanalysis.

Bergeret's theory has the advantage of having developed by taking into account every historical contribution to psychology, going to the sources, stripping down and reworking to their correct dimension numerous characterological, psychiatric, and psychoanalytic models of personality structure. Bergeret does not proffer new categories but expounds instead a new dynamic conception for approaching personality, based on Freud. He reorganizes the criteria that describe personality in a synthetic perspective, within a psychoanalytical framework.

His extensive research led him to formulate a *basic hypothesis*, summarized below, of a structural organization at the heart of personality that comes from a psychogenetic evolution and which, in a normal situation, is stable and defined.

Basic hypothesis

From birth, and perhaps even before birth, an individual's mental life is organized around the very first relations with the parents, together with ensuing frustrations, traumas, and conflicts which engage the defences of the Ego. According to Bergeret, personality comes from a stable and deep *basic structure*, which translates into relational and psychological life using elements of *character* or *symptoms*.

The criterion of *normality* requires from the subject adaptability to both internal and external reality. But this state of normality does not mean an attitude of simple submission but rather a functional and successful dynamic adaptability within the fixed basic structure. The three basic fixed structural lines are:

- *neurotic structures*
- *psychotic structures*
- *borderline organizations*

Character is then the expression of the *basic structure* when its function is *normal*. When its function is morbid, then the *imbalance* becomes *symptoms*, resulting in a break with normality and illness. To understand this point of view, we can use the image proposed by Freud in his *New Conferences* (1932): "When a crystallized mineral block breaks, the fracture lines define the internal structure of this mineral." Personality according to Bergeret should therefore be "organized" upon a modality of privileged function of the *neurotic* or *psychotic* type, each modality having its own normality.

When the subject is unable to adapt the basic organization to new internal or external circumstances, the organization is overwhelmed and the impulses of the *Id* clash with reality. The loss of harmony provokes an evolution towards *neurosis*, in the subject with a *neurotic base structure*, whereas in a subject with a *psychotic base structure*, a development towards psychosis occurs. The terms neurosis and psychosis are used to indicate an *illness* or a state of *imbalance*. In both cases, with treatment, an adequate balance can be restored. A more serious pathology would develop when the base structure alters from psychotic to neurotic, and the other way round.

Between the two basic structural lines – *neurotic* and *psychotic* – lies a middle area called *limit-state* or *borderline* which represents a specific tendency and not a passage between the other two structures, even if it could develop towards either direction. In this case the subject benefits neither from the neurotic state, with its conflicts between Superego and impulses, nor from the psychotic, with the split of the Ego and its relative stability. To this organization corresponds an adaptment of *pseudo-normality*, which makes such a basic structure unstable. This imbalance can take a neurotic, psychotic, or psychosomatic direction. It can also develop towards two more stable systems of defence: the characterial organization or the perverse.

The *limit-state* or *borderline* is really a type of uncomfortable narcissistic organization which requires certain reactive formations costly for the subject, whose behaviour appears to be normal but in fact risks a *depressive* or *phobic* pathology. This is a type of adaptment centred on a fundamental *narcissistic* need to conform to an ideal or to a "group-which-reassures". The individual plays sometimes the role of *hyper-normality* to avoid falling into depression.

In brief, Bergeret tries to establish a synthesis between:
- *structure* of personality: constant and essential base;
- *character*: function is manifestation (not morbidity) of the structure, that is, a normal adaptment;
- *symptomatology*: morbid function; *imbalance* between *defence* and *adaptment*, hence illness and poor adaptment.

Organization of the Ego in the basic structures

In the *neurotic* structure, the organization of the Ego is focused around the *genital* and the *Oedipal*. The conflict lies between the Ego and the impulses. The principal defence mechanism is that of *repression*. Respect for reality impels the removal of representations of the impulses. The presence of an *object libido* and of secondary type mental processes confirms the close connection to reality.

In the *psychotic structure*, the Ego is not facing repression, but *denial* of a large part of reality. The *narcissistic libido* and the *primary process* with their immediate and dictatorial modalities are in first place. Defences are costly and archaic. The principal defence mechanism is *projection*, with a split Ego. From this usually arise *depersonalization* and *split personality*.

IV. THE ENGLISH PSYCHOANALYTIC SCHOOL

Anna Freud and defence mechanisms

According to Anna Freud [96], the word "defence" appears for the first time in 1894 in Sigmund Freud's work *Defence Psychoses*. Later it was replaced by "repression", then brought back in 1926 in *Inhibition, Symptom and Anxiety*, in which repression becomes one of the means of defence. Anna Freud exhaustively researched the problems of the principal defence mechanisms, and her concepts still form the basis for students today. Following the works of her father, Anna Freud identified nine methods of defence: "repression, regression, reactive formation, isolation, retroactive annulment, projection, introspection, self-obsession, transformation into the opposite... We can also add sublimation, or the shifting of instinctual scope."

To capture the essence of these notions we quote Anna Freud: "Each defensive action has the object of assuring the Ego's security and avoiding dissatisfaction." And: "Satisfaction given by fantasy loses, in the adult, its meaningless character... When the adult, for greater pleasure, abandons himself to delusions of fantasy, the road to psychosis opens up before him."

THE CONCEPT OF DEFENCE

For further instruction we draw upon the recent book by two Italian authors, Lingiardi and Madeddu [148]. A defence is a psychological mechanism, which "mediates between desires, needs, affections, and drives of the individual on the one hand and between internal prohibitions and external reality on the other." The defence mechanism therefore represents a way of feeling and thinking with more or less voluntary consequential behaviour, in response to the perception of a mental danger, or to alleviate anxiety generated by conflicts, or even to conceal unease.

According to context, that is, according to the gravity or inflexibility of the clinical case, these mechanisms can be more adaptive or less. Against an internal excitation caused by a strong drive or by the delusion to which it is connected, mature and adaptive defences can arise that accentuate gratification and awareness: for instance, altruism, anticipation, humour, sublimation. As we shall see with the psychoses, other defences are clearly less adaptive. A defence mechanism is positioned "on the border between a world of internal impulse and a relational external world. Defences may sometimes creatively soften the demands of both, serving a subtle process of adaptation. Sometimes they form rigid and painful protective barriers: we could say that they represent the regulators of mental homeostasis" [148].

According to George Vaillant, *The Wisdom of the Ego*, defences have certain fundamental properties:

1) they constitute a creative synthesis;
2) they are relatively unconscious and involuntary;
3) they distort internal and/or external reality;
4) they distort the relationship between affect and idea and between subject and object;
5) they are more often healthy than pathological;
6) they appear strange to everyone else except those who use them;
7) they evolve over time.

We draw again from the above mentioned book [148] the classification of defence mechanisms, in relation to the broad psychopathological categories (Table 41).

DEFENCE MECHANISMS		
Neuroses	**Borderline cases**	**Schizophrenia**
repression	projective identification	projective
identification		
reactive formation	primitive idealization	split
retroactive annulment	denial	raving projection
transfer	omnipotence	distortion
isolation	undervaluing	hallucination
intellectualization	split	denial
		acting out

Table 41

CURRENT DEFINITIONS OF DEFENCE MECHANISMS
(Collected from books by Italian authors [6] and by the French psychiatrist and graphologist Claude Villard [244].)

Repression
The defence mechanism par excellence and the most frequent. The Ego rejects or maintains in the unconscious certain thoughts, images, or illusions belonging to a prohibited impulse, with great expense of energy.

Annulment
"Defensive inversion of an action that brings anxiety." The action is nullified by the conscious or directly inverted to its opposite. Symbolic annulment is the root of obsessive repetition.

Reactive formation
Attitudes, needs, or behaviour in antithesis to the real and unconscious ones.

Idealization
The object invested with mental energy is overvalued and magnified beyond its real limits (such as being in love).

Identification
Process of unconscious imitation that tends to blend the subject and object.

Denial
Tendency to resolve emotional conflict by rejecting it on the conscious plane, and in this way alleviate anxiety. One of the more simple and primitive mechanisms.

Projection
Elements of the Ego are denied then reflected outwards and attributed to others.

Transfer
An emotion connected with an internal object is transferred onto an external object, which replaces it. This defence mechanism is typical of phobic neurosis.

Conversion to the opposite
A drive transforms itself into the opposite, passing from an active attitude to a passive: such as sadism into masochism, aggression into submission, jealousy into admiration.

Rationalization
Attempt to justify with a logical and coherent explanation behaviour whose real motivations cannot be admitted.

Compensation
Advanced by Alfred Adler, according to whom the mechanism of compensation or overcompensation would be linked to an *inferiority complex*, innate and *normal*, and difficult to resolve.

Sublimation
According to Freud the mechanism consists in deflecting a disapproved impulse towards a non-sexual direction: the unacceptable drives are therefore purified and idealized, for example in artistic or intellectual activities.

Identification with the aggressor
Frequent according to Anna Freud in the two year old child: to face up to an excessive threat or a demanding authority, the child identifies with the aggressor, imitating him physically or morally or using symbols to which he is assimilated (wolf). This role is essential in the formation of the Superego.

Projective identification
Typical of Melanie Klein's *schizo-paranoid position*. Parts of the Self and the internal objects are split and projected onto the external object to possess and control it.

DEFENCE MECHANISMS IN PSYCHOSIS

The defence mechanism around which the psychotic experience revolves is one of *psychotic denial*, although this mechanism can also be found in neurosis. The patient effects this mechanism in response to traumatic sensory data or to conceal a narcissistic wound. Sometimes the mechanism aims to alleviate unease but it can also lead to the denial of reality. For example the *denial* of one's own image can lead to the destruction of one's photographs, the denial of one's name, manner of dress, or physical appearance, all of which are normally means of protecting one's self-esteem.

The authors already cited [148] refer to the case of a 24 year old woman who completely identified with her twin brother who had committed suicide, from whom she appropriated his name as well as manner of dress. On the anniversary of his death, she too killed herself.

STYLE OF WRITING

Various French graphologists, among them Claude Villard [244] and Flore Duruy [87], have focused on Anna Freud's insights from a graphological point of view. It is obvious that the defence mechanism can be deduced by in-depth writing analysis. In this case we must not focus on a small sign, but always on certain syndromes that concern the graphic context. Defence mechanisms will certainly be easier to deduce in writings with a strong psychotic force, but evaluating their positive or negative role will be much harder, just as evaluating their role and intensity in more *normal* writing is. Such evaluation can be a great help in career advice and in the study of group dynamics. By observing writing according to a longitudinal perspective, one can identify the defensive changes that are of greatest diagnostic value.

Melanie Klein and the positions of early development

We had been struck for some time by the impossibility of attributing graphologically any pre-genital fixation in the writing of young people who, for example, had shown completely immature and even psychopathic behaviour, and about whom one could have made a hypothesis of fixations at an even earlier development stage. It seemed that we could therefore try to identify certain connections between the Kleinian positions and graphology.

Our research on the writings of artists and poets brought some confirmation of this view, and we had mentioned them in a report to the Congress at Jerusalem in 1987. There is no doubt that looking at artists permits a macroscopic observation of mechanisms which are often on the border between pathology and originality and so exalt their underlying mental dynamic. The late lamented Dr Gille-Maisani encouraged us in these studies though he never had the opportunity himself to pursue them. We would therefore like to trace in writing the possible influence of vicissitudes connected to the positions described by Melanie Klein and later by Hanna Segal, without however entering into the complexity of Klein's theories, and concentrating on the *positions* themselves.

Melanie Klein, in comparison with Freud, advanced the phases of development. Already at birth the breast-feeding baby has a primitive Ego that feels pain and can activate defences, that already possesses *aggression*. Klein outlined two stages of development during the first six months of life, which she called *positions*.

Schizo-paranoid position

This primary phase is found in the first three months of life and its defence mechanism is characterized by *division* or *split*. The mother object, or partial mother, is viewed in a divided way: on the one hand idealized because it is the source of satisfaction and nourishment, on the other hand the child's aggression and feelings of persecution caused by frustration are projected onto it. Another defence mechanism originates from this position, *projective identification*.

"The condition for a constructive development of the schizo-paranoid position is the supremacy – in this period of childhood development – of good experiences over bad, so that trust in the persistence of the object's goodness can grow and consolidate. This is the condition whereby the processes of the Ego's split can be weakened, permitting an integration of aggression instead of its projection" (Klein).

In the adult the double mechanism generates intensified feelings: on the one hand a defensive reluctance, pessimism, a continued emotional and intellectual diffidence, and not least suspicious attitudes supported by strong egocentric narcissism, on the other hand a projection of aggression onto the object, bringing up feelings of jealousy and envy and the manifestation of sadistic impulses.

It is clear that a *fixation* in this position opens the way to grave psychopathological disorders: psychopathy or perversion. With adequate defence mechanisms and a favourable environmental context, however, these conditions could soften into the depressive position – with the danger of being overcome by it as well as successfully working it through – or sublimate through positive and creative works the destructive and persecutory impulses.

DEPRESSIVE POSITION

When the integrative processes become more stable and continuous, a new phase of development begins, the *depressive position*. This position has been defined by Melanie Klein "as a phase of development in which the child recognizes an object as a whole and places itself in relation with it" (Hanna Segal [219]). If, at around the age of six months, the baby can integrate its own aggression, instead of dividing and projecting it, and understand the object mostly in its "good" aspects, it is on course to face and overcome the depressive phase.

In the contrary case, inability to work through the depressive position causes anxiety that leads to *projective identification*. "The projected parts of the Self are broken up and are projected onto the object disintegrating it, and then reintrojected always in a disintegrated form ... the division takes over the Ego. It is impossible to recognize the mother as a whole object." This is when a fixation to the previous position occurs.

Melanie Klein maintains that envy is "a trap which imprisons desires for life" and thus impedes fulfilment. Excessive envy does not permit an adequate oral gratification and therefore acts upon stimuli, in the sense of intensifying the senses and genital tendencies. This means that the child turns to genital gratification too soon and therefore the oral relation is genitalized, while the genital tendencies remain excessively coloured by demands and anxiety of an oral type.

We quote from Bergeret's illuminating texts on this mechanism [23]: "Melanie Klein presents different clinical examples of *limit-depressive* states in which the depressive and paranoid tendencies meet. On one side fears and paranoid suspicions are reinforced as defences against the depressive position, on the other we see the sublimation of the loved object reaching its peak." The object is transformed and therefore divided from the real image. Internalized and idealized rather than sublimated images are created:

the mother, or certain religious images or symbols, or else "artistic inspiration, or an *imaginary companion*". These correspond to the *symbolic equations* described by Hanna Segal, which are distinct from the symbol: "It is dealing with how to avoid pain and frustration, to negate it as much as possible, at least at that moment; the stance is not to admit it or accept it as reality, and certainly not to overcome it and benefit from more developed mental resources."

GRAPHISM

We do not intend to show the identification of these complicated mechanisms with a table. Psychological deduction must come to our aid more than ever. In a special way, recognition of actual defence mechanisms is the dynamic of the instances: *Ideal of the Ego*, *Superego*, and *Ego Ideal* can all give indications.

A writing sample coloured by the *schizo-paranoid* position obviously contains signs of aggression as well as of split personality and projective exaltation, and if it has not begun to work itself through the *depressive* position, the writing will show signs of rigidity and harshness. In children, a writing style with many white spaces and aggressive strokes, of marked egocentricity, can be a good example. In adults, the writing of great commanders well "positioned on the line" (according to a Morettian type), rigid or systematized, often with a neat and sharp stroke, can represent an early fixation to this position.

Writing coloured by the *depressive* position shows that the struggle around the relation with the object is full of conflict. Destructive feelings such as envy mix with feelings of strong dependence of the *anaclytic type*, linked to the anxiety of abandonment. In cases of *fixation* there are great risks, and it is difficult to work through the pain linked to the depression.

ARTISTIC PROCESS AND KLEINIAN POSITIONS

To grasp these aspects in a living way, avoiding the wider theoretical explanations which are for specialists, we will now look at a number of case studies on artists, drawn from our own extensive research (which will be presented elsewhere). The cases are of artists or poets whose well-known attitudes and precise biographical data supply adequate material to trace the Kleinian double process.

Working through and overcoming the depressive position represents for Melanie Klein the favoured ground for the processes of sublimation and artistic creation. The artist, struggling with the demands of the depressive position, which is not always adequately worked through, is driven to denigrate his work, which unconsciously symbolizes the mother, and early anxieties connected to the loss of the object are rekindled. This is especially so if other subsequent traumas have strengthened the precariousness of such an image.

Also at the moment of separation from his work, which he must *exteriorize* and show to the outside world, the artist is struggling anew with the difficulty of separation from his own "good object". Mechanisms bearing negative anticipation of *projective identification* intervene, and the artist is overcome by feelings of hate or envy. We draw from several passages in our report to the World Congress of Graphology in London in 1996 on "The creative process through artists' writing", to illustrate this problem area.

Many precocious artists have lived through the diffusion of their work in a state of paroxysmal loss. Youthful creative production rises in them as a cathartic surge, in which the tragic and persecutory violence of impulsive and relational life is marked by the *paranoid-schizoid position*, and in which the "symbolic equations" described by Hanna Segal can cause, in her words, "release from the destructive envy of the maternal content, in favour of the work as a receptacle of all the violent substance and wounds of accusation."

Rimbaud with his book *Saison en enfer* could be their prototype (Fig. 97); his writing does not contain either oral or anal fixation, but his well-known pathologic style of life indicates a psychotic nucleus in his make-up. We believe that in his writing the *schizoid* aspect emerges through the tendency to detachment between letters and the trenchant stroke, and the *paranoid* aspect is very obvious in the elaboration of ample forms, a proud and even vulgar writing (see Moretti's "Enflée" writing in Cristofanelli [69]).

Among contemporary painters, Jackson Pollock also represents a vibrant affirmation of the cathartic aspect of artistic madness. Living the lifestyle of a painter damned, Pollock expressed intensively in his *action paintings* his anger, as a reaction to American society and to his own anxiety of life,

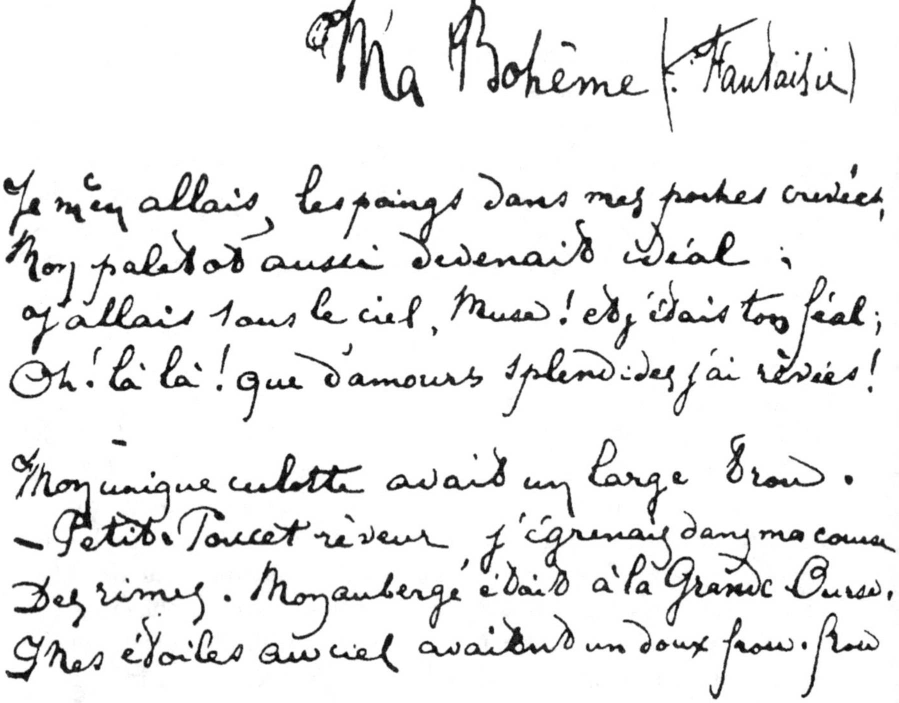

Ma Bohème (Fantaisie)

Je m'en allais, les poings dans mes poches crevées;
Mon paletot aussi devenait idéal;
J'allais sous le ciel, Muse! et j'étais ton féal;
Oh! là là! que d'amours splendides j'ai rêvées!

Mon unique culotte avait un large trou.
— Petit-Poucet rêveur, j'égrenais dans ma course
Des rimes. Mon auberge était à la Grande-Ourse.
Mes étoiles au ciel avaient un doux frou-frou

Et je les écoutais, assis au bord des routes,
Ces bons soirs de septembre où je sentais des gouttes
De rosée à mon front, comme un vin de vigueur;

Où, rimant au milieu des ombres fantastiques,
Comme des lyres, je tirais les élastiques
De mes souliers blessés, un pied près de mon cœur!

                                    Arthur Rimbaud

Figure 97
The poet Arthur Rimbaud's writing at 15, marked by the schizo-paranoid position

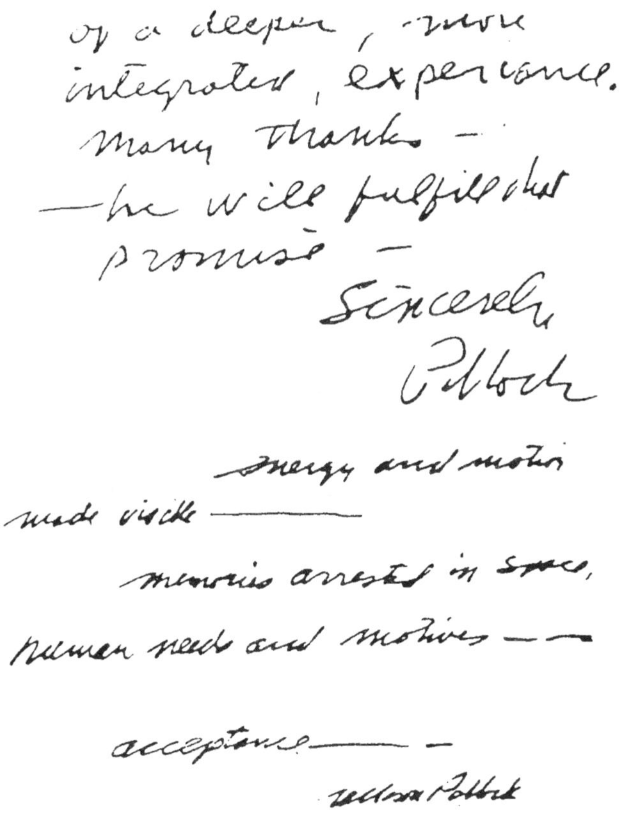

Figure 98
The painter Jackson Pollock's writing, marked by the schizo-paranoid position

finally committing suicide. His writing (Fig. 98) reflects the extreme ambivalence of his being, with different graphic styles, and strong anal and paranoid tendencies. Pollock, known for his "automatic" painterly style, embodies the *second phase* of the creative process according to the French psychoanalyst Didier Anzieu [7], a phase characterized by delusive tension and an insatiable imagination. The "unconscious mental agent" invades the Ego and sets itself up as a "code" or guide in the action of *doing*, in such

a way that the artist is more "worked" by his own creative act than an
artisan of his own work. Depression is latent, and the writing expresses the
difficulty of working through the *depressive position* while the Superego
becomes self-destructive and is unable to come to terms with social reality.

In the case of Paul Klee (Fig. 99) his writing expresses his struggle with
the *depressive position* which tends to reactivate the anguish of loss of the
object. Klee's biography informs us that fortunately he did not experience
any grave emotional trauma that would have activated such anguish.

The dynamism, rhythm, and strength of the stroke indicate that the
danger has been overcome and that Winnicott's "*sufficiently good*" mother
image has encouraged the creative thought of the child, and has predisposed
him to internalize the *paternal function*, that is to understand the *codes* and
so move from *creativity* to the work of *creation*. A vulnerable and troubled
Ego is obviously noticeable in Klee (irregularities, speed, extended, different
types of connections, flattened ovals, centripetal and centrifugal final strokes,
not forgetting the loneliness of the capital "P" in his signature). There is
no doubt, however, that the Ego is endowed with an exceptional and
perceptive critical faculty, attention, and concentration (rhythms of black
and whites, words diminishing, precise stroke).

On the other hand, the wealth of impulses and delusive tension
(effervescent rhythm, capital letters rooted in the zone of the unconscious,
centrifugal and pointed finals) clashes with a precarious *Ideal Ego*, which
does not rest on a solid primary narcissism (superelevated but narrow letters,
middle zone small and rather *tormented* according to Gille-Maisani), and
so does not show any feeling of omnipotence.

Conflicts between the *Ideal Ego* and *Superego* then become sharp. The
Ideal Ego demands its freedom, trying to shake off frustrations and feelings
of abandonment, but the *Superego* reacts by imposing its ethic and twists
back against the Ego in a masochistic way. The risk of self-destruction
which Ania Teillard [228] had predicted lies in wait (stroke tension, falling
endings and bars, diminishing letters, sharpness).

According to the dynamic of the Freudian instances, the great mediator
the *Ideal of the Ego* intervenes, which reinforces the precarious identifications
of the *Ideal Ego* but also suggests aesthetic stylizations which the *Ego*'s
intelligence will interpret as profoundly thought out inspirations. Thanks

to the support of the *Ideal of the Ego* (firmness of verticals, precise stroke, haughty capitals, extended *t*-bars), the torments of the artist's soul can be channelled into his work. The signature "Klee" with its clearly stylized design is highly symbolic of the painter's *Ideal of the Ego*.

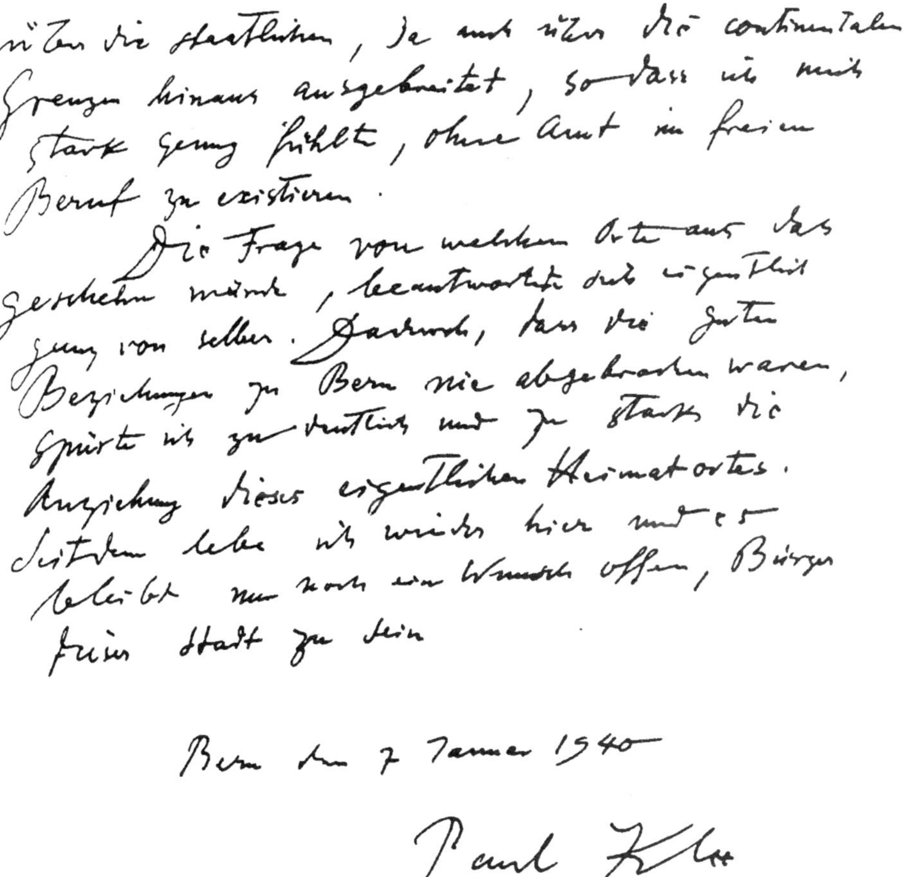

über die staatlichen, ja auch über die continentalen Grenzen hinaus ausgebreitet, sodass ich mich stark genug fühlte, ohne Amt im freien Beruf zu existieren.

Die Frage von welchem Orte aus das geschehen würde, beantwortete sich eigentlich ganz von selber. Dadurch, dass die guten Beziehungen zu Bern nie abgebrochen waren, spürte ich zu deutlich und zu stark die Anziehung dieses eigentlichen Heimatortes. Seitdem lebe ich wieder hier und es bleibt nur noch ein Wunsch offen, Bürger dieser Stadt zu sein

Bern den 7 Januar 1940

Paul Klee

Figure 99 (reduced)
Paul Klee: his writing is marked by the *depressive position*, but works through this successfully (from Will Grohmann, *Paul Klee*, Flinker, Paris, 1954)

Chapter Fourteen

PSYCHOPATHOLOGIES AND GRAPHOLOGICAL CORRELATIONS

In this chapter we will examine more carefully the principal psycho-pathologies for which precise graphological correlations have been shown. We have to remind ourselves, however, that the Deontological Code approved at a national level in many countries, and active also at the European level, does not allow graphologists to issue a psychopathological diagnosis. All the same, psychotherapists now more frequently call on graphological assistance for a wider diagnostic investigation, or to trace the development of a subject.

It is obvious that the main conditions behind a psychopathological development are noticed in writing. In particular, anxiety, distress, excitability, regression, sense of guilt, and the persecution of the Superego are very clearly shown. This said, there are some general graphological categories, such as discordance, rigidity, monotony, and incoherent layout, which immediately alert the graphologist to a subject at risk.

When we examine psychopathological configurations from a graphological point of view, we should ask some questions. How do we guide the young and how do we direct them towards integration into the workplace if they have pathological tendencies? How do we evaluate the incidence of these tendencies and in particular within determined positions or roles? What value does a graphological investigation have from a diagnostic or prognostic point of view? What are its advantages or disadvantages?

We shall focus therefore in a rather analytical way on the following tendencies: the hysterical, obsessive, phobic, paranoid, schizoid, manic-depressive, and borderline or limit-case. We shall at the same time show the theory and writing aspects together in order to bring to life personality and writing. We shall also present a number of summary tables. We shall use the classic terminology, but nowadays disorders are being reclassified according to diverse psychiatric categories, and we recommend following the latest version of DSM IV [78].

I. HYSTERIA AND HYSTERICAL TENDENCY

According to Bergeret the hysterical *structure* is characterized "by the strength of the erotic element, whose aspects dominate the life and relations of the hysteric." The emotional objects are variable and fluctuating, repression being the principal defence mechanism. According to Sheldon such immature personalities are not productive. Hysteria represents a compromise between sexual or aggressive tendencies and the defences of the Ego. It expresses itself through body language with somatic symptoms or behavioural disorders. It is more frequent in the female, though not absent in the male.

The classic hysteria which Charcot treated in 1878 with hypnosis is today uncommon in its basic form but has taken on more camouflaged forms, in which very ambivalent, transient, and theatrical behaviour patterns alternate.

A typical graphic configuration would be: *effervescent, irregular,* and even *destructured.* Writing is often "agitated" with a very unstable middle zone – or zone of the Ego – which passes from ample letters to atrophied, filiform, or childish ones, with various excessive strokes in the outer zones, verticals and loops out of proportion or contorted, full ovals: all signs of a demanding phallic type based on an oral fixation, that is, on a weak Ego, dependent, immature, which absorbs the other and drains him/her.

The instability and the highly exaggerated tendencies are the two dominant graphic aspects which express the weakness or childishness of the Ego, with a capricious emotional greed, an apparent sociability in which the need to please and seduce is driven by great emotional demands. If depressive elements are added, they lead to emotional blackmail and sometimes even suicide. The defence mechanisms of *repression* (with or without *conversion*), of *denial*, and of *reactive formation*, can sometimes produce the reverse behaviour.

One could possibly identify four different styles of hysterical personality, which we have called *basic, deceitful, rigid,* and *gifted.* More than graphological *signs,* we shall identify a number of typical but not unique graphic *syndromes* for these configurations, which we have come across in our experience.

Basic hysterical personality (Fig. 100a)

Invasive, tiring, always present, of indiscriminate sociability but also attracting sympathy from the need for attention, this type is well known and also feared in the workplace, and often creates confusion and discord in the family. The writing is recognized at first glance:
- confusion in the management of space;
- great irregularities and destructuring in the middle zone;
- hypertrophy of lower extensions and capitals;
- exaggerated free strokes;
- imprecise and variable forms.

Deceitful hysterical personality (Fig. 100b)

More deceitful and elusive, this personality does not display theatrical public behaviour, but turns to eccentricity, sometimes with a "dreamy" atmosphere in a type of eternal adolescence. Often the person is a mythomaniac with an imaginary life confused with reality, and can also be aggressive, in which case forms of diffidence overlap with paranoiac attacks, or self-harm. In general, however, the condition is expressed through various psychosomatic conditions. In writing the following configuration may be seen:
- middle zone is small and irregular with filiform gestures within the words;
- light, precise, and sharp-pointed stroke;
- full and/or atrophied ovals.

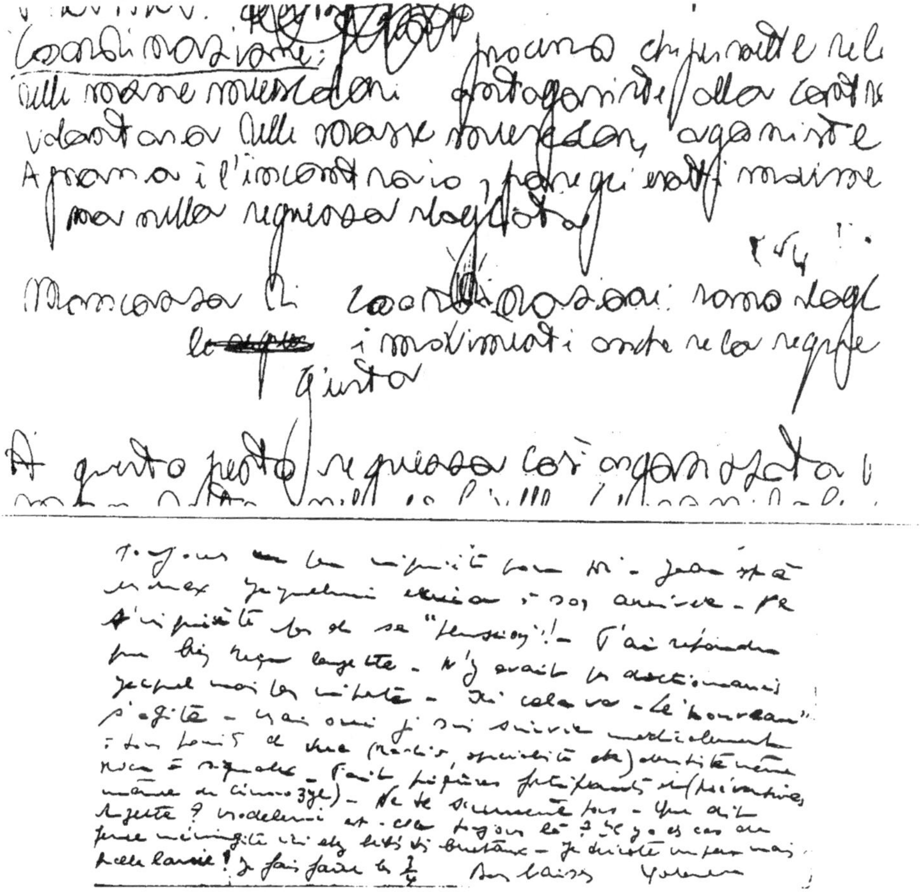

Figure 100 (reduced)
(a) Young woman aged 23: basic hysterical tendency, original intelligence
(b) Woman aged 35: clearly hysterical with paranoid tendencies of persecution and hypochondria, notwithstanding a high level of education

Rigid hysterical personality with conversion (Fig. 101a)

In this type of personality a rigid framework forces repression of the emotional and erotic nature, and psychosomatic illness can take over completely, as the fixation is symbolized through the body. Sometimes hypochondriac, sometimes hyperactive with rigid principles, this type represses many dissatisfactions, especially emotional and sexual. They can be found in power and management roles, where they substitute diplomacy with dogged utilitarian egocentricity.

In cases of successful repression we speak of the hysteric's "beautiful indifference". This is found for example in anorexic young people, nowadays frequent, who display hyper-normal public behaviour.

Writing draws closer to a paranoid configuration:
- large;
- rigid pattern, sometimes artificial or mechanical;
- precise and incisive stroke;
- hypertrophy or atrophy of the lower extensions;
- *Persona* aspect with overcompensation.

Gifted hysterical personality (Fig. 101b)

This type of hysterical personality shows outwardly a particular, *original*, existence, living in accord with their sensitivity and sensuality and with their psychosexual conflicts. Sometimes they sublimate their impulses to an intellectual and artistic level (artists, writers, poets, directors …) or heighten them in perverted and even wicked behaviour, using the defence mechanisms of sublimation or perversion. Such persons often have a certain charisma.

The writing is often of high Formlevel, that is, developed and very personalized, with pasty and firm but also spasmodic stroke, and with overblown and discordant lower extensions. Sometimes the writing is sloppy in a childish way and almost neglected.

Figure 101 (see opposite page ☛)
(a) and (b) Women, rigid hysteria with conversion
(c) Gifted hysterical tendency of the poet Verlaine (signature enlarged)

Souvenir
et un affectueux
baiser à petite
Michèle de Nounou
sa Nounou

Spero di rivederla pre-
sto a Firenze.
Buon Natale e felice An-

Mon Dieu, mon Dieu, la vie est là
Simple et tranquille.
Cette paisible rumeur là
Vient de la ville.

P. Verlaine

Socialization

There are obviously mixed forms of hysterical personality, some milder and others so marked that we can speak of hysterical psychosis, as for example in the cases of great mythomaniacs.

How do we socialize hysterical people into the work environment? If one needs to direct young people, apart from giving advice on possible treatment, one should point them towards professions that do not require teamwork. In a team they are apt to be dissatisfied, self-justifying, and overbearing, with inadequate communication, and so become highly irritating. It is better to place them in a situation where they can use any inventive talent, or develop for example manual, artistic, or entertainment abilities, or else commercial or presentational skills.

If oral fixation is important we can suggest aesthetic, culinary, or hotel work; also language teaching and dental work. In each case we need to evaluate the likely capacity for autonomy and sense of responsibility. When the person is already in work it is necessary to control the tendencies to seduction and confusion, and to give the subject precise work with deadlines,

---

HYSTERICAL PERSONALITY

Behaviour
Emotional greed – need to please and seduce – dependence
Emotional instability – depressive tendencies
Apparent sociability – exhibitionism – theatricality
Erotization of relationships – sexuality disorders

Psychology
Psychoneurosis of a very archaic form: conflicts between the Id and the defences
of the Ego expressed through the body, going as far as convulsions, paralysis,
blindness, catatonia
Weakness of the Ego – ambivalence
Oral and phallic fixation
Unresolved Oedipal phase: imprecise and precarious identifications

Defence mechanisms: Repression, denial, reactive formation

Psychotic form: Loss of sense of reality

Table 42

allowing a certain amount of independence but demanding forcefully the end resul . This person is not at all dependable and tends to waste time.

If the person is intelligent and aggressive, sudden changes of attitude are to be feared, which could fluctuate between ready availability to bad temper and vindictiveness, both dictated by envy. This behaviour clearly points to paranoia.

HYSTERIA: GENERAL GRAPHOLOGICAL CONNECTIONS

Proteiform – arrhythmic: exuberance and weakness
Badly structured middle zone – filiform in the body of the words
Excessive or atrophied extensions and loops
Puffy ovals and other childish components
Light and pale stroke
Sometimes stiffening, or the reverse, an elusive aspect

Table 43

II. OBSESSIVE NEUROSIS

This is a psychoneurosis of defence, because the obsessive expends energy in defending himself from his own obsessions. It is characterized by three components:
-   regression to the sado-anal stage;
-   the Ego's excessive defence against the impulses;
-   strict Superego.

The obsession consists in the involuntary and anxious eruption in the conscious sphere of thoughts or feelings recognized by the Ego as morbid, although they come from the subject's own psyche. Notwithstanding the subject's efforts in getting rid of them, they tend to assert themselves. Obsessive ideas, doubts, scruples, and a tendency to brood occur. Rituals that represent a barrier against anxiety intervene in an attempt to prevent compulsive mental automatism, but without success. This type of neurosis is absolutely conscious and stressful, and appears unexpectedly for no apparent reason.

There are various types of obsession: idealistic, on the metaphysical level, and impulsive (of phobic type: pyromania, kleptomania, exhibitionism). The characteristic defence mechanism is the *reactive formation*, followed by *isolation, annulment* through rituals, *transfer* of anxiety onto affections. This neurosis is the most "organized" and very resistant to therapy. Indeed the obsessive is opposed to analytical treatment.

OBSESSIVE PERSONALITY

Behaviour: Order, meticulousness, frugality, obstinacy, rigidity
Indecision, scrupulousness, eagerness for checking
Excess in either cleanliness or filth
Meanness with a spattering of prodigality
Aggression, will to dominate, sadomasochism
Emotional barrenness, detachment from the emotional object
Frenzied work
Taste for games, risk, and money
Anal reactive: milder behaviour but with a pungent critical sense

Psychology: Perfectionism characterized by doubts and checking
Rigid Superego, self-punishment, hypochondriac tendency
Regression leads to fixation at the sado-anal stage
Psychasthenia (weakness of psyche)
Sometimes schizoid tendency, withdrawal from reality

Table 44

OBSESSION: GRAPHOLOGICAL CONNECTIONS

Graphic environment: Rigid page layout, or neglected and dirty
Tendency to rigidity and to methodical arrangement
Tendency to feathery movement (defensive)

Writing   Small, dark, precise, squeezed, compact, rigid
Pasty or smeary, pointed, closed or with bows
Edgy tendency, with hooks
Methodical small initial profiles
Anal reactive: light, grey, precise, compact
Signature similar to text, protected
Signs of anxiety and uncertainty

Table 45

At the occupational level, some character traits are appreciated: the sense of reality, of order, method, detail, precision, arrangement. There is however a tendency to give more importance to form than to content. The will seems directed towards limited objectives and lacks boldness. Obsessive types travel along well-worn paths. On the emotional plane they are closed, cold, ambivalent (sadomasochistic), and have a fear of feelings.

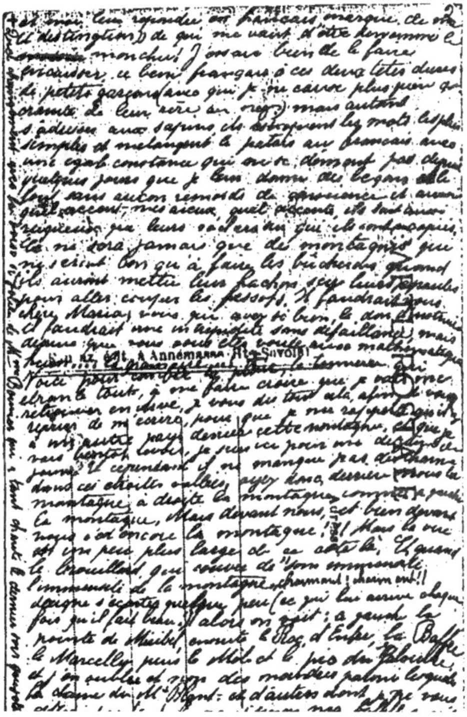

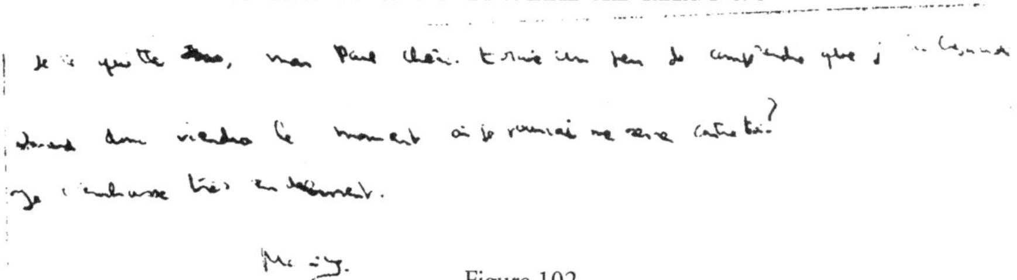

Figure 102
(a) Highly obsessive woman (reduced)   (b) Woman with phobic tendencies

III. PHOBIC NEUROSIS

This neurosis stems from childhood disorders of the libido. It corresponds to what Freud called "anxiety hysteria", also termed "phobic hysteria". It is produced by the *transfer* defence mechanism; anxiety (that can be intense and paralysing) shifts the conflicts onto precise objects or situations:

Objects: knives, feathers, velvet

Animals: dog, cat, snake, spider

Situations: means of transport (claustrophobia, agoraphobia)

Functions: fear of blushing, fear of being unable to swallow or breathe

Compulsions: fear of harming self and others, suicidal or homicidal fears

Phobic behaviour

This consists of endless flight to avoid the deep cause of the phobia. The phobic tends to create systems of reassurance to face the situation with the help of another person or through a reassuring object. As the phobia is a mental representation there are few signs of it in writing.

PHOBIC PERSONALITY

Behaviour (similar to the hysteric)
Theatricality, mythomania
Lack of authenticity in relationships
State of alarm: always on edge, fear of but also search for the object of phobia
Inability to confront the unknown

Psychology
Weak Ego, inconsistent, passive
Inhibited sexual activity
Flight through fear of professional and social commitment
Reaction: endless hyperactivity, or conscious reactive depression with suffering

Defence mechanisms
Transfer, avoidance

Table 46

Hypochondriac neurosis

Exasperating preoccupation for own health; the sick person is conscious of it but is unable to get better, consulting many doctors and wanting to be heard, with a continual narcissistic demand often linked to anxiety or phobic neurosis. Patients are fastidious, demanding, dependent, immediately displeased.

GRAPHOLOGICAL CONNECTIONS

Phobic neurosis
From the writing it is not possible to draw any distinguishing diagnosis
Signs of hysteria and anxiety

Hypochondriac neurosis
Signs of narcissism – anality – obsessive tendencies – masochism

---

Table 47

IV. PARANOIA

The term *paranoia*, like *hysteria*, has entered current vocabulary to designate certain character traits. The person who makes himself "interesting" by making up stories, by exhibitionist and sometimes violent tantrums, who changes tone and mood at any moment, is regarded as *hysterical*. The hot-headed or irritable subject, who believes in his own importance and always accuses others for his own troubles or illnesses, always ready to judge or call to judgement, is labelled *paranoiac*.

Paranoia is not only a *character*, which as such belongs to *psychology*, but is also a *delirious psychosis* within *psychopathology*. In general it represents an *emotional pathology* which distorts an initially rich intelligence by subjecting it to aberrant mechanisms. Etymologically paranoia means: one whose mind is "against".

The paranoid character (Table 48, Fig. 104)

This type of character often exists without any delirium and can be encountered in obsessive or melancholic persons as well as psychopathic.

Historically this type has been seen in two forms: the *sensitive* form (according to Kretschmer) and the *aggressive-revengeful* form.

Kretschmer's *sensitive paranoia* is easily seen in debilitated persons, focusing on themselves, indecisive and full of scruples, with a fragile Ego, hyper-emotive, unable to confront emotional or social trauma. These persons go around with a feeling of failure, which turns more towards *depression* than revolt. We know only too well the phrases typical of these subjects, "Everything is always going wrong", "I'm unable to do such things", and "I cannot decide what to do." Bergeret modified the usual classification of the *sensitive* character as *paranoid* and placed it instead in the *borderline* cases. This new viewpoint implies significant consequences on the plane of psychosocial prevention as well as on the psychotherapeutic plane. We believe that Bergeret's new classification is very fitting.

The remaining *aggressive-revengeful paranoiac* character, frequent in the male gender, has four precise characteristics which are very obvious in writing (Fig. 103).

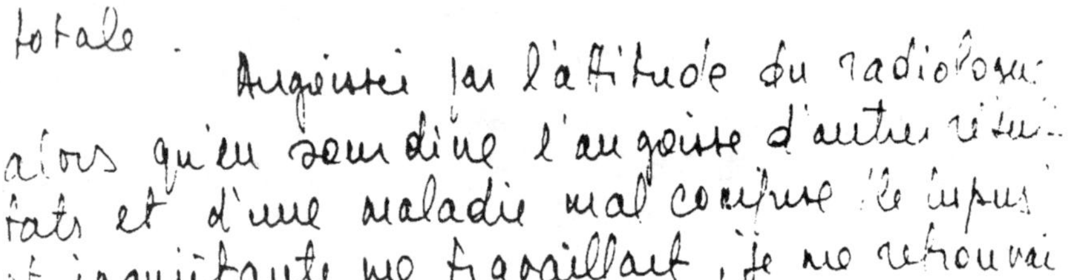

Figure 103 (reduced)

Gabrielle, aged 32, is a drama teacher being treated for a severe phobia, with personality disorders close to depersonalization; asexual appearance, aggression repressed and projected outward: believes she is being followed to be killed. The writing shows rigidity of a paranoiac type, but it is impossible to deduce the essence of the illness.

(a) Enlargement of the Ego
- pride bordering on megalomania; almost continual exaggeration;
- egocentricity and excessive love of oneself, absence of self-criticism;
- disdain for others and vanity often masked by false modesty;
- stubbornness and fanaticism, with attitudes at times stoic and at others extravagant, with a tendency to proselytize and to mental exhibitionism, as well as despotism.

(b) Diffidence
- constant attitude of suspicion;
- excessive fear of others' aggression, distancing oneself when being addressed; excessively obsequious, or with hidden or open aggression;
- touchiness and feeling of persecution.

(c) Errors of judgement: essential trait in the paranoiac structure
- methodical dialectic and logic, based on *passion*; distorted recollections and arbitrary selection from elements of reality;
- *a priori* belief, without any doubt, nor self-critical when partly to blame;
- hyperemotional nature behind the appearance of a purely rational attitude; a chronic hyperpassionate subject;
- logical reasoning on false premises which spring from an emotion of the moment closed to the opinion of others.

(d) Mental rigidity
- authoritarian, emotional and relational inflexibility, haughty demeanour, dry temperament and rarely sanguine;
- inadequate social adaptability caused by mistaken evaluation of reality and incapacity to adjust one's own value system;
- closed, absence of group spirit and collective discipline;
- loner, little sociability; frequent feeling of revolt, and "mental wandering";
- vindictive and touchy attitude;
- "iron constitution", hiding one's own physical disorders.

Psychodynamic aspects

In the psychotic structure, the paranoiac is the least regressive on the plane of the libido. *Fixation* is at the beginning of the *anal stage* after its effect takes place, a set-back before the manifestation of the second anal stage (*retention*); the character therefore forms with aggressive fixations, and with primitive experiences of frustration and vindication. The defence structure of the paranoiac is against passive desires directed towards the mother as well as the father. Often parents are couples with inverted roles: the mother has the real authority even if the father is treated as if he came first. Latent homosexuality is frequent in paranoia due to the father usurping the mother's functions, with her complicity. It is here that the basic sexual identity disorders originate, and the consequent frequent need for social climbing.

Even in language, by using a detached, admonitory, and demonstrative style, the trace of "protective failure" emerges, as does that of negated passive desires. More or less oral or anal forms can be found in paranoia. Freud describes the three stages in the fundamental mechanism of paranoia:

(1) Negation of affection and reversal of impulse: "*it is him that I love*" becomes "*no I don't love him, I hate him.*" (2) Projection and reversal of the object. "*I hate him*" becomes "*it is he who hates me.*" (3) The final sentiment is seen as external and therefore justified: "*because he hates me, I hate him.*"

Socialization

Paranoiacs' high self-regard, disdain for others, the arrogance that often swells into mental exhibitionism and megalomania, are not obvious ways of attracting sympathy. Emotional and relational inflexibility make paranoiacs socially inadequate, arid, closed to collective values and unable to discuss their own value system, authoritarian, touchy and vindictive, and sometimes with a rebellious spirit based on mental delusion. Stubbornness and fanaticism determine stoic or eccentric attitudes, which sometimes lead to despotic proselytizing tendencies. Many sectarian leaders are examples of this.

In the work environment the true paranoiac causes mayhem. As an employee he feels frustrated, suspicious, he can appear obsequious to superiors, but nourishes rancour, does not adapt himself to team work, and scatters discord. His haughty and scolding attitude is extremely annoying. In a position of power, the risks of despotism are great, but that is not all. He tends to surround himself with fawning underlings, to the disadvantage of talented persons whose competition and possible aggression he fears. Even if he is able to achieve great undertakings through tenacity and ambition for career and power, in the end he tends to be destructive.

Such characters, we need to keep in mind, are always ready to exhibit sadistic attitudes and to crush anyone in difficulties. Independent autonomous work is advisable. Fixation at the *anal* stage leads very much towards precise and detailed work in which, if their feelings do not come into play, they may demonstrate remarkable ability. If they have more creative gifts, they can become writers, poets, and artists, but these activities are all undertaken in an extremely individual way, and they remain greatly isolated in a world they scorn.

In the worst cases, the defence mechanisms of *projection* and *denial* can trigger extremely contemptible behaviour (anonymous letters, menaces, slander). They can lead to "vampirism" in which the creative energy of others is exploited in order to crush them better, to cold and premeditated murder, and sometimes to self-accusation in cases of sexual crimes.

To summarize, we find in the writing of a paranoiac: a rigid tension of stroke and space, with both hypertrophied and systematic gestures. There are also traces of an overcompensated inferiority complex, anal obsession, and latent homosexuality. The overall inflexibility differentiates this diagnosis from insanity, which also generates hypertrophy and fullness of form.

Hysterical people quite often experience moments of paranoia, sudden and real attacks of feeling persecuted with consequent vindictive feelings (they feel persecuted, and become persecutors). Such feelings can poison personal relationships. We believe that the mechanism of envy evidenced by Klein suffuses these subjects.

Paranoiac delusion

In general paranoiac delusion presents itself as a delusion of social relations, it is chronic and is lived in complete awareness. The character's grounding is very favourable because its ruthless logic favours doggedly subjective interpretations, which enrich themselves in such a way as to make the delusion seem stable, well organized, and even contagious. The symptoms of delusion revolve around an intellectual construct with the following points of fixation: interpretation, persecution, feelings of omnipotence. They mostly concern *delusions of passion* in which the exaltation of a leading idea invests a particular sector:

Delusion of vindication: fighting an injustice whether true or false; it concerns legal or medical affairs, or metaphysical or empirical areas, for example inventions.

Delusion of erotomania: the certainty of being loved by a particular person generates a dangerous vicious circle: hope, ill-feeling, hate, and reprisal.

Delusion of jealousy: the couple live in a triangular situation with a fixed idea of the rival lying in wait; proofs are sought and the imagined rival is persecuted.

Delusion of interpretation: type of ratiocinative madness; based on erroneous intuition, everything is interpreted according to the direction of the delusion (distorted memories or expectations, megalomania, persecution). Less coherent than the other more clearly passionate delusions, its outcome is however insidious and progressive, with grave danger of medical or legal repercussions.

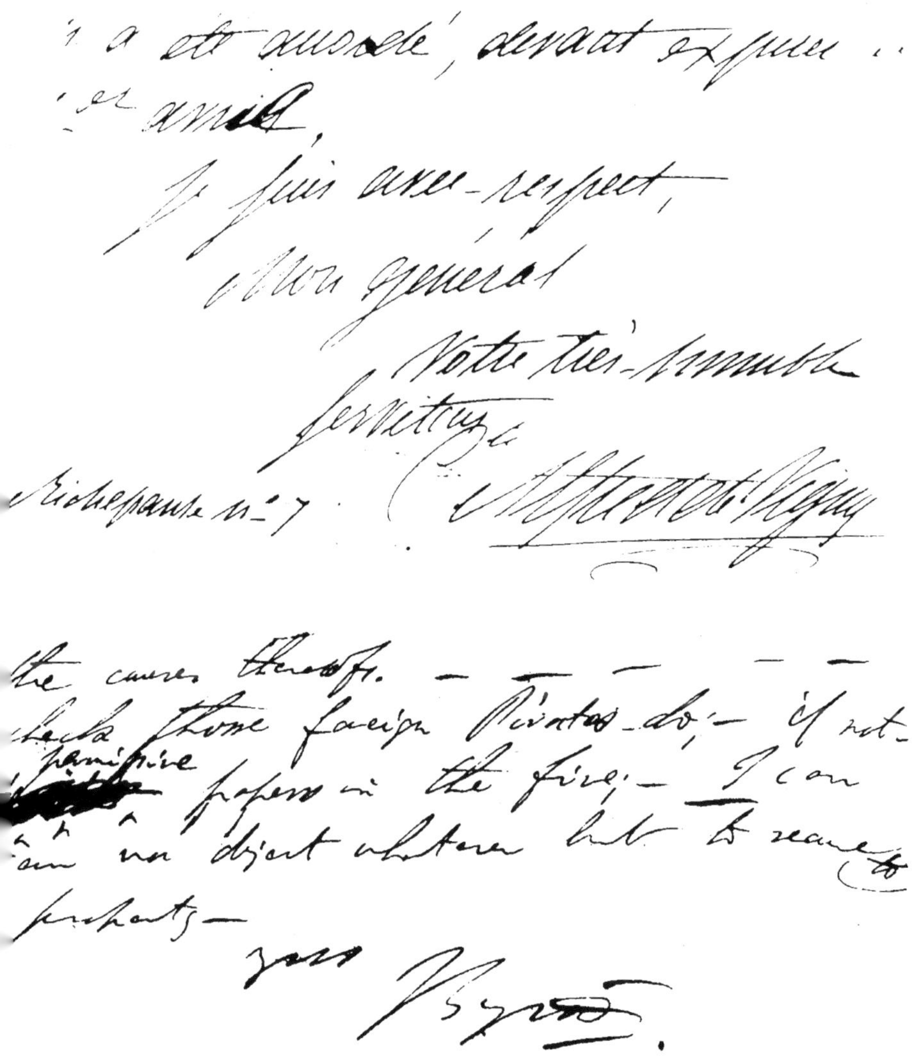

Figure 104 (reduced)
Paranoiac syndrome, the poets Alfred de Vigny and Lord Byron. Vigny: obsessive background, schizoid. Byron: hysterical background, "with sexual complexes: pasty and spasmodic stroke, anality, narcissism" (Gille-Maisani [108])

PARANOIAC PERSONALITY

Paranoiac behaviour
Exalted closed-off pride, distrust and disdain for others
Wrong judgements and passionate, rigid hyperlogic
Fanaticism and despotism
Social and emotional inadequacy
Ambition, vindication and social overcompensation
Solitude, irritability, wish for vengeance

Psychology
Fixation to first anal stage
Emotional frustration and narcissism
Overcompensated inferiority complex
Latent or practising homosexuality

Psychotic form: very structured psychotic delirium

Deliriums: jealousy, erotomania, vindication, interpretation

Defence mechanisms: projection, negation

Table 48

PARANOIA : GRAPHOLOGICAL CORRESPONDENCES

Tension and inflexibility: space, movement, stroke, and form
Hypertrophy of capital letters
Narrowness of dimension, often methodical slanting
Tangled lines
Excessive dashes instead of full stops

Table 49

Criminal behaviour

We give a number of writing samples of criminals with their basic psychopathological characteristics. Very often psychopaths show alterations in rhythm and pressure. According to Roda Wieser [250] their "basic rhythm" is defective because of excessive inflexibility, or in the reverse case, excessive weakness, and their writing tends to be discordant. According to a study conducted in France in 1977 on crime and delinquency by

M. Peyrefitte, the Minister of Justice, "there are two factors connected to a latent violence that is not mentally integrated and requires an outlet in action: the subject's passivity, and a continuing dependent relationship."

In Fig. 105, we reproduce writing samples of murderers taken from Wieser's book. In Figs 106–7 we reproduce criminal cases already in the public domain. (For reasons of discretion it is difficult to offer present day writing samples.)

Psychosis of character

Bergeret makes an interesting insight on the *psychosis of character*. According to him the subject affected by psychosis of character does not deny reality, but makes grave errors in evaluating it, with a process of dual split of the internal and external elements of reality, separated into the gratifying and the disturbing. It is a type of character framework seen in politicians, artists, writers, and we have also identified it in writings of so-called "terrorists", which unfortunately cannot be reproduced.

MAXIMILIEN ROBESPIERRE (Fig. 108a)

We take from Bergeret [23] this eloquent portrait of the chief agent of the French Revolution. The brief life of Robespierre (1758–94) has attracted contrasting and passionate evaluations. Nothing was ordinary in his birth, education, sex life, friendships, metaphysical stance, defence, fall, and death. Bergeret noted a diversity between the often painful and wretched external realities with which he fought and his *internal ideals*. This is not a type of paranoiac megalomania, but of "pomposity" connected to an effort of *manipulation of the object* (whereas megalomania denies it).

He is the first of four children, born a few months after his parents' unsuitable marriage. His mother dies in her fifth confinement after a rapid series of pregnancies. His father refuses to attend her funeral, abandons the children, and disappears to squander his family fortune and die soon after; he was a boisterous psychopath. Maximilien is brought up by his maternal grandparents, and enters college in Arras, where he presents a detestable character.

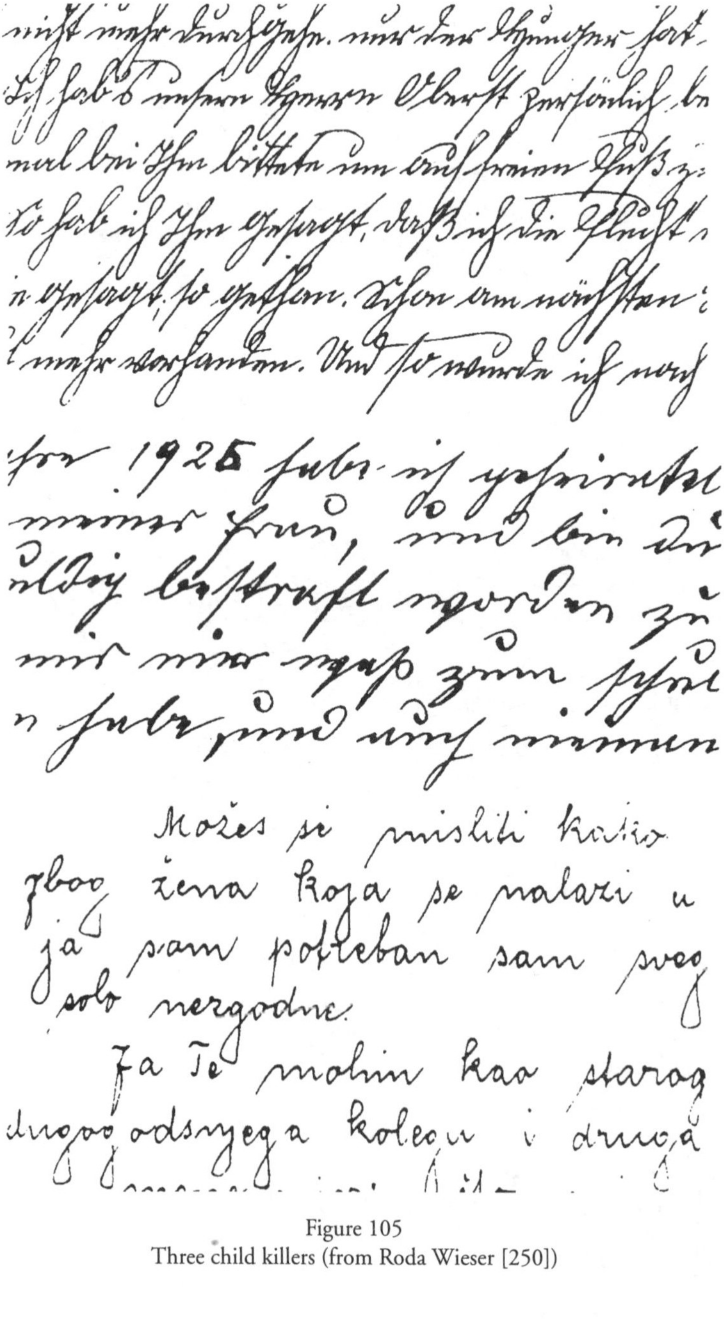

Figure 105
Three child killers (from Roda Wieser [250])

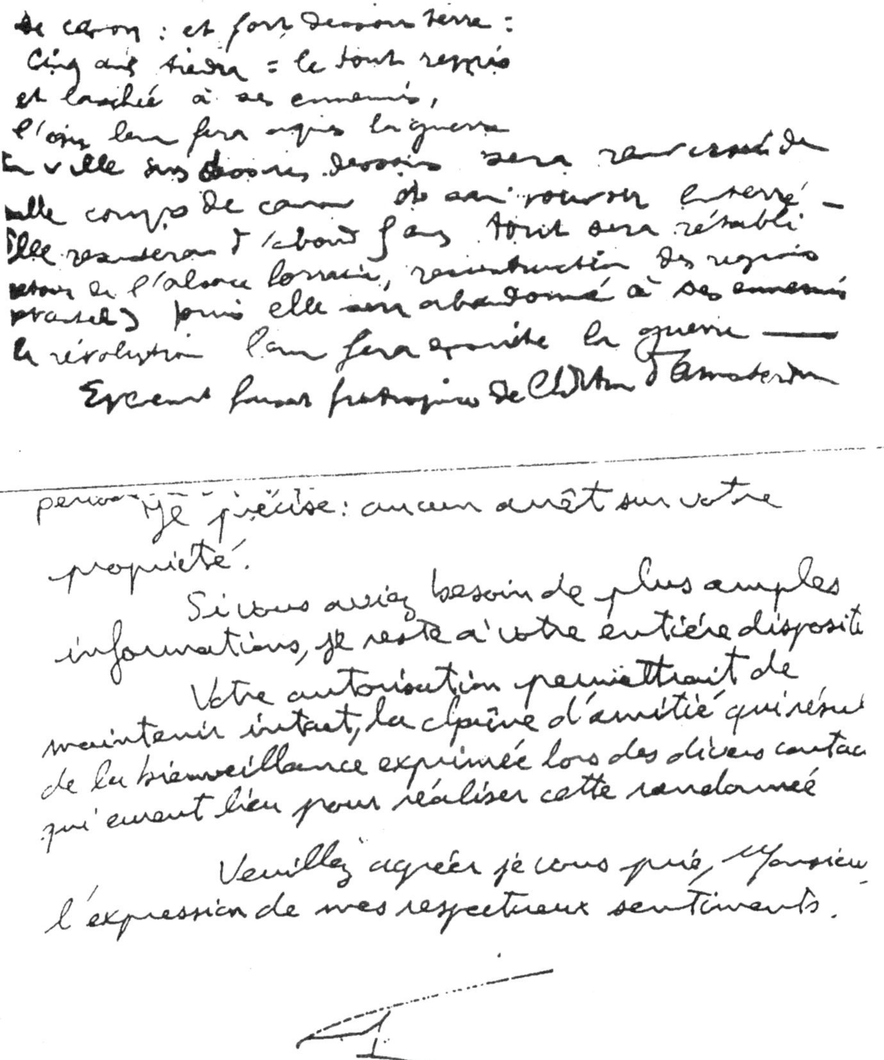

Figure 106
Writings taken from Colo et al. [61]
(a) Doctor Petiot accused of 23 murders (claimed responsibility for 63), committed during the Second World War, and appropriating the victims' property: satanic, sadistic, considered a "depressive paranoiac"
(b) "The assassin of the full moon": assaults, rapes, and murders; dual personality

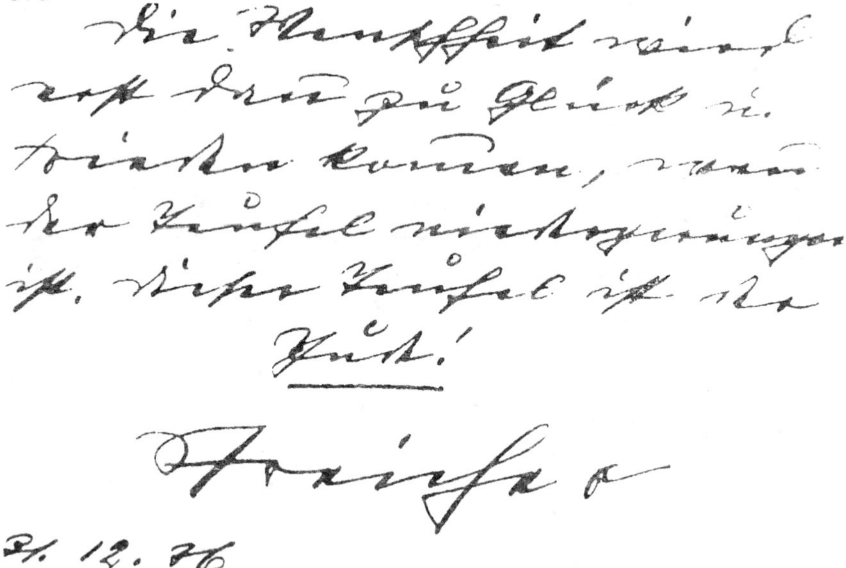

Figure 107

We draw from Ania Teillard [227] the terrifying writing of Julius Streicher, schoolmaster turned major war criminal, exterminator of Jews: "the heightened passion is reflected in the overall angular, heavy, and slanted writing; the fanaticism, in the black stroke, compact and overconnected … all the characteristics of the sado-anal complex … falseness and cunning in the covering strokes, regressive strokes, and closed ovals"

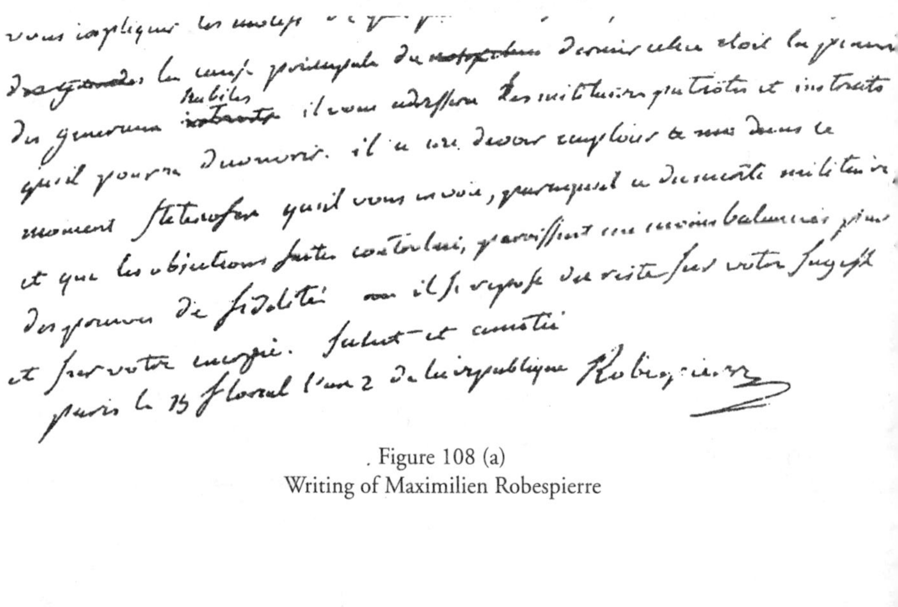

. Figure 108 (a)
Writing of Maximilien Robespierre

He wants to stand out, to surpass others, he studies energetically, obtaining a scholarship at a great Parisian Lycée, suffers from feeling "different" from others, is inspired by Rousseau, and fantasizes during his solitary walks. He becomes a lawyer in Arras and occupies himself in literature and philosophy. He enters politics and is elected as a deputy of the Third Estate. Mirabeau said of him: "This young man will go far, he believes everything he says." His sincerity excuses his violence and in 1791 he is nominated public prosecutor to the Criminal Tribunal of the Seine, in a position of "executioner".

In his aggressive diatribes he declared himself to be a sacrificial victim for the nation: "I see with trepidation the painful work to which my position condemns me, but I am called to a tumultuous destiny; I have to follow its course to the ultimate sacrifice which I will offer to the fatherland." He quickly detaches himself from his first friends and becomes, says Michelet, the "great obstacle of those he has left". He accepts the presence of the King, then seeks his death. A member of the Committee of Public Safety, he does not take part in the revolutionary tribunal. If privately petitioned by families, he often gives prisoners freedom. According to Bergeret, Robespierre had nothing of the pervert.

His hypersensitive *narcissism* does not tolerate face to face accusation. He is desperate to be "loved", but in his public contact he perceives everything to be persecutory, and he is subject to such strong tension that he becomes prey to defensive impulses which wear him out, despite the stimulation of an *Ideal of the Ego* beyond measure. When he is alone, he feels anguish and vacillates, but facing a group of people his violence is reborn. With a sufficient emotional maturity and the capacity to "love", Robespierre would have been able to use his exceptional intelligence and his "incorruptibility".

His clearly psychotic character derives from: an anxiety of losing the illusory object, a fusion of the protecting and gratifying maternal and paternal images, and seeking a delusive link to the positive *internal* representation, a Supreme Being. This gave rise to splits, reactive formations, incredible projections and projective identifications, intolerable due to his strongly heightened "narcissism", dangerous in such a disturbed period. He truly suffered in the situation in which he found himself. An ascetic, he had two platonic fiancées, and was inadequate and stiff on the emotional plane; in the name of justice, inflexible.

He treated the Assembly as "conspirators, dictators, enemies of the people, tormentors, traitors ...Death is the beginning of immortality." According to Bergeret he was not a paranoiac with a strict Superego. He did not go beyond the stage of the Ideal of the Ego, so he did not attain the Oedipal organization to meet the opposite sex. In his defensive process the object representations underwent sudden distortions but not his Ego. He did not deny reality but split it, and sought neither satisfaction nor power, but an inaccessible reassurance.

A prophetic forecast: Adolf Hitler

The historian Antonio Espinosa, in his book *Hitler, il figlio della Germania* (Mondadori, 1991) recounts that in 1914 Hitler, an as yet unknown young man, asked a graphologist to study his writing, when he was only 25. His personality was described in the following sentences: "a tormented instability and extreme irritability"; "mostly an aggressive behaviour, which due to lack of any goodness of spirit and consideration, could unleash itself without restraint on others." "An extremely fine degree of intelligence, not in the sense of critical method but with shrewdness, ability, spontaneous sharpness, and imagination, able to react to the most varied situations." His personality was "anything but mediocre and colourless", on the contrary it revealed itself as "powerful even if it had many negative aspects", but in addition he showed an "aggression that might have led him to bellicose conflicts with the world around him." We may speculate as to whether this graphologist belonged to the Klagesian School. We reproduce Hitler's handwriting, including a sample of the same year, in Fig. 108b.

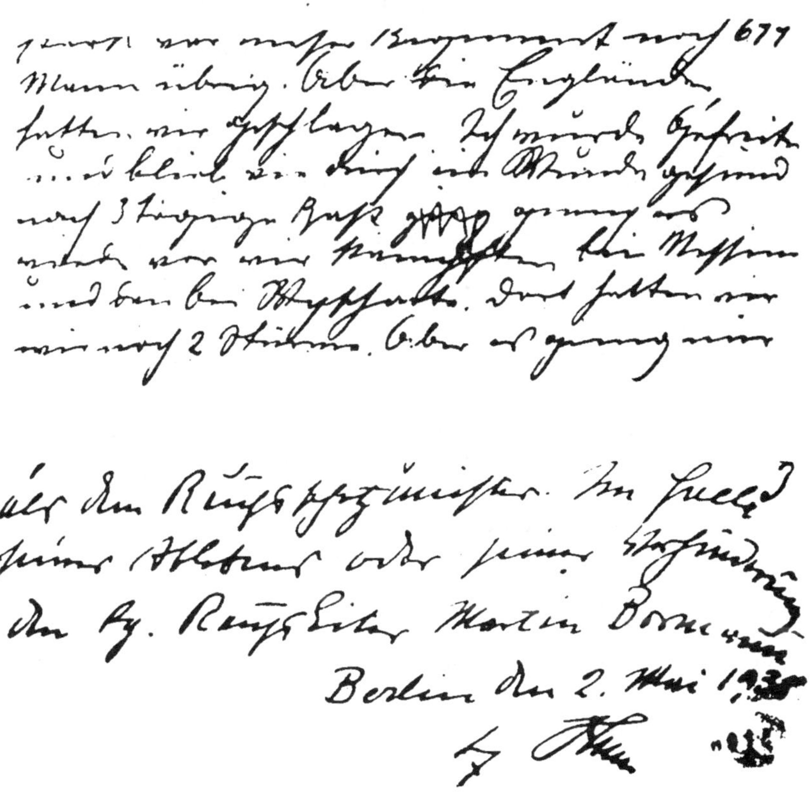

Figure 108 (b) and (c)
Writings of Adolf Hitler in 1914 and 1935 (Werner Maser, *Hitler segreto*, Garzanti, 1974)

V. SCHIZOPHRENIA

"The unreal invades a personality which then detaches itself from reality and dissolves. There is a dissociation: or better, a discordance between the emotional, psychomotor, and rational components of the personality" (Rosine de Goursac, GGCF).

This is a type of *chronic* and *developing* psychosis mostly affecting younger subjects between the ages of 15 and 35. The influence of sociocultural factors, isolation, uprooting, etc., added to genetic and biochemical factors, unleashes its disruption. The basic formation is often Jung's "introvert" and Kretschmer's "schizoid" type, a formation on which various character disorders prey.

Many artists, poets, writers, and musicians with schizoid tendencies have found a balance through art. A number of occupations or hobbies, as well as certain more or less solitary sports (sailing, mountaineering, flying), help to distance the reality of daily life. Adolescents often go through a transitional "schizoid" phase. The disorganization that occurs in schizophrenia affects all aspects of character, the following being the more salient points:

Intellectual dissociation

Intelligence remains potentially intact but it is used in an inadequate way. The thought process is blocked, thoughts become vague, untidy, confused. Language disorders occur such as not speaking, talking nonsense, swearing, or using arbitrary linguistic constructions. Logic is altered and disturbed by magico-symbolic thought with empty abstractions.

Disorganization of emotional life

Emotional and relational life is characterized by contradictions between inertia and impulsiveness, by bizarre behaviour, and communication with others is completely out of line. Emotion is repressed: the subject wants to be cold, unfeeling, indifferent. If emotions burst out, the subject releases substantial energy in violent and maladjusted impulses. Always there is an underlying indifference, negativity, and dissociation from practical life. Sexuality is disturbed, with strong oral and anal regressions.

Psychomotor discordance

Ambivalence provokes constant oscillation between the execution and the suppression of movements: paradoxical expressions of mimicry, of smile; mannered, affected, and excessive expressions; stereotype gestures, empty and fantastic rituals; intentions of murder, suicide, mutilation, aggression contrast with inertia, inflexibility, catatonia.

Schizophrenic delirium stems from a thinking disorder, from delusive convictions which, for the patient, become more real than reality. The subject enters an *autistic, archaic* world: a world of alienation, feelings of being influenced, loss of personal identity.

The neuropsychiatrist Massimo Santi Reitano [211] sums it up thus. "A serious mental illness rests on a triad of: conceptual disorder, dissociation, and perceptual disorder.

The word psychosis (according to DSM IV) nearly always refers to disorders centred on ideas, the word schizophrenia refers to disorders which can be organized around the three so-called primary symptoms: delusion, dissociation of ideas and emotions, hallucinations.

The graphic expressions, the graphological qualities of expression of the patient affected with paranoiac schizophrenia, catatonia, feeblemindedness, or by paranoia, borderline syndromes, or mood disorders, have great diagnostic value. Nearly always the symptomatic expression of these patients is very well recognized in their graphic traits, with characteristics which sometimes can be considered almost pathological."

Writing (Figs. 109–10)

The seriousness of the disorder does not always appear in the writing. In some cases, psychotic schizophrenics could be mistaken for *neurotics*. However, following the development of the illness over months, graphology can be more prognostic than diagnostic. The graphologist can sound the alarm by observing the sudden change in writing of an adolescent, for example, and can also check for possible improvements.

Drawings by schizophrenics represent a privileged expressive production which, when imaginative capacity still exists, can allow access to their world. Also, drawing can be therapeutic for them, as can poetic composition.

A number of graphic signs are frequent and have been collated by Gille-Maisani; these signs mainly concern graphic categories reflecting overall aspects of the writing. In the first French edition of *Psychologie de l'écriture* of 1969 [105] Gille-Maisani refers to his personal observation after giving tests to patients in a hospital in Quebec. He chose around ten cases which he affirmed are "among the most typical for showing the potential and present limits of graphology for the study of schizophrenia." From these he distinguished the following types of patient: *straightforward schizophrenics, catatonics, paranoid schizophrenics*. His observations can be summarized thus:

- the *organization* of writing is in general maintained, and when a process of *disorganization* occurs it is not mistaken for pre-senile degeneration or regression to a childish phase. The prognosis is serious if graphic disorganization occurs in a young person with previously satisfactory organization;
- *monotony*, a *stereotyped* aspect, and *weak* stroke are the most recurrent signs of the illness, in drawing as well as writing;
- finally, the *lack of compensation mechanisms*, such as occur in the writing of neurotics, facilitates a precisely different diagnosis regarding the psychosis.

Thea Stein-Lewinson in particular studied pathological writings and developed *graphometric scales* through which a *pathological index* is obtained. According to her, it can forecast the development of schizophrenia. For a list of studies that have appeared in graphological literature we refer to our own article [36]. More recent studies have shown that certain parental characteristics promote the appearance of the illness in their children, and a *schizophrenogenic* father or mother can be sketched (see E. Manetti [161a]).

SCHIZOID PERSONALITY

Intellectual dissociation
Disorganization of emotional life
Psychomotor discord

Behaviour
withdrawal into own world; distance from reality
thought without logic, abstract, formal
morbid rationality
lack of emotion
lack of interest, lack of the joy of living
bodily neglect
stereotyped language or "babbling"

Psychodynamics
Family with schizophrenic disorders
Poor, unhappy family: unable to fulfil the child's needs
Schizophrenogenic father: insecure of own masculinity, with paranoiac and
    tyrannical tendencies, need for admiration
Schizophrenogenic mother: overprotective, cold, anxious, guilt-ridden,
    with unclear messages

Defence mechanisms
Annulment – division – projective identification – denial – acting out

---

Table 50

GENERAL GRAPHOLOGICAL CORRESPONDENCES: SCHIZOPHRENIA

Space too invaded or too impoverished
Monotonous, rigid
Stereotyped forms; drawings without movement
Weak stroke, dominance of lines and extensions
Cut up movement, inadequate, hindrance of progress to the right
Tendency to wrong number of verticals (*m* with four downstrokes)
Often weak, uncertain pressure, inconsistent *t*-bars
Tremors (sometimes due to inability to understand written or verbal messages)
Lack of compensatory signs

Table 51

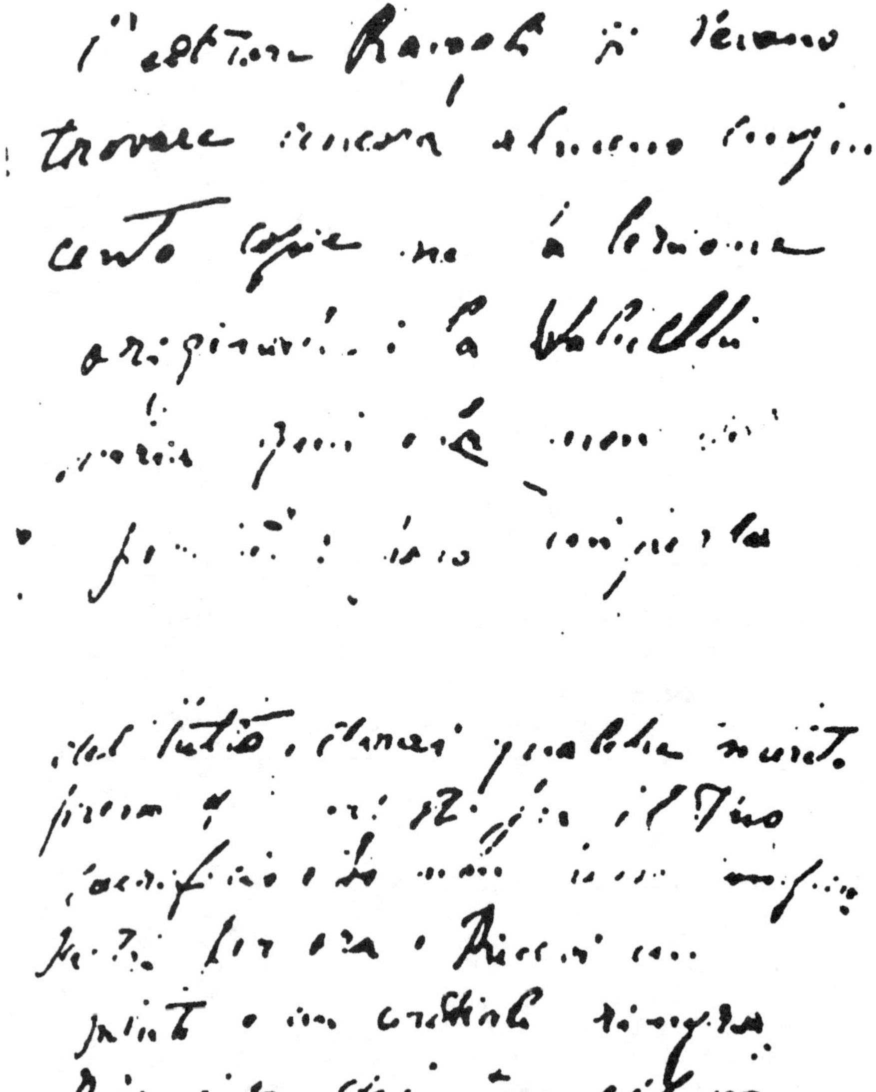

Figure 109
Writing of the poet Dino Campana: schizoid tendency marked by the
schizo-paranoid position

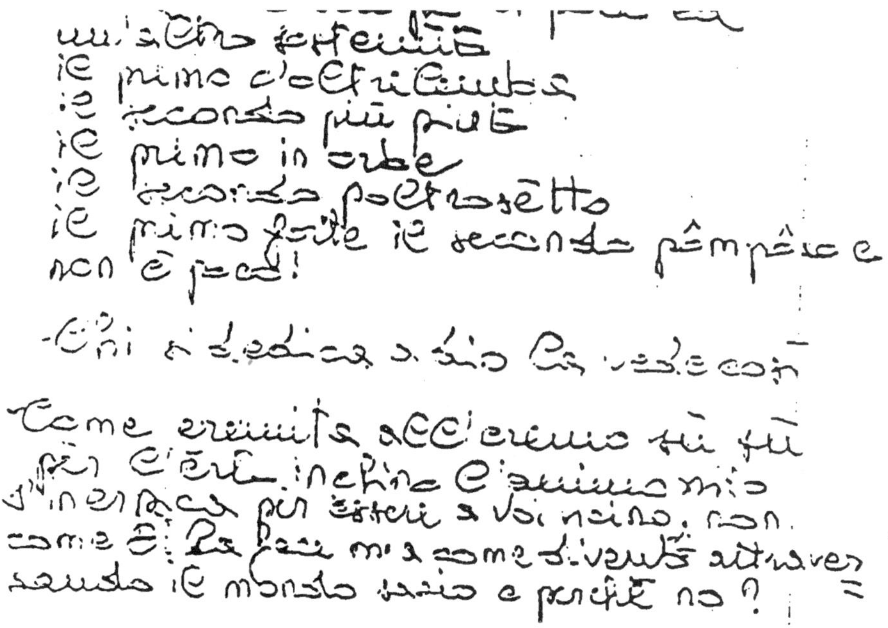

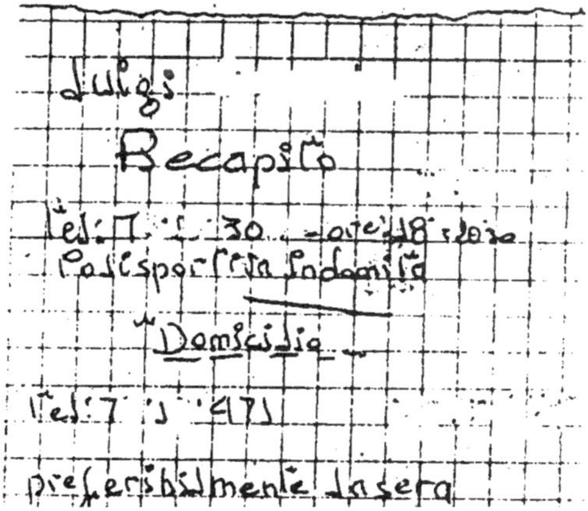

Figure 110
Schizophrenia, writings marked by the schizo-paranoid position
(a) mental patient well adapted with his delusions, he draws and writes: affected writing
(b) young worker with abnormal behaviour: regressive writing

VI. DEPRESSION

The depressive character, manic-depressive psychosis, limit or borderline cases, are all structural forms of a basic anxiety: fear of *loss of the object*. "Depression is a black cloud on things": these words from "The exercise books of Thea", written by a young woman in a mental institution, are heartbreaking when we learn that she died in good health at the age of 34 in 1970, not by suicide. The depressive character is according to Bergeret "a basic element of narcissistic makeup and its mental function is underlined by ambivalence." Anxiety, the fear of losing the loved òbject, the terror of being abandoned, of defeat, are the foundations of the depressive personality. In depression, the Superego is no longer a structuring guide but a castrating persecuting judge, as Melanie Klein put it.

Depressive tendencies are in general easily picked out in writing: lack of tone in the stroke, descending lines or words, very strong signs alternate with weak or nearly disappearing ones, signs of regression, of lack of impulse, all signs of a suffering and fragile Ego. The writing of the *manic-depressive* expresses the two poles of this cyclical illness, from the overflow of instinctive and emotional impulses and the anguished flight from ideas, to the depressive sense of loss which can lead to suicide. In writing we find paradoxical and opposing movements: for example, weak and slow, but excessively progressive and overconnected, with sudden gaps, or a fluctuating movement with exaggerated gestures.

The serious manic-depressive is not easily integrated in the world of work. We do know, however, that some people can live with this real handicap, at the price of great suffering.

Bergeret insists that the *limit-state* organization (see next section) "is underlined by the depressive threat": the inherent narcissistic retrogression opens the way to strong imbalances which could be misunderstood as neurotic and psychotic indicators, leading to a wrong therapy. Bergeret has therefore developed a "theory of limit-depression".

It is not possible to encompass the variety of depressive personalities in a summary diagram, we only give a general view in Table 52. The depressive component, which can be momentary or more structured and lasting, that is to say reactive or inherent, often overlaps with other psychopathological configurations.

Dr V. Mirabel's concluding sentence at a recent conference sums up the dilemma of depression [76]. "Depression is strongly linked to a neurobiological profile, but also to vicissitudes in the subject's emotional history: it would be futile to focus only on one half of the problem." We agree with him that the present DSM classifications [78] establish "a theory of illness fixed to behavioural criteria ... This classification develops a concept too full of the diagnosis of pure depression and suppresses the concept of neurosis, including hysterical neurosis." Furthermore, he continues: "we are also fortunate at the end of this century to have at our disposal efficacious and easily administered anti-depressant drugs."

To identify the risk of depression one needs to catch signs of anxiety and insecurity, and the lack or rigidity of defence mechanisms. Graphologists have always been involved in the problem. We cite a recent work of Florence Despras who outlines some writing profiles of depressives [76], specifying that there are danger signals but that there is no typical writing for the depressed. We also cite the work of the Italian graphologist Angela Mele [167] who has particularly concentrated on this problem.

DEPRESSIVE PERSONALITY: GENERALITIES   (from Dr V. Mirabel)

Negative perception of self – sense of impotence – desperation – loss of emotion with consequent acute sense of blame – pervasive anxiety – perception of imminent danger

Behaviour
Strong mood changes – psychomotor slowing down – somatic disorders – intellective disorders: of concentration, attention, and memory, or motor agitation – insomnia – anorexia – ideas of suicide

Grave risk
Melancholic attacks – suicide

Psychodynamic of borderline (see next section)
Pathology of narcissism and archaic defence mechanisms of introspection and projection (according to M. Klein, Lebovici, Racamier, Bergeret)

Table 52

GENERAL GRAPHOLOGICAL CONNECTIONS: DEPRESSION

Tendency to descending writing
Irregularities in the slant
Disturbance of movement: tension, braking after initial impulses
Dominant and disturbed "whites": gaps, chimneys
Extremely changeable stroke, twisting
Badly formed middle zone, messy, squeezed
Presence of Superego, sense of guilt, frustrated narcissism

Table 53

VII. LIMIT OR BORDERLINE CASES

Limit cases are so called because their psychopathological configuration lies at the boundary between neurosis and psychosis. They seem to represent a real illness of the present time, at least this "structure", or "a-structure" as Bergeret defines it, is built on a psychological configuration that at first sight cannot be placed in the theoretical framework of illness.

According to Bergeret [25] a precocious emotional trauma always plays the role of "prime disorganizer" of the development of the subject. The Ego in the "limit state" presents an empty, hollow aspect and sees itself as systematically disinherited or guilty. Such a personality is defined as "anaclytic", that is a personality that "needs the presence of others to feel narcissistically complete". These are persons who only appear to be adapted. Bergeret defines them as "sufficient" or "not too bad" people, who present themselves as:

- sufficiently adaptable rather than adjusted;
- sufficiently charming because of an ardent need for respect and affection;
- sufficiently energetic because they have manic defences.

The French psychiatrist Green has spoken of their "Messianic reverie" which behind a feigned humility hides a powerful ambition. They play at being hypernormal. As a means of defence, they function along two tracks:

they display a syndrome of " flight from identity", with an intolerance of anxiety, poor control of impulsiveness, and blocking sublimation. They are also called "as if" personalities: that is with a passive mental flexibility, suggestible, childish, with hidden aggressive tendencies, and sometimes the makeup of a "False Ego" as described by Winnicott. Denial and projective identification are defence mechanisms that can have long-term success.

In writing we do not find the presence of a very strong Superego, which is not well formed in the limit state, but we do see the *Ideal of the Ego*. Spatial organization, stroke, and forms lack structure and firmness, but sometimes a richly subtle vibration emanates in an almost unfathomable style. The Ideal of the Ego exalts itself with ample gestures in the capital letters.

Bergeret explains the role of the Ideal of the Ego in the following way: "It is through heroic and excessive ambitions to "surpass" with the intent of keeping hold of love and the presence of the object, that such people confront their relational life, much more than through their guilt of having 'been bad' in a genital and Oedipal manner, and being punished for this with castration." Because of this, a great danger arises of failure in idealistic ambitions, and the consequent depressive reaction stems from self-disgust (narcissistic line) which can be projected upon others. The lack of Superego makes the person intolerant to contradictions and uncertainties, and leads the subject just "to act".

The defence mechanisms in the "limit states" take into consideration the neurotic leaning and so we find: *repression* (less accentuated than in neurosis), *avoidance* (similar to phobia), rejection of the representation of the paternal image, and the mechanisms of *projective identification* described by Melanie Klein regarding the *schizo-paranoid positions*. All the same, *projective identification* can also have positive relational aspects. The psychoanalyst Racamier distinguishes a projective identification that is malign, violent, confused with the object, and a benign one, more moderate and temporary, with communicative value. In therapeutic work it is therefore very useful to identify immature defensive processes.

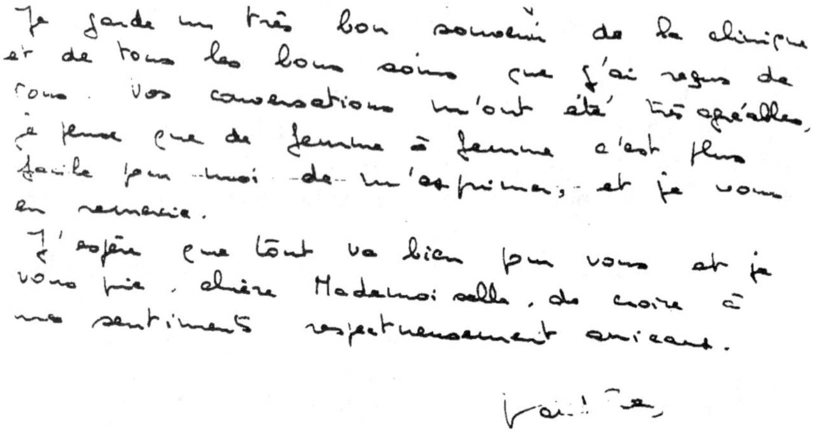
Je garde un très bon souvenir de la clinique et de tous les bons soins que j'ai reçus de vous. Vos conversations m'ont été très agréables, je pense que de femme à femme c'est plus facile pour moi de m'exprimer, et je vous en remercie.
J'espère que tout va bien pour vous et je vous prie, chère Mademoiselle, de croire à mes sentiments respectueusement amicaux.

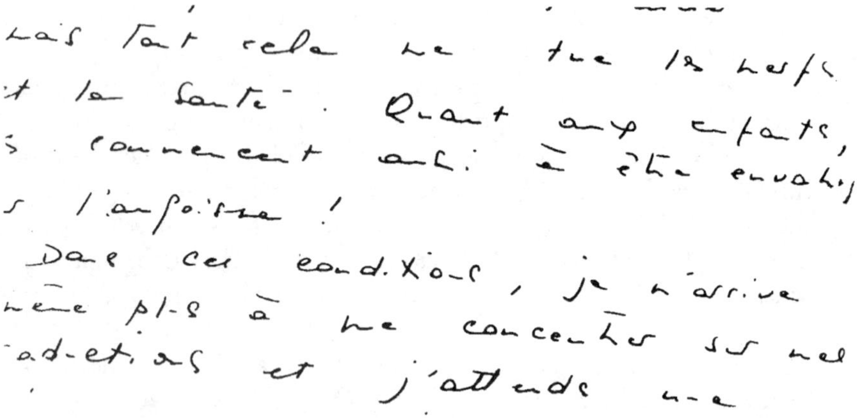
mais tout cela ne tue les nerfs et la santé. Quant aux enfants, s commencent aussi à être envahis r l'angoisse !
Dans ces conditions, je n'arrive même plus à me concentrer sur mes méditations et j'attends une

Figure 111 (reduced)
(a) 37 year old woman, with three children, divorced, clerk: depression a reaction to anorexia, very much attached to father
(b) 35 year old woman, three children, separated, serious anxiety crisis, fighting against depression and family problems, intelligent and educated

Figure 112 (*see opposite page* ☛)
53 year old woman, single, teacher: recurrent nervous depression, condition has become chronic after retiring; once a very authoritarian person now unable to organize herself; closed writing, diagonal. One can posit a hysterical background, rigid with conversion

3

"les neiges"

et bergeries

puisqu'on a 2 février.

dans un lycée agricole.

près de Montélimar ce soir chercher

Nous allons souhaitant

Hélène à Perpignan traumatisée

ne pas la trouver trop cette joie de maison

Elle s'était fait mal une

les vacances loin. le Divorce

familiale

Pour moi je n'oublie pas

au sujet des affaires. J'ai beaucoup

laquelle je ne pas vous avez reçu

eu Septembre car de temps

peut-être jours. De i' Nöel !

les jours de contenu ont

été nombreux

car

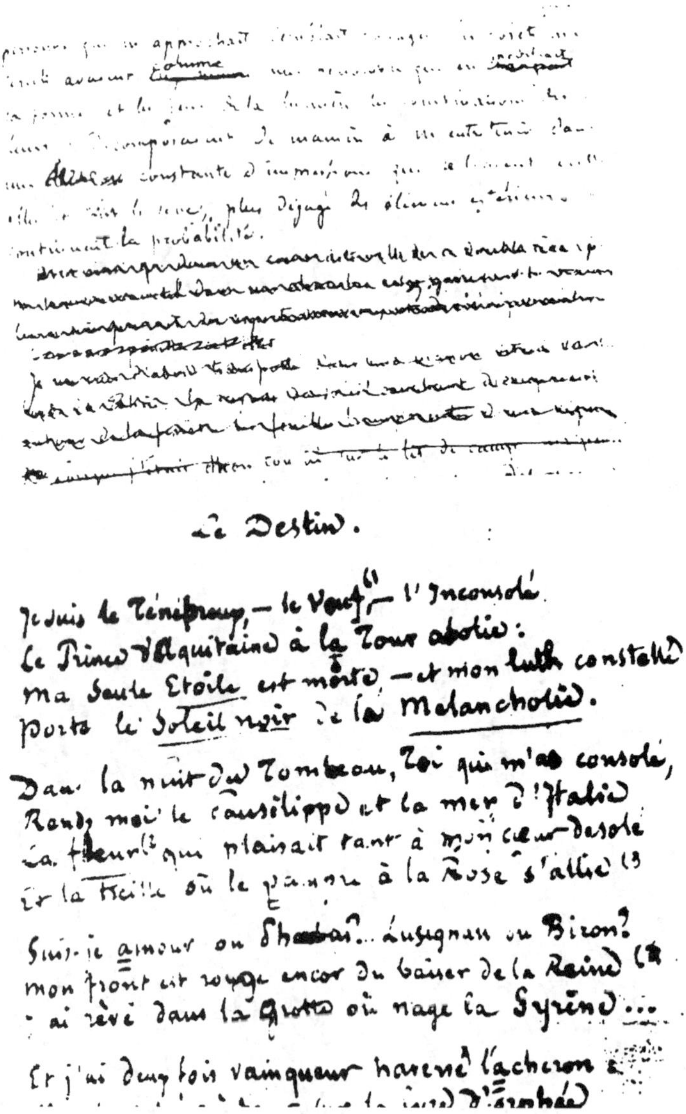

Figure 113
Writing of the poet Gérard de Nerval, committed suicide by hanging in 1855
(a) From the manuscript of "Aurelia"
(b) Manuscript poem. Schizo-paranoid and cyclothymic tendencies; sometimes in asylums, visionary and observer of his own madness: "the dream is a second life" (Raymond Jean, *Nerval*, Seuil)

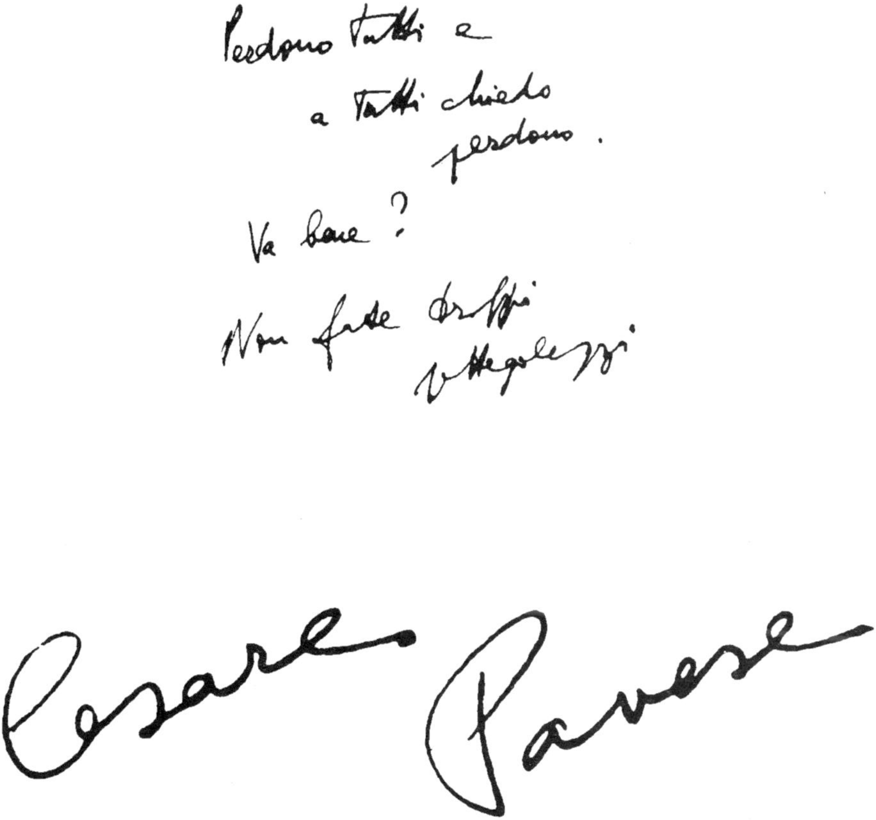

Figure 114
Writing of the poet Cesare Pavese: note found after his suicide (from the newspaper
La Repubblica, 10 March 1990). Below is his signature at a previous time

Chapter Fifteen

PERSONALITY THEORY AND THE JUNGIAN SCHOOL

In addition to Freud, Jung's ideas on personality theory have stimulated many graphologists to pursue interesting research. The first pioneer Ania Teillard, with her brother, published in Leipzig in 1929 [168] the main correlations between graphology and the theory of personality according to both Freud and Jung, later updated in the French edition published in Paris in 1948. Following her method, Dr Gille-Maisani carried out wide-ranging studies, and more recently other methodologies have been proposed by the graphologists Claude Boureille [41–2] and Catherine Colo [60], while Monique Genty [100] has developed a theoretical and philosophical study on the subject.

We also refer to the observations of Marie-Louise von Franz [94], one of the most authoritative followers of Jung, a person of great scientific and humanist culture, who in her work as a psychoanalyst has obtained remarkable findings related to the mechanism of the psychic functions identified by Jung, in particular the role of the lower function. Ania Teillard, Marie-Louise von Franz, and Claude Boureille, have all practised psychoanalysis and have developed experimental methods of verification for Jung's theories, drawn from observations of their patients.

I. CARL GUSTAV JUNG (1875–1961)

The historian Ellenberger [89], comparing Jung's infancy to that of Freud, asked whether their different family backgrounds could explain one of the reasons why Jung did not give any weight to the theory of Oedipal conflict. Jung's relationship with his parents lacked affection. Freud, on the contrary, the adored son of a young and beautiful woman, was directed to an inevitable conclusion.

Jung's life and thought were certainly influenced by his Swiss origins and family environment. Both parents had been born when their respective families had lost their economic status, but his paternal grandfather (also Carl Gustav) had been one of the most renowned doctors in Basel, Rector of the University, Grand Master of the Swiss Masons, a scientific popularist and a theatrical author. His maternal grandfather Preiswerk, a theologian and Hebrew scholar, was the President of the Pastoral Council of Basel, and both he and his wife, and other relatives, seemed to possess paranormal faculties. We can therefore understand Jung's interest and open-minded attitude towards the metaphysical, the irrational, and oriental culture, interests which influenced his entire work. On the other side, his attachment to his roots and traditions supplied him with a solid, realistic, and scientific base.

Carl Gustav Jung was born in the canton of Thurgau, graduated in medicine in Zurich in 1900, and joined the Burghölzli, a hospital for mental disorders and university clinic, directed by Eugen Bleuler. He soon aligned himself with Freud's new theories, so much so that Freud considered him his heir. However, Jung's own critical thought brought about a gradual detachment and subsequent rupture with Freud. After his separation from the Freudian movement, Jung developed his own system, which he called *analytical psychology*.

In 1913 he left both the Burghölzli and the Psychoanalytical Association to dedicate himself only to private patients. He spent a period of research and internal analysis which later formed the kernel of the Jungian analytical treatment. This process was drawn from observations that he made at the Burghölzli, where he had noted the frequency with which ancestral and universal symbols appeared in the hallucinations of patients. From these findings arose the notion of archetype and an unconscious different from that of the individual, which Jung called *collective unconscious*.

Analogous to Freud's experience of self-analysis, Jung experimented on himself to discover his own knowledge of archetypes. To begin with this process was slow, but it quickened so much that he began to fear for his sanity. Fortunately he found in his profession and family a sustaining strength and anchor to reality. After this Jung dedicated himself to writing, travelling, teaching, and to psychotherapy.

II. JUNGIAN THEORY

Psychic energy or *libido*

In Jung the *libido* moves from the Freudian concept of mostly *sexual energy* to that of *psychic energy*. "For Libido I mean the psychic energy ... an energetic value capable of communicating itself to any sphere of activity: power, hunger, hate, sexuality, religion, etc."

Even if analogies can be established between "physical energy" and "psychic energy" and the principles of conservation, transformation, and degradation, there are substantial differences between them: psychic energy cannot be measured and in addition to having "a cause, it also has a scope". Its quantity remains *constant* and with certain stimuli its strength can be mobilized by emerging from the unconscious. Jung set up the *verbal association test* as the cardinal instrument to demonstrate this process.

The quality of psychic energy, however, does fluctuate. Jung calls the direction that psychic energy takes *progressive* when it expresses itself in a process of balancing the adaptation to the outside world. When the individual remains stagnant or regresses, becoming prey to internal conflicts and to reactivated unconscious elements, the direction will instead be *regressive*. A state of regression can be temporarily beneficial in finding a contact with one's own internal reality necessary to development, but this development must not be confused with the process of *progression*.

Collective unconscious, archetype, and symbol

Jung distinguishes the personal unconscious, which comprises forgotten, repressed objects, the thoughts or perceptions which remain beneath the conscious, and the collective unconscious, which comprises ancestral images that we already possess from birth. In Ellenberger's words [89]: "The Jungian concept of the unconscious differs from the Freudian in three fundamental ways: the unconscious for Jung has an autonomous course of development; it is complementary to the conscious; it is the seat of universal primordial images, the archetypes."

Through his clinical experience of schizophrenic patients and through his cultural research on the study of myths and religions, Jung brought to attention the presence of universal imagery. "Archetypes are predispositions to act out certain types of attitude and behaviour in response to given stimuli-signals" explains Bianca Iaccarino [116]. The *archetypes* are for Jung *primordial images*, collective and common to peoples and epochs, "engrams" or "handy mnemonics, constituted by the condensing of countless processes similar to each other."

The archetype must not be confused with the *symbol* that comes from "the dynamic interaction between given psychic predispositions and given experiences." Through the symbol, however, we can reach the archetype of the collective unconscious. For example, the concept of *four* is an *archetype* that has innate resonance for us: the *cross* is a *symbol* of it. In dreams symbols are in general individual and must be interpreted according to their associations for the dreamer. Sometimes, however, they can take on a universal significance. Jung cites, in this connection, the "monster" whose universal significance is transmitted to us by fairy tales, legends, or mythology.

Structure of the psyche

We reproduce a diagram taken from one of Marcelle Desurvire's courses (Table 54) which derives from Jung, showing the elements of the mental dynamic structure.

THE CONSCIOUS

Jung said that the conscious is by nature a type of superficial layer, a floating epidermis over the unconscious that extends into the depths, like a vast ocean in perfect continuity. The conscious *Ego* is seen as the meeting point between the external or spatial world, and the internal or objective mental world. It is formed by a condensation of data or sensations, perceptions, emotional states, memories. Around our *Ego* interlace a number of aspects – which Jung also called "archetypes" – which modify their relationship with the *Ego* during the course of life: *Persona, Shadow, Anima or Animus, Archetype of the Spirit, Self.*

PERSONA

In classical tragedy the mask worn by the actor was termed *persona*. This concept, transferred into normal life, therefore describes a social mask, made up of conformity and convention, that the individual uses in a given social or professional environment, or caste, party, group, etc. It represents a protective system, but also a means of concealing one's own nature, sometimes ending in self-deception and complete identification with an unreal interior image.

Various social or racial prejudices often stem from such an attitude. It leads easily to ideas of utopia or megalomania, or a systematic depreciation of differences from oneself, producing a rigid personality who has created a fictitious "character". Even the identification with a *social persona* such as doctor, student, artist, manager, yuppy, is unpromising for psychological development.

Table 54

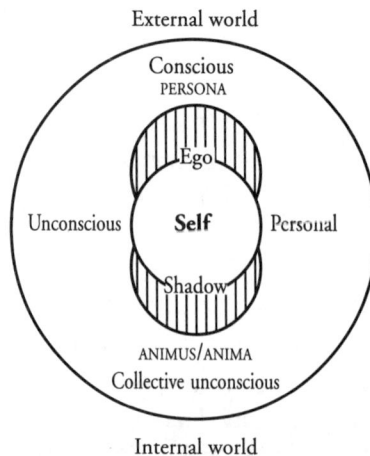

Shadow

Represents the dark side of the unconscious, containing personal characteristics (whether negative or positive) rejected as truly our own by our conscious. The Shadow risks slipping from conscious control, driving one to iniquity, or being projected onto another person who assumes the role of scapegoat. The aspects of the Shadow generally elude consciousness but if, with an effort, they reach the conscious, this process of acceptance is positive for the development of the personality.

Anima

Describes the feminine unconscious component in the man's personality. The identification with the Anima reinforces in the man a form of hypersensitivity and effeminacy, sometimes wilful or melancholic. In artists the Anima is the source of receptivity and inspiration.

For Jung the meeting with the "image of the Anima" in a man is represented by a female figure, archetype of an ideal figure. Such an ideal is projected onto the woman he loves, who may not in fact correspond to the required qualities, thus provoking negative effects.

Animus

Describes the masculine unconscious component in the woman's personality. The identification with the Animus can lead to combative, polemic, and intransigent behaviour. The idealization of the father figure, the hero, or the genius can be a source of strength but it can also lead to disastrous projections. If the Animus can be integrated harmoniously in the woman it represents the principle of the *logos*, which in addition to producing rationality, touches creative resources in the unconscious.

Polarity (introversion–extroversion)

During the course of his analytical experience and his exploration of myths, stories, and legends, Jung observed that the process of adaptability of individuals to their surroundings takes different forms. On the one hand the *introversion–extroversion* polarity divides people into two different *attitudes* or temperaments, and on the other, the tendency to rely mainly on a given *psychic function* determines the formation of different *types*. Although the terms *introversion* and *extroversion* have entered popular language, less well known is the concept of *psychic function* which represents the manner of confronting and assimilating life's experience, while the type of attitude, *introvert* or *extrovert*, indicates the direction in which psychic energy will be directed.

It is important to clarify the concepts of this polarity in the Jungian vision. We must not equate extroversion with *exteriorizing* and introversion with *interiorizing* (in today's jargon). These concepts cover a very deep psychological dimension which focuses on the relations between *Ego-object-subject*, that is the type of mechanism through which the subject interacts with reality and with everything outside the self. In studying two types of patients, hysterics and schizophrenics, Jung identified what seemed to be caricatures of two opposite relations of the individual with the environment. In the first case, there was a charged emotional relation with the therapist, in the second, there was extreme apathy with hardly any exchanges. Jung called the first attitude extroversion, the second introversion.

Although it seems that behaviour in each individual has a biologically determined tendency, this behaviour, together with psychic functions, is influenced greatly by the environment, which can sometimes overturn innate tendencies or change functions.

We quote from Marie-Louise von Franz [94] the following description: "In the extrovert the conscious libido flows as a matter of course towards the object, but it is accompanied by a hidden unconscious counteraction towards the subject. In the case of the introvert the opposite occurs: he has the impression of being permanently oppressed by the object, from which he has continually to withdraw. Everything catches him unaware and he is constantly overwhelmed by impressions, but is not aware of drawing psychic energy secretly from the object, pouring it back into the object itself, through his unconscious process of extroversion."

The two attitudes, introvert and extrovert, constitute ways of routine reaction and condition all psychic processes; not only noticeable behaviour, but also the way of evaluating every experience, as well as "the way with which *compensation* of the unconscious occurs with work", as Jung said. In practice the two temperaments will determine different behaviour in accordance with more developed functions, with the possible combination of eight different psychological types (see below). The two attitudes are nonetheless present in each individual. Introversion is generally more differentiated and available to the conscious for adapting to reality, extroversion is more childish and archaic and can become forced and less natural when it is obliged to reveal itself.

These attitudes constitute one of the fundamental aspects of mental organization, but their way of functioning is complex. It is more interesting to consider their methods of action and compensation than the prevalence of a given attitude over the other.

INTROVERSION OR TENDENCY TO TURN TOWARDS THE SUBJECT

Jung's description derives from Schiller: "The introvert must exteriorize everything that is internal and structure everything that is external. … Everyone knows those characters who are closed, impenetrable, often shy, who tend to defend themselves from external demands … and to create instead within themselves a position of security and power."

For the introvert, what matters is the *subjective* value he attributes to objects and interests. He is reserved, exclusive, and could pass as egocentric and selfish, instead he is profoundly attached to what he has chosen. In Ania Teillard's words, "the extrovert fears losing contact, the introvert is afraid of conflict." He will therefore react by withdrawing into an internal world, an imagined world. If he lacks "the mobility and adaptability of the opposite type, he has instead greater depth of feeling and thought."

As we have already said, one must not mistake *introversion* – the attitude of a subject directed towards his own subjective interior world – for a tendency to *interiorize*. We can find many people with a subjective bias who may at times shut off their own problems but who are otherwise pleasingly sociable and even worldly.

INTROVERSION OR TENDENCY TO TURN TOWARDS THE OBJECT

Jung proposed a definition symmetrical to that for introversion. The extrovert "must interiorize everything that is external and structure everything that is internal." In the pure state the main characteristic is socialization: openness, readiness to face external situations, desire to influence and to be influenced by circumstances, to cultivate friendships and all kinds of relations without much discrimination, delight in making an impression and showing off, with a "collective" position on ethics and morality and a propensity for altruism. So as not to compromise this optimistic and matter-of-fact attitude, the extrovert avoids self-knowledge. The internal world appears disquieting and when he feels disturbed he throws himself into external contact. "When not too pushy or superficial, this type is obviously a useful and positive member of society", said Jung.

It is important to emphasize that the extrovert's prerogative is to regard the object – outside the self – rather than the subjective and internal world, but he will not always live an outward life; he could also be shy or complicated, at times even asocial, and may tend to live alone. The extrovert deals in concrete matters, never reflective thought. He may for example withdraw to an island where he can build his own style of life (he may once have been a colonialist). In other cases the extrovert dedicates himself to technical work which absorbs him completely. He could be a coach-builder or a mechanic who lives around his workshop, or a technocrat who has respect for his attainment but does not waste time in extensive social exchanges.

The functions of the psyche

Jung observed that mental illness appears to be a maladjustment to reality. He therefore asked himself which were the psychological functions that allow us to adjust. He identified four psychic functions: *Thinking* – *Sentiment* (or *Feeling*) – *Sensation* – *Intuition*. Each of these functions conditions a particular type of adjustment to reality, one function being predominant in any individual, and is itself directed by a prevailing attitude of either *extrovert* or *introvert*. Jung places these psychic functions in two categories, rational and irrational.

RATIONAL FUNCTIONS: *THINKING* AND *SENTIMENT*

These two are considered *rational* because both establish scales of values and make judgements: *mental* ones for *Thinking*, indicating the meaning of the perceived object, and *sentimental* ones for *Sentiment*, indicating the value which such an object has for us, that is, the relationship between subject and object.

IRRATIONAL FUNCTIONS: *SENSATION* AND *INTUITION*

These two are *irrational* because they are functions of sense perception: *pure perception* for Sensation, the sort which verifies the objects that surround us and acts as "the function of reality", and *unconscious perception* for *Intuition*, which supplies a form of instinctive understanding coming from the unconscious, allowing us to pick up on things beyond appearances and to glimpse possibilities and potential hidden behind objects, beings, situations, and appearances. We quote the definition given by André Lalande [126]: "*Intuition* is what we call that type of *intellectual sympathy* by which we are carried inside an object to harmonize with its indefinable uniqueness."

According to Jung the process of an individual's adjustment occurs through the *principal* or *primary function* supported by the *secondary* or *subsidiary function*. The other two functions generally remain more or less unconscious, and therefore less marked and more archaic. The fourth or *inferior* function is the one least accessible to the conscious; indeed it operates in the unconscious, by which it can be enslaved, as in cases of neurosis.

LAW OF OPPOSITIONS

The *rational* functions – Thinking and Sentiment – are always in opposition to each other, in the sense that if one is the *principal* or *primary* function, the other is automatically the *inferior* function. The same law holds for the *irrational* functions – Sensation and Intuition.

III. JUNG'S PSYCHOLOGICAL TYPES

Combining the four primary and four secondary functions and the two possible attitudes – *extrovert* and *introvert* – gives us sixteen different *psychological types*. In other words, Jung defines the types by a combination of their primary and secondary functions.

Thinking and Sensation Extrovert – Thinking and Sensation Introvert
Thinking and Intuition Extrovert – Thinking and Intuition Introvert

Sentiment and Sensation Extrovert – Sentiment and Sensation Introvert
Sentiment and Intuition Extrovert –Sentiment and Intuition Introvert

Sensation and Thinking Extrovert – Sensation and Thinking Introvert
Sensation and Sentiment Extrovert – Sensation and Sentiment Introvert

Intuition and Thinking Extrovert – Intuition and Thinking Introvert
Intuition and Sentiment Extrovert – Intuition and Sentiment Introvert

Ania Teillard [227] gives a suggestive representation of the psychological types when she imagines a dinner party in which the behaviour of each different type is observed, with their qualities and weaknesses, from the sociable hostess, a *Sentiment extrovert* type, to the ethereal poet who has forgotten the invitation, an *Intuition introvert* type.

In the preface to von Franz [94], Daniele Ribola describes the practical value of the Jungian typology in communication between individuals, in education, and in therapy. To understand individuals according to psychological type, we must be fair and not consider them inadequate because they do not conform to the dominant values of a given collective. We should respect their particular character and not push them into a false adjustment. In some cases, says Marie-Louise von Franz, "the theory of types takes on enormous practical importance because it is the only means of preventing complete misapprehension of some people. It gives us a key for understanding people whose spontaneous reactions otherwise appear incomprehensible."

We can observe the complex play of the functions through the role of the "inferior function" which allows a very clear understanding of the personality. Von Franz says: "The inferior function is the door through which all the subconscious images enter the conscious. Our conscious realm is like a room with four doors. It is by the fourth door that the Shadow, Animus or Anima, and the personification of self enter."

We should remember that Jung stated that his typology was *psychological*, and that he intended to clarify the dynamic between the various psychic mechanisms and not describe manifestations deriving from a physical or constitutional base. Such a psychological dynamic must be considered as autonomous and independent from bodily mechanisms.

Psychological characteristics of the Jungian types

The merit of Jung's typology is that it leads to the analysis of the relations between *conscious* and *unconscious* in the totality of psychic life, to catch the deepest psychological dynamic. Some of Jung's followers have in fact placed more importance on investigating the dynamic rather than the structural aspect of this typology.

In identifying a psychological type we must not only determine the *principal, subsidiary*, and the *lower* functions but also evaluate their respective strengths and the roles which they play in connection to each other. (For example, the presence of an adequately developed *Intuition* function, as well as providing a pointer on the overall picture for an individual, is a favourable condition for the subject's evolution or for the success of an analytical treatment).

In addition, the inherited model of classifying the functions has its limitations, like all such schemes: it is not rare for example to observe the contemporaneous development of Sensation and Intuition in plastic artists, as we shall discuss later. In compensation strategies, the sudden emergence of the lower function makes the typology much more complicated than it appears at first sight. If a balance between introvert and extrovert behaviour and between the various functions has not been reached by the second part of life, serious conflicts could occur.

We shall describe the types following von Franz's model, indicating the principal and lower functions. Graphological correspondences are then evaluated, mostly by reasoning on the psychic dynamics, and not around a list of fixed signs.

A. The four irrational types

Sesnation extrovert
Lower function: INTUITION INTROVERT

The predominantly extrovert attitude leads the individual towards the object and the external, while the principal function serves to embrace reality in the way it is perceived, realistically and concretely. Sensations from the surrounding world are observed and absorbed, making them objective, picking out every detail and quickly sniffing out the practical possibilities. Each problem is reduced to objective causes, from external influences. Facts rather than theories are preferred and intuition is confused with a strange imagination.

In general the Sensation type appreciates every pleasure in life: comfort, aesthetic appearance, good cooking. If they are of a rough nature, the seeking of sensations becomes dominant, to the disadvantage of reflection and dignity. They can then become unpleasant and without scruples: in Jung's words "the object is brutally violated and exploited." An eloquent illustration of this is the squalid personality of the captain and exploiter of young girls in the novel *Teresa Batista stanca di guerra* by the Brazilian author Jorge Amado.

"The Sensation extrovert type", says von Franz, "acts like the best photographic equipment, so to speak; capable of responding to external facts objectively and quickly. That is why this type is present among the best Alpine climbers, engineers, and men of affairs, all of whom have an accurate and wide sense of external reality in all its differing aspects" (see Fig. 116).

Role of the lower function

(The quotations in this and similar sections below on the role of the lower functions are from von Franz.) Considered as "insane fantasy" at the conscious level, the intuition repressed in the unconscious breaks out in projections such as: jealousies, anxieties, phobias, obsessions, "dark suspicions", "gloomy premonitions". Often, these very concrete personalities are attracted by supernatural aspects, they frequent or support sects of a metaphysical flavour, and are prey to strange superstitions. "Great danger occurs when the lower function gains a hold over the whole personality."

Example: *Sensation* extrovert – *Thinking* type

Sensation	→	extrovert	(primary function)
Thinking + *Sentiment*			(subsidiary functions)
Intuition	→	introvert	(lower function)

The subsidiary function *Thinking* increases the realistically objective direction and deliberate rationality of the subject. In this category we find industrialists, politicians, businessmen. The subsidiary function *Sentiment* imparts a more communicative sensibility.

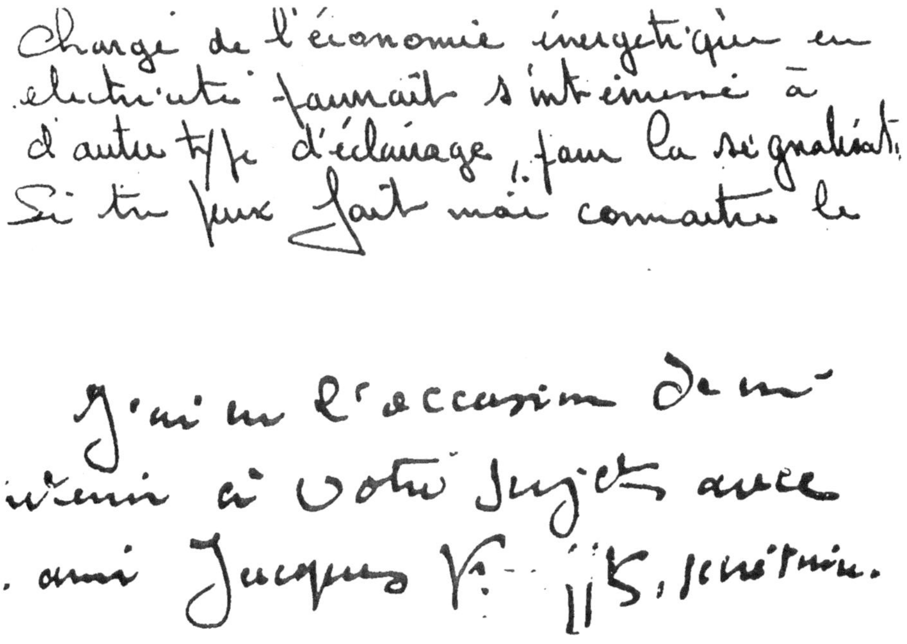

Figure 116 (reduced)
(a) French industrialist: Sensation extrovert – thinking
(b) Theatrical author: Sensation extrovert – sentiment

SENSATION INTROVERT
Lower function: INTUITION EXTROVERT

In contrast to the Sensation extrovert, this type responds to the subjective and internal impressions that the facts produce. Their reactions do not always adjust to circumstances. Their irrational and at the same time intense side often makes them misunderstood. Being sensitive and impressionable, they are vulnerable and easily hurt. They receive deep and instant impressions that seem to sink into their internal life, while from the outside they appear to have no reactions, or very slow ones.

Thomas Mann in his novel *Death in Venice* presents us with a protagonist whose personality corresponds completely to the Sensation introvert type. He is a shy person, an observer of the slightest nuance, who receives subjective impressions discomforting in their intensity.

Sometimes this type can express their universe of impressions in an artistic field: painting, writing, photography, among others. Marie-Louise von Franz speculates that Thomas Mann himself may have been of this type. His *stroke* appears as if drawn on blotting paper, with its *bitter* pressure and an almost compulsive-phobic graphic rhythm (Fig. 117). However, Thomas Mann's secondary function, *Thinking*, allows him to organize the pressing multitude of internal images and weave an underlying plot. Therefore, almost equally, *Thinking* and introverted *Sensation* interlace, while in the unconscious the lower function *Intuition extrovert* projects a disquieting light.

Role of the lower function

Just as for the Sensation extrovert type, the intuition repressed in the unconscious has a dangerously destructive character. It allows the dangerous, gloomy, morose sides of reality to be seen. But its extrovert form can make it particularly disruptive.

"The lower intuition of this type is similar to that of the Sensation extrovert: it has a magical, fairy tale, fantastic character. However, it is mostly attuned to an external, impersonal, collective world ... I have seen material in a Sensation introvert type which I could define as prophetic:

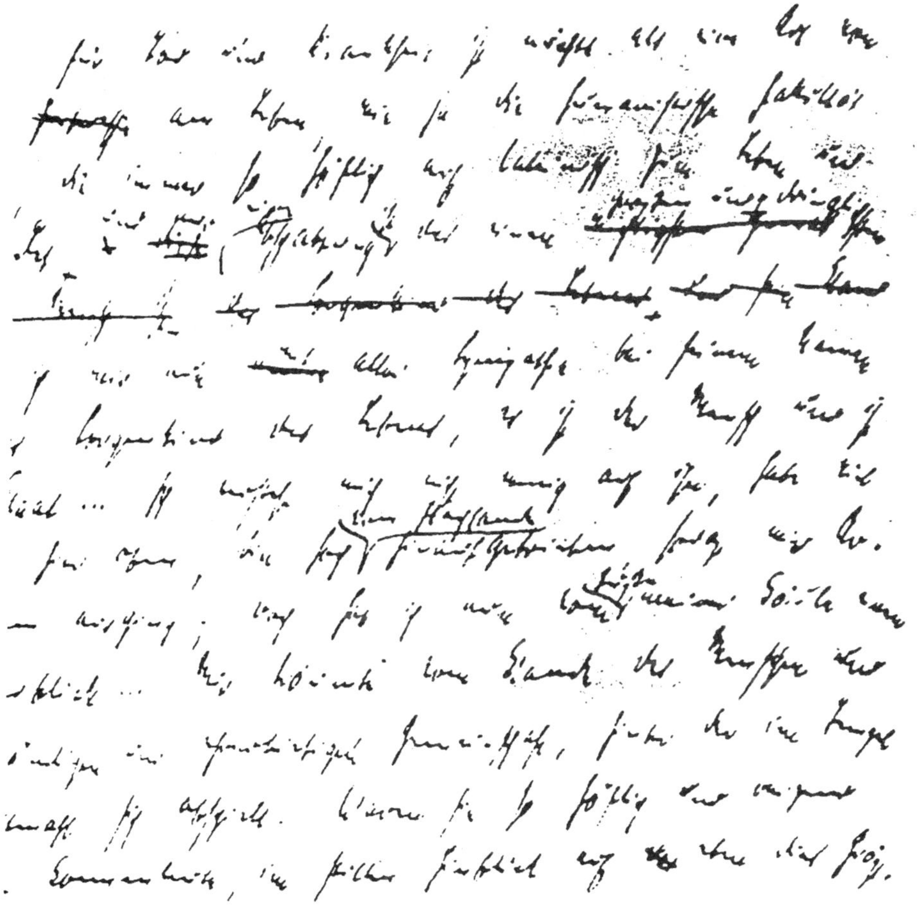

Figure 117
Writing of the author Thomas Mann: Sensation introvert and Thinking are practically
in symbiosis: The writing reflects the subject's ability to absorb a great number of
sensations and emotions that are immediately developed cerebrally and sensitively.
The artist practically lives on these two functions, the others remain more unconscious.
In the unconscious, however, these nurture both artistic talent and adaptive discomfort.

archetypal fantasies that do not principally represent the problems of the dreamer, but the problems of the age."

This type has great difficulty in catching the flash of their intuitions, sometimes "extraordinary emerging internal fantasies", because their anchor to concrete reality impedes any vision of the future. Once in a while a number of surprising premonitions may be suggested by the unconscious, but they will mostly be totally wrong as well as pessimistic.

INTUITION EXTROVERT
Lower function: SENSATION INTROVERT

Intuition is not only pure perception or contemplation, according to Jung, it also represents "a creative and active process", it supplies images, ideas of relations, suitable for "choosing the maximum possibilities, because it is above all through the contemplation of possibilities that the faculty of anticipating things is fulfilled."

The present situation is quickly felt as prison, as such types always seek new ways of escape, new outlets for exterior life. They are not troubled by observation of the minutiae of reality, but are, so to speak, illuminated by a global and unrestrained vision of events. "To make intuition work and to receive suggestions from the unconscious, situations must be seen in a vague way and from a distance."

Intuitive extroverts therefore show enthusiasm for projects of whose development they have insight. However they always tend to seek new horizons without gathering the fruits already sown, and sometimes run after the impossible. To this type belong women who foresee the development of their husband's career, and who with the help of the function Sentiment know how to arrange the appropriate connections. Nowadays we find women executives who have insight of possible developments in their own career, often supported by a high level of subsidiary function Thinking.

To this group therefore belong people who sniff out hidden potentials and opportunities which appear blocked: great inventors, persuasive politicians, businessmen or contractors, journalists, editors, share dealers, as well as participants of avant-garde cultural movements. They will often pick out and exploit the abilities of introverts who are least able to manage the marketing of their work. But if they have the gift to foresee and encourage the creativity of others, they can also belong to the category of artists themselves: "It is the creative artist, in general, who can create the future. A civilization without creative people is a doomed civilization." The poet Marinetti exhibited both aspects of this type, being creative himself as well as discovering and supporting talented people and sociocultural movements (Fig. 118).

The Intuition extrovert artist, however, will have great difficulty in staying in the present to gather the fruit of his toils, always following new images and at risk of losing himself on the concrete plane. At times success itself seems to be a constraint, he does not want to adjust to the demands of the market and an already conquered public, preferring to burn the opportunities of the moment and to pursue new experiments.

Role of the lower function

Given the lower function Sensation, this type is not very concerned by the demands of the physical body. Disregarding basic needs, "the type is extremely unilateral, unaware of having endosomatic reactions. The lower function, like all lower functions, is slow, heavy, and laden with emotion. Being introverted, the function is withdrawn from the external world and its activities. It possesses a mystic character, common to all lower functions."

These quotations, as already stated, are drawn from von Franz. We recommend her book [94] to the reader to benefit fully from so suggestive a treatment of observed cases. The reader will then be able to meet the entrepreneur, the great exploiter of lucrative plans, who under the influence of his own dreams has had to *learn* how to contact nature and the horse (see p. 322) – that is to bring to life his lower sensation – to free himself from symptoms that had brought him into analysis.

Archaic sensations, relegated to the unconscious, determine obsessive ideas: the object not taken into consideration at the conscious level sometimes becomes obsessive in the unconscious. So we find absurd phobias and bodily sensations, of a hypochondriac sort, which can represent a "vendetta" by the unconscious. Another vendetta could be revealed in

projections: an attachment to a possible partner with the knowledge of
failure, or taking on another person's guise, an artist for example, or
projecting one's own creativity onto another at the risk of losing one's own
(we can speculate that Mozart's father, dedicating himself to the son,
neglected his personal creative development).

INTUITION INTROVERT

Lower function: SENSATION EXTROVERT

This type, just like the intuition extrovert, sees the potential in situations,
but mostly internalizes them, acting more as a prophet or seer. Jung describes
the type thus: "On one side the mystic dreamer and seer, and on the other
the man of fantasy and the artist ... the voice preaching in the wilderness."
A long way from banal and touchable reality, as artist, poet, musician, or
misunderstood genius, they are in contact with the collective unconscious
from which they can restore images in visionary or fantastic art, for example.
   The Intuition introvert with no artistic gifts has difficulty in
communicating the internal and subjective vision, and is often undervalued
and misunderstood through a lack of vital contact to reality, even if flashes
of inspiration hit the target with perceptions and insights outside the norm.
To a woman the type confers a certain mystery, and if she is charming she
will stir up passions. On the physical side, the Intuition introvert is
neglectful, and prefers to safeguard the interior world by limiting comfort,
food, and material goods.

Role of the lower function

   "The lower sensation of an intuition introvert is extremely intense, but
emerges only from time to time, and then disappears again from the
conscious field." Often they do not notice a real event happening around
them, and when they do they explain it in the wrong way. In the sexual
field the unconscious is vindictive, leading to painful sensory activities,
with instinctive and immoderate attachments to particular persons.

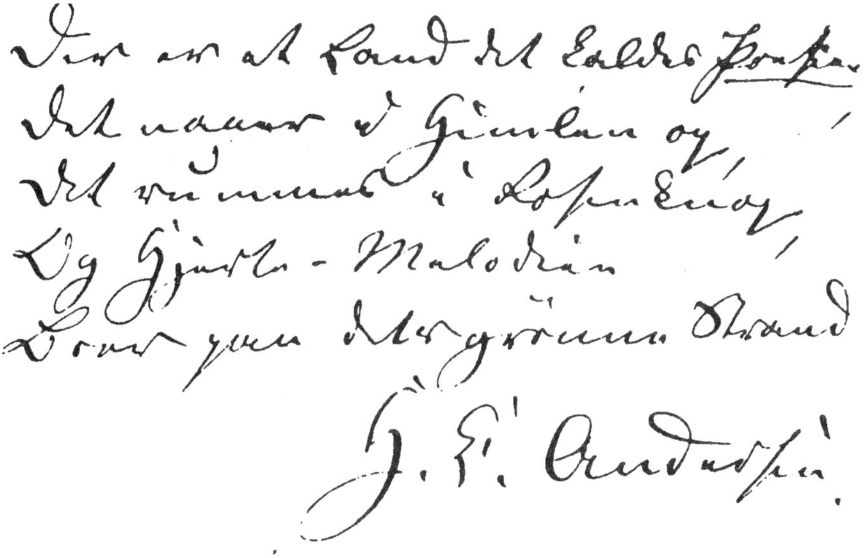

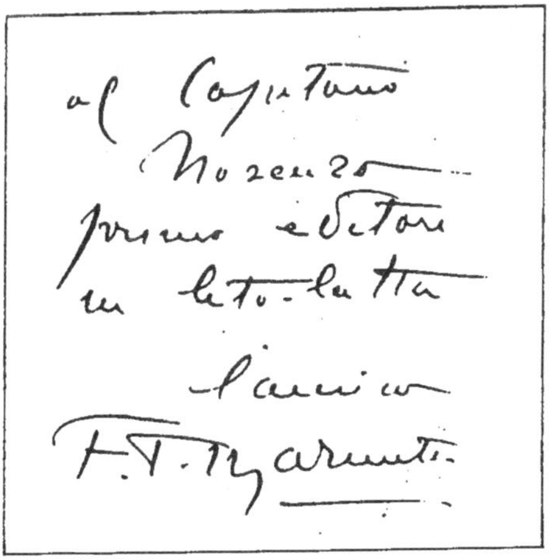

Figure 118 (reduced)
(a) Hans Christian Andersen: Intuition extrovert – sentiment (from *La Graphologie*)
(b) F. T. Marinetti: Intuition extrovert – thinking

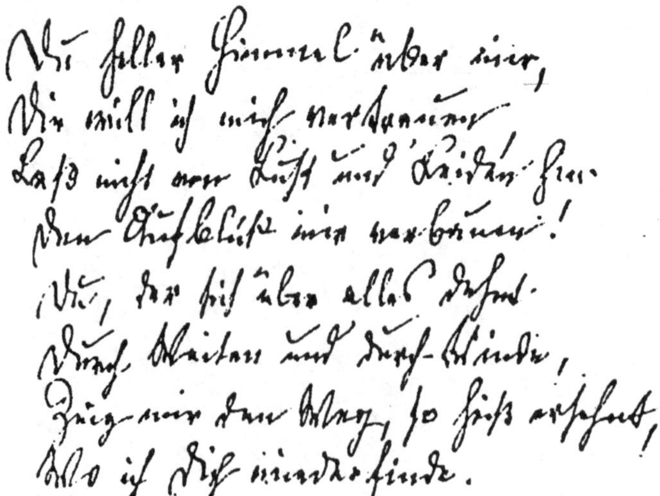

Figure 119
Oscar Wilde: Intuition introvert – thinking
Lou Salomé: Intuition extrovert – thinking and sentiment

B. The four rational types

THINKING EXTROVERT
Lower function: SENTIMENT INTROVERT

This type is directed towards an external world, in its objective and concrete aspects. Their thought is typically empirical, impersonal, and constructive, preferring facts to theories, logical deductions, verified and accepted methods, avoiding abstraction and theory. "As far as he is able to assume decisive positions, the Thinking extrovert type introduces clear order into external situations", not because he might have subjective and personal opinions, but because he observes the situation objectively, ascertains the facts, and then intervenes.

This way of proceeding could be inflexible, but it could also be that of an ardent declaimer and propagandist. In this category we find lawyers, engineers, financiers, administrators, business people, managers, and scientists, as well as the strategic politician and committed trade unionist.

Role of the lower function

In this type, immersed in objective reality (although not through sensory strength as is in the case with the Sensation extrovert), the role of feelings repressed in the unconscious is very eloquent, and they erupt in an unexpectedly childish fashion. "Of course they feel drawn towards certain ideals or persons, but these feelings never appear in their daily activities. An individual could spend a lifetime solving problems, reorganizing companies, formulating facts with clarity: only towards the end of life will he start to question with sadness the reason he has truly lived. At that moment he will fall into his lower function."

His feelings can be deep but they remain unexpressed and difficult to understand, because he invests, in an absolute manner, in a number of particular areas, and no others. Though faithful and loyal, his lower sentiment can also assume a barbarous attitude "gushing with destructive fanaticism". In other cases he can suddenly become a convert to mystic interests, or be prone to sentimentality, with strong bonds to the world of childhood. We recommend Marie-Louise von Franz's treatment on the subject, with many evocative examples.

THINKING INTROVERT
Lower function: SENTIMENT EXTROVERT

Introversion guides thinking in a completely opposite way to that of the extrovert, so this type is based upon theoretical, abstract concepts and personal ideals, sometimes even daring and profound. This is the prototype of the "philosopher". "When a person states that one must never begin with facts but should first clarify one's presuppositions, this person belongs to the thinking introvert type."

An engineer of this type will choose the research laboratory as a work place, whereas the extrovert will prefer to experiment directly in the test centre, with a team of technicians. The introvert professor will teach theoretical physics whereas the extrovert will teach experimental physics. However if his secondary function is *Sensation* he will be driven to experiment practically on his theories, whereas if the secondary function is *Intuition* he will prefer to delegate the experiments to others, and follow his own research.

The lower function leads the subject to coldness. He shows taciturn behaviour and with the passing of time can become rigid and fixed in his own ideas and manias. "The most frequent psychopathic nature", according to Dr Gille-Maisani, "is paranoia: solitary pride and poor adaptability."

Role of the lower function

Marie-Louise von Franz helps us understand this particular type: "the lower Sentiment of the Thinking type is comparable to the lava flow of a volcano. It proceeds at the speed of only five metres an hour, but destroys everything it meets … The love of this type does not know constraint … It is completely directed for the good of the other but its form is primitive. (We recall the professor who falls in love with the femme fatale in the film *The Blue Angel*.)" The lower function of Sentiment is not dependable: the subject can surround himself with people of value as well as those who are totally inadequate.

SENTIMENT EXTROVERT
Lower function: THINKING INTROVERT

Drawn towards the external world, this type is open, affable, welcoming, well adjusted, sociable. They know everybody and have many friends; in addition they establish suitable relationships, being able to estimate the positive and negative aspects of people, and create a pleasant social atmosphere to make everyone feel they are valued friends.

This trait is often found in women, in the best housewives and mothers, who immediately see the need to offer help and sometimes are ready to make sacrifices for others. Sentiment extroverts spread their convivial nature with generosity, and are unconcerned about breaking a contact because they know it can be restored. This mixture of sentiment with extroversion represents one of the types most indispensable to the social fabric. In consequence of a strong reliance on relationships and social contacts, however, there is the danger of suffering a profound sense of loss when a partnership breaks down.

An excess of smothering sometimes produces a suffocating atmosphere, and often this type falls into banal and conventional superficial social relationships. Sentiment, in this case, is so externalized that it becomes empty and artificial. A painful example of the suffocating feeling of this type is the mother (Fig. 26) who stifles her daughter (a Thinking introvert) by her aspirations for a good social position and wealthy husband, while crushing the fundamental intellectual qualities of the daughter, whose only wish is to study. She succeeds in making her daughter feel guilty of the sacrifices she has made for her and influences her towards the wrong choices.

Role of the lower function

If badly directed, the introvert side of thinking can produce *panic fear* faced with its own interior world, leading to escape mechanisms and brooding. The logic of this type always comes from sentiment; thinking remains childish with negative aspects which they avoid facing. However, if they can acknowledge their negative thought patterns, "these do not act like black magic but on the contrary lose all their destructive power ... Such thoughts are generally based upon a cynical view of the world: the dark side of life represented by illness, death, and similar things. In the background is a sort of second philosophy of life, cynical and negative. These thoughts are introvert, and therefore are very often turned against the subject."

SENTIMENT INTROVERT
Lower function: THINKING EXTROVERT

Difficult to know, closed, taciturn, and inaccessible, their tranquil appearance hides great passions. Everything develops beneath the surface, intense emotions are concealed. The subject is capable of great sacrifice and heroism and exercises a "secret positive influence ... Often these people are the ethical backbone of a group."

This type is frequent in women who present a slightly tragic aura, whereas the Sentiment extrovert is all charm. "Their character is tense and passionate", says Jung, "it can lead them to acts of cruelty and vengeance", the classic example being the stepmother who adores her own son while making the son of the first wife suffer.

Role of the lower function

"In surprising contrast to their quiet exterior and reserved aspect, persons of the sentiment introvert type are interested generally in an incredible number of outside situations ... When their extrovert thinking is being used creatively, they encounter the same difficulty as extroverts: they allow themselves to be excessively stimulated by an overload of information or facts in such a way that their extrovert thinking is sometimes lost in a quagmire of details from which they cannot extricate themselves." The lower function thinking extrovert tends to be tyrannical and arrogant, but in better cases it can be simple, clear, and rational.

The example of Freud

According to Marie-Louise von Franz, Freud was a *Sentiment introvert* with Thinking extrovert as lower function: "In all his works his fundamental ideas are few: through these he plumbed an enormous depth of materials, and the entire system is completely directed towards the external object." (Jung himself had already noted that the Freudian system was typical of extrovert thinking.) Paradoxically Freud's peculiarities, his audacious theories, would then proceed from his lower extrovert thinking, as also his well-known intolerance to contradiction. We can now ask ourselves if Thinking extrovert might instead have been Freud's principal function, which led him to revolutionary ideas, a thinking also intolerant towards different opinions and combative in defence of his own.

Graphology can perhaps help to solve the problem, by considering an example of his handwriting (Fig. 120). The graphic syndrome is: over-connected, slanted, fast, narrow, angular, with heavy and pointed pressure. The unstoppable activity and drive towards the final aim, with an intensity of thought that plumbs conscious and unconscious, takes up and stitches together theories through observation and practical action; and these are characteristics of extrovert thinking.

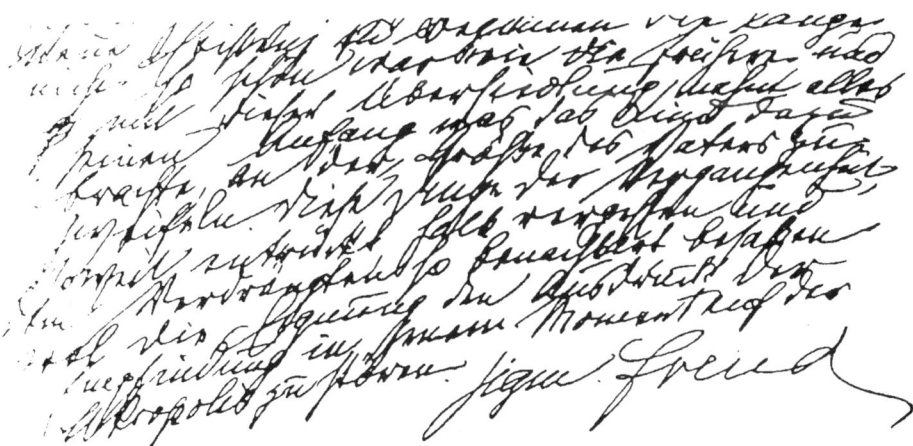

Figure 120 (reduced)
Sigmund Freud's writing (see also Fig. 28)

It is the writing of an experimenter, instinctive and realistic, who follows the logic of his own ideas and convictions, in symbiosis with them, barring the road to any contradictory intrusion (presence of hooks and curls of subjectivism, as described by the Italian master G. Moretti), and thus with Thinking extrovert dominant. We therefore think that Freud's Jungian type was:

Thinking	→	extrovert
Sensation + *Intuition*		
Sentiment	→	introvert

Graphological correspondences

Given the great difference between, for example, an extrovert and an introvert thinking type, graphology can clarify the dominant attitude, bearing well in mind the need to consider the tendency to turn to the *object* or to the *subject*, and not confusing externalization with extroversion, as is usually done in common speech today.

Small writing does not necessarily indicate introversion. It is so, if it is *precise* (defensive stroke); the psychic energy is directed towards the subject. It is not so, if it is *pasty* (participating stroke): the psychic energy is directed to the object.

A *large* to *medium* writing does not necessarily indicate extroversion. It is so only if it is full and has a pasty stroke. It is certainly not if it is also narrow and of precise stroke, with brief final gestures. Blurred stroke does not in itself give indications of the basic attitude.

Do not undervalue the "Sentiment" type, or overvalue the "Thinking" type.

In Fig. 121, we see the writing of the famous French psychiatrist Françoise Dolto, who through feeling and instinct made vibrant contact with young boys in difficulty, eliminating parental intervention. In the same way she was able to communicate through radio programmes with every French mother. We also give the writing of two art critics (Fig. 122). Through Jungian typology we distinguish their approach to art: one is more cerebral, the other more intuitive. Then we have two non-figurative painters (Fig. 123). Lastly there are examples from Ania Teillard (Fig. 124) and Jung (Fig. 125).

GUIDE TO CORRESPONDENCES

Extrovert A tendency to be *wide*, veering to exuberance: in the management of space, in size, in free strokes. *Stroke predominantly pasty.*

Introvert Tendency to *concentration*, veering to inhibition: in the management of space, in size, in free strokes. *Stroke predominantly precise.*

Sensation Nourished stroke, stability on the line, full lower extensions.

Intuition Light stroke, irregularity, white spaces, airy gestures.

Thinking Minute strokes, simplification, progression.

Sentiment Ample strokes in the middle zone, garlanded, slanted.

Ania Teillard: "Generally speaking: *Thinking* makes the stroke smaller and concentrated; *Sentiment* makes it larger, wider, and softer; *Sensation* makes it heavier and stable; *Intuition* lightens it, giving it movement, rhythm, and sometimes instability."

Table 55

Conclusion

We conclude this chapter with one of Jung's last paragraphs from *Psychological Types* [117]:

"To recap, I would like to insist on the fact that each of the two general attitudes, that is introversion and extroversion, is manifested in a very particular way according to the dominance of one of the four functions. In reality there are no pure introverts or pure extroverts, but function types introvert and function types extrovert, such as thinking types, sensation types, etc. We have thus a minimum of eight clearly distinguishable types. Of course this number can be multiplied each time that the single functions are divided, for example each one into three sub-groups, which is empirically not impossible. It would be easy for example to subdivide intellect into its three well-known forms: the intuitive-speculative form, the logical-mathematical form, and the form based essentially on sensory perception. Other functions too can be subdivided in the same way: so, intuition has itself an intellectual aspect, and one based on sentiment. With these subdivisions it is possible to establish an indeterminate number of types, so that establishing new types always becomes more a question of subtlety."

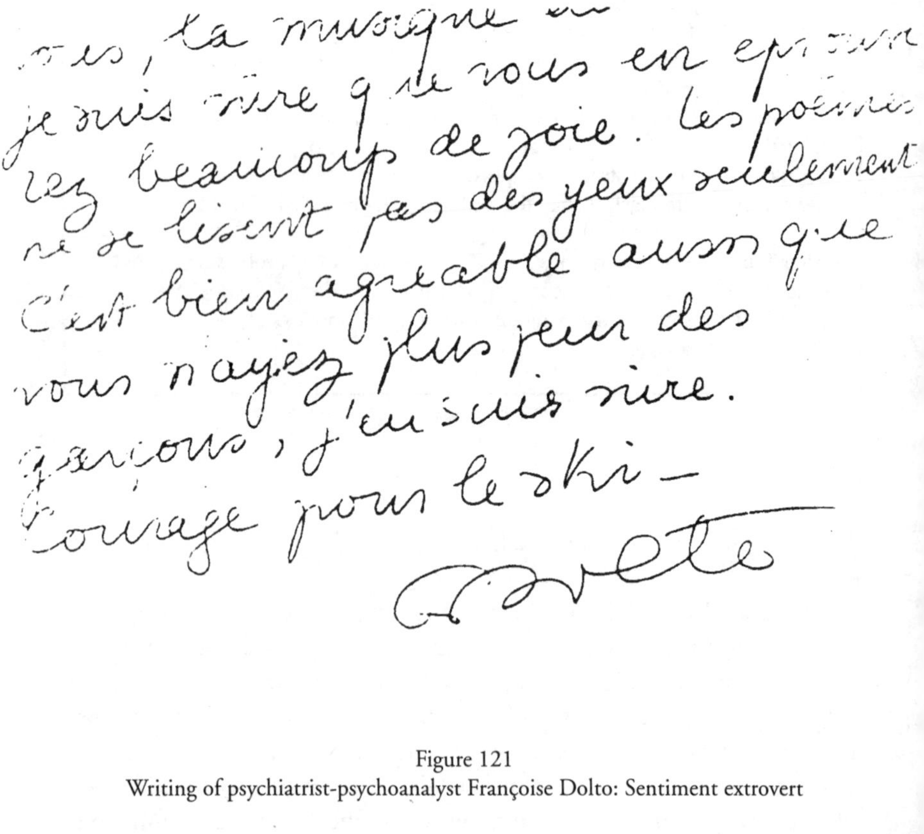

Figure 121
Writing of psychiatrist-psychoanalyst Françoise Dolto: Sentiment extrovert

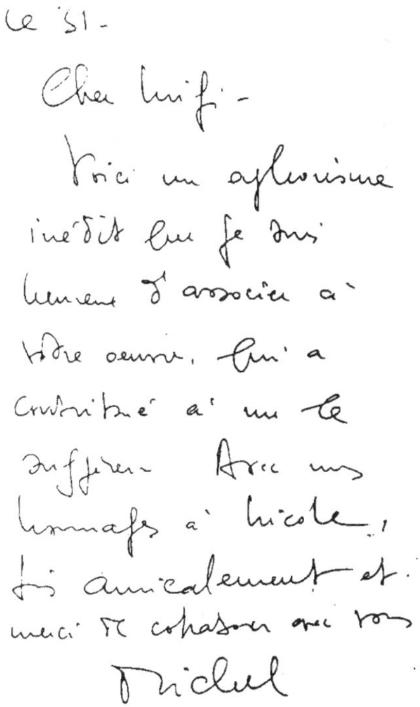

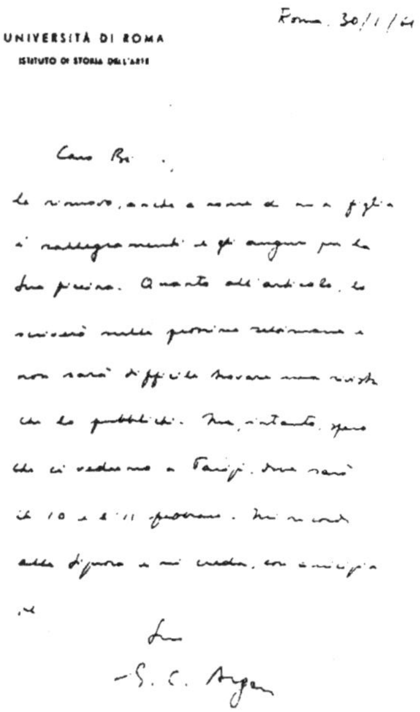

Figure 122 (reduced)
Art critics
(a) Michel Tapié: Intuition extrovert – thinking, sentiment; he anticipates situations, discovers artists, travels, gathers little on the practical plane
(b) Giulio Carlo Argan: Thinking introvert – intuition; he develops a history of art, he teaches

Figure 123 (overleaf ☛)
(a) Jaroslav Serpan, painter, poet, and biologist: Thinking and Sensation
(b)   Lucio Fontana, painter: Sentiment and Intuition extrovert

Ceci dit, ... vous espérons en bonne
forme et ... réjouissons de la perspective de
... revoir ailleurs ... ... de ville.
... bonnes choses de ... 2 à ...
tous, ... attendant Ste Après et ... amis
amicalement
Slar

(J'espère ... ... indulgence
...)—

io seguito lavorando sempre fior...
...ti...ute! e spero che tu stai
facendo scintille—!! cari ...
tutti a ... famiglia tuo

... ...

... novembre ho nostalgia di
Paris!! ci vedremo!!—

Figure 123

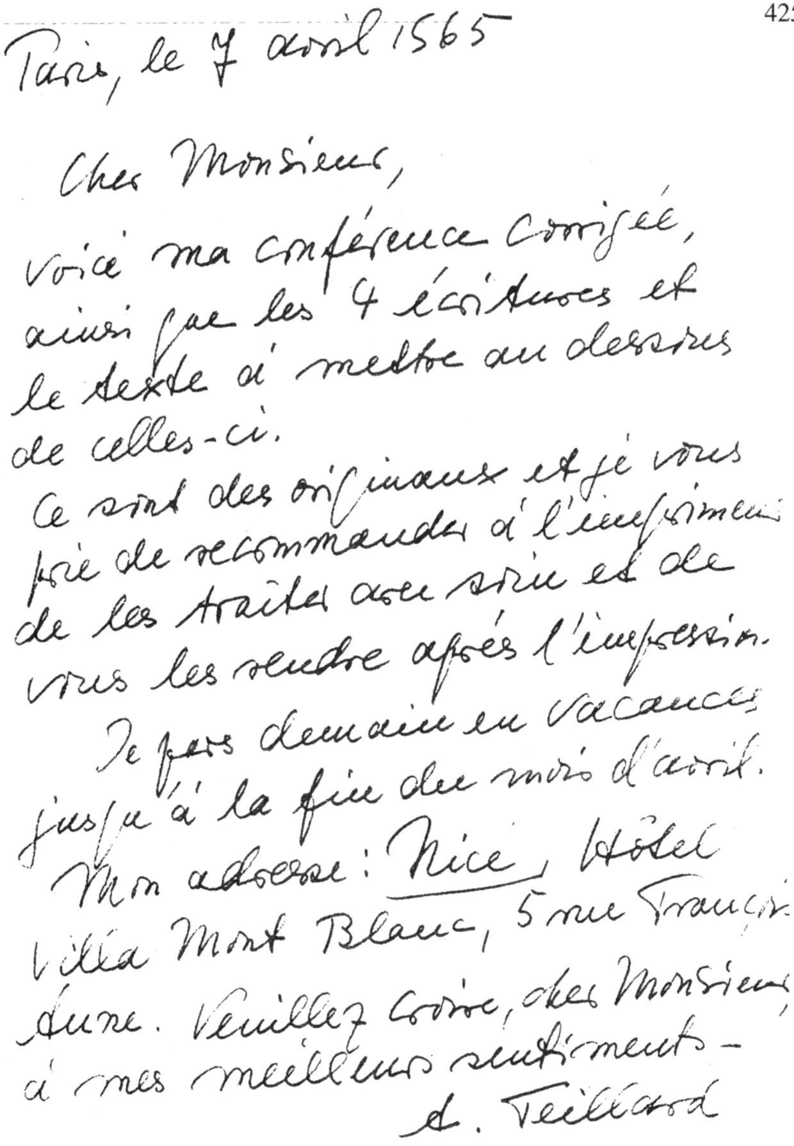

Paris, le 7 avril 1565

Cher Monsieur,

voici ma conférence corrigée,
ainsi que les 4 écritures et
le texte à mettre au dessus
de celles-ci.

Ce sont des originaux et je vous
prie de recommander à l'imprimeur
de les traiter avec soin et de
vous les rendre après l'impression.

Je pars demain en vacances
jusqu'à la fin du mois d'avril.
Mon adresse: Nice, Hôtel
Villa Mont Blanc, 5 rue François
Aune. Veuillez croire, cher Monsieur,
à mes meilleurs sentiments —
A. Teillard

Figure 124 (reduced)
A splendid sample of Ania Teillard at 76 years: presence of the four functions with
Sentiment extrovert dominant. The structured and yet caustic aspect of her thought
reflects her lower function well

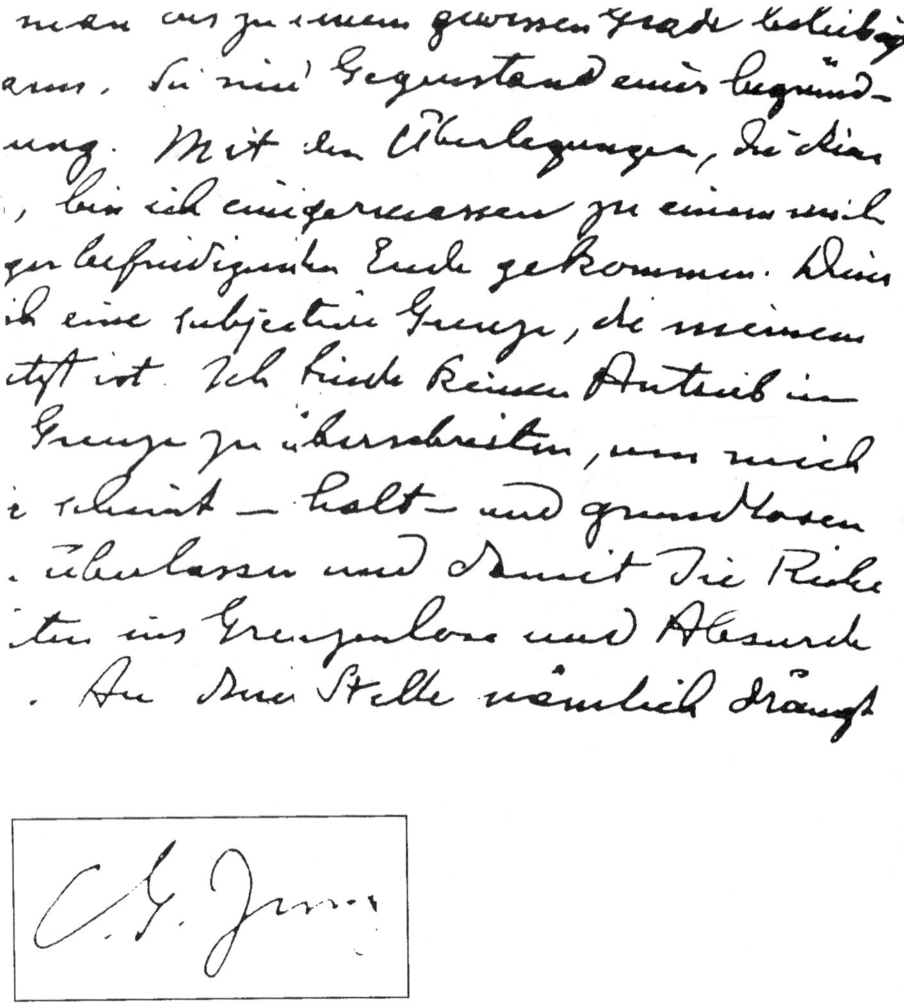

Figure 125
Carl Gustav Jung's writing

APPENDICES

APPENDIX I
Judicial Graphology

As already mentioned in the Introduction, judicial work is a fundamental though completely distinct field in graphology. A consultant graphologist is not necessarily a handwriting analyst and vice-versa. All the same, a grounding in graphology, meaning *observation* of the gestural dynamics and of the single graphic gesture, rather than a psychological interpretation, is essential. At a famous conference Dr Schima with simplicity and clarity went to the heart of the problem: without entering an in-depth study of writing characteristics, we must answer two questions. What does the analyst need to carry out his work, and what can the judge expect from the analyst?

We have seen that graphic activity, from drawing to writing, is an imperative and complex human activity, a physiological necessity as well as a psychological expression, which forms a unique and irreplaceable source of investigation. The graphic expression of each person is as unique as fingerprinting: it gives off rich conscious and unconscious impulses, so that the expert can discover whether they are signs of spontaneity and authenticity or of suspicious artifice. It is clear that this subject requires specific treatment elsewhere, but for the moment, to complete this book, we give a general view of expert handwriting analysis.

Training of judicial experts

The expert's training, apart from basic graphology, involves a mastery of instrumental techniques not easily accessible to those not attuned to the work. At the moment a number of newly qualified graphologists, and some without qualifications, throw themselves into judicial expertise, as manna waiting for them alone. We must drive in the fact that a handwriting analyst takes on a heavy responsibility if he expresses hasty judgements on false presumptions. This gold-rush is wholly dangerous.

Each judicial interpretation presents its own problems and has to be treated in a specific way. Contrary to what beginners believe, we cannot adopt a common approach. Supervision, though essential to the beginner, is not enough because each of us develops the connections of a given problem in silence by ourselves, and this solitary work is not transmissible (the same occurs during the progress of a detailed graphological analysis). To a colleague who has the same methodology we can certainly say "that is wrong" or "that is not the right way", but we cannot give the correct formula for proving the thesis. This work is of a very personal nature, and cannot be passed from one expert to another, but must be thought out afresh for each new problem, whether checking a will, a signature, or anything else.

An expert must have the ability to pick out the graphic dynamic of a particular writing. This is achieved with experience, in the graphologist's case by having prepared at least 500 psychological profiles, and observed and considered 3,000 writing samples (the preparation required for obtaining a diploma). There is also the experience of the old fashioned expert whose graphic skills have been acquired within a family of writing experts absorbed in "the job".

The best preparation for an expert is therefore solid experience in the fields of graphology and technical expertise, over a strong cultural base. We can thus identify the following requirements.

GRAPHOLOGICAL TECHNIQUES

Basic graphology
- how to pick out the gestural dynamics and the graphic context
- knowledge of the basic textbooks used by the different graphological schools

Evolutive graphology
- how the graphic gesture is formed during the developing stages of childhood
- elements of graphometry
- the ability to evaluate "elementary" writing

Specialised graphology (disorganised writings)
- elements of deterioration of graphic gesture in the major illnesses and in old age
- recognition of writing disorders: difficulty in execution, lack of drive, smudging, jerks, absence of connections, body size excessively small or large, etc

TECHNICAL KNOWLEDGE

Judicial procedure

Technical instruments

- use of microscope, direct and radiant light, ultraviolet or infrared exposure, etc.
- evaluation of mechanical or chemical anomalies: deletion, restarting, retracing
- ability to work from a photographic or enlarged document
- ability to perform chemical analysis on paper, ink, etc.

Expert methodologies

- being able to justify the chosen methodology
- presentation of an expert report clearly and intelligibly for the non-specialist (the judge, the lawyer, and the client)
- producing a photographic illustration

Historical knowledge

- bibliography of basic historical textbooks
- knowledge of palaeography
- ethical principles

Types of expertise

Expert investigations can be of different types: they can be *documentary*, *graphic*, or *graphopathological*. In the latter case investigations are strictly reserved to graphologists who are also doctors, psychiatrists, or psychologists. Their graphological training must be very oriented towards clinical psychology. Graphopathology investigates deterioration in the writing as an indication of psycho-physiological personality changes, that is alterations of the function of transmission of the graphic impulse, related to the central nervous system or peripheral areas. Dr Perrella states: "Writing can be regarded as a true seismograph of the mental and physical state of the writer."

Principles of the great masters

The expert must study the established principles of the great masters, among whom are Hilton, Conway, Klages, Crépieux-Jamin, Moretti, Solange Pellat, Locard, Gayet. One must also remain up-to-date with the vast modern bibliography, among which are the works by Perrella, Vettorazzo, Buquet, and others. Knowledge of the principal rules relating to the field of graphology and criminal law are essential. To serve justice, a combination of prudence, strict ethics, and technical training gives great weight to the professional in this field.

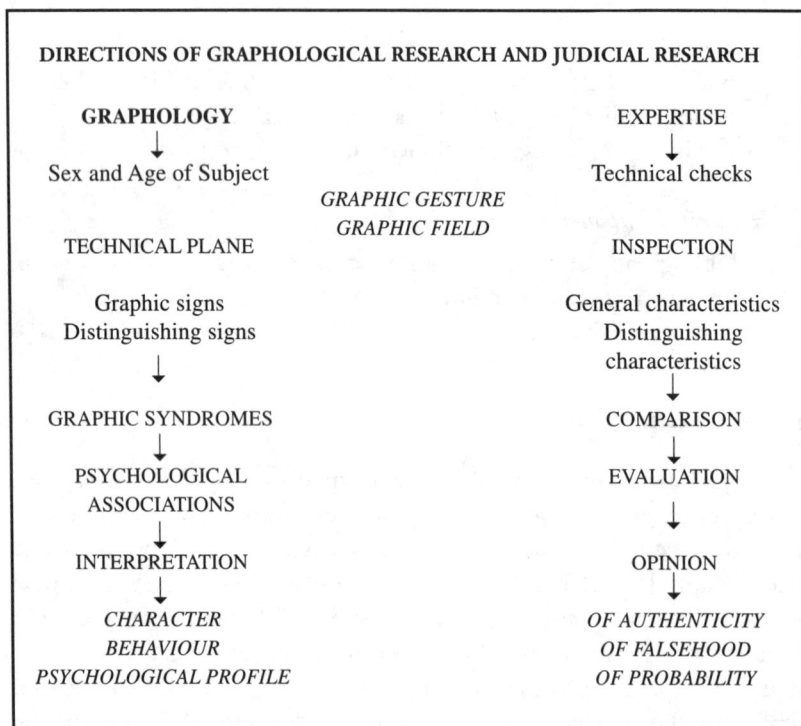

DIRECTIONS OF GRAPHOLOGICAL RESEARCH AND JUDICIAL RESEARCH

GRAPHOLOGY		EXPERTISE
↓		↓
Sex and Age of Subject		Technical checks
	GRAPHIC GESTURE	
	GRAPHIC FIELD	
TECHNICAL PLANE		INSPECTION
Graphic signs		General characteristics
Distinguishing signs		Distinguishing
↓		characteristics
		↓
GRAPHIC SYNDROMES		COMPARISON
↓		↓
PSYCHOLOGICAL		EVALUATION
ASSOCIATIONS		↓
↓		
INTERPRETATION		OPINION
↓		↓
CHARACTER		*OF AUTHENTICITY*
BEHAVIOUR		*OF FALSEHOOD*
PSYCHOLOGICAL PROFILE		*OF PROBABILITY*

Table 56

APPENDIX II

Lexicon

This lexicon is very concentrated and reduced to essentials in a search for the basic meaning of the signs, at a medium to high graphological level for an adult reader. We have tried here to establish certain criteria of average sizes, which will always be modified by the basic school model of a country. For some signs brief graphological interpretations are suggested and sometimes associations with other signs.

Apart from the great classic works of the various European schools, we have consulted the coursework of Marcelle Desurvire (consultant graphologist and psychologist in Paris), the books of Bresard, Faideau, Torbidoni and Zanin, and Cristofanelli, the coursework of comparative graphology at the Moretti Institute, edited by Nazzareno Palaferri, the publications of the Groupement des Graphologues-Conseils de France, and the *Manual of Graphology* by J. Peugeot, A. Lombard, and M. de Noblens [200]. We have included material from Dr Gille-Maisani's *Psicologia della scrittura* [105], and also have drawn on our own experience in rethinking interpretations.

For ease of use, we list the signs in alphabetical order, but add the category under which they are discussed in Chapter Four and the text figures showing characteristic features of that sign. Finally, remember that a lexicon is only a guide and can be properly used only by specialists with professional experience.

ACCELERATED (*Speed*: Figs 2, 22a, 34a–b, 123b)
A rate of about 150 letters a minute.
The writing contains some signs of slowing down (see Slowed down) but the speed remains quick and capable of acceleration.
Fluent thinking, objectivity.
Harmonious adjustment, self-control.
Appropriate and efficient activity.

ACQUIRED (*Form*: Figs 7d, 12c, 16, 110a)

Often treated as *artificial* writing, from which it must be distinguished. It comes from a process of self-control, more or less voluntary, or under the influence of an involuntary defence mechanism, which determines a need for "constructing" a writing. Heiss's "rhythm of structuration of form" prevails, and a slight tendency to an architectonic form of letters. When the process is entirely voluntary, it is "acquired" in the full Klagesian sense (see Chapter Three), with special reference to judicial graphology. Today we often see "acquired" writing in people who want to protect themselves, showing their need for structure, for "construction", and hiding, or believing they hide, their vulnerability. It is important to know the social and cultural level of the writers to understand their type of "reaction".

Repressed spontaneity.
Need to create an image of ideal self.
Search for construction, structuring, mastery of self.
Desire to please.
With other signs: *sense of pattern, propriety, artistic tendencies.*
Sometimes associated with *stylized* writing.
Underneath there is the stimulus of a strong defence mechanism (compensation, sublimation, rationalization, etc.). Small signs which escape this control will reveal the tendencies that are repressed (for example, large, heavy, sharp-pointed, aggressive commas).

AERATED (*Layout*: Figs 29a, 30a, 54, 122)

Balance between whites and blacks, space between words of around two letters, lines well spaced and never tangled, overall harmony.

Adaptability adjusted to the circumstances and the facts of life.
Clear and critical intelligence, objective and independent judgement.
Able to synthesize, open to intuition and the creative spirit.
Balance and control in relations, respect for others.

Ania Teillard: common in the Jungian type Thinking Intuition.

Gille-Maisani: "Writing acquires its true value in a sober, combined, and harmonious graphic context" (e.g. the writings of certain creative intellectuals).

AMENDED (*Continuity*: Fig. 77)

A letter or part of a letter is amended in an often unnecessary way, the stroke returns on its own track to the left. Excludes corrections through forgetfulness or spelling mistakes. Check whether the tendency is linked to motor difficulties. Examine how systematic it is in the context, with clarity of intent or from an unconscious action.

Doubt, hesitation, scruple.
Wish for precision, for perfection, love of detail at the expense of the whole.
Anxiety, inhibition, obsessive tendency, withdrawal.

AMPLE (*Form*: Figs 15, 44)
The ovals and loops are quite large but not inflated. Klages treated this as a full form, the opposite of thin or linear.
With movement and irregularity of size: *imagination, fantasy.*
With small writing: *imagination, intellectual spark.*

ANGULAR (*Form*: Figs 16, 104a, 107)
Writing is termed angular when the curves are replaced by angles and the necessary angles are accentuated. With an angular writing, it is important to assess whether it freezes graphic flexibility or imparts a firmness that sustains the general graphic context.
Firmness, leading on to rigidity.
Very rational and logical.
Adherence to rules and principles.
With firm pressure: *reason, decision, firmness, resistance, loyalty, intransigence, severity, rigidity, discipline, professional ethic.*
With muddy pressure and stereotyped rhythm: *sado-anal complex.*
With measured speed: *untiring activity.*
With narrow writing: *closed mind, diffident, repression, fixed ideas, egocentric.*
With regressive angles: *objection, negativity, obstinacy.*

ANIMATED (*Speed*: Figs 19, 24, 27, 37)
For Crépieux-Jamin the characteristics of this sign were agility and mobility of outline, with thrusting and progressive forms, quick combinations, variable slant, ascending lines, all in a discreet way. The sign is more specifically described, from particular viewpoints, by Heiss [113], de Gobineau [110, and see Movements of H. de Gobineau below], and Bresard [46]. See also ch. 4, Movement, in *Manual of Graphology* [200].
Imagination, activity, enthusiasm.

ARCADES (*Form*: Figs 39, 42, 45, 100a, 122)
The letters *m* and *n* or the connecting strokes are arcaded. We must distinguish whether this is a survival of infantile components, a writing of elementary level anchored to the basic school model, or a personal adult choice. In the case of adult writing, we repeat here the fundamental meanings given by G. Beauchâtaud [18], *Pretence – Construction – Preservation*, and we have added *Concealment*.

Pretence
Education and principles.
Dignity, sense of own status.
Formality, servility, obsequiousness, snobbery.
With showy superelevations: *pride, pretension, vanity, arrogance, disdain.*

Construction
Fidelity to the model, concrete sense, sense of form.
With combined or artistic forms: *sense of beauty, talent, creative originality, love of composition (literary or artistic), constructive.*

Preservation
Tendency to meditation and introspection.
Prudence, reserve, self-reliance.
Closed to outside influences, impenetrable, individual.

Concealment
Lack of spontaneity, secretive, love of mystery.
With low creeping arcades and wavy lines: *diplomacy.*
With signs of concealment: *hypocrisy, deceit, bad faith.*

For Pulver, "the final arcade curved to the right" showed inhibition: "either it is hardly noticeable and remains suspended above the baseline, or instead it is completely defined and thrown back under the last letter." For Hegar, "the arch in space" is a sign of creativity.

ARTIFICIAL (*Form*: Figs 16, 45)
Bizarre, involved forms, systematic complications, opposed to the conventional models or unusual.
With original, rapid, harmonious writing: *creative gifts, desire to evolve originally.*
With very structured, original writing: *individual searching on a principled basis, choice of a role.*
In an average or mediocre context, with large middle zone: *snobbery, exhibitionism, social mask.*
With childish components (large middle zone, inflated letters, twisted uprights): *playful, childish, fantasy, magic world, passive, dependent, oral* (designers, writers, artists).
With signs of anxiety (retouching, heavy full stops, twisted or crowded letters): *overcompensation from sense of guilt, phobias.*
With contrary or unusual (proteiform) forms, spasmodic pressure: *invented personality, varying from insincerity to pathological simulation.*
With rigidity, spasms, superelevations: *paranoia, sado-masochism, perversions.*
With gestures of inhibition and block: *desires beyond one's own possibilities.*

BACKWARD (*Direction*: Fig. 110b)
A general obstruction to forward movement (Gille-Maisani [105]). Leftward slant, letters squeezed up, unconnected or with rightward flow blocked, leftward final strokes, uprights curving to the left in the middle zone, margin on the right, signature on the left (unless culturally influenced). Also expressed through a "gesture-type of reversal": *t*-bars, final strokes.

Fear (which causes anxiety and reflex of reversal).
With signs of diffidence: *obstinacy.*

N. Palaferri [189], see *Riccio della stentatezza.*

BLURRED (*Pressure*: Fig. 103)
The edges of the strokes are badly defined or broken, giving a porous effect. One needs to see different examples and check the type of pen and paper to eliminate incidental factors.
Softness.
Difficulty in putting self forward, weak Ego.
Mental and/or physical weakness. Old age. Depression.
Sensuality. Dubious morality.

Gille-Maisani: "Hegar counted a blurring on the left edge as a sign of fixation to the mother, to the past."

BOW TIES (*Form*: Figs 96a, 114)
A method of closing the ovals, "by means of small loops or rings in the upper part" (Vels [235]). The closure can be complete or leave a small opening. Whichever style, bow ties are always an added method of closure, never a feature of the school model. The movement which determines this sign is centripetal or inhibited. All the same we must take account of the way the school model outlines the ovals. In Italy they begin and end at the top right in the model (see Chapter Seven), so in Italy we use bow ties to mean that movement which accentuates the normal closure of the oval, with supplementary loops or loops that complete the entire rolling up movement. For example, the outline of the *a* starts from the bottom and develops in an anti-clockwise way to end at the bottom.
Suspicion through instinct of preservation.
From discreet to closed.
With full regressive movement: *need to captivate, lack of candour, hiding own thoughts.*
With lasso movements and complications in the paraph: *negotiating skills, intrigue.*

B. Angiolini and C. de Loisy (study for the GGCF): "According to the graphic syndrome in which it appears: reserve of strength; element of protection, of stability; shell which lets one stay centred on oneself."

CARRIED AWAY (or EXPLOSIVE) (*Speed*: Figs 37b, 107)
Gille-Maisani [105]: "product of rapid and violent movements whose fullness and shape seem to concentrate then explode in an unexpected way." The outline is closed and dynamic at the same time.
Strong temperament, powerful will.
Commanding attitude, inflexible tendency.

CHILDISH (*Form*: Fig. 7c)
Gille-Maisani [105, ch. 18–24] distinguished the sign *childish* from *children's writing*, which latter encompasses the more positive aspects of children's writing. If the outline is inharmonious and regressive it is called *childish*, if it is harmonious it is called *children's writing*. In both cases the writing exhibits pre-adult components in an adult hand, sometimes of high level too. It is important to find out the educational level of the subject and to distinguish this from *unorganized*. We have often met this sign in writings of artists, otherwise large and clear (a very playful aspect).

We may prefer to use the single term *childish*, which is more in current use, and leave it up to the graphologist to assess the level of immaturity or of innocence implicit in the graphic context.

Interpretations can be varied and the diagnosis difficult. Rigidity, monotony, and angularity, point to a mainly pathological evaluation, whereas clarity, spontaneity, and harmony point to naivety.
Immaturity of instinct, of emotion, of intellect.
Dependence, poor adaptability, neurotic aspects.
Young character, natural, open humour.
Honesty, idealism.
Creative spontaneity.
Pregenital fixations.
Psychopathic, mental deficiency.

Gille-Maisani: "We should not be surprised to find almost always some childish traits in writings of scientists, whether theoretical or applied: they express the fundamental honesty of these subjects, bordering sometimes on innocence, and their not wholly mature emotions, given the high development of their logical thought."

CLOSED (*Form*: Figs 29c, 13b)
Opposite of open.
Ovals firmly closed, but without any ties or loops: *reserve, discretion, modesty.*
Ovals closed high and to the right: *natural and prudent reserve, secrecy.*
Ovals closed high and to the left: *reasoned reserve in response to a context seen as hostile, hiding of interior conflicts, affected independence, tenderness not expressed.*
Ovals closed below, especially if the movement of the oval is done in a reverse direction: *concealment, hypocrisy, falsity.*

CLUBBED (*Pressure*: Fig. 40)
Final stroke in the form of a club with an abrupt stop.
Brutal aggression, imposition of own feelings and wishes, with greater or lesser violence.
Passion or intransigence.
Sign of block (in inhibited writing).

COMBINED (*Continuity*: Figs 27, 118, 119)
Connections between letters are original and personal, without artifice or ostentation. For Crépieux-Jamin this sign was the highest grade of organization of writing.
Flexible, intelligent, cultured, quick and original thinking.
Inventive mind.
An excess of originality can come at the expense of sobriety, which demands graphic efficiency:
Mental, associative, and ideative sparkle.
Difficulty in reining in, or in finishing things.

COMFORTABLE (*Continuity*: Fig. 22a–c)
The writing progresses with a simple spontaneity, free yet under control. The movement is flowing, with balance between tension and slackness.
Discreet spontaneity, simplicity.
Internal balance.

COMPACT (*Layout*: Figs 1, 2, 102a)
The "blacks" prevail over the "whites". Distance between words is about one letter width. Lines are very close together and are sometimes tangled. Sometimes there are no margins or indents, and sometimes the lines are close but the words are wider spaced (Fig. 2).
Concentration of mind and energy.
Solid, precise thinking, but contending with emotive impulses.
Relational skills, reassuring presence.
Involved in concrete action. Long-term resistance.
With tension and angularity: *intensity but defensive against the outside.*
With constricted movements: *closed, subjective, obsessive.*

COMPLICATED (*Form*: Fig. 101b)
Addition of gestures unnecessary for formation of letters. Consider the age of the document in question and the cultural level of the writer. The complication is analysed according to the type of movement which causes it: looped, flying, regressive, centripetal, etc. See also Gille-Maisani [105], *Macchinosa.*
Difficulty in synthesis and in analysis of the essentials.
Coyness, frivolity.
Pedantry, obsession.
Concealment.

CONCAVE (*Direction*: Fig. 39)
The base line curves down to the middle of the line then curves up again, both ends being at the same level.
Effort in countering discouragement.

CONFUSED (*Form*: Figs 88, 93b)
Legibility is compromised by one or more causes: "agitation, complications, obstruction of words or lines, many abbreviations, disorder, tangled lines, but above all imprecise forms that make the text unclear and hinder or retard the reader" (Crépieux-Jamin [65]). Often seen in clinical cases, in old people, or in children with mental or motor difficulties. *Tendency to conceal one's thinking, through withdrawal or fear, or through negligence and laziness.*

CONGESTED (*Pressure*: Figs 41, 111, 114, 117)
The ovals and loops tend to be filled with ink.
With pasty stroke: *difficulty in expressing emotion.*
With subtle stroke: *restlessness, conflicts.*

CONNECTED (*Continuity*: Figs 4, 19, 21, 52)
Four to six letters are drawn without lifting the pen. Interruptions are mainly made to put in accents or dots. In adult hands, assess the relation to the school model and the educational level. In children, the connection can conceal pick ups which can persist sometimes into adolescent or adult writing.
Quick thinking, deductive logic, faculty of synthesis.
Spontaneity and foresight.
Continuous effort towards fulfilment of tasks, efficiency in actions.
With school model forms: *application, conformism.*
In a poor graphic context: *lack of initiative, routine.*

CONSTANT (OR CADENCED) (*Continuity*: Figs 16, 32e)
Regular progression of stroke, giving uniformity of size, inclination, speed, and pressure. The general movement is lively but without jerks, like the balanced swing of a pendulum.
Stability, resistance, constancy. Moral courage.

CONTRARY (OR IN REVERSE) (*Direction*: Figs 32c–d, 100a)
The formation of each letter or part of letter is contrary to the expected base model, and systematically so. The sign concerns in particular the ovals, which are traced clockwise, and the extensions of *d* and *t*, which are drawn from bottom to top. Occasional contrary signs appearing in a good graphic context are signs of originality and often of culture (Fig. 124).

Gille-Maisani extended the notion of "contrary" to almost all the categories, in particular:
Contrary continuity: alternation of stops and forward strokes in an illogical way.
Contrary pressure: sometimes appears "deviated", sometimes systematic irregularities take on the aspect of "discordance".
Difficult character, twisted mind.
Anal personality, paranoiac tendency.

Gille-Maisani: "Interpretation of these different movements always lies in tying them to the underlying signs (artificial, regressive, irregular, simplified, thrown forward, mannered, etc.) in relation to the characteristics of the entire writing."

CONTROLLED (*Speed*: Figs 9, 12a)
The outline shows movements of braking and control, especially at the ends of words.
Reflection, prudence.
Discipline, self-control, introversion.
Inhibition, shyness, watchful Superego.

CONVENTIONAL (*Form*: Fig. 112)
This aspect varies greatly according to nationality and sociocultural background and can only be identified securely after wide experience.
Conformist in attitudes and ideas.

CONVEX (*Direction*: Figs 52, 54, 108a)
The base line rises and then towards the middle curves down, both ends of the line being on the same level.
Difficulty in maintaining effort, enthusiasm is dampened.
Interior struggle.

Peugeot [200]: "Convex writing can also indicate the struggle against discouragement, delusion, disenchantment."

COPY-BOOK (*Form*: Fig. 96e)
A writing anchored in the basic model. Elementary school teachers often retain in their own writing a strong influence from the model that they have to teach. Also those who have studied less remain tied to the school model.
Respect for rules, conformity, lack of personality.

COVERING STROKES (*Continuity*: Figs 107, 112)
Tendency to go back on the stroke just made, instead of proceeding to the right.
Strong self-control, fear of revealing oneself.
Repressed spontaneity, inhibition.
With other confirming signs: *tendency to hide one's thoughts.*
Sometimes we find the "shark's tooth" sign, given a negative valuation by Pulver (more common in the German base model): *unscrupulous greed and slyness.*

According to Ursula Avé-Lallemant it represents in childhood one of the "alarm signals" and can be interpreted as a search for stability to compensate for insecurity. In a rapid script "the lack of courage is transformed into a lack of candour, indicating psychologically a denial of reality" (see Cristofanelli [69]).

CRENELLATED (*Form*: Figs 38c, 47)
The ovals remain open at the top or to the right, without loops. It is an aspect of *open* writing.
Spontaneous trust, sincerity, abandon.
Altruism, generosity, spontaneous devotion.
Suggestible, lack of self-defence.
In a relaxed context and with flying strokes: *lack of discernment, inconsequence, distraction.*
Psychology: search for support (anaclytic position), search for competence and results, idealistic yearnings, ambition for power, potency of the imaginary (from research for the GGCF by S. Binet de Vauclair and C. de Carayon).

DESCENDING (*Direction*: Figs 83, 102b, 111)
The base line descends from the horizontal and so the end of the line is lower than the beginning.
Fatigue, melancholy, depressive tendency.
Feeling of impotence.

DEVIATED (*Pressure*: Figs 40a–b, 45, 101a–b)
In general, the opposite of *in relief.* The usually thin strokes are heavy and the thick strokes are lighter. Pay attention to the symbolism of the zones. Often occurs in a horizontal direction, especially with heavy connections. Always see whether the deviation is intermittent or systematic.
Internal tension, appearance of confronting situations.
Internal security, will used in ways not always appropriate.
Closed.
In a harmonious context the valuation is generally positive: *action.*
With horizontal deviation in the middle zone: *compensation, sense of doubt, care for the everyday, energy to do one's best for others.*
In an inharmonious context the valuation is generally negative and increases the discords of the character.
With other confirming signs: *reserve, asperity, lack of warmth and feeling.*
Psychology: *Superego, inferiority complex, discontent, frustration, search for compensation, unease, illness, trauma.*

DIMINISHING (*Dimension*: Fig. 32/4)
The height of the letters lessens from the start to the end of the word, or from the start to the end of the line.
Sharp, able, psychological feeling.
Concealment, sometimes fatigue.

DISCORDANT (see Chapter Two: Figs 105–7)
Discordance is rare in the general population. Some frequent aspects are: uncontrolled disorder, excesses in dimension, interruptions of speed, continuity, and direction, excesses or changes of pressure, and sometimes polymorphism (even on a monotonous base).
Imbalance, twisted mind, deviation, uncommon sexual practices.

See Gille-Maisani [105], the section on discordant writing and hypotheses of deviation.

DISHARMONIOUS (or **DISHARMONIC WRITING**) (*Continuity*: Figs 13c, 110b)
Sign reintroduced by Gille-Maisani that offers important clues for psychopathological research (see [105]). Forms are personalized with a good graphic level, but the rhythm of movement is upset by systematic retouching, unnecessary and discordant, a sort of gesture-type or "graphic tic": corrections, jumping letters, spasms, bizarre gestures whose sudden impulse interrupts the rhythm and creates inhibition.
Imbalance of character, nervousness, instability, excessive emotivity.

Gille-Maisani: "In a superior graphic context occasional discordant notes reveal sufficiently well a personality which, according to Magnan's terminology, presents a brilliant side but developed in a disjointed manner, a 'sort with gaps in the thinking matter'. Persistent discordance and retouching and their appearance in particular letters are 'graphic tics', true motor impulses … The habitual predominance of the nervous temperament reveals the 'instability' of the disharmonious personality, with its emotivity and changeable will."

DISORDERLY (*Layout*: Figs 104b, 106)
The layout lacks order, the movement is poorly controlled, forms are neglected, the stroke is untidy.
Untidy, improvident, negligent person.
Nonconformist, fantasist.

Crépieux-Jamin distinguished two kinds of disorder: "active disorder, with strong, excessive, rash movements, caused by the passions; passive disorder resulting from inattention, laziness, apathy, improvidence, negligence, etc."

Moretti grounded the concept of disorder on irregularity in the size of letters, and sudden changes of pressure and proportion, in an inharmonious context.

Cristofanelli: "Moretti saw some positive value in a script only slightly disorderly. It is similar to *rhythmic irregularity*."

DISORGANIZED (*Continuity*: Fig. 109)
Writing which has lost the main features of organization, due to illness or old age. Sometimes anxious people mask their tremors and unconnected letters by heavy pressure with the pen.
Senility, debility, illness.

Crépieux-Jamin [65]: "A writing is disorganized when, on comparing it with other documents in the same hand, there is a notable loss of its former qualities."

DIVING (*Direction*: Figs 27, 31b, 36a, 102, 108c, 117)
The last letters of the line are squeezed together and descend below the average level of the line. This effect can happen systematically or at intervals. It can start before the right margin or it can extend beyond the margin. It tends to reduce clarity and harmony. The causes can be varied, depending on the other dominant elements in the writing: difficulty in stopping, impudence, passion, avarice, etc.
Negligence, carelessness, lack of organization.
Pushy, invasive.
Frenetic activity, thrust, obstinacy.
Diffidence, avarice.
Fatigue, depression.

Gille-Maisani: "Sometimes the diving words, through the sudden change of direction, form, and continuity, seem to be by a different hand compared to the rest of the line. *Change of pace* in writing indicates a dual personality: hindrance, inconstancy, cyclothymic, social mask, duplicity, according to each case."

DOUBLE CURVES (*Form*: Figs 30b, 47, 106)
Connections between letters are curved whether they are made from the top or bottom of the letters, avoiding angles: in effect, the connections alternate between garlands and arcades. "If the height of these letters lessens through a tendency for the writing to elongate, we will have a contour that represents the prototype of undulation" (see ch. 20 in Gille-Maisani [105]).
Search for conciliation, shunning conflict. Adaptation.
Difficulty in taking a position. Impressionable.
Imagination, ability, mimicry.
Opportunism.

The firmness or weakness of stroke, rhythm, or monotony, lead to many different interpretations.

DYNAMIC (*Speed*: Fig 118)
Fast speed with ample stroke, rightward slant, ascending, well-nourished, in a harmonious context. Excludes spasmodic pressure or sharp points.
Quick thinking, able, persuasive.
Need for freedom, vital thrust, love of life, optimism.
Practical energy.

DYNAMIC DISCONNECTION (*Continuity*: Figs 18, 35, 36b, 100: see also Static disconnection and Unconnected)
There is an implicit connection in the spaces, hardly visible, or virtual, which makes a disconnection dynamic, that is sharing in the general rhythm. One must assess the movement, speed, pressure, and structure of the forms.
Analytic mind.
Independence, autonomy, individualism.
Intuition.
With light pressure:
Penetrating analysis, original thought, intuition.
Openness, sensibility, receptivity, availability.
Discretion, selective contacts, refined air.
Cautious instinctive life, frailty.
Action based on inner motivation.
With heavy pressure:
Deep, intense, controlled thinking.
Concentration of interior forces, certainty in choices.
Selective but warm contacts.
Motivated action, with ability to make things happen.

ENLARGING (*Dimension*: Figs 12b, 32e)
Size of letters tends to grow towards the end of the word, and sometimes the words themselves enlarge towards the end of the line.
Poor discernment through naivety or impulsiveness.
Enthusiasm, open mind.
Naivety, rashness, credulity.

FALSE CONNECTIONS (*Continuity*: Figs 38a, 90b)
The connection between letters is executed in two parts, with an intervening lift of the instrument. Check if it comes from residual childhood motor difficulties. Other causes: fatigue, motor difficulty, lack of education, unease (sometimes in young persons when first starting work).
Difficulty in coordinating thought and action, and in structuring thought.

FILIFORM (*Form*: Figs 8a, 111b)
The letters of the middle zone are reduced to a thread, especially *m* and *n*. Filiform can derive from a curved or angular writing, from garlands or from arcades. One must check whether the tension is taut or slack, variable, agitated, etc. Filiform can represent:
1. A chosen form and therefore a simplification: *efficient use of energy and time, adaptive, intellectual agility, emotional disengagement.*
2. A reduction of form and therefore an imprecision: *escape, carelessness, nonchalance.*
3. A denial of form and therefore a constraint or an escape: *poor grasp of reality, unconscious pathogenic influence.*

These three aspects can also be present all together. Any interpretations, whether positive or negative, in the areas of intellect, emotion, or career, must take into account the fact that filiform expresses an ambivalence at a deep psychological level and therefore positive and negative aspects can coexist.
Adaptment, ability, capacity for change, activity, lively intelligence, clear imagination, invention, improvisation of solutions, inspiration, dreams.
Emotional evasion, need for freedom, but correct social behaviour towards friends and family. Ability to take advantage of circumstances.
Lack of responsibility, headstrong, superficial, agitated.
Manipulative, ambiguous, concealing, escape from reality.
Pathology: *physical weakness, exhaustion, pretence.*
Unexpected filiform words: *hysteria* (Klages).
The presence of *Anima* in men and *Animus* in women is common: *uncertain identification, difficulty in choice of objects.*
See also Chapter Four Section X.3's extensive summary of the study of Kergall and Pinon [118].

FIRM (*Pressure*: Figs 70b, 124)
The full weight of the pressure goes from top to bottom of the downstrokes independently of the thickness of the stroke. The stroke is firm, without softness or instability.
Energetic, hands on character, cold blood, will, action.
Discipline, authority (without being authoritarian), loyal, constant.

FLATTENED OVALS (*Form*: Fig. 7d)
The ovals of the letters *a, d, g, o,* and *q* are widened horizontally. This sign is usually seen in a controlled graphic context in which form predominates, expressing inhibition. At times it can express a superficial search.
Reserve, shyness, scruple.
With other confirming signs: *concealment, lies.*

FLEXIBLE (see "WAVY" p.469)

FLYING STROKES (*Speed*: Figs 52, 97)
Some strokes and especially the *t*-bars are thrown forward with dynamic speed.
Spontaneity, expansion, extroversion.
Dynamism, reactivity.
Difficulty of control, impulsivity, provocation.
Violence.

Crépieux-Jamin [65]: "There is a mystic form to flying writing ... according to the graphic context it shows the excitation of a very vivid imagination, or a tendency to high aspirations, to visions of utopia, ... to imbalance."

FRAGMENTED (*Continuity*: Fig. 109)
Single letters are formed with separated elements, a sort of excessive disconnection. This can affect only certain letters or the whole writing. The formation can be more or less voluntary, even specially chosen for artificiality, or may stem from motor difficulties.
Hesitation, inhibition.
Construction.
Sickness.

Crépieux-Jamin: "Concerns a more or less extensive interruption in the outline of the letters. This sign is linked to respiratory or circulatory disturbances."

Manual of Graphology [200]: "The fragmentation of letters can even be a means of constructing a writing. The choice of such letters is not neutral, they are essentially the round letters, that is to say the affective letters, and *m*, very symbolic, followed by *p*, which represents affirmation since it can be completed by a single vertical thrust."

FULL (*Dimension*: Figs 44, 96a, 116, 118a: see also Triple width)
Airy letters, especially the ovals and loops which are ample and inflated.
Expansion, imagination, prodigality.
If clearly plump (see Chapter Ten, children's items F2): *dependent, childish.*

GALLOPING (*Direction*: Figs, 54, 102, 108c, 117)
Single words rise or fall, but they all begin on the same horizontal line, so that they look like a line of curved (Roman) tiles on a roof.
Rising: *renewed effort but controlled impetus.*
Falling: *struggle against depression, sense of failure.*

GARLANDS (*Form*: Figs 16a, 19, 23a, 96a, 118: *see also* Looped garlands)
Predominance of curves open at the top, so that the letters *m* and *n* look like *u*. Initial and final strokes of letters or words as well as connections between letters are in the form of a festoon.

Receptive, open attachment, sociable, spontaneous sympathy.
Love of contact, richness of feeling.
In initial strokes it is associated with "caressing" writing: *gaiety, amiability, sympathy.*
In final strokes: *cordiality, pleasant extroversion.*
In connecting strokes: *sweetness, sensibility, openness, flexibility.*
Deep, static garlands: *passive sympathy, calm, indolence, contemplation, melancholy.*
Soft, unstable garlands: *impressionable, indecisive.*
Garlands sticking strongly to the line: *sensuality, materialism.*

GRACEFUL (*Form:* Figs 96c, 101e, 118a)
There are three types of graceful form:
1. Light and pleasing curves that prolong the lower extensions of *p, q,* and *f: charm and gentle flattery.*
2. Initial strokes in the shape of a semicircle: *possessiveness which turns on feelings and not on material goods.*
3. Noose-like stroke in the paraph and certain final letters; *f* or *p* in the form of an 8: *enfolding caress.*

Torbidoni and Zanin [230]: see "I ricci dell'Ammanieramento": they emphasize the flattering aspect and the need to put on appearances. (See also p.430 above, "Strokes of concealment")

GROUPED (*Continuity:* Figs 9, 11b, 123, 124)
Three or four letters are linked together in logical sequences which allow for adequate pauses. Consider the syllables and the accents to assess the logic of the pattern. If the sequences obey no logic, one cannot attach much positive value to this sign. Also examine the influence of other signs: punctured, false connections, amended, inhibited, suspended, jerky, etc.
Good coordination of ideas and action, intellectual adaptability.
Flexibility, aptitude to variety, inventive.
Initiative, independent judgement, critical observation.

HETEROCLINE (*Slant:* Figs 41, 87)
Strong changes of slant which give the writing an air of torment. (First called *tiraillée* by Oscar Del Torre, then taken up by Gille-Maisani.)
Difficulty in concentration, indecision.
Internal contradictions, oppositions between contrary feelings.
Exhaustion of energy by internal conflicts.
At times: *frenzied creative search.*
Psychology: *ambivalence* (often in adolescence).

HOMOGENEOUS (*Continuity*: Figs 2, 7c, 9)
Unity between the various graphic elements: movement, form, dimension, direction, inclination, rhythm, blacks and whites, text and signature, without monotony. In general this sign represents an element of harmony in assessing the graphic context.
Deep unity of personality, true to oneself.
In excess it borders on rigidity: *systematic conceptions, lack of flexibility, tendency to preach.*

HOOKS (or **HOOKED WRITING**) (*Direction*: Figs 96c, 101a)
Initial and final strokes of letters have a little regressive turn, like a hook. As with all small signs, it must be considered in the graphic context.

Initial hook
Obstinacy, perseverance, tenacity, egoism.
When associated with a lasso: *acquisitive and far-sighted tendency.*

Gille-Maisani: "On the psychological plane tenacity and egoism are two aspects of the force of the instincts of the Ego."

Final hook
Note whether it is formed by itself or is part of a "connection in space".
In north-east direction: *aggression.*
In centripetal direction: *dissimulation.*

HOPPING (*Continuity*: Figs 10a, 23c)
A dancing aspect: general liveliness of outline with irregular connections and poor stability of line.
Lively perception, intuition.
Rapid thought and action.

HORIZONTAL (*Direction*: Figs 22b, 31e)
The direction of the line is horizontal across the page. Lines are parallel with each other. If very systematic see Rigid.
Self-control, defensive balance, serene humour.
Will, fidelity to decisions taken, holding to the chosen view.
If lacking movement and with soft stroke: *apathy, indifference.*

INFLATED (*Form*: Figs 70a, 116, 118)
Curves, loops, and ovals are overblown.
Exalted imagination, enthusiasm.
Exaggerated feelings, pride.
Vital, sanguine, exhibitionist.
In upper zone: *exaggeration, illusion, irrepressible fantasy world.*

In middle zone: *need to attract attention, emotional demands, heightened desires, mythomania.*
In lower zone: *exhibitionism, lack of shame, eroticism, hysteroid aspects.*
In children's forms it becomes *plump* writing, still present in 70% of writings at 11 years
in the graphometric scale (see Chapter Ten, children's items F2).
Immaturity, emotional vindication.
With excessively full movement, in creative persons: *imaginative world, sparkling fantasy.*

IN RELIEF (*Pressure*: Figs 1, 12b, 27, 30d, 118)
Contrast of pressure between the down and up stroke with well-defined contours. Hegar
[112] did not always give relief a positive value: "we often find strong relief in the writings
of criminals."
Energy, vitality, psychological balance.
Self-reliance, resistance to outside influences.
Observant.

INVASIVE (*Layout*: Figs 100a, 102a)
The graphic space is so excessively filled that neither harmony nor sobriety is respected.
Also, margins and indents tend to be absent. One must consider the age of subjects and
the cultural and educational norms of their homelands.
Taking up space or butting into others', through lack of respect or critical discernment, caused
by difficulties in disengaging from one's Ego.
With large movements: *extroversion dominates, need for social role.*
With concise movements: *closed to others, obsessively egocentric.*

IRREGULAR
Variations which alter the regularity and homogeneity of the writing. They can involve
one or more categories, particularly Continuity, Speed, and Pressure. Do not confuse
irregularity with motor difficulties caused by age, illness, or graphic level.

Crépieux-Jamin [65]: "Every irregularity of the stroke shows an emotion. The more
moderate and repeated the irregularities are, the more qualitative the emotions to which
they correspond."

Pulver [207]: "Irregular writing has a very wide range of meanings. Generally it can be
said that emotions and spontaneity are predominant, while discipline, rationality, balance,
and perseverance are lacking."

Continuity
A small irregularity in connection between letters, which airs the writing, is a positive
sign.
Emotivity, sensitivity.

Dimension (Figs 5a, 99)
See if the irregularity – in width, in height, and in spacing – affects mainly the middle zone or the outer zones.
Changeable sense of self. Sensibility. Emotivity.
Uncertainties, inhibitions.
(Can reach) *elation or depression.*
Irregularity in the general fullness of the stroke: *inner tension, highs and lows.*
Excessive irregularity and disorder: see Disorderly, Discordant.

Layout (Figs 43–4)
Irregular margins, spaces, order.
Movement, poor concentration, poor discipline, negligence.
Instability, susceptibility.
Unpredictable and baffling actions.

Slant (Fig. 10: see also Heterocline)
Light variations in letter slant.
Intellectual and emotional sensibility.
Mental curiosity, eclecticism.
Ability to see things from different viewpoints.
Clear and frequent variations: *nervous, sensitive, indecisive, mental ambivalence between reason and feeling.*

Pulver [207]: "All variations in slant are graphic expressions of ambivalence. These changes are above all important in the middle zone, because it escapes self-control; then come variations in slant in the zone of the lower extensions."

JERKY (*Continuity*: Figs 29e, 37a–b, 40)
Connections between letters are abrupt, taut, with jerks. The gesture is not sufficiently mastered, preferring angles to curves and causing irregularity in the connections.
Overemotive, internal tension.
Susceptibility.
Difficulty in controlling impulses and nervous reactions.
Subjects are always exposed, tense, with poor adjustment. We should look for diverse causes: weariness, illness, old age.

LARGE (*Dimension*: Figs 11, 23a, 26)
The middle zone is higher than 3.5 mm.
Self-importance, need for expansion.
Tendency to be subjective.

Ania Teillard: strong libido, Sentiment and Sensation type, extrovert.

LASSOS (*Form*: Figs 28b, 107)
A lasso is formed by a forward stroke turning back on itself, completing a closed loop.
Skilful, inventive.
Desire for recognition, for love. Seduction.
Intrusive, egoist.
At the base of *t*: *tenacity, stubbornness.*
High whiplash: *authoritarian energy.*
In a paraph: *business ability.* If very complex: *intrigue, scheming.*

Gille-Maisani: "the term lasso was coined by Abbé Michon who defines the paraph thus: *long pen stroke which turns back on itself.*"

LEFTWARD SLANT (*Slant*: Figs 8a, 116a)
The axis of the letters forms an angle of more than 90° with the base line. There are three levels of evaluation:
1. *Vigilance: defence, emotional control, reserve, apprehension, shame.*
2. *Opposition: reactive feeling, reluctance, shyness.*
3. *Repression: difficulty in exteriorizing, conflicts, closure.*
If the movement is rhythmic, the significance of movement and rhythm prevails over that of leftward. This means a truly personal writing style in which impetus and watchful control coexist.
Frequent in left-handed and perhaps in ambidextrous people and in thwarted left-handers. With other confirmatory signs: *risk of psychopathy.*

Klages considered this sign, in its negative aspect, to be a sign of *concealment*, and in its positive aspect a vanquishing of the self, where the Ego transmutes itself in an impetus of *abnegation.*

LIGHT (*Pressure*: Figs 38a, 41a, 119a)
The stroke tends to float on the surface. It may contain light relief and some spasms which differentiate it from *pale* pressure. The writing can be precise or pasty. The associated signs will have special bearing on the interpretation. It is found in the Jungian types Thinking and Intuition.
Subtle perception (stroke of *sensitives*).
Refinement, spirituality.
Vulnerability, worry, fragility.
With other signs: *weakness, lack of vitality.*
In a poor or inharmonious context: *Superficial, suggestible, escapist, passive.*
With relaxed stroke: *weak-willed.*
With full and garlanded writing: *ability to disentangle situations.*
With little development of the lower extensions: *poor sense of reality.*
With filiform: *easily swayed or seduced* (criminology).

With large, garlanded letters: *often found in merchants.*
With spasms: *irritable, nervous contractions.*
Pathology: *states of exhaustion, convalescence, heart trouble; with subtle and wide garlands, obesity.*

LIMPID (*Form*: Figs 7c, 121, 123b)

A positive, qualitative sign, in conjunction with an aerated layout. The writing is legible with no ambiguity or complication and the forms are not stunted. The overall impression is of clarity. Often the writing is simple, but not simplified.
Moral rectitude, balanced judgement, sincerity, simplicity, clear head, intelligence, organization, scientific spirit.

LOOPED GARLANDS (*Form*: Figs 26, 103, 124)

The downstrokes of garlands loop back, presenting a series of regressive rings. This can also apply to *lassos*, with similar interpretation. According to Gille-Maisani [107] the loops are "typically *Melodic-Rhythmic*" (after Leone Bourdel), and such a temperament "represents par excellence the utilitarian temperament: the individual adapts to circumstances (Melodic) to impose his own agenda (Rhythmic)."
Sociable, adaptable, able, dextrous.
Practical intelligence, willing, liberal.
Calculating, plotting, egocentric avidity.
In an inhibited context: *shame, interiorization.*
In a lively context: *active, talkative.*
Heavily placed on the line: *strong realism in human relations* (Jungian type Sentiment Sensation).

LOOPED OVALS (*Form*: Figs 29c, 100a: see also Bow ties)

The basic movement of this sign is close to that for bow ties and often the two signs occur together. The rolled up movement applies above all to the ovals. We propose to reserve the term for writings where leftward coiling occurs in ovals that is unnecessary for their closing.
Self-centred, egoist.
Concealment of thoughts and actions.
With anomalies of pressure and rhythm: *sexually-based pathologies.*

Ania Teillard [227], under Twisted in the lexicon: "the rolling up can take the form of little coils on single gestures."
Harmless subterfuge or lies.

LOW (*Dimension*: Figs 30a, 96a)

The writing expands in the middle zone. The extensions tend to disappear in the outer zones, whatever the general dimension.
The Ego predominates. Impulses are reduced. Contemplative tendency. Renunciation.

MARGINS (*Layout*: Figs 2, 9, 45, 53)
The formation of the margins can be related to the age of the subject and to the school model and cultural habits of the country of the writer. For this entry, we follow the French norms; for other countries see Chapter Fourteen.

Upper margin
Very large (about a quarter of the page height): *burden of authority and of social and family upbringing. Respect for convention. Overhanging Superego.*
Large (distance between the top of the page and beginning of the text is larger than the total space of three lines of text): *respect for authority, for good education, and for conventions. Ability to distance oneself from surroundings.*
Small or absent (according to cultural context, for instance in Italy the perception of "space of the page" as something to do with organization is little felt): *easy manner, extrovert spontaneity, intrusiveness.*

Lower margin
A good spatial awareness means that the writing does not go down to the bottom of the page.
Absent: *difficulty in detaching oneself from the context, improvidence.*
Large: *formal, aesthetic more than logical.*

Left margin
Very wide, with only a small right margin (over a quarter of the page width): *distance from the past, from origins, escape or fear.*
Wide, with only a small right margin (a quarter of the page width): *detachment from the past, open to the future and to action* (in a context without inhibition).
Medium or proportional (for a standard A4 page, about 4 cm): *integration of the past with freedom of action, self-control, courtesy and good education, critical and organizational capacity.*
Absent or minimal (to be assessed by the age and cultural context): *attachment to the past, to the mother, to traditions.*
Irregular: *easy manner, fantasy.*
Progressive (increases line by line): *enterprise, impatience, extroversion.*
Very progressive: *flight from the past, psychological problem linked to infancy.*
Rigid: *conformism, closed mind, Superego.*

Right margin
Important mainly in comparison with the left margin. The right margin is not particularly significant in teaching.
Wide (larger or equal to a quarter of the width of the page): *low enterprise, fear of the future.*
Protected (present in a discreet way to prevent unnecessary word breaks): *self-control, logical organization.*

Absent (without touching the edge of the page, otherwise see Invasive): *extroversion, initiative.*

Progressive (increases line by line): *difficulty in maintaining impetus, fears.*

Regressive (lessens line by line): *initial fears overcome, extroversion and initiative increase with time.*

MEDIUM (*Dimension*: Figs 2, 122a)
The middle zone is around 2.5 mm high.
Measured self-awareness, natural openness.
Balance between the Ego and surroundings.

Torbidoni and Zanin [230]: "This graphic aspect more than any other recalls the classical axiom that virtue lies in the mean."

METHODICALLY IRREGULAR (see RHYTHMIC)

MIXED (*Form*: Figs 21, 99)
Half curved and half angular. A prevalence of curves leads to softness while a prevalence of angles lead to firmness.
In a good graphic context: *flexible intelligence, productive activity, adaptability.*

MOVEMENTS OF H. DE GOBINEAU
Reared up movement (*cabré*): close to the sign Leftward slant.
Obstructed movement (*barré*): close to the sign Controlled.

NARROW (*Dimension* and *Form*: Figs 12b–c, 13b, 16b, 101b)
The base of each letter is very reduced and the main body is higher than it is wide. This sign is independent of a compact or aerated aspect, which both concern the spaces between letters and lines. Crépieux-Jamin called it "contracted" (*étrécie*): "it seems to gain in height what it loses in width."
Reflection, restraint, inhibition.

NUANCED (NUANCÉE) (*Continuity*: Figs 53, 54)
The writing shows gentle irregularities in various categories, but without damaging an overall regularity of movement. Very often there are light differences in pressure.
Delicate sensibility.
Subtlety in perceptions and emotions.

OPEN (*Form*: Figs 10, 40b)
Tendency to leave the ovals *a, o, d, q* open. If this is constant, the writing is Crenellated.
Open, receptive, lack of defence.
With opening high to the right: *emotional spontaneity, rash, without calculation.*
With large high opening and rounded and large writing: *impressionable receptivity, tendency to reveal one's mental state, uncritical, talkative.*

With opening to left: *reluctant to reveal, tactful, shy, very reserved over personal things.*
With opening at the bottom and with contrary stroke: *lack of sincerity, hypocrisy, disloyalty.*
NB In left-handed subjects, note the logic of the movement!

ORGANIZED (*Continuity*)
Writing which has attained motor flexibility and an adequate graphic level in relation to the cultural background (see Chapter Two, Section V).

ORDERLY (*Layout*)
A sign listed by Crépieux-Jamin which substantially agrees with his definition of *harmony* (see Chapter Four, Section III).

OVERCONNECTED (*Continuity*: Figs 4, 34c, 43)
Words are very connected internally and some final or free strokes connect to the following word. The valuation of this sign as creative or cavilling must be taken from the context. Also we must determine the cultural habits of the period or the school model of the country (Anglo-Saxon writing for example).
Associative thinking. Tendency for paradox.

OVOID (*Form*: Figs 38b, 118, 121)
The ovals are precisely oval, particularly the *o*, with a gentle slant of the vertical axis. Ovoid takes on its full positive value in a harmonious context with a steady stroke. This sign is typical of instinctively organized persons, or those who exercise a suitable and timely initiative to achieve results.
Flexible and intelligent adaptability.
Concrete imagination, realism.
Productive activity, openness.
General balance, stability.

Suzanne Bresard [46]: "rich, precise forms taken to their essence … symbolizing a maximum vital weight with minimum stroke and maximum dynamic advance."

PALE (*Pressure*: Fig. 32d)
The quality of stroke is neutral and colourless, without nuance or relief.
Lack of personality, insignificant.
In a young subject: *shyness and modesty.*

PASTY (*Pressure*: Figs 25, 124a)
Dense stroke of a certain thickness with little difference between the solid and the subtle. The pressure can be either light or heavy.
Emotionally effusive, sensory, sensual in a broad sense.
Aesthetic sense (colours, pleasing effects), *artistic sense, sensitivity to surroundings.*

Found in Jungian types Sensation and Sentiment (e.g. the painter Pissarro).
With very developed lower extensions: *preponderance of instinctual life, sensuality, carelessness, nonchalance.*
With banal writing: *materialism.*
With firm and resolute outline: *passionate character, strong libido.*
With inclined outline and very long lower extensions: *depravity, lack of restraint in actions and gestures.*
With leftward writing and large and rigid letters: *male homosexuality.*
With thick writing: *heavy sensuality, materialism.*

POINTED (See Sharp-pointed)

POISED (*Speed*: Figs 7c, 22b, 35)
A speed of around 130 letters a minute. The movement is controlled and smooth, the forms respected, slowing down does not imply constriction but adequate pauses. It goes together with moderate dimension, homogeneity, and general sobriety.
Reflection, observation, realistic imagination.
Seriousness at work, good sense, moderation.
Calm and self-control in the face of the unexpected.
In a monotonous context: *passive, weak will, indifference.*

PRECIPITATED (*Speed*: Figs 4, 19, 23c)
A speed of more than 200 letters a minute. The movement is excessively fast, to the detriment of the forms.
Transports of passion, enthusiasm, febrile activity.
With homogeneous and well laid out writing:
Lightning thought and simultaneous action.
Initiative and activity.
Impetus and zeal.
With little homogeneity, irregularities, and jerks:
Mental vivacity not always mastered, brio.
Excitability, restlessness, agitation, activism, escape.
Difficulty in containing oneself, irritable, lack of scruple.
With spasmodic or clubbed pressure: *risk of violence.*

PRECISE (*Pressure*: Figs 2b, 9, 123b)
Stroke is precise, subtle, without smudges or shakes, and with clean edges.
Concentration, precision, firm convictions.
Reason prevails over feelings and instincts. Moderate energy.
With thin writing: *abstract thinking.*
With angular writing: *cold, severe, ascetic.*
Jungian type Thinking Intuition.

PROGRESSIVE (*Direction*: Figs 7a, 18, 19, 27, 124a)
The movement of the graphic outline is pushed markedly towards the right, tending to eliminate returns to the left, to quicken the formation of single letters, combinations, and connections.
Speed of thought and action.
Openness, desire for contact, generosity.
Enterprise, faith in the project and its outcome.
With uneven pressure and careless forms: *escape in advance, improvidence.*
With angular, trenchant, or clubbed pressure: *prevarication, poorly controlled aggression, likes to be instrumental in big decisions.*
With excessively large or superelevated forms: *pride, exaltation.*
(See Pulver [207] ch. 17, Right and Left Tendencies.)

PROLONGED DOWNWARD (*Dimension*: Figs 49b, 100)
The lower extensions descend below the base line to a distance greater than twice the middle zone.
Predominance of instinctual forces, sense of reality, pragmatic tendencies.

Ania Teillard [227]: "Sensation type. … With strong pressure and well developed loops: predominant sexuality."

Manual of Graphology [200]: "One should note the frequent emphasis on lower extensions in writings of average sociocultural milieu."

PROLONGED UPWARD (*Dimension*: Fig. 114)
The upper extensions reach a height from the base line greater than twice the middle zone.
Intellectual tendencies, idealism.

PROLONGED UPWARD AND DOWNWARD (*Dimension*: Figs 118, 119b)
Both the upper and lower extensions reach a distance from the base line greater than twice the middle zone.
Multiple interests, contradictory tendencies, aspirations, dissatisfaction, splitting of energies.

PUNCTURED (*Continuity*: Figs 43, 54, 111b)
Excessive and unexpected spaces between letters.
Nervous interruption. Open to events, flight, emptiness.
In a creative context: *intuition, ideas.*
In an inhibited context: *autism, split.*

RAPID (*Speed*: Figs 4, 14, 19, 27, 41a, 42, 43)
Speed of around 180 letters a minute. The movement runs in a fluid rush without any notable slowing down.
Lively mind, easy and quick thinking, imagination.
Activity, fast reactions, ability to find solutions, dynamism.
Easy manner, impatience, instability.

Manual of Graphology [200]: "On the moral plane, if it is true that certain imprecisions, evasions, and a moderate clarity are more excused in a fast graphic context than in a slow one, we must tone down such interpretations and not give in to a facile and dangerous Manicheism, either one way or the other."

REGRESSIVE (*Direction*: Figs 105, 107, 110b)
The outline tends to retard movement to the right. The writing includes unnecessary returns to the left. Seen especially in the formative movements of loops and ovals.
Introverted thinking, closing of self.
Little spontaneity, prudence, mistrust, shyness.
With aggressive pressure and lasso gestures: *egoistic attitudes and tendency to monopolize.*
With very angular writing: *poor adaptability, stubbornness.*
With squeezed, narrow, and angular writing: *sado-anal complex.*
With signs of insincerity (ambiguous letters, covering strokes, arcades): *calculation, concealment, deceit, larceny.*

Pulver: "The regressive tendency as a result of strong influence of the past is important in writings of many psychopathics, especially in cases of regression."

RHYTHMIC or METHODICAL IRREGULARITY (Moretti) (*Continuity*: Figs 6a, 14, 27, 42)
Shows a light variability of stroke that confers rhythm to the writing, not disorder. The irregularities must be methodically repeated. According to Moretti, the sign occurs in three areas:
1. Size in the middle zone: *flexibility, intuition, mental agility, richness of ideas.*
2. Slant: *psychological intuition, ease in personal relations, practical solutions.*
3. Base line is unsteady: *emotional spontaneity* (for Moretti a sign of *musical creativity* if not disorderly).

RIGHTWARD SLANT (*Slant*: Figs 27, 52, 104, 112)
The axis of the letters forms an angle of between 45° and 70° with the base line.
Spontaneity, sociability, participation, imprudence.
Deep convictions, subjective and partial tendency.
Tendency to impose self on others.
With light pressure: *sensibility, impressionability.*
With pasty pressure: *sensuality, passion.*

With angular writing: *obstinacy, relentless fury.*
With soft writing: *sluggish.*
With prolonged upper and lower extensions: *tendency to dissipate energies, dependence on the instincts and on feeling.*

RIGID (*Direction*: Figs 12, 112)
The appearance of the lines is identical to each other, without flexibility. In general the layout is also formal, the slant of the letters is strictly parallel, and the outline tends to be angular.
Intransigent will and rigour.
Sectarian opinions, harshness.

RISING (*Direction*: Figs 87, 121)
The line rises in a clear progression from the horizontal, so that the end of the line is higher than the beginning (but check the position of the paper while writing).
Thrust, enterprise, enthusiasm, optimism.
With excessive rising movement and disorder: *excitable.*
With soft stroke and slackened speed: *fatigue, depression.*

ROUND (*Form*: Figs 16a, 30b, 44)
Ovals are round, almost circular, and the writing tends to curved forms.
Adaptable, sociable, lazy.
With warm stroke: *cordial.*
With regressive tendency: *egoism.*

SCRIPT (*Form*: Fig. 67a)
Close to the typographic model, script is taught in several countries. Therefore we must know the school model and preferably the educational level and occupation of the writer. In general the letters, in the style of lower-case print, are unconnected, but not consciously. English script in fact adopts certain specific connections. We should look for a reason for this choice, because interpretations can be made in various ways:

lack of the writing habit or fidelity to the school model: *desire for clarity.*
through free choice: *desire for originality or aesthetic effect.*
book reader: *learning, aesthetic value.*
defence or mask: *compensation.*

SECONDARY CONNECTION (*Continuity*: Figs 27, 36a)
The connection between two letters stretches horizontally, taking up roughly the space of one letter.
Persistence in own ideas and actions.
Ethics. Strain.

Connected with heavy pressure: *strong presence, security, activism, will which follows its own lines, search for contact*. In a poor graphic context: *closed, heavy mind, obtuse, limited*. Connected with light pressure: *refined and subtle, ability to plan and carry out a course of conduct*. In a poor graphic context: *wordy, pondering, humdrum, sectarian*.

SHAKY (*Continuity*: Figs 37a, 105c)
The stroke is agitated by little tremors on the verticals or horizontals. The causes range from poor writing ability to cramp, illness, old age, drugs, etc. Without any specific cause, the evaluation is:
Nervous, excited, tense.
Hysteria.

SHARP-POINTED (*Pressure*: Figs 4, 9, 39)
Finals and *t*-bars are pointed, flying, rapid.
Intellectual domineering, critical sense.
Sarcasm through nervousness or poor character.
Sometimes hypocritical, or ironic.

SIMPLE (*Form*: Figs 7a, 12a)
Writing with precise, considered gestures, close to the base model. Unnecessary signs are excluded, too elaborate forms or excessive superelevations.
Simplicity, modesty, discretion, shyness, measure.
Frank, sincere.
Productive and harmonious activity.
Without rhythm or air: *conventional, indifferent, lack of imagination, obsessive tendencies.*

SIMPLIFIED (*Form*: Figs 4, 36b, 37a, 38c, 41a)
Letters are reduced to their essentials while preserving their legibility. A full positive value for this will depend on the rhythm, given that simplification itself excludes loops and full curves, the typical signs of imagination, which will be expressed instead through the rhythm.
Culture, quick mind, clarity.
Synthesis, speed of association.
Natural justice, need for objectivity.
Note: do not confuse *simple* with *simplified*. For example, an original and aesthetic simplified writing comes close to being *stylized*, which *simple* never does.

SLACK (*Speed*: Fig. 10)
The writing lacks structure, clarity, and consistency, with weak pressure and uncertain direction.
Changeable, impressionable, inactive.
Depressive states, internal imbalance.

SLOW (*Speed*: Figs 32b, 105c, 110b)
Speed of less than 100 letters a minute. One must carefully assess objective factors linked
to age, educational level, state of well-being, or accidental causes. The absence of the main
signs of rapidity (simplification, progressive and inclined movement), with numerous signs
of slowing down, indicates a slow speed. The graphic context will mostly determine the
interpretation.
Inhibition, passivity.
Insincerity, concealment, hypocrisy (see Pulver's signs of insincerity).

SLOWED DOWN (*Speed*: Figs 7d, 8b, 40a, 41b, 105)
More than a truly separate sign, this term signifies the occasional slowing down which can
occur with other signs of speed. It is handy to consider it as a separate sign as a way of
showing the various sorts of slowing down, distinguishing it from slow writing which
does not involve other sorts. We here suggest a listing of gestures of slowing down.

Gestures of perfection
Attempts at precision and accuracy in forms, or corrections.
Need for clarity and precision.
Prudent and punctilious character, perfectionist.

Gestures of inhibition
Breaks in the movement, suspensions, point-like forms in the connections of letters
and words.
Hesitation, scruples, insecurity, anxiety.
Nervous emotion, excitability, fright.

Gestures of ornament or elaboration
Mainly in initial and final strokes of words, they add an unnecessary element to the
detriment of simplicity and spontaneity.
Search for effect, adulation, coquetry.
In graceful writing with firm rhythm: *sociable, gentle fantasy.*

Gestures of conservation
Excessively looped forms.
Instinct for conservation, possessive emotions and values.
Tendency to ruminate.

Gestures of a psychosexual nature
Spindles, spasms of pressure, inflated forms. Deviant mental energy.
Sensuality and overexcitement, obsessive fixation.

Gestures of concealment
Artificial with regressive forms, discordances, covering strokes. Mask.
Hiding through fear, insecurity.
Concealment, duplicity.

Gestures of unease
Tremors, blotches, twisting, smudges.
Fatigue and melancholy.
Drug addiction.

SMALL (*Dimension*: Figs 12a, 123b)
The middle zone is less than 2 mm.
Modest opinion of self, need for concentration, search for objectivity.

Ania Teillard: Introversion Thinking type.

SMEARY (*Pressure*: Figs 32b, 106a, 107, 109)
Thickened stroke and filled in ovals. Check that there are no accidental causes (unsuitable pen or paper). Given its negative signification, this sign should be used with caution.
Sensuality, greed, disorder, obscenity.
In some pathologically disturbed persons: *hypertension, neurasthenia, exhaustion, old age.*

SOBER (*Dimension*: Figs 36b, 37a, 122b)
Dimension and proportion are controlled and nothing excessive disturbs the graphic balance. The sign excludes monotony.
Balance, control, reflection and introversion, modesty.

SPACED OUT (*Layout*: Figs 34b, 41a, 52)
The whites prevail over the blacks. The distance between words is more than about three letters, the lines are far apart, sometimes chimneys appear in the white spaces.
Distancing self from events.
Abstraction, synthetic vision, concentration.
Selective contact, solitude sought or endured.
Balance and adaptability (depending on graphic context).
With high Formlevel: *search for the absolute, spirituality.*
With low Formlevel: *emptiness, dispersion.*
With signs of inhibition: *mental inhibition, isolation.*
With irregularities of spacing: *uncertainty, changefulness.*

Faideau [91]: "White space always represents breath, with a spiritual connotation."

SPASMODIC (*Pressure*: Figs 37b, 97, 105b, 107)
Irregular extra pressure. The stroke widens, even in a light script, in the form of spasms, which can be brief and passing or long and continuous. Often found with certain illnesses and in puberty or menopause.
Tendency to nervous disturbance, overexcitement.
Spasms on accents, *t*-bars, and punctuation: *nervous reaction* (in a tense subject).
With discordances: *strongly aggressive, poor self-control, activity interrupted, sexual disturbances* (fears, repressions).

SPINDLE-SHAPED (*Pressure*: Fig. 40)
Contains spasmodic swellings in the form of spindles. It is a type of spasmodic writing.
Sensuality, greed, glutton for pleasure.

SQUEEZED (*Dimension*: Figs 7d, 13b, 28b, 96c)
The space between letters (see Triple width) or parts of letters is reduced to a minimum, no matter what the height and width of the letters. We are only concerned with the letter space. *Narrow* writing, on the other hand, develops height at the expense of width and fullness.
Caution, circumspection, reserve.

STATIC DISCONNECTION (*Continuity*: Figs 45, 96c)
The letters or parts of letters are placed on the line with definite stops or suspensions of the gesture. The graphic structure reveals a search for compensation. When well compensated the common signs are: predominance of form, strict organization and precision, verticality, differentiated pressure.
Basic vulnerability which marks a block or inhibition.
With soft pressure and lack of precision: *inhibition lacking in reaction.*

STRAIGHTENED (*Slant*: Figs 12a, 23a)
The outline is gently inclined but many letters tend to straighten towards the vertical. This can be an occasional tendency with certain words, or frequent.
Checking, vigilance.
Doubts, hesitations, denial.

STRUCTURED (*Form*: Fig. 45)
Can take on two aspects: the letters are turned into structures or designs, or certain structures appear in the text, between words, between lines, or in the margins. Structured writing adds an individual element to the message beyond language, in the realm of symbolism.
Aesthetic and artistic gifts.
Penchant for allusive and symbolic communication.
Expressive sparkle, creative freedom.

Gille-Maisani: a writing "whose harmonious and careful outline, original but without discordance, comes closer to a true design than to simple calligraphy. Structured writing is an instinctive artistic manifestation, we see noble forms, a pure and nuanced stroke, sometimes exaggerated in its relief or size, but always harmonious and rich in life."

STYLIZED (*Form*: Figs 36b, 119)
Writing simplified in a personal way, with regards for elegance of form, remaining legible, precise, and authentic.
Distinctive mind, original personality, personal and synthetic opinions.
With aerated writing: Jungian type Thinking Intuition.
With sober forms: scientific or philosophical spirit.

SUPERELEVATED (*Dimension*: Figs 23a, 104a)
Some letters or parts of letters increase in height, notably the vertical of *p*, the first downstroke of *m* and *n*, and *s* and *j* in French.
Susceptibility, amour propre, aspirations.
Compensation or overcompensation, pride, grandeur.
Psychology: strong Ideal of the Ego.

SUSPENDED (*Continuity*: Figs 54, 111)
A letter or part of a letter hangs suspended, not reaching the base line or remaining incomplete in its vertical or horizontal development.
From timidity to inhibition.
Apprehension, prudence.
Reduced spontaneity, difficulty of action and communication.
With other confirming signs: *concealment.*

SYSTEMATIC (*Form*: Figs 105, 112)
In French, the term assumes a negative connotation of reduction to a system, whereas Italian tends to emphasize the positive value of methodical organization. In graphology the term is used in the French way.
One-dimensional personality.
Poor adaptability, set purpose.
In a homogeneous, simple, firm, and precise context: *trustworthy.*
In an inharmonious context with complications, artifice, illegible letters, or irregularities: *lying, concealment.*

TANGLED LINES (*Layout*: Figs 28, 100, 105, 120)
The lower extensions of one line extend into or actually entangle with the upper extensions of the next line. The gap between the lines is no longer a neutral space.
Subjective thought. Lack of synthesis and clarity. Difficulty with abstraction.
Prevalence of emotion and instinct over thought. Lively mind.

Sometimes: *bodily agitation.*
Psychology: *primary narcissism, fear of separation.*

Janine Caradec (study for the GGCF): "Thinking comes through images, parallels, and associations; confusions and mixings that can germinate a new theory" (e.g. Freud, Picasso).

The Morettian term is *confused* (It. *confusa*), which has another meaning (see p.426). For Palaferri, it represents the graphic projection of the person through undifferentiated processes which entwine the emotional, spiritual, and rational spheres.

THICK (*Pressure*: Fig. 13c)
The stroke reaches 3 or 4 mm in thickness, even in a writing only 2 mm high.
Congestion, laziness, awkward spirit, materialism, sensuality.
With signs of weariness: *sluggish temperament.*
In inharmonious context: *sensuality, dubious morality.*

THIN (*Pressure*: Fig. 23b)
Dry stroke, mainly with a precise, narrow writing. This sign always has a negative connotation.
Reason predominates over feeling, meanness, logical more than imaginative.
With angles: *harshness, discontent.*
With inclined and rigid writing: *fanaticism.*

THROWN (*Direction*: Figs 37a, 38c–d, 119b)
Some strokes are prolonged upward with a thrown movement that lightens the pressure. Some letters are especially involved in their final part: *d, r, v.* If this is found often in a sober and calm writing, it is all the more revealing.
Mental activity, imagination.
Spiritual and contemplative nature.
High idealism.

TORMENTED (*Form*: Figs 41b, 114)
A disturbed movement pervades the writing: unevenness in size and direction, retouching, sudden stops and suspensions. They cause complications within letters, twists of stroke, covered strokes, regressive returns, often of small size.
Complex mind and character.
Tension and anxiety, internal conflicts.

Gille-Maisani: "Tormented writing comes from a complex personality, in which internal oppositions cause high anxiety. They are unhappy people, sometimes psychasthenic or masochistic. They often have poor social relations as a result of their internal confusion. But sometimes, after great struggle, this personality can gain a creative balance which is enriched by the internal oppositions."

TRENCHANT (*Pressure*: Fig. 12b)
The stroke is hard and incisive, the opposite of light, nuanced, pasty, and velvety.
Imperious will, ability to get things done, zealous social climbing.

Gille-Maisani: "Strong personality, with peremptory gestures and cutting tone of voice, who decides without fear, with no regard for those around, in an absolutist way."

TRIPLE WIDTH (*Layout* and *Dimension*: Figs 11b–c, 15a, 22a, 44)
A balance between the three widths (letter, between letters, and between words) means that each is proportionate to the others.
Balanced character and behaviour.
Firm intelligence.

Cristofanelli: "Non-homogeneity in the widths occurs when individual widths are not constant at their respective level, and shows lack of balance and stability, alternation of closed and open attitude, introversion and extroversion of feeling, instability."

Lena: "We find a correlation between balance in triple width and good academic results … *Homogeneity in triple width* clearly shows in creative subjects."

Wide letters
Lower-case letters, particularly those containing ovals, are wider than they are high, but without excessive broadening.
Mental and emotional understanding, broad conscience.

Wide letter spacing
Distance between letters is about the width of an average *o* or *a* of the writing in question.
Open, generous, extrovert, enthusiastic, prodigal.

Wide space between words
Distance between words is about the width of four *o*'s of the writing in question.
Rational and critical faculty.

TWISTED (*Direction*: Fig. 90)
The vertical axis appears wavy or twisted. It presages the hormonal changes in preadolescence and adolescence, as well as the menopause. If it otherwise occurs in an adult writing, it indicates a pathological state: nervous, psychological, or circulatory disturbances.
Emotional, afraid.
Tired, anxious, overburdened.

TWISTED (Moretti) (*Slant*: Fig 96a)
The axis of the letters "bends brusquely towards right or left and the extensions meet in a band very near the middle zone of the writing or immediately inside it" (Cristofanelli [68]).
Need for control, verification, and objectivity.
Aptitude for the mechanical.
Tension, irritability.

TYPOGRAPHIC (*Layout* and *Form*: Fig. 45)
Involves two different categories. One should assess the levels of motor agility, of original or constricted combinations, rigidity, or even extravagance.
Layout: margins reflect the layout of a typical printed page, with equal and regular spaces to right and left.
Form: form is close to the typographic model in capitals and lower-case letters.
Search for clarity, precision, and method.
Defence, fear, difficulty in acting with spontaneity.
Concealment, artifice.

UNCONNECTED OR JUXTAPOSED (*Continuity*: Figs 12c, 37a)
Absence of letter connection. See whether there is any dynamic movement that may give a virtual connection between the letters, or whether the letters are placed side by side in a static way.
From individualism to egoism.
From analysis and intuition to inhibition and moral isolation.
With low Formlevel and light pressure: *poor adaptability, defensive egoism. Lack of logic, broken thought. Emptiness.*
With low Formlevel and strong pressure: *tension, obsessive thoughts. Marked selectivity. Ambivalence.*

UNDULATING (*Form*: Figs 18, 36a, 34b, 53, 122a)
Between garland and filiform. The writing is a cadenced and flexible festoon which derives from the garland form.
Ability to outflank obstacles.
Intellect, culture.
With graceful appearance: *artistic sense.*
With marked difference in height between the middle zone and the outer zones: *ardour, ambition, initiative, idealism.* Or: *nervous tension, anxiety, dissatisfaction, sense of resentment or guilt* (often with inferiority complex).
In a soft, imprecise context: *overadaptment, weak Ego.*

UNORGANIZED (*Continuity*: Fig. 87b)
Refers to childish or illiterate writings which have not reached the level of graphic organization and motor flexibility. The graphometric studies of Ajuriaguerra on children's writing have led to another view of childish writing (see Chapter Ten).

VELVETY (*Pressure*: Figs 47, 111a)
Sign introduced by Ania Teillard. The stroke is slightly pasty but not heavy and with little relief. It goes with a smooth stroke, connected to grouped letters, rounded, garlanded, or wavy. It is the opposite of precise stroke, in relief, spasmodic or trenchant, angular, rigid. Different from unfocused and pasty writing, which is less attractive and with a poorer quality of stroke.
Spontaneity and affective sensibility.
Sociable, desire for participation, seduction.

VERTICAL (*Slant*: Fig. 96a–c, e)
The letter axis forms a right angle with the base line.
Self-control, emotional stability, rationality.
Independence, individualism.
With firm pressure: *will, energy.*
With spaced writing: *conscious isolation.*

VERY SLANTED TO THE RIGHT (*Slant*: Fig. 23c)
The slope of the letters forms an angle of less than 45° with the base line, in other words a very inclined writing.
Passion, impulse, fanaticism.
In a lifeless context: *suggestible, depression.*

WAVY or **FLEXIBLE** (Moretti) (*Slant*: Figs 14, 37a)
Observe the meeting point of the axes of the letters. Cristofanelli [68]: "The level is that much higher the more the projections of the letter axes meet further away from the zone of text." In other words a higher value is given to a more gently waving writing.
Psychological intuition, penetration, empathy.

WAVY LINES (Crépieux-Jamin) (*Direction*: Fig. 22c)
The base line proceeds in an alternate concave and convex wavy movement, in variously pronounced degrees.
Flexibility in conduct and convictions.
Variable temper, emotional.
Diplomacy, opportunism.

Manual of Graphology [200]: "Some slightly wavy lines are signs of adaptability."

WEAK (*Pressure*: Figs 10, 89b)
Development of a slow and curved outline, monotonous or pasty, without vigour.
Weak character, inactive, patient but passive.
Letting go, careless, sulky, obstinate.
With angles at the base of the *t*: *spirit of contradiction.*

WELL-NOURISHED (*Pressure*: Figs 7d, 31e, 116)
Well-fed, well-inked stroke, between light and pasty.
Good vital balance, will, energy.
Activity, sense of reality.
With dynamic rhythm: *ardent, enterprising, fearless.*
Found in Jungian types Sensation and Feeling.

WIDE (*Dimension*: Figs 7b, 8a: see also Secondary connection, Triple width)
Two linked graphic aspects, which accentuate expansion to the right, produce wide writing.
1. The base of the letter is *wide*: its body is wider than it is high (*primary width*).
2. The connection between letters is wide, so the words are wide (*secondary width*).
Spontaneity, sociability, enterprise, imprudence.

APPENDIX III

Bibliography

[1]   AGI, 'Codice deontologico dei grafologi', *Attualità grafologica* 43 (Associazione grafologica italiana) XI/2, April–June 1992.

[2]   AGNELLINI, M. (ed.), *Firma d'Artista, 2600 firme di pittori e scultori dell'ottocento italiano*, Le Guide della Fenice, Fenice 2000, Milan, 1995.

[3]   AJURIAGUERRA, J. de, *Manuel de psychiatrie de l'enfant*, Masson, Paris, 1971.

[4]   ——, AUZIAS, M., and DENNER, A., *L'Écriture de l'enfant*. I. *L'Évolution de l'écriture et ses difficultés*. II. *La Rééducation de l'écriture*, Delachaux and Niestlé, Neuchâtel–Paris, 1971.

[5]   —— and MARCELLI, D., *Psicopatologia del bambino*, Masson, 1984.

[6]   AMMANITI, M., ANTONUCCI, F., and JACCARINO, B., *Appunti di psicopatologia*, Bulzoni, Rome, 1975.

[7]   ANZIEU, D., *Le Corps de l'œuvre*, NRF, Gallimard, 1981.

[8]   ——, *Le Moi-Peau*, Dunod, Bordas, Paris, 1985.

[9]   AURIGEMMA, L., *Prospettive junghiane*, Boringhieri, Turin, 1989.

[10] AUZIAS, M., *Les Troubles de l'écriture chez l'enfant*, Delachaux and Niestlé, Neuchâtel–Paris, 1970, 1981.

[11] ——, *Enfants gauchers, enfants droitiers*, Delachaux.

[12] AVÉ-LALLEMANT, U., *Graphologie des Jugendlichen*. I. *Langschmitt Analyse*, E. Reinhardt, Munich–Basel, 1970.

[13] ——, *Comment interpréter l'écriture de vos élèves*, Bordas, Paris, 1987.

[14] BACHELARD, G., *L'Intuition de l'instant*, Éditions Gonthier, Paris, 1972.

[15] ——, *La Poétique de l'espace*, PUF, Paris, 1972.

[16] BARTHES, R., *L'Empire des signes*, Flammarion, Paris, 1970.

[17] BASTIN, C. and CASTILLA, D. de, *Graphologie, le psychisme et ses troubles*, Robert Laffont, Paris, 1990.

[18] BEAUCHÂTAUD, G., *Learn Graphology*, Scriptor Books, London, 1988.

[19] BEAUCHESNE, H. and GIBELLO, B., *Traité de psychologie infantile*, PUF, Paris, 1991.

[20] BELIN, C., 'Graphologie et médecine', in [91].

[21] —— and AUBERT, M.-F., 'La Personnalité des violeurs au travers d'expertises et d'examens graphologiques', *La Graphologie* 189, 1988.

[22]   BERGER, R., *Manuel d'écriture courante et ornementale*, Payot & Cie, Lausanne, 1937.

[23]   BERGERET, J., *La Personnalité normale et pathologique*, Dunod, Paris, 1974.

[24]   —— et al., *Psicologia patologica*, 3rd edn, Masson Italia, 1988.

[25]   ——, *La Dépression et les états limités*, Payot, Paris, 1984.

[26]   ——, in *Adolescenza terminata, adolescenza interminabile*, Borla, Rome, 1987.

[27]   BERNSON, B., *Présence de Bernard Bernson, par ses élèves*, EMU, Paris.

[28]   BERNSON, M., *Dallo scarabocchio al disegno*, Armando Editore, 1968.

[29]   BESSON, J. and NOBLENS, M. DE, 'Test de l'arbre et écriture', *La Graphologie* 189, 1988.

[30]   BIDOLI, S., *La psicologia della scrittura*, Longanesi, Milan, 1979.

[31]   BINET, A., *Les Révélations de l'écriture d'après un contrôle scientifique*, Alcan, Paris, 1906.

[31a] BLANQUEFORT D'ANGLARDS, M., *Motivations et compensations*, Masson, Paris 1994.

[32]   BOILLE, N., *Les Écritures italiennes*, GGCF, 1987.

[33]   ——, 'La Méthode graphométrique d'Ajuriaguerra appliquée aux écritures italiennes: résultats statistiques et nouvelles perspectives', *La Graphologie* 197, 1990.

[34]   ——, 'Il problema dell'identità dell'adolescente e il suo inserimento scolastico', *Scrittura* 80, 1991.

[34a] ——, 'Stile cognitivo e comportamentale e patologie della personalità in disgrafici', paper given at the 3rd Congress of Studies, International Centre of Medical Graphology, Rome, 1992.

[35]   ——, LONGO, M. A., MAZZOLI G., and POMA, C., 'Immaturité et compensation dans le recrutement professionnel des jeunes en Italie', *La Graphologie* 213, 1994.

[36]   ——, 'Handicap psichico: possibilità di espressione grafica e intervento pedagogico', *Grafologia medica* 1, 1992; and 'Visione storica degli studi grafologici sulla schizofrenia', *Grafologia medica* 3, 1996.

[37]   ——, *Oltre il bianco. Panorama sulla grafologia*, Edizioni Sestante, Ripatransone, 1998.

[38]   BOSE, C. DE, 'Le Rythme dans la méthode du professeur Heiss', *La Graphologie* 107, 1967.

[39]   ——, 'Méthode graphologique de Müller–Enskat', *La Graphologie* 152–4, 1978–9.

[40]   ——, *La Graphologie allemande, ses tendances, ses lignes de force*, Masson, Paris, 1992.

[41]   BOUREILLE, C., 'L'Introversion et l'extroversion dans l'écriture', *La Graphologie* 153, 1979.

[42]   ——, 'Application graphologique de la théorie jungienne de l'introversion et de l'extraversion', *La Graphologie* 162, 1982.

[43]   BRABANT, G. P., *L'Écriture considérée comme un secteur du comportement*, L'Évolution graphologique, Paris, 1960.

[44]   BRACONNIER/MARCELLI, *I mille volti dell'adolescenza*, Borla, Rome, 1988.

[45]   BRAVO, A. and TARANTINO, V., *Il tremore in scrittura*, Istituto grafologico giudiziario, 1986.

[46]   BRESARD, S., *La Graphologie, méthode d'exploration graphologique*, Scarabée & Cie, Paris, 1984.

[48]   ——, *La Graphologie*, Masson, Paris, 1990.

[47]   —— and WILLI, M., 'Recherche pour un lexique de graphologie illustré', *La Graphologie* 167–8, 1982; 170–1, 1983; 178–9, 1985; 184, 1986; 188, 1987; 191–2, 1988; 203, 1991.

[49]   BUQUET, A., *L'Expertise des écritures*, CNRS, Paris, 1990.

[50]   ——, *L'Expertise des écritures manuscrites*, Masson, Paris, 1991.

[51]   CALLEWAERT, H., *Graphologie et physiologie de l'écriture*, Louvain, Paris, 1962.

[52]   CAROTENUTO, A., *Trattato di psicologia della personalità e delle differenze individuali*, Cortina, Milan, 1991.

[53]   CARTON, P., *Diagnostic et conduite des tempéraments*, Le François, Paris, 1972.

[54]   ——, *Le Diagnostic de la mentalité par l'écriture*, Le François, Paris, 1973.

[55]   CASELLI, R., 'La scrittura invadente', *Il gesto creativo* (Arigraf), 1996.

[56]   CASTILLA, D. DE, *Le Test de l'arbre, relations humaines et problèmes actuels*, Masson, Paris, 1995.

[57]   CHARDON, C. and GILBERT, P., 'Écriture et personnalité des cadres', *La Graphologie* 177, 1985.

[58]   COBBAERT, A.-M., *La Graphologie, connaître et interpréter les écritures*, Ariston, Geneva, 1973.

[59]   COBLENCE, C., articles on Michon, *La Graphologie* 165–7, 1982.

[60]   COLO, C., *Types psychologiques de Jung et applications graphologiques*, Masson, Paris, 1993.

[61]   ——, GOURSAC, R. DE, LIEVRE, F., and PINON, J., *L'Agressivité dans l'écriture et le comportement*, GGCF, Paris, 1991.

[62] CONFICONI, I., *I tratti della personalità*, Libreria G. Moretti, Urbino, 1996.

[63] CORMAN, L., *Le Test du gribouillis*, PUF, Paris, 1966.

[64] COSSEL, B. VON, 'Le Théâtre de la drogue', *La Graphologie* 128, 1972.

[65] CRÉPIEUX-JAMIN, J., *ABC de la graphologie*, [1929], 8th edn, PUF, Paris, 1983.

[66] ——, *Il carattere dalla scrittura*, Quattro Venti, Urbino, 1985; trans. of *L'Écriture et le caractère*, 1888.

[67] CRISTOFANELLI, P., 'Autoritratto grafologico di Girolamo Moretti', *Scrittura* 4, 1986.

[68] ——, *Grafologia. Dalla scrittura alla personalità*, Calderini, Bologna, 1989.

[69] ——, *Segni del vissuto*, Libreria G. Moretti, Urbino, 1995.

[70] CROTI, E., *Test di scrittura*, Librex, Milan, 1985.

[71] [= 38]

[72] [= 40]

[73] DEGUY, M., 'L'Écriture des écrivains', *La Graphologie* 179, 1985.

[74] DELACHAUX, S., *Écritures des enfants, tempéraments, problèmes affectifs. Le caractère des enfants révélé par leur écriture*, Delachaux and Niestlé, Neuchâtel, 1960.

[75] DELAMAIN, M., 'Typologie et graphologie', *La Graphologie* 137, 1975.

[76] DESPRAS, F., 'Commento su scritture: dopo la conferenza del Dr. V. Mirabel: "La dépression, maladie de la fin du XXe siècle" ', *La Graphologie* 227, 1997.

[77] DEL TORRE, O., *Grafologia moderna. Trattato di perizia grafica*, Ed. Mediterranee, Rome, 1962.

[78] DSM IV, *Manuale diagnostico e statistico dei disturbi mentali*, Masson, Milan–Paris–Barcelona, 1996.

[79] DESURVIRE, M., *Étude de la personnalité, les théories*, Masson, Paris, 1992.

[80] ——, *Graphologie et recrutement*, Masson, Paris, 1992.

[81] ——, *Le Trait*, GGCF, Paris

[82] DUBOUCHET, J., *L'Analogie des phénomènes physiques et psychiques et l'écriture*, Parthénon, Brussels, 1961.

[83] ——, *L'Écriture des adolescents. Etude psycho-pédagogique*, Le François, Paris, 1967.

[84] ——, 'Graphologie par le trait de Walter Hegar', *La Graphologie* 142, 1976.

[85] DUGUEYT, C. and MONNOT, J., 'Dynamique et symbolique de la signature', *La Graphologie* 197, 1990.

[86]   DUPUIS, C., 'Différentes formes d'insincerité et leur traduction dans l'écriture', *La Graphologie* 213, 1994.

[87]   DURUY, F., 'Étude sur la répartition du noir et du blanc dans l'espace graphique à travers quelques mécanismes de défense du moi', *La Graphologie* 153, 1979.

[88]   ELEFTERIOU, F., 'L'Incidence du chômage sur l'écriture', *La Graphologie* 187, 1987.

[89]   ELLENBERGER, *La scoperta dell'inconscio*, Boringhieri, Turin, 1972.

[90]   ELLISON, O., *Les Écritures anglo-saxonnes*, extract of monograph, GGCF, Paris, 1985.

[91]   FAIDEAU, P., *La Graphologie. Histoire, pratique, perspectives*, M.A. Éditions, 1983.

[92]   —— and DUGUEYT, C., *La Pression déplacée*, GGCF, Paris

[93]   FRAISSE, P. and PIAGET, J., *Traité de psychologie expérimentale*, PUF, Paris

[94]   FRANZ, M.-L. VON, *Tipologia psicologica*, Red Edizioni, 1988.

[95]   FREEMAN, L., *La storia di Anna O.*, Feltrenelli.

[96]   FREUD, A., *Le Moi et les mécanismes de défense*, PUF, Paris, 1949.

[97]   FREUD, S., Complete works.

[98]   ——, *Delirio e sogno nella gradiva*, Newton Compton Ed

[99]   GAFFURI, G., *Il reattivo dell'albero nella diagnosi di schizofrenia*, Edizioni Omnia Medica, Pisa, 1970.

[100]   GENTY, M., *L'Être et l'écriture dans la psychologie junghienne*, Masson, Paris, 1991.

[101]   GIACOMETTI, F., PALAFERRI, N., and GALEAZZI, G., *Che cos'è la grafologia*, 3rd edn, Sansoni, 1990.

[102]   ——, 'Problemi scientifici della grafologia dell'età evolutiva', *Quaderni di scrittura 3*

[103]   GILBERT-DREYFUS, J., 'Considérations d'ordre général et psychologique sur l'obésité', *La Graphologie* 146, 1977.

[104]   [= 57]

[105]   GILLE-MAISANI, J.-C., *Psicologia della scrittura*, Liguori, 1990; trans. of *Psychologie de l'écriture*, 1st edn, Payot, 1969. English Edition *Psychology of Handwritnig* Scriptor books 1992

[106]   ——, *Écritures de poètes de Byron à Baudelaire*, Dervy livres, Paris, 1977.
          ___,*Poets Handwritings* Scriptor Books, London, 1995

[107]   ——, *Types de Jung et tempéraments psychobiologiques*, Maloine, Paris/ Edisem, Quebec, 1978.

[108]   ——, *Poésie, musique et graphologie*, Dervy livres, Paris, 1988.

[109]   ——, *Temperamenti psicobiologici e gruppi sanguigni. Espressione grafologica e artistica*, Teda Edizioni, Castrovillari, 1992.

[110]   GOBINEAU, H. DE and PERRON, R., *Génétique de l'écriture et étude de la personnalité. Essais de graphométrie*, Delachaux and Niestlé, 1954.

[111]   GUAITOLI, A. R., *Per un ascolto attivo del disagio emozionale nelle grafie degli adolescenti*, Tesi e Quaderno di Ricerca Arigraf, 1996.

[112]   HEGAR, W., *Graphologie par le trait. Introduction à l'analyse des éléments de l'écriture*, Vigot, Paris, 1938.

[113]   HEISS, R., *Die Deutung der Handschrift*, Claassen, Hamburg, 1976.

[114]   HERTZ, H., *La Graphologie*, PUF, Paris, 1947, 1975.

[115]   HILLMANN, J., *Fathers and Mothers*, Spring Publications, 1973; trans. *Pères et mères*, Imago, Paris, 1978.

[116]   IACCARINO, B., 'Origini culturali del simbolismo in Freud e Jung', *Rivista di psicologia analitica* 2/II, October 1971.

[117]   JUNG, C. G., *Tipi psicologici*, Opere complete, ed. L. Aurigemma, vol. 6, Boringhieri, Turin, 1969.

[118]   KERGALL, N. and PINON, J., *L'Effet filiforme ou réflexions à propos de la filiformité*, GGCF, Paris, 1982.

[119]   KLAGES, L., *L'anima e lo spirito*, Bompiani, Milan, 1940.

[120]   ——, *Handschrift und Charakter*, Barth, Leipzig, 1917.

[121]   ——, *Valore e limiti della grafopsicologia*, Mursia, Milan, 1964.

[122]   ——, *Perizie grafologiche su casi illustri*, Adelphi, Milan, 1994.

[123]   KLEIN, M., *Invidia e gratitudine*, Giunti-Barbera, Florence

[124]   ——, *La psicoanalisi dei bambini*, Martinelli, Florence, 1970.

[125]   LAGACHE, D., *La Psychanalyse*, PUF, Paris, 1956.

[126]   LALANDE, A., *Dizionario critico di filosofia*, Istituto editoriale internazionale, 1975.

[127]   LAMI, C. and MAUBLANC, H. DE, 'Construction et juxtaposition de tendance statique', *La Graphologie* 169, 1983.

[128]   LAPLANCHE, J. and PONTALIS, J.-B., *Enciclopedia della psicanalisi*, Universale Laterza, 1974.

[129]   LAUBIE, M., 'Etude graphologique de la communication dans un groupe de jeunes malades atteints de psychose dissociative chronique', *La Graphologie* 169, 1983.

[130]   LAUFER, M., *Adolescenza e breakdown evolutivo*, Bollati Boringhieri, Turin, 1986.

[131]   LEBOVICI, S., DIATKINE, R., and SOULE, M., *Traité de psychiatrie de l'enfant et de l'adolescent*, PUF, Paris, 1985.

[132]   LECERF, A., *Cours supérieur de graphologie*, Dangles, Paris, 1947.

[133]   LEFEBURE, F., 'Graphologie et médecine', in [91].

[134]   —— and VAN DEN BROEK D'OBRENAN, C., *Le Trait en graphologie, indice constitutionnel*, Masson, Paris, 1986.

[135]   —— and GILLE-MAISANI, J.-C., *Graphologie et test de Szondi. I. Le Moi. II. Dynamique des pulsions*, Masson, Paris, 1990.

[136]   ——, *Test du paysage d'André Arthus*, Masson, Paris, 1992.

[137]   ——, *Le Dessin de l'enfant: le langage sans parole*, Masson, Paris, 1993.

[138]   LEIBL, M., *Grafologia psicologica*, Cisalpina-Goliardica, Milan, 1976.

[139]   LENA, S., 'I segni discendenti e aste rette durante l'età evolutiva', *Scrittura* 13, 1975.

[140]   ——, *Creatività e scrittura*, Istituto grafologico G. Moretti, Urbino, 1985.

[141]   ——, 'Creatività e scrittura. Una ricerca sperimentale nel secondo ciclo delle scuole elementari', *Scrittura* 57, 1986.

[142]   ——, *Grafologia dell'età evolutiva e della consulenza scolastica*, Istituto grafologico G. Moretti, Urbino, 1987.

[143]   ——, 'Che cosa rivela la scrittura? Appunti per una epistemologia della grafologia', *Scrittura* 95, 1995.

[144]   ——, 'Storia di un'educazione mancata', *Scrittura* 96, 1995.

[145]   LEROY-GOURHAN, *Le Geste et la parole*, Albin Michel, Paris, 1964.

[146]   LEWINSON, T. S. and ZUBIN, J., *Handwriting Analysis*, King's Crown Press, New York, 1942.

[147]   LIEVRE, F., 'Signature et mise en œuvre du potential', *La Graphologie* 177, 1985.

[148]   LINGIARDI, V. and MADEDDU, F., *I meccanismi di difesa*, Raffaello Cortina, Milan, 1994.

[149]   LOMBARD, A., *Écritures d'enfants*, GGCF, Paris.

[150]   ——, 'L'Écritures des adolescents', *La Graphologie* 157, 1980.

[151]   ——, 'L'Écritures des adolescents', *La Graphologie* 164–5, 1981–2.

[152]   ——, 'Recherche sur la vitesse', *La Graphologie* 195, 1989.

[153]   ——, 'La maladie de Parkinson; étude graphologique de 30 cas', *La Graphologie* 211, 1993.

[154]   [= 200]

[155]   LONGO, M. A., *Manuale pratico di grafologia*, Hermes, Rome, 1995.

[156]   LURÇAT, L., *Étude de l'acte graphique*, Mouton, Paris, 1974.

[157]   Lurija, A. R., *Neuropsicologia del linguaggio grafico*, Messaggero, Padua, 1984.

[158]   MAERO, M., *Il test della scrittura*, Associazione italiana grafoanalisi per l'età evolutiva, Turin, 1980.

[159]   MAGNAT, G.-E., *Poésie de l'écriture*, Sack, Geneva, 1944.

[160]   MANETTI, E., 'Sconforto e sfida creativa nell'orientamento dei giovani', *Il gesto creativo* (Arigraf), 1995.

[161a]   ——, 'La schizofrenia: sofferenza e psicosi', *Grafologia medica* 3, 1996.

[161b]   MARCHESAN, R., *Introduzione alla psicologia della scrittura*, Istituto di indagini psicologiche, Milan, 1955.

[162a]   MARCHESAN, M., *Psicologia della scrittura. Segni e tendenze*, Istituto di indagini psicologiche, Milan, 1984.

[162b]   MATHIEU, H., 'Balance et clé de voûte; des revers de Steinizer à l'agapé de Roda Wieser', *La Graphologie* 145, 1977.

[163]   ——, *Le Graphologue, son art et son client. Raisons, hérésies de la graphologie*, Masson, Paris, 1993.

[164]   [= 127]

[165]   MAUBLANC, H. DE, *L'Écriture par la méthode Saint-Morand*, Masson, Paris, 1990.

[166]   —— and FEST, C., *Graphologie planétaire et tests. Orientation, psychopathologie*, Masson, Paris, 1990.

[167]   MELE, A., 'La grafologia in campo psicopatologico: la depressione', *Grafologia e sue applicazioni*, Oct.–Dec. 1996.

[168]   MENDELSSOHN, ANJA [A. Teillard] and MENDELSSOHN, G., *Der Mensch in der Handschrift*, Seeman, Leipzig, 1929.

[169]   MICHON, J.-H., *Système de graphologie. L'Art de connaître les hommes d'après leur écriture*, Lecuir, 1875, repr. Payot, 1970.

[170]   MONCEAU, C., 'Réflexions autour d'une possibilité de rapprochement entre les interprétations de l'œuvre d'art et l'écriture', *La Graphologie* 194, 1989.

[171]   MONNOT, J., 'La Signature abstraite', *La Graphologie* 150, 1978.

[172]   ——, 'Les Marges du haut et du bas', *La Graphologie* 186, 1987.

[173]   ——, 'Dynamique et symbolique de la signature', *La Graphologie* 197, 1990.

[174]   MORETTI, G., 'La filigrana dello spirito. Ludwig Klages e la sua grafologia vitalistica', in [122].

[175]   ——, *Il corpo umano dalla scrittura. Grafologia somatica*, Studio grafologico 'Fra Girolamo', Ancona, 1961.

[176]   ——, *Trattato di grafologia*, 13th edn, Messaggero, Padua, 1985.

[177] MUEL, A., 'Méthode statistique d'analyse graphique appliquée à un groupe de garçons inadaptés: les lignes descendantes', *La Graphologie* 126, 1972.

[178] MÜLLER, W. H. and ENSKAT, A., *Graphologische Diagnostik. Ihre Grundlagen, Möglichkeiten und Grenzen*, 2nd edn, Huber, Berne, 1973.

[179] MUSSCHOTT, F. and DEMEYER, W., *Le Test du dessin de l'arbre*, Editest, Brussels.

[180] NEZOS, R., 'Les Ecritures anglaises', *La Graphologie* 199, 1990.

[181] ——, *Graphology*, 3rd edn, Scriptor Books, London, 1992.

[182] [= 200]

[183] OBRECHT, M., *Les Écritures allemandes*, GGCF, Paris, 1990.

[184] OLIVAUX, R., *Pédagogie de l'écriture et graphothérapie*, Masson, Paris, 1988.

[185] ——, *L'Analyse graphologique*, Masson, Paris, 1990.

[186] ——, *Disgrafie e rieducazione della scrittura*, AGI, Ancona, 1993.

[187] OLIVERIO-FERRARIS, A., *Il significato del disegno infantile*, Boringhieri, Turin, 1978.

[188] PALAFERRI, N., *Quantificazione grafologica morettiana*, Istituto grafologico G. Moretti, Urbino, 1976.

[189] ——, *Gli altri segni morettiani*, Istituto grafologico G. Moretti, Urbino, 1979.

[190] ——, *Grafologia comparata*, Istituto grafologico G. Moretti, Urbino, 1980.

[191] ——, *Dizionario grafologico*, Istituto grafologico G. Moretti, Urbino, 1983.

[192] PELLAT, S., *Les Lois de l'écriture*, Vuibert, Paris, 1927.

[193] PÉRIOT, M. and BROSSON, PAUL, *Morpho-physiologie de l'écriture. Méthode rationelle de graphologie basée sur la physiologie du geste graphique et la physiologie du tempérament*, Vuibert, Payot, Paris, 1957.

[194] PERRELLA, R., 'La psicologia nelle perizie grafiche', *Scrittura* 13, 1975.

[195] ——, 'La perizia grafica nella giurisprudenza', *Scrittura* 22, 1977.

[196] ——, 'La capacità di intendere e volere dell'autore di un testamento olografo in grafopatologia', *Scrittura* 49, 1984.

[197] PEUGEOT, J., 'La Dyslexie et l'écriture des enfants dyslexiques', *La Graphologie* 105, 1967.

[198] ——, 'Possibilités et limites de l'approche graphologique des enfants', *La Graphologie* 157, 1980.

480 APPENDIX III

[199] ——, *La conoscenza del bambino attraverso la scrittura*, La Scuola, Brescia, 1985.

[200] ——, Lombard, A., and Noblens, M. de, *Manual of Graphology*, Scriptor Books, London, 1997; trans. of *Manuel de graphologie*, Masson, Paris, 1986.

[201] ——, 'Alcuni aspetti clinici dell'handicap grafomotorio psicogeno nell'età evolutiva', *Grafologia medica* 1, 1992.

[202] [= 118]

[203] PLOOG, H., 'L'Écriture en Allemagne', *La Graphologie* 199, 1990.

[204] POMA, C., 'Tre esempi di applicazione della grafologia come strumento per la selezione del personale', *Il gesto creativo* (Arigraf), January 1992.

[205] POPHAL, R., *Zur Psychophysiologie der Spannungserscheinungen in der Handschrift*, Greienverlag, Rüdelstadt, 1949.

[206] PRENAT, M. T., *Graphométrie. Approche de la personnalité profonde*, Masson, Paris, 1992.

[207] PULVER, M., *The Symbolism of Handwriting*, Scriptor Books, London, 1994; trans. of *Symbolik der Handschrift*, Orell Verlag, Zurich, 1931.

[208] QUATTROCCHI, G., 'Paolo Colombetti "grafologista" torinese', *Scrittura* 96, 1995.

[209] RACAMIER, P.-C., *Les Schizophrènes*, Payot, Paris, 1980.

[210] RATZON, H., 'Sur la graphologie de l'écriture hébraïque', *La Graphologie* 176, 1984.

[211] REITANO, M. S., 'Disturbo mentale e prestazione grafomotoria', *Grafologia medica* 3, 1996.

[212] RETHORE, J., 'Présentation de six écritures de trisomiques', *La Graphologie* 182, 1986.

[213] RILEY, M., 'Du diagnostic graphologique sur un type d'écriture à facture contemporaine', *La Graphologie* 195, 1989.

[214] ROSSI LECERF, J., *Grafologia, scrittura e personalità*, Seda, Milan, 1979.

[215] ROTTENBERG, H., 'Les Problèmes d'une relation père-fils à travers une correspondance entre Léopold et Wolfgang Amadeus Mozart', *La Graphologie* 204, 1991.

[216] RUZZA, S., *Storia della grafologia*, Istituto grafologico G. Moretti, Urbino, 1978.

[217] SAINT-MORAND, H. DE, *Cours de graphologie. Les bases de l'analyse de l'écriture*, Vigot Frères, Paris, 1937.

[218] SAUDEK, R., *The Psychology of Handwriting*, Books for Professionals, 1978.

[219]   SEGAL, H., *Introduzione all'opera di Melanie Klein*, Martinelli, Florence, 1971.

[220]   SEILER, J., *De Lavater à Michon*, vol. I, Éditions Universitaires, Fribourg, 1995.

[221]   SIMETI, F., 'Sindromi neuropatologiche infantili e quadri grafici', *Scrittura* 46, 1983.

[222]   SIMON, A. M., LASCARD, S., and ASSELOT, H., 'Moirages et mirages, observation du trait dans l;ecriture de quelques somatisants ulcéreux', *La Graphologie* 218, 1995.

[223]   Société française de graphologie (summary of A. LOMBARD), 'Recherche européenne sur la communication des adolescents en classe de terminale', *La Graphologie* 157/9, 1980.

[224]   STORA, R., *Le Test du dessin de l'arbre*, J. P. Delarge, Paris, 1975.

[225]   TAJAN, A. and DELAGE, D., *L'Analyse des écritures. Techniques et utilisations*, Seuil, Paris, 1972.

[226]   TARANTINO, V., 'Memoria e motricità grafica', *Grafologia medica* 1, 1992.

[227]   TEILLARD, A., *L'Anima et la scrittura*, Boringhieri, Torino, 1980. Ed. orginale: *Der Mensch in der Handschrift,* Seemann, Lipsia 1929.

[228]   ——, 'Portrait graphologique [Paul Klee]', in W. Grohmann, *Paul Klee*, Flinker, Paris, 1954, p. 444.

[229]   TISSERON, S., 'Le Dessin du dessin', in *Art et fantasme*, Champ Vallon, Paris, 1983.

[230]   TORBIDONI, L. and ZANIN, L., *Grafologia. Testo teorico-pratico*, La Scuola, Brescia, 1986.

[231]   TORBIDONI, L. (ed.), *L'equilibrio psichico dalla scrittura*, Bulzoni, Rome, 1978.

[232]   TRILLAT, R., *Graphologie pratique*, Vigot, Paris, 1953.

[233]   TRIPIER, G., 'L'Attitude actuelle face au malade alcoolique', *La Graphologie* 161, 1981.

[234]   URBANI, P., *Interpreta la scrittura, scopri con la grafologia te stesso e gli altri con test ed esercizi*, Le Comete, 1996.

[235]   VELS, A., *Escritura y personalidad. Las bases cientificas de la grafologia*, Herder, Barcelona, 1982.

[236]   ——, *Diccionario di grafologia*, Herder, Barcelona, 1983.

[237]   VENTURINI, O., 'Studio grafologico su scritture di soggetti anziani', *Scrittura* 36, 1980.

[238]   ——, 'I segni grafici della capacità di intendere e di volere', *Rassegna di studi grafologici* (Istituto italiano di grafologia di Trieste) V/1, 1986.

[239]   VERBIST, A., 'Expertise graphométrique des déviances influant sur le comportement professionnel', *La Graphologie* 196, 1989.

[240]   VETTORAZZO, B., *Grafologia giudiziaria e perizia grafica*, Giuffrè Editore, 1987.

[241]   VICTOR, F., *L'Écriture projection de la personnalité*, Payot, Paris, 1956.

[242]   VILLARD, C., 'Graphologie et médecine', in [91].

[243]   ——, 'A propos des écritures primaires', *La Graphologie* 139, 1975.

[244]   ——, 'Névroses, psychoses, mécanismes de défense et intégration du moi', *La Graphologie* 145, 1977.

[245]   VILLETTES, V. DES, 'L'Écriture des bègues', *La Graphologie* 188, 1987.

[246]   VINH BANG, *Évolution de l'écriture de l'enfant à l'adulte*, Delachaux and Niestlé, Neuchâtel–Paris, 1959.

[247]   VOLMAT, R., 'Dépression masquée et équivalents dépressifs dans l'écriture', *La Graphologie* 196, 1989.

[248]   VYGOTSKI, L. S., *Lo sviluppo psichico del bambino*, Payot, Editori Riuniti, 1975.

[249]   WIDLÖCHER, D., *L'Interprétation des dessins d'enfants*, Dessart and Mardaga, Brussels, 1975.

[250]   WIESER, R., *Der Verbrecher und seine Handschrift*, Altdorfer Verlag, Stuttgart, 1952.

[251]   ——, 'Raidissement et rythme de base', *La Graphologie* 102, 1966.

[252]   WILLI, M., *L'Énergie dans les écritures artificielles*, GGCF, Paris, 1986.

[253]   WINNICOTT, D. W., *Sviluppo affectivo e ambiente*, Armando Editore, 1986.

[254]   ——, *Gioco e realtà*, Armando Editore, 1974.

[255]   ——, *Il bambino deprivato*, Cortina, 1986.

[256]   WITKOWSKI, F., *Psychopathologie et écriture*, Masson, Paris, 1989.

[257]   WITTLICH, B., 'Altération de l'écriture sous l'influence de l'alcool', *La Graphologie* 107, 1967.

[258]   YALON, D., 'L'Ordinateur auxiliaire du graphologue?', *La Graphologie* 184, 1986.

[259]   ZAMPIERI, M. C., 'Adolescenti e paura', *Scrittura* 71, 1989.

[260]   ZUCCHI, I., 'Grafologia familiare tra innato e acquisito. Casi esemplificativi', *Scrittura* 64, 1987.

[261]   ——, *Psicologia della motricità grafica*, Libreria G. Moretti, Urbino, 1990.